The Earthscan Reader in Poverty and Biodiversity Conservation

The Earthscan Reader in Poverty and Biodiversity Conservation

Edited by Dilys Roe and Joanna Elliott

publishing for a sustainable future

London • Washington, DC

First published in 2010 by Earthscan

Earthscan Ltd, Dunstan House, 14a St Cross Street, London EC1N 8XA, UK
Earthscan LLC, 1616 P Street, NW, Washington, DC 20036, USA

Earthscan publishes in association with the International Institute for Environment and Development

For more information on Earthscan publications, see www.earthscan.co.uk
or write to earthinfo@earthscan.co.uk

ISBN   978-1-84407-842-4 hardback
         978-1-84407-843-1 paperback

Typeset by Piers Aitman
Cover design by Andrew Corbett

A catalogue record for this book is available from the British Library

Library of Congress Cataloging-in-Publication Data
The Earthscan reader in poverty and biodiversity conservation / edited by Dilys Roe and Joanna Elliott.
    p. cm.
Includes bibliographical references and index.
ISBN 978-1-84407-842-4 (hardback) -- ISBN 978-1-84407-843-1 (pbk.)
1. Biodiversity conservation. I. Roe, Dilys. II. Elliott, Joanna.
QH75.E236 2010
333.95'16--dc22
2009049946

At Earthscan we strive to minimize our environmental impacts and carbon footprint through reducing waste, recycling and offsetting our CO_2 emissions, including those created through publication of this book. For more details of our environmental policy, see www.earthscan.co.uk.

This book was printed and bound in the UK
by CPI Antony Rowe.
The paper used is FSC certified.

Mixed Sources
Product group from well-managed forests and other controlled sources
www.fsc.org Cert no. SGS-COC-002953
© 1996 Forest Stewardship Council

FSC

Contents

Part 1 — Linking Biodiversity Conservation and Poverty Reduction: Where, How and Why?

Part 2 — Conservation's Place in International Development

Part 3 — Conservation Policy and Protectionism

Part 4 — Conservation NGOs and Poor People

Part 5 — New Developments: Ecosystem Services, Carbon and Climate Change

Part 6 — Moving Beyond the Debate:
The Need for Conservation–Poverty Partnerships

List of Figures, Tables and Boxes

Figures

Tables

Boxes

About the Editors

Dilys Roe is a senior researcher in IIED's Natural Resources Group, where her work focuses on the links between biodiversity, livelihoods and development. Since 2004 Dilys has coordinated the Poverty and Conservation Learning Group – a network of conservation, development and indigenous/local community organizations that is intended to improve dialogue on poverty–conservation linkages, promote better understanding of different perspectives and experiences of these links and help inform policy on these matters. While the majority of Dilys's work focuses on biodiversity–development/conservation–poverty issues, she also has a research interest in community-based natural resource management and community-based conservation; and pro-poor tourism. In addition to her work at IIED Dilys has worked periodically as a consultant biodiversity adviser to the UK Department for International Development and is also a doctoral candidate at the Durrell Institute for Conservation and Ecology (DICE) at the University of Kent.

Joanna Elliott is Vice President for Program Design at the African Wildlife Foundation, where she works closely with field-based conservation teams in nine priority landscapes across fourteen African countries to connect their practical work on conservation-livelihood linkages to the work of multilateral and bilateral donors and related aspects of the global policy environment. In addition to her work with AWF, Joanna is a Visiting Fellow in IIED's Natural Resource Group and a member of the PCLG Secretariat. She has also worked as a consultant rural livelihoods adviser to the Department for International Development where she was responsible for the DFID Wildlife and Poverty Study in 2002.

Chapter Sources

Part 1 — Linking Biodiversity Conservation and Poverty Reduction: Where, How and Why?

2   Adams, W.M., Aveling, R., Brockington, D., Dickson, B., Elliott, J., Hutton, J., Roe, D., Vira, B. and Wolmer, W. (2004) 'Biodiversity conservation and the eradication of poverty', *Science,* 306: 1146–1149
3   Fisher, R.J., Maginnis, S., Jackson, W., Barrow, E. and Jeanrenaud, S. (2008) *Linking Conservation and Poverty Reduction: Landscapes, People and Power,* Earthscan, London
4   Agrawal, A. and Redford, K. (2006) *Poverty, Development and Biodiversity Conservation: Shooting in the Dark?,* WCS Working Paper no 26, Wildlife Conservation Society, New York
5   Sunderlin, W.D., Angelsen, A., Belcher, B., Burgers, P., Nasi, R., Santoso, L., and Wunder, S. (2005) 'Livelihoods, forests and conservation in developing countries: An overview', *World Development,* 33(9): 1383–1402

Part 2 — Conservation's Place in International Development

6   Organisation for Economic Co-operation and Development (OECD) (2002) *Integrating the Rio Conventions into Development Co-operation,* The DAC Guidelines, OECD, Paris
7   Department For International Development (DFID) (2002) *Wildlife and Poverty Study,* DFID Rural Livelihoods Department, London
8   Lapham, N.P. and Livermore, R.J. (2003) *Striking a Balance: Ensuring Conservation's Place on the International Biodiversity Assistance Agenda,* Conservation International, Washington, DC.
9   Secretariat of the Convention on Biological Diversity (CBD) (2007) *Report of the Ad Hoc Open-ended Working Group of Review of Implementation of the Convention,* Second meeting, UNESCO, Paris, 9–13 July 2007
10 Sanderson, S. and Redford, K. (2003) 'Contested relationships between biodiversity conservation and poverty alleviation', *Oryx,* 37: 1–2

11 Sanderson, S. (2005) 'Poverty and conservation: The new century's "peasant question?", *World Development*, 33: 323–332

12 Bass, S. (2006) *Making Poverty Reduction Irreversible: Development Implications of the Millennium Ecosystem Assessment*, Environment for the MDGs series, IIED, London

Part 3 — Conservation Policy and Protectionism

13 McShane, T.O. (2003) 'Protected areas and poverty – the linkages and how to address them', *Policy Matters*, 12: 52–53

14 Colchester, M. (2004) 'Conservation policy and indigenous peoples', *Cultural Survival Quarterly*, 28: 17–22

15 Naughton-Treves, L., Buck Holland, M. and Brandon, K. (2005) 'The role of protected areas in conserving biodiversity and sustaining local livelihoods', *Annual Review of Environment and Resources*, 30: 219–252

16 Brockington, D. and Igoe, J. (2006) 'Eviction for conservation: A global overview', *Conservation and Society*, 4: 424–470

17 Adams, W.M. and Hutton, J. (2007) 'People, parks and poverty: Political ecology and biodiversity conservation', *Conservation and Society*, 5(2): 147–183

18 Mascia, M. and Claus, C.A. (2009) 'A property rights approach to understanding human displacement from protected areas: The case of marine protected areas', *Conservation Biology*, 23(1): 16–23

Part 4 — Conservation NGOs and Poor People

19 Coordinating Body for the Indigenous Organizations of the Amazon Basin (COICA) (1989) 'Two agendas on Amazon development', *Cultural Survival Quarterly*, 13(4): 75–78

20 Romero, C. and Andrade, G. (2004) 'International conservation organisations and the fate of local tropical forest conservation initiatives', *Conservation Biology*, 18(2): 578–580

21 Chapin, M. (2004) 'A challenge to conservationists', *World Watch*, Nov/Dec: 17–31

22 Oates, J.F. (2006) 'Conservation, development and poverty alleviation: Time for a change in attitudes', in *Gaining Ground: In Pursuit of Ecological Sustainability* (ed. D. Lavigne), International Fund for Animal Welfare, Canada

23 Kaimowitz, D. and Sheil, D. (2007) 'Conserving what and for whom? Why conservation should help meet basic needs in the tropics', *Biotropica*, 39(5): 567–574

Acknowledgements

This book was inspired by our interactions with members of the Poverty and Conservation Learning Group (PCLG) – many of them authors of the various readings we highlight here. We would like to thank them for that inspiration, and in particular those that commented on our choice of materials and made helpful suggestions for additional or alternative readings. PCLG has received financial support from a number of sources – the Ford Foundation and Irish Aid in particular, but also IIED's other core donors including DFID and Norad. Joanna Elliott's time was donated by the African Wildlife Foundation.

We would like to thank the authors and publishers of the readings reproduced here – for their permission to use their material and, in some cases, for their patience and acceptance of the abridged or extracted versions we have produced. We would also like to thank Tim Hardwick at Earthscan for seeing the merit in our proposal and the three reviewers to whom he sent the proposal, who also provided further encouragement that this was a worthwhile project to pursue. Finally a big thank you goes to Khanh Tran-Thanh, for her help with various production tasks for this project.

Our biggest thanks, however, go to Alessandra Giuliani, PCLG Research Assistant, who has worked tirelessly to acquire permissions, reformat papers and generally coordinate the production of this book. Without her this project would not have been possible.

List of Acronyms and Abbreviations

ACSC	Advancing Conservation in a Social Context
ADB	Asian Development Bank
APF	African Parks Foundation
ASB	alternatives to slash and burn
AWF	African Wildlife Foundation
BINGO	big international non-governmental organization
CAMPFIRE	Communal Areas Management Programme for Indigenous Resources
CBD	Convention on Biological Diversity
CBNRM	community-based natural resource management
CDF	Comprehensive Development Framework
CDM	Clean Development Mechanism
CEESP	Commission on Environmental, Economic, and Social Policy
CEPF	Critical Ecosystems Partnership Fund
CI	Conservation International
CIDA	Canadian International Development Agency
CIFOR	Center for International Forestry Research
CITES	Convention on International Trade in Endangered Species of Wild Fauna and Flora
COICA	Coordinating Body for the Indigenous Organizations of the Amazon Basin
COP	Conference of the Parties
CRS	Creditor Reporting System
CSP	Country Strategy Paper
DEFRA	Department for Environment, Food and Rural Affairs
DFID	Department for International Development
DLC	Digital Library of the Commons
EKC	environmental Kuznet's curve
ES	environmental services
FAO	Food and Agriculture Organization of the United Nations
FBPA	forest-based poverty alleviation
FCO	Foreign and Commonwealth Office
FCPF	Forest Carbon Partnership Facility
FFEM	French Global Environment Facility
FFI	Fauna & Flora International
FGLG	Forest Governance Learning Group

FPIC	free, prior and informed consent
FPP	Forest Peoples Programme
FSC	Forest Stewardship Council
FT	forest transition
GCF	Global Conservation Fund
GDP	gross domestic product
GEF	Global Environment Facility
GHG	greenhouse gas
GTZ	Gesellschaft für Technische Zusammenarbeit
HCVF	high conservation value forest
HIPC	Highly Indebted Poor Country
IASCP	International Association for the Study of Common Property
IASNR	International Association for Society and Natural Resources
ICCA	Indigenous and Community Conserved Areas
ICDP	integrated conservation and development project programme
ICO	international conservation organization
ICRAF	International Centre for Research in Agroforestry
IFAD	International Fund for Agricultural Development
IIED	International Institute for Environment and Development
ILO	International Labour Organization
INC	Intergovernmental Negotiating Committee
IPCC	Intergovernmental Panel on Climate Change
IPGRI	International Plant Genetic Resources Institute
IUCN	International Union for the Conservation of Nature (World Conservation Union)
IWMI	International Water Management Institute
LLS	Livelihoods and Landscapes Strategy
MA	Millennium Ecosystem Assessment
MCA	Millennium Challenge Account
MDG	Millennium Development Goal
MINEF	Ministry of the Environment and Forestry
MPA	marine protected area
NGO	non-governmental organization
NKMCAP	Noel Kempff Mercado Climate Action Project
NTFP	non-timber forest product
ODA	Organization of Development Assistance; also official development assistance
OECD	Organisation for Economic Co-operation and Development
OTEP	Overseas Territories Environment Programme
PA	protected area
PALNet	Protected Areas Learning Network
PCLG	Poverty and Conservation Learning Group
PEN	Poverty Environment Network
PEP	Poverty Environment Partnership

PES	payments for ecosystem/environmental services
PiP	Parks in Peril
PPA	Programme Partnership Agreement
PRS	poverty reduction strategy
PRSP	Poverty Reduction Strategy Paper
RECOFTC	Regional Community Forestry Training Centre for Asia Pacific
REDD	reduced emissions from deforestation and degradation
RNHP	Regional Natural Heritage Programme
R-PIN	readiness plan idea note
RUPES	Rewarding Upland Poor for Environmental Services
SCB	Society for Conservation Biology
SDC	Swiss Agency for Development and Cooperation
SEA	strategic environmental assessment
SSWG	Society for Conservation Biology's Social Science Working Group
SwedBio	Swedish International Biodiversity Programme
TEEB	The Economics of Ecosystems and Biodiversity
TFAP	Tropical Forestry Action Plan
TFCA	United States Tropical Forest Conservation Act
TILCEPA	Theme on Indigenous and Local Communities, Equity, and Protected Areas
TNC	The Nature Conservancy
TSP	Target Strategy Paper
UN	United Nations
UNCED	United Nations Conference on Environment and Development
UNDP	United Nations Development Programme
UNEP	United Nations Environment Programme
UNFCCC	United Nations Framework Convention on Climate Change
USAID	United States Agency for International Development
USFWS	United States Fish and Wildlife Service
WCD	World Commission on Dams
WCPA	World Commission on Protected Areas
WCS	Wildlife Conservation Society; also World Conservation Strategy
WDPA	World Database on Protected Areas
WPC	World Parks Congress
WRI	World Resources Institute
WSSD	World Summit on Sustainable Development
WWF	World Wide Fund for Nature

Chapter 1

Biodiversity Conservation and Poverty Reduction: An Introduction to the Debate

Dilys Roe and Joanna Elliott

Linked Challenges

The larger challenge is to allow human society to meet its potential and share the fruits of economic growth while sustaining a biosphere that not only sustains full ecological functions but retains its living diversity. (Adams et al., 2004)

In the last decade biodiversity loss and persistent poverty in developing countries have each been recognized as major international problems that require urgent attention – not just for moral or ethical reasons but to address fundamental concerns about world security and biosphere functioning.

Poverty reduction was brought to broad public attention in the United Nations Millennium Declaration and associated Millennium Development Goals and has been adopted as a priority objective by the majority of official development agencies. The poverty reduction ambitions that have been articulated, while often simply restating development goals that have been set (and missed) over the last 30 years, are unusual in that they now have an unprecedented level of international commitment and monitoring. As a consequence, all sectors of society are urged to contribute to their achievement. Conservation agencies find themselves among the many organizations struggling to determine how their work could – or indeed whether it should – fit into this international effort.

At the same time, biodiversity loss is proceeding at an unprecedented rate. This loss applies to genes, species, habitats and ecosystems and affects not just the number or scale of these living natural resources but also their variety. The findings of the Millennium Ecosystem Assessment (MA), published in 2005 highlight that the ecosystem services that underpin all life on Earth are in a state of actual or potential collapse. Just as international targets have been set for poverty reduction, the scale and rate of biodiversity loss led the UN Convention on Biological Diversity (CBD) to adopt a target in 2002, endorsed by the World Summit on Sustainable Development (WSSD), to significantly reduce the rate of biodiversity loss by 2010.

While these international challenges have been identified and brought to public and political attention by different communities of interest – the conservation community on the one hand and the development community on the other – the links between them have been recognized in the international policy statements that guide action to address them. Poverty reduction is one of 21 targets within the set of eight Millennium Development Goals (MDGs), as is – since 2006 – reducing biodiversity loss.[1] Similarly, the full (and often overlooked) text of the CBD 2010 biodiversity target reveals the motivation for addressing biodiversity loss: '*as a contribution to poverty alleviation* [emphasis added] and to the benefit of all life on earth'. Beyond the CBD, at the UN World Summit in 2005 which was intended to review progress towards the achievement of the MDGs, the secretariats of the five major biodiversity conventions – CBD, the Convention on International Trade in Endangered Species of Wild Fauna and Flora (CITES), the Convention on Migratory Species of Wild Animals (CMS), the Ramsar Convention on Wetlands and the World Heritage Convention – issued a joint statement emphasizing the important role that biodiversity plays in the achievement of the MDGs: 'Biodiversity can indeed help alleviate hunger and poverty, can promote good human health, and be the basis for ensuring freedom and equity for all' (Biodiversity Liason Group, 2005).

The MA further emphasizes the link between biodiversity conservation and poverty reduction. The conceptual framework of the MA (Chapter 25 of this volume) views biodiversity as underpinning the delivery of a range of ecosystem goods and services on which human well-being depends – poverty being 'the pronounced deprivation of well-being' (Millennium Ecosystem Assessment, 2005a). The MA further notes that 'the harmful effects of the degradation of ecosystem services are being borne disproportionately by the poor, are contributing to the growing inequities and disparities across groups of people, and are sometimes the principal factor causing poverty and social conflict' (Millennium Ecosystem Assessment, 2005b). These findings are reaffirmed in progress so far on another international study, the G8-initiated *The Economics of Ecosystems and Biodiversity* (TEEB) (Sukhdev, 2008).

Historical Recognition of Links

Acknowledgement of the link between biodiversity and poverty, and more broadly between environment and development, is not new. As early as the 1940s there was increasing recognition that conservation provided revenue-generating opportunities (trade, tourism) that could contribute to local economic development in poor countries (Adams, 2004). The Third International Conference for the Protection of Fauna and Flora in Africa in 1953 emphasized the need for stricter measures to control local hunting because wildlife was an important food supply for local people (Caldwell, 1954). Similarly, in development circles, Anderson and Grove (1987) note that advisers to post-war colonial governments in Africa drew up development plans that had a significant linked conservation component.

The *World Conservation Strategy* (WCS), (IUCN et al., 1980) was the first influential document to bridge the conservation-development divide, highlighting both the potential synergies and trade-offs between conservation and development and echoing earlier concerns (e.g. Strong, 1977) about the ideological chasm between conservation and development practitioners. The WCS also suggested that much habitat destruction and overexploitation of living resources by individuals, communities and nations in the developing world was a response to relative poverty (IUCN et al., 1980). This link between poverty and ecological degradation was reiterated in the *Global 2000 Report* (CEQ, 1981).

Building on the advances made by the Stockholm conference and the WCS, a World Commission on Environment and Development was established in 1982, producing the report *Our Common Future* (WCED, 1987) and laying the ground-work for the UN Conference on Environment and Development in 1992 (the 'Earth Summit') at which the United Nations Convention on Biological Diversity (CBD) was adopted.

In the intervening period conservation policy and practice was paying increasing attention to the need to ensure benefits for local people and to recognize indigenous peoples' rights over land and resources. The third World Parks Congress in 1982, for example, was seen by some as a turning point in conservation practice, through its encouragement of local participation, sustainable use and joint management arrangements (Wilshusen et al., 2003). In 1985 WWF recognized the need to take poverty and local economic development around protected areas seriously, with the launch of its Wildlife and Human Needs Programme comprising 20 projects that sought to combine conservation and development in developing countries. A growing number of integrated conservation and development projects (ICDPs) and community wild-life management programmes were being implemented at this time, notably in Southern Africa, including the Communal Areas Management Programme for Indigenous Resources (CAMPFIRE) in Zimbabwe and the Luangwa Integrated Resource Development Programme in Zambia (Roe, 2008).

Development theory in the 1980s was also emphasizing the need for local participation, decentralization and local empowerment (Ellis and Biggs, 2001). This theory and practice of participation provided the driving force for the conver-gence of conservation and development discourses that lay behind the rise of the community conservation paradigm (Campbell and Vainio-Mattila, 2003; Adams, 2004).

Enchantment with integrated conservation and development and with community conservation was short-lived, however, among both conservation and development practitioners. Within the conservation community a backlash against community conservation and in favour of a return to more 'traditional' protected area approaches to conservation emerged (e.g. Kramer et al., 1997; Brandon et al., 1998; Oates, 1999; Terborgh, 1999). In development circles a combination of the new focus on poverty reduction coupled with high perceived costs of community-based conservation and changes in aid delivery mechanisms away from project funding towards direct budget support result in a decrease in funding for such activities (Roe and Elliott, 2004; see also Chapter 7 in this volume).

Focus of Current Debate

Despite the apparent consensus at international policy level on the links between biodiversity conservation and poverty reduction, and the high levels of commitment to both the MDGs and the CBD, the dual concern with a return to protectionism on the one hand and with the overriding priority of poverty reduction on the other hand has raised the level of the debate about the nature of links at the practical level and about the roles and responsibilities of different interest groups in addressing them. Roe (2008) identifies three specific areas of the debate of the last decade, each of which has generated a powerful exchange of ideas and opinions reflected in the choice of articles for this Reader:

(1) The current lack of attention given to biodiversity conservation on the development agenda, with the prioritization of poverty reduction and, particularly, the emphasis on the first Millennium Development Goal and on national poverty reduction strategies (Sanderson and Redford, 2003; Roe and Elliott, 2004; Sanderson, 2005). Funding for conservation has declined over the last two decades (Brockington et al. (2008) note that during the 1990s funding for conservation declined by 50 per cent) while official development assistance agencies have emphasized that decision-making over resource allocation for biodiversity conservation in developing countries is now held firmly by national governments facing tough choices in funding competing priorities with limited fiscal resources (DFID, 2002). This area of debate is addressed in **Part 2** of the Reader.

(2) The apparently increasing protectionist focus of conservation policy (Brechin et al., 2001; Wilshusen et al., 2001; Hutton et al., 2005), and its implications for communities resident in and around protected areas, in particular regarding involuntary displacements and evictions (Cernea, 2003; Colchester, 2003; Brockington and Igoe, 2006). Again, this debate is not new. As early as the 1950s a polarized debate about the purpose of conservation – to protect species, or to benefit people – had begun to emerge (Holdgate, 1999). Within the last few years, however – and particularly following the fifth World Parks Congress in 2003, this debate appears to have become more vociferous, and, at times, acrimonious. This area of debate is addressed in **Part 3** of the Reader.

(3) The activities and accountability of big international conservation NGOs, and their impacts on local and, particularly, indigenous communities (Bray and Anderson, 2005; Chapin, 2004; Khare and Bray, 2004; Romero and Andrade, 2004; Dowie, 2005). For example, despite individual and collective policy statements (Box 1.1), Brockington et al. (2008) note 'The poverty and conservation debate is hotly contested between those who feel that conservation should address poverty issues and those who do not.' This area of debate is addressed in **Part 4** of the Reader.

Box 1.1 *Conservation Organizations Commit to Address Poverty*

During the UN World Summit in 2005 a number of leading international conservation organizations (Conservation International, Fauna & Flora International, The Nature Conservancy, BirdLife International and Wildlife Conservation Society) made the following announcement:

'As those standing in your midst can testify, conservation work is crucial to sustainable development. Therefore:

- We commit to demonstrating that biodiversity conservation contributes to human well-being, and that to be truly sustainable, our efforts must improve human well-being, empower communities, and create new opportunities to increase incomes while strengthening the natural resource base;

- We renew our commitment to work with indigenous and local communities, and respect local knowledge in pursuit of the common goal of protecting the environments on which they depend;

- We pledge to work within our missions to address the root causes that lead jointly to poverty and ecological disruption.

We invite our colleagues in the broader development community to make a similar acknowledgement – that alleviating poverty in a lasting manner is fundamentally linked to investing in environmental sustainability and to accounting for the actual value of ecosystem services.

After all, creating a better life for present and future generations is an objective we all share.'

Source: Joint Environmental Community Call: www.nature.org/pressroom/press/press2088.html

---

Climate change has added an extra layer of complexity to these three areas of debate, not least because of the refocusing of already limited donor environmental agendas on climate change to the exclusion of other environmental issues. At the same time efforts to tackle climate change mitigation and adaptation promise to provide a catalyst for addressing some fundamental issues about natural resource governance, power relationships, accountability and transparency that have dogged the conservation–poverty debate.

Biodiversity conservation both affects and is affected by climate change and this relationship has implications for poor people. On the one hand, biodiversity can help poor people adapt to climate change: for example, through natural protection against floods and increased resilience provided by diverse traditional crops (Reid and Swiderska, 2008). On the other hand, because of the potential threats to biodiversity posed by climate change, there are calls for renewed support for, and expansion of, protected areas (Hansen et al., 2003). Discussions about the potential of reduced emissions from deforestation and degradation (REDD) as a formally approved climate change mitigation strategy have fuelled concerns around the potentially negative implications of state-enforced forest conservation on indigenous and local communities and around appropriate governance and accountability arrangements when large sums of money are at stake. The debate about REDD is captured in **Part 5** of the Reader, which addresses new developments in conservation policy, particularly the question of the potential impact of innovations in payments for environmental services.

Scope of the Reader

This Reader is intended to provide a flavour of the different elements of the conservation–poverty debate and help its audience locate these within their wider contexts. Understanding the origins and evolution of the conservation–poverty debate is critical to understanding and resolving the current claims and counterclaims that are being made, and moving beyond polarizing debate to constructive solutions. The recent focus of the climate change agenda on REDD makes this search for solutions particularly important because of the implications for conservation and, subsequently, for its impacts on poor and vulnerable people.

Although the roots of the conservation–poverty debate lie in much older discussions of the links between environment and development, this Reader focuses on the period since 2000 for three reasons:

- In this period poverty reduction has been voiced as an international imperative through the MDGs, and development agencies have switched their focus from broad sustainable development to poverty reduction.
- Concerns over protected area impacts and governance have been increasingly raised in international conservation circles, notably at the 2000 IUCN World Conservation Congress in Aman and the 2003 World Parks Congress in Durban, the latter of which was widely acclaimed (both positively and negatively) for its unprecedented attendance by representatives of indigenous and local community groups.

- In this period the debate has moved out of academia and into the mainstream through the publication of a series of articles in the popular press critical of conservation NGOs.

At the outset we should make clear that the focus of this Reader is very much on the links between *conservation* and poverty rather than on *biodiversity* and poverty. The two are quite different – 'biodiversity' refers to diversity in composition, structure and function of genes, species and ecosystems; 'conservation' refers to a set of objectives or management interventions designed to maintain that biodiversity and to prevent its degradation or loss. The role and value of biodiversity in supporting the livelihoods of poor people has itself been widely debated for over 25 years: (Prescott-Allen and Prescott-Allen, 1982; Scoones et al., 1992; Nasi and Cunningham, 2001; Rietbergen et al., 2002; Angelsen and Wunder, 2003; World Resources Institute, 2005; Millennium Ecosystem Assessment, 2005b). There is dispute as to whether, or under what conditions, biodiversity can actually lift people out of poverty (World Resources Institute, 2005); act as a safety net, preventing them slipping further into poverty (Angelsen and Wunder, 2003); or even act as a poverty trap (Ambrose-Oji, 2003; Bass et al., 2009). This issue could be the subject of an entire Reader in itself. Here we simply touch on it in Chapter 5, which discusses this issue in the context of forests and highlights the distinction we try to make here between the use of forest *resources* as a poverty alleviation strategy and the use of forest *conservation* as a poverty alleviation strategy.

We should also note that many of the readings featured in this book use the term 'biodiversity conservation' but it is clear that the conservation activity under consideration is largely focused on maintaining a maximum 'volume' (species numbers, habitat extent etc.) of the resource base, rather than necessarily maximum 'variety' or diversity per se.

The terms poor people, poverty and poverty reduction are also worthy of some discussion because they are used and understood differently by different groups, as is reflected in their usage in the readings. When international development agencies talk about 'poor people' they are generally referring to the 1.2 billion defined as chronically poor on the basis of an income level of less than one dollar a day. This figure, set by the World Bank, is intended to represent the minimum amount required for a person to meet his or her daily physical needs. This monetary figure is a crude – but easy to measure – indicator of poverty and is currently the basis for defining the scope of the first Millennium Development Goal which includes a target to 'halve the number of people living in extreme poverty'. Beyond this international poverty indicator, different countries set their own national poverty lines based on more locally relevant indicators – but again generally based on a minimum income level, or sometimes a food consumption level.

Thus 'poverty reduction' literally means reducing the number of people that fall beneath a recognized poverty line. But it is often used to indicate a general increase in well-being, whether or not this actually is sufficient to move people from being classified as 'poor' to 'not poor'. Technically speaking this is poverty alleviation rather than poverty reduction.

Further, people's own perceptions of what poverty means and who is poor vary hugely according to their sociocultural norms and traditions: in this sense the definition of poverty will always depend on what people, in a particular society, at a particular point in time, perceive as poor. Inequality can be as significant a measure of well-being as absolute levels of poverty (Angelsen and Wunder, 2003).

In its 1980 *World Development Report*, the World Bank described poverty as 'a condition of life so characterized by malnutrition, illiteracy, and disease as to be beneath any reasonable definition of human decency' (World Bank, 1980). Increasing income may help to tackle this condition but is not the only means of doing so. Poverty could also be alleviated by providing poor people with free access to healthcare, education, water and sanitation and so on, or by building up the asset base available to poor people, including environmental assets, so that these support livelihoods and economic growth (Pearce, 2005). More recent definitions have thus tended to move beyond the income focus and there seems to be a general consensus, as evidenced by the World Bank (2001), Poverty Environment Partnership (DFID et al., 2002), and the poor themselves (Naryan et al., 2000), that poverty means not just lack of income but also lack of civil and political rights, assets and services; i.e. the opposite to the constituents of human well-being as defined by the MA.

Structure of the Reader

The Reader is structured to reflect the different strands of the modern conservation–poverty debate as discussed above. **Part 1** provides an overview of the links between biodiversity conservation and poverty reduction – the different perspectives and positions held as to the nature of the links. **Part 2** documents the declining focus of development agencies on biodiversity conservation. **Part 3** moves the focus from development to conservation and explores the impact of international conservation policy – particularly protected areas – on poor people, and the conditions under which these impacts are positive or negative. **Part 4** focuses particular attention on conservationists and conservation NGOs – presenting claims and counterclaims about their impacts on local people and their roles in addressing poverty reduction. **Part 5** looks at new developments in conservation policy – particularly the recent focus on ecosystem services and the role of payments for ecosystem services as a conservation strategy. Payments for reduced emissions from deforestation and degradation (REDD) are one application of this strategy, which could bring substantial funds for conservation – but at the same time raise concerns from those concerned with the welfare of forest-dependent communities. Many of the debates about REDD and its social impacts revisit concerns raised earlier within the conservation–poverty debate.

By way of conclusion, **Part 6** highlights a number of readings around one of the often proposed ways forward in the conservation–poverty debate. It focuses on the theme of partnerships – between social and natural scientists, between those who 'do' conservation and those who 'do' development, between those who implement conservation and those who feel its effects on the ground.

We recognize that the limited number of readings presented in this book (many of which are, by necessary extracts or abridged versions of the originals) means that we can only scratch the surface of the conservation–poverty debate. We therefore provide details of further readings in the Introductory Editorials for each Part of the Reader, as well as a final section of the Reader detailing useful resources for those interested in pursuing aspects of the debate further. These resources are largely drawn from the website of the Poverty and Conservation Learning Group – www.povertyandconservation.info – itself a treasure trove of information on organizations, initiatives, readings and events of relevance to this subject.

Notes

1   The relevant target for MDG7 was previously to 'reverse the loss of environmental resources' but in 2006 a variation of the 2010 biodiversity target was adopted, with additional biodiversity indicators.

References

Adams, W.M. (2004) *Against Extinction,* Earthscan, London.

Adams, W.M., Aveling, R., Brockington, D., Dickson, B., Elliott, J., Hutton, J., Roe, D., Vira, B. and Wolmer, W. (2004) 'Biodiversity conservation and the eradication of poverty', *Science,* 306: 1146–1149.

Ambrose-Oji, B. (2003) 'The contribution of NTFPs to the livelihoods of the 'forest poor': Evidence from the tropical forest zone of South-West Cameroon', *International Forestry Review,* 5(2): 106–117.

Anderson, D. and Grove, R. (1987) 'The scramble for Eden: Past, present and future in African conservation', pp. 1–20, in Anderson, D. and Grove, R. (eds), *Conservation in Africa: People, Policies and Practice,* Cambridge University Press, Cambridge.

Angelsen, A. and Wunder, S. (2003) *Exploring the Forest–Poverty Link: Key Concepts, Issues and Research Implications,* CIFOR, Jakarta.

Bass, S., Steele, P. and Grieg Gran, M. (2009) *Natural Riches and the Poor: Escape Route or Poverty Trap?,* IIED, London.

Biodiversity Liaison Group (2005) *Biodiversity: Life Insurance for Our Changing World,* Secretariat of the Convention on Biological Diversity. Available at www.cbd.int/doc/statements/mdg-2005-en.pdf (accessed 26 November 2009)

Brandon, K., Redford, K. and Sanderson, S. (1998) *Parks in Peril: People, Politics and Protected Areas,* Island Press, Washington, DC.

Bray, D.B. and Anderson, A.B. (2005) *Global Conservation, Non-governmental Organizations, and Local Communities: Perspectives on Programs and Project Implementation in Latin America,* Working

Paper 1, Florida International University Institute For Sustainability Science in Latin America and the Caribbean, Miami.

Brechin, S., Wilshusen, P.R., Fortwangler, C. and West, P.C. (2001) 'Beyond the square wheel: Towards a more comprehensive understanding of biodiversity conservation as a social and political process', *Society and Natural Resources*, 15: 41–64.

Brockington, D., Duffy, R. and Igoe, J. (2008) *Nature Unbound: Conservation, Capitalism and the Future of Protected Areas*, Earthscan, London.

Brockington, D. and Igoe, J. (2006) 'Eviction for conservation: A global overview', *Conservation and Society*, 4: 424–470.

Caldwell, K. (1954) 'The Bukavu Conference', *Oryx*, 2: 234–237.

Campbell, L.M. and Vainio-Mattila, A. (2003) 'Participatory development and community-based conservation: Opportunities missed for lessons learned?', *Human Ecology*, 31: 417–437.

CEQ (1981) *Global 2000 Report to the President*, US Council On Environmental Quality, Washington, DC.

Cernea, M. (2003) *Biodiversity Conservation Versus Population Resettlement: Risks to Nature and Risks to People*, Paper Presented at the International Conference On Rural Livelihoods, Forests and Biodiversity, 19–23 May 2003, Bonn, Germany.

Chapin, M. (2004) A challenge to conservationists, *World Watch*, Nov/Dec, 17–31.

Colchester, M. (2003) *Salvaging Nature: Indigenous Peoples, Protected Areas and Biodiversity Conservation*, World Rainforest Movement and Forest Peoples Programme, Moreton-in-Marsh.

DFID (2002) *Wildlife and Poverty Study*, Department for International Development, London.

DFID, EC, UNDP and WB (2002) *Linking Poverty Reduction and Environmental Management: Policy Challenges and Opportunities*, Department for International Development (DFID), European Commission (EC), United Nations Development Fund (UNDP) and the World Bank (WB).

Dowie, M. (2005) 'Conservation refugees: When protecting nature means kicking people out', *Orion Magazine*, November/December, 16–27.

Ellis, F. and Biggs, S. (2001) 'Evolving themes in rural development 1950s–2000s', *Development Policy Review*, 19: 437–448.

Hansen, L.J., Biringer, J.L. and Hoffman, J.R. (2003) *Buying Time: A User's Manual for Building Resistance and Resilience to Climate Change on Protected Areas*, WWF, Gland.

Holdgate, M. (1999) *The Green Web: A Union For World Conservation*, Earthscan, London.

Hutton, J., Adams, W.M. and Murombedzi, J. (2005) 'Back to the barriers? Changing narratives in biodiversity conservation', *Forum for Development Studies*, 2: 341–370.

IUCN, UNEP and WWF (1980) *World Conservation Strategy: Living Resource Conservation for Sustainable Development*, IUCN, Gland.

Khare, A. and Bray, D.B. (2004) *Study of Critical New Forest Conservation Issues in the Global South*, Ford Foundation, New York.

Kramer, R.A., Van Schaik, C.P. and Johnson, J. (eds) (1997) *The Last Stand: Protected Areas and the Defense of Tropical Biodiversity*, Oxford University Press, New York.

Millennium Ecosystem Assessment (2005a) *Ecosystems and Human Well-Being: Conditions and Trends*, World Resources Institute, Washington, DC.

Millennium Ecosystem Assessment (2005b) *Ecosystems And Human Well-Being: Biodiversity Synthesis*, World Resources Institute, Washington, DC.

Nasi, R. and Cunningham, T. (2001) *Sustainable Management of Non-Timber Forest Resources: A Review with Recommendations for SBSTTA*, Secretariat to the Convention On Biological Diversity, Montreal.

Naryan, D., Patel, R., Schafft, K., Rademacher, A. and Koch-Schulte, S. (2000) *Voices of the Poor: Can Anyone Hear Us?*, World Bank, Washington, DC.

Oates, J. (1999) *Myth and Reality in the Rainforest: How Conservation Strategies are Failing in West Africa*, University of California Press, Berkeley.

Pearce D.W. (2005) *Investing in Environmental Wealth for Poverty Reduction*, Report Prepared for the Poverty Environment Partnership, UNDP, New York.

Prescott-Allen, R. and Prescott-Allen, C. (1982) *What's Wildlife Worth? Economic Contributions of Wild Plants and Animals to Developing Countries*, Earthscan, London.

Reid, H. and Swiderska, K. (2008) *Biodiversity, Climate Change and Poverty: Exploring the Links*, IIED Briefing, International Institute for Environment and Development, London.

Rietbergen, S., Bishop, J. and Mainka, S. (2002) *Ecosystem Conservation: A Neglected Tool for Poverty Reduction*, WSSD Opinion Series, IIED, London.

Roe, D. (2008) 'The origins and evolution of the conservation–poverty debate: A review of key literature, events and policy processes', *Oryx*, 42(4): 491–503.

Roe, D. and Elliott, J. (2004) 'Poverty reduction and biodiversity conservation: Rebuilding the bridges', *Oryx*, 38: 137–139.

Romero, C. and Andrade, G.I. (2004) 'International conservation organizations and the fate of local tropical forest conservation initiatives', *Conservation Biology*, 18: 578–580.

Sanderson, S. (2005) 'Poverty and Conservation: The new century's 'peasant question'', *World Development*, 33: 323–332.

Sanderson, S. and Redford, K. (2003) 'Contested relationships between biodiversity conservation and poverty alleviation', *Oryx*, 37: 1–2.

Scoones, I., Melnyk, M. and Pretty, J. (1992) *The Hidden Harvest: Wild Foods And Agricultural Systems: A Literature Review And Annotated Bibliography*, IIED, London.

Strong, M. (1977) 'The international community and the environment', *Environmental Conservation*, 4: 165–172.

Sukhdev, P. (2008) *The Economics of Ecosystems and Biodiversity: Interim Report*, European Commission, Brussels.

Terborgh, J. (1999) *Requiem for Nature*, Island Press, Washington, DC.

WCED (World Commission on Environment and Development) (1987) *Our Common Future: Report of the World Commission on Environment and Development*, Oxford University Press, Oxford.

Wilshusen, P.R., Brechin, S., Fortwangler, C. and West, P.C. (2001) 'Reinventing a square wheel: Critique of a resurgent "protection paradigm" in international biodiversity conservation', *Society and Natural Resources*, 15: 17–40.

Wilshusen, P.R., Brechin, S., Fortwangler, C. and West, P.C. (2003) 'Contested nature: Conservation and development at the turn of the twenty-first century', pp. 1–22, in Brechin, S. Wilshusen, P.R. Fortwangler, C. and West, P. (eds), *Contested Nature: Promoting International Biodiversity with Social Justice in the Twenty-First Century*, State University of New York Press, Albany.

World Resources Institute (2005) *World Resources 2005: The Wealth of the Poor – Managing Ecosystems to Fight Poverty*, UNEP, UNDP, WRI and World Bank, Washington, DC.

World Bank (1980) *World Development Report, Part II: Poverty and Human Development*, World Bank, Washington, DC.

World Bank (2001) *World Development Report 2000/2001: Attacking Poverty*, World Bank, Washington, DC.

Part 1

Linking Biodiversity Conservation and Poverty Reduction: Where, How and Why?

Editors' Introduction

There is no single relationship between biodiversity conservation and poverty reduction. Nadkarni (2000), for example, describes six different poverty–environment relationships: from a vicious cycle of poverty leading to environmental degradation and thence to more poverty; to a win–win scenario where environmental conservation contributes to poverty alleviation. There is certainly no linear relationship – the Millennium Ecosystem Assessment (MA) concludes that while many millions of people have benefited from the transformation of ecosystems and exploitation of natural resources, the benefits have not been evenly or equitably distributed, with the poor being the biggest losers (Millennium Ecosystem Assessment, 2005).

Other commentators have noted the dynamic and context-specific nature of the conservation–poverty relationship (Kepe et al., 2004; Redford and Sanderson, 2006; BirdLife International, 2007). Nevertheless the debate about the relationship is all too often characterized by generalities, or by focusing only on one part of a larger and more complex issue (Rangarajan and Shahabuddin, 2006).

The tendency to generalize, or to disregard the complexities of the debate, is an outcome of the widely divergent characteristics of the organizations (and individuals) involved, including variations in:

- the missions and objectives of the organizations tackling conservation and/or poverty reduction on the ground;
- the academic disciplines of professional staff;
- the level of remoteness from the conservation or poverty intervention – directly affected communities, for example, are likely to have very different opinions from remote policy-makers or external 'experts'; field practitioners from academics or theoreticians; and
- the varying worldviews of different stakeholders and the ways in which this affects their understanding and experience of terms such as 'poverty' or 'well-being'; 'conservation' or 'exploitation'; 'natural' and 'social'.

The readings we present in **Part 1** provide general background to the conservation–poverty debate. More importantly, all four chapters seek to define the debate, stripping it to a place of clarity in underlying positions taken and in interpretation of available evidence of linkages. The authors acknowledge that 'Biodiversity conservation scientists face a dilemma' (Chapter 2) and 'conservationists face three challenges' (Chapter 3), and in turn seek typologies in underlying hypotheses (Chapter 2) or inferences (Chapter 4) to enable improved understanding. Their efforts are responses both to the growing importance and volume of the debate as to the nature of poverty–conservation linkages, and to the increasingly acknowledged complexity of these linkages and the subjectivity of available evidence.

In Chapter 2 Adams et al. (2004) present a conceptual typology of the hypotheses underlying the positions taken by different protagonists. It helpfully distinguishes between global and local costs and benefits of conservation, and global, national and local levels of response. It then defines four distinct ways of looking at poverty–conservation linkages in order to enable 'understanding of their mutual positions'. The chapter was written by a group of UK-based academics, policy analysts and conservation practitioners soon after the World Parks Congress in Durban in 2003.

In Chapter 3, Fisher et al. (2008) identify three challenges to conservationists and call for the 'reinvigoration of sustainable development'. The reading is taken from a book written by a group of IUCN conservation specialists with broad experience of conservation policy and practice. They acknowledge the complexities of assessing causal linkages and their implications, identifying the often contradictory assertions made in linking conservation, environmental degradation, poverty and wealth, showing that these are generally case specific. They conclude 'Sustainable development needs negotiated outcomes that are equitable, economically viable and socially sustainable. It is easier to achieve this type of outcome at broader geographical scales rather than at the site level'.

In Chapter 4, Agrawal and Redford (2006) examine the evidence base for asserting conservation–poverty linkages. They review 37 empirical studies, concluding that they depend on simplified understandings of poverty–conservation linkages, that they are not comparable and are therefore hard to generalize conclusions from, and that overall they are a poor insight into conditions under which poverty alleviation and biodiversity conservation may be compatible goals. They demonstrate the trade-offs that underlie the complexities of poverty–conservation linkages, for example how alleviating one aspect of poverty may worsen another, and suggest that going forward the challenge is to identify how some aspects of poverty can be alleviated while different components and attributes of biodiversity conserved. The authors advocate a new research agenda: 'Without great attention to change over time, the goal of policy-relevant understanding of the relationship between biodiversity conservation and poverty alleviation is likely to remain chimerical'.

In Chapter 5, Sunderlin et al. (2005) focus on the specific case of forests – the extent to which they can support poverty alleviation and the compatibility of this with conservation. The authors conclude that the location of chronic rural poverty and forests tend to overlap, that it is important to distinguish between the use of forest resources to prevent rural people from falling into (deeper) poverty versus their role in lifting people out of poverty, and that there are intrinsic qualities of forest resources and the context in which they are used that tend to run counter to poverty alleviation. They advocate site-level research to support efforts to reconcile forest-based poverty alleviation and forest conservation.

References

Adams, W.M., Aveling, R., Brockington, D., Dickson, B., Elliott, J., Hutton, J., Roe, D., Vira, B. and Wolmer, W. (2004) 'Biodiversity conservation and the eradication of poverty', *Science,* 306: 1146–1149.

Agrawal, A. and Redford, K. (2006) *Poverty, Development and Biodiversity Conservation: Shooting in the Dark,* WCS Working Paper no 26, Wildlife Conservation Society, New York.

BirdLife International (2007) *Livelihoods and the Environment at Important Bird Areas: Listening to Local Voices,* BirdLife International, Cambridge.

Fisher, R.J., Maginnis, S., Jackson, W., Barrow, E. and Jeanrenaud, S. (2008) *Linking Conservation and Poverty Reduction: Landscapes, People and Power,* Earthscan, London.

Kepe, T., Saruchera, M. and Whande, W. (2004) 'Poverty alleviation and biodiversity conservation: a South African perspective', *Oryx,* 38(2): 143–145.

Millennium Ecosystem Assessment (2005) *Ecosystems and Human Well-being: Biodiversity Synthesis,* World Resources Institute, Washington, DC.

Nadkarni, M.V. (2000) 'Poverty, environment, development: A many-patterned nexus', *Economic and Political Weekly,* 35(14): 1184–1190.

Rangarajan, M. and Shahabuddin, G. (2006) 'Displacement and relocation from protected areas: Towards a biological and historical synthesis', *Conservation and Society,* 4(3): 359–378.

Redford, K. and Sanderson, S. (2006) 'No roads, only directions', *Conservation and Society,* 4(3): 379–382.

Sunderlin, W.D., Belcher, B., Santoso, L., Angelsen, A., Burgers, P., Nasi, R. and Wunder, S. (2005) 'Livelihoods, forests and conservation in developing countries: An overview', *World Development,* 33(9): 1383–1402.

Chapter 2

Biodiversity Conservation and the Eradication of Poverty

William M. Adams, Ros Aveling, Dan Brockington, Barney
Dickson, Joanna Elliott, Jon Hutton, Dilys Roe, Bhaskar Vira
and William Wolmer

It is widely accepted that biodiversity loss and poverty are linked problems and that conservation and poverty reduction should be tackled together. However, success with integrated strategies is elusive. There is sharp debate about the social impacts of conservation programmes and the success of community-based approaches to conservation. Clear conceptual frameworks are needed if policies in these two areas are to be combined. We review the links between poverty allevia- tion and biodiversity conservation and present a conceptual typology of these rela- tionships.

Biodiversity conservation scientists face a dilemma. There is increasing concern that global efforts to maintain biodiversity are in conflict with those to reduce poverty.[1] The decline of populations, extinction of species, and habitat transforma- tion demand urgent action.[2] The leading response to these threats since the late 19th century has been the creation of protected areas.[3] Technical capacity to design effective protected-area systems is increasing,[4] allowing the identification of coverage and remaining gaps in the international protected-area system.[5] This, combined with positive assessments of the effectiveness of protected areas is encouraging the consolidation and expansion of the network of protected areas.[6] The 2004 World Database on Protected Areas includes over 105,000 sites covering an area of 19.7 million km.[2,7] The establishment and effective management of a global series of protected areas was a key element of the 7th Conference of the Parties (COP) to the Convention on Biological Diversity (CBD) in 2004.[8]

The problem with this strategy is that its impacts on poverty are often negative. The creation of protected areas causes the foreclosure of future land-use options, with potentially significant economic opportunity costs.[9] The creation of protected areas can have substantial negative impacts on local people. The eviction of former occupiers or right holders in land or resources can cause the exacerbation of poverty, as well as contravention of legal or human rights.[10–14] Globally, it is

Reprinted from *Science*, vol 306, Adams, W.M., Aveling, R., Brockington, D., Dickson, B., Elliott, J., Hutton, J., Roe, D., Vira, B. and Wolmer, W., 'Biodiversity conservation and the eradication of poverty', pp. 1146–1149, copyright © (2004) with permission from AAAS.

recognized that the costs of biodiversity conservation are not distributed in proportion to their benefits.[15] Typically, many of the costs of protected areas in poor biodiverse countries are paid by local people.[16] The 7th CBD COP called for an assessment of the economic and sociocultural costs of protected areas (including the cost of livelihood opportunities forgone), and policies to ensure that they are equitably compensated.[8] By the start of the 21st century, a remarkable international agreement on the urgency of global poverty elimination had made the relation between biodiversity conservation and poverty reduction an important element of debate about conservation policy.[1, 13]

The meaning of poverty may be intuitively obvious, but its measurement is complex. Common definitions are based on monetary (such as per-capita income) or non-monetary (such as health or mortality) criteria, although broader approaches have been suggested.[17, 18] In 1999, 1.2 billion people worldwide had consumption levels below $1 a day and 2.8 billion lived on less than $2 a day.[17] Poverty is not a static condition, but it is estimated that between 300 and 420 million people live in a state of chronic poverty (always or usually poor).[19] The first of the United Nations Millennium Development Goals (MDGs), agreed on in 2000, was to halve, between 1990 and 2015, both the proportion of people whose income is less than $1 a day and the proportion of people who suffer from hunger.[20]

National poverty reduction strategies are central to attempts to achieve poverty elimination.[21, 22] There is a clear need for these to be integrated with national sustainable development strategies.[1, 23] The UN MDGs are premised on such integration, with the area of land protected to maintain biological diversity being an indicator of performance against MDG Goal 7 ('to ensure environmental sustainability'). However, the co-listing of poverty elimination and environmental goals does not mean that integrated solutions are possible or that protected areas can contribute to growth and poverty reduction in poor countries. Indeed, the separation by the MDGs of environmental sustainability issues from development goals alarms some observers.[24] It has even been suggested that the urgent global push for poverty reduction has subsumed or supplanted conservation goals.[1]

Combining Conservation and Development Goals

The combination of poverty elimination and biodiversity conservation goals has been approached in various ways. The specific problem of the social impacts of protected areas has been recognized by conservation planners for two decades. The principle that the needs of local people should be systematically integrated into protected-area planning was agreed to at the third World Parks Congress in Bali in 1982.[25] In 1992, the president of IUCN–The World Conservation Union argued that 'if local people do not support protected areas, then protected areas cannot last'.[26] IUCN's director general now suggests that protected areas should be seen as 'islands of biodiversity in an ocean of sustainable human development' with their benefits extending far beyond their boundaries,[27] but this is still an aspiration. Delegates from the human rights and minority peoples' movements prominently voiced concern at the persistence of such impacts at the fifth World Parks Congress in September 2003.[28] There are coherent calls for better understanding of the social impacts of protected areas.[29, 30]

Beyond protected areas, the question of whether it is possible to combine poverty elimination and biodiversity conservation relates to the more general debate, familiar to conservation scientists, about the environmental dimensions of development. In the 20th century, the dominant approach was to push for economic growth first and assume that environmental problems (and indeed improved social welfare) could be sorted out later. Economists argue that as economies grow, they can invest in cleaner technologies and less resource-depleting processes: Arguably, an 'environmental Kuznets curve' can be observed in industrialized and newly industrialized countries, with improvements in factors such as air pollution.[31] In the 1950s and 1960s, development planners paid scant attention to environmental impacts, whether focusing on poverty elimination, the creation of high-productivity agriculture, or physical infrastructure such as dams or industrialization and the associated problems of pollution.[32, 33]

Critics of this technocratic top-down development focused on its environmental and social failures.[33, 34] The need to improve the environmental record of development gave rise to the second approach to the environmental aspects of development, in the concept of sustainable development, which underpinned the 1980 *World Conservation Strategy* document.[33] As developed since, notably at the World Conference on Environment and Development in Rio de Janeiro in 1992 and the World Summit on Sustainable Development in Johannesburg in 2002, the concept of sustainable development was extended to make explicit reference to justice, equity and the elimination of poverty. World leaders agreed that biodiversity and resource conservation must be fully integrated into strategies for economic development and are essential elements of sustainable livelihoods at local scales.[35] It is widely argued that biodiversity underpins the livelihood strategies of the rural poor.[16] These political and policy insights have been accompanied by the emergence of new academic subfields that offer integrative transdisciplinary insights into social-ecological systems.[36]

Sceptics point to the large element of wish fulfilment in arguments about the possibility of win–win solutions in sustainable development.[1, 33, 37, 38] A strong body of opinion, however, maintains that poverty elimination and conservation can happen together. The term 'pro-poor conservation' has been used to identify conservation strategies that are designed to deliver both poverty reduction and biodiversity protection.[39, 40] But is this confidence in win–win solutions justified? Lasting positive outcomes of conservation-with-development projects are elusive.[41, 42] Projects that seek to integrate conservation and development have tended to be overambitious and underachieving.[41–44] Although it is desirable to satisfy the goals of biodiversity and poverty reduction simultaneously, it may only be possible under specific institutional, ecological and developmental conditions (such as in long-lasting field projects in small human communities in fragile ecosystems[1]). The links between biodiversity and livelihoods, and between conservation and poverty reduction, are dynamic and locally specific.[34, 45] In most cases, hard choices will be necessary between goals, with significant costs to one goal or the other. The acceptability of these costs will vary for different organizations and actors.

Diverse Relations Between Conservation and Poverty Reduction

Clarity over the choices between biodiversity conservation and poverty elimination goals is essential. The desire to package projects as delivering win–win solutions plays down the incompatibilities between goals. Equally, exclusive conservation or development goals can be blind to alliances that favour both.[1] We therefore offer a conceptual typology of the relationships between poverty reduction and conservation in order to promote a clearer understanding of them. The typology presents four different ways of looking at the connections and disconnections between poverty reduction and conservation, reflecting positions in the current debate. It includes both the moral and pragmatic dimensions of arguments for the conservation of biodiversity and the reduction of poverty. Disentangling these makes for clarity.

1. *Poverty and conservation are separate policy realms.* This position sees poverty elimination and conservation as quite different problems comprising distinct sectors of policy concern. Thus, conservation is a legitimate objective that can be pursued independently of any benefits in poverty reduction (and vice versa). Under this position, conservation strategies would focus on the establishment of protected areas or approaches such as direct payments.[46] If poverty is recognized as an important cause of conservation failure, the response is the designation of further critical biodiverse habitat and the stronger defence of protected areas, rather than the dissipation of scarce conservation resources to maintain diversity across landscapes or in poverty alleviation activities.[37, 38] This position sees conservation benefiting poverty reduction indirectly where it secures ecosystem services that yield economic benefits to society, such as enhanced water yields from forested catchments.[47, 48] There may also be local opportunities for win–win strategies that combine biodiversity and poverty reduction (such as protected-area tourism arrangements[49]). However, this position holds that trying to combine conservation with poverty reduction everywhere risks misallocating limited conservation resources and compromising biodiversity preservation.[37, 38] The key to the success of conservation is the establishment and effective management of a complete global network of protected areas selected because of scientific criteria and owned or legally

established by the state or legitimate private owners. Success is measured in terms of biodiversity criteria, not of measures of social development.[6]

2. *Poverty is a critical constraint on conservation.* This position makes the empirical, pragmatic argument that poverty limits conservation success to a sufficient degree that biodiversity conservation will fail if it does not successfully address poverty elimination. Such a position might be expected in a scenario where poor people were overharvesting wild species, poaching critical species, or colonizing and cultivating biodiverse land, and if the political or economic costs of stopping them (such as by a conventional strict protected-area strategy) were prohibitive. Poverty reduction would be undertaken in this instance simply as a means to achieve more effective conservation. This position holds that to achieve its goal, conservation must provide (and be seen to provide) effective contributions to poverty reduction, including both net benefits to the poor and the avoidance of significant local costs to any social group. Conservation organizations will invest in addressing the poverty of critical protected-area neighbours and actors with the power to disrupt conservation programmes. Examples of policy action include classic park outreach strategies (such as service provision to neighbouring villages, employment for local people, and participation in park planning processes) and income-generating projects (such as sharing revenue from wildlife tourism in protected areas, integrated conservation–development projects, or the provision of locally acceptable alternatives to lost resources).[41, 43]

3. *Conservation should not compromise poverty reduction.* This position recognizes that conservation agencies have conservation as their primary goal, but it holds that in pursuing that goal they should, at a minimum, not increase poverty or undermine the livelihoods of the poor. This position was adopted at the fifth World Parks Congress in 2003, but has its critics.[27] Examples of strategies resulting from this position might include codes of conduct for conservation organizations, social impact assessment of protected areas,[29, 30] and the payment of the full local opportunity costs of conservation in protected areas.[50] Conservation strategies might also seek to generate positive economic benefits for local communities within constraints of biodiversity conservation targets, for example through non-extractive use (such as ecotourism[49]) or harvesting within sustainable limits (such as safari hunting, medicinal products, or biomass products[51, 52]). This position differs from the empirical claim in position 2 that poor people, if ignored, will undermine conservation. Rather it reflects independent moral and political obligations on conservation agencies to take account of human poverty. It is a claim that recognizes that conservation action can be sustained despite negative social impacts.[53] It applies even where it is possible to do conservation effectively without benefiting poor people.

4. *Poverty reduction depends on living resource conservation.* This position rests on the empirical claim that financially poor and socially and politically marginalized people depend on living species in biodiverse ecosystems for livelihoods and ecosystem services, and that their livelihoods can be improved through

appropriate conservation activities.[33] Conservation is therefore a tool for achieving poverty reduction, with the sustainable use of natural resources being a foundation of strategies for achieving poverty reduction and social justice. Biodiversity benefits not immediately necessary to this goal are a secondary gain. This position might lead to the rejection of a protected-area strategy because, except under special circumstances (for example, where shares of ecotourism revenues exceeded all other forms of land use), protected areas were unlikely to achieve poverty reduction goals. Alternative approaches would include the sustainable use of living resources to optimize economic return and/or positive impacts on the rural or urban poor.[54] Examples of policy include conservation programmes outside protected areas; for example, to promote the local management of common-pool resources within the constraints of ecological sustainability such as fisheries, wildlife, grazing, or forestry that are targeted at improving the livelihoods of the poor.[54-56] Conservation in response to this position tends toward the maintenance of yields of harvestable species and ecosystems rather than the preservation of biodiversity. Outcomes may deviate to a greater or lesser degree from biodiversity conservation targets. This principle is reflected in the 'ecosystem approach' adopted by the CBD in 2000.[57]

Conclusion

No position outlined here suggests that either the conservation of biodiversity or the elimination of poverty are improper goals. All positions are consistent with the call for conservation organizations to identify and monitor the social impacts of their work, and to take corporate responsibility for operating in a socially accountable manner.[29] They are also all consistent with the need for poverty alleviation efforts, and wider projects for the development of humankind, to have regard to their demands, or footprint, on the biosphere.[3, 58, 59]

Different agencies (and different individuals) are likely to wish to adopt different positions. For example, differences in thinking about the balance to be struck between poverty reduction and biodiversity conservation underlie different positions in the 'parks versus sustainable use' debate.[37, 38, 54, 60] Those advocating strictly enforced protected areas in poor developing countries to guarantee the maintenance of populations of vulnerable species (such as forest primates) are adopting position 1, treating the problems of extinction and poverty as separate. Those advocating programmes to tackle the poverty of people living around such parks in order to persuade them not to trespass or hunt are adopting position 2, seeing poverty as a critical constraint on conservation. Those who would seek to increase the flow of revenues from such parks to a level that would fully compensate all stakeholders for associated opportunity costs of the park are adopting position 3, attempting to ensure that conservation does not increase poverty in any way. Those who propose conservation strategies building on the needs of local communities for sustainable harvests of wild species resources, and not necessarily a formally declared protected area at all, are adopting position 4, seeing conservation strategies based on sustainable use primarily as a means to reduce poverty.

Policy that fails to take account of the diverse relationships between conservation needs and the demands of poverty reduction, and the related consumptive demands of the growing world economy, risks failure.[1] Organizations committed to the preservation of species and those committed to sustainable rural livelihoods based on natural resource use are likely to engage with issues of poverty and biodiversity in very different ways. Their interactions will be facilitated if they can understand their mutual positions. The recognition of different starting points in the way in which biodiversity conservation and poverty elimination goals are prioritized is essential if there is to be success in identifying common ground and differences between biodiversity and development organizations. Such recognition will facilitate the task of those who believe that the goals must be achieved together.

It is premature to abandon attempts to combine conservation and development. The elimination of poverty and the preservation of biodiversity are two distinct objectives. Each may be driven by different moral agendas, but there is considerable overlap in practice.

At the local scale, the policy need is to reconcile the interests of different stakeholders in the management of the natural resources of biodiverse ecosystems.[45] The larger challenge is to allow human society to meet its potential and share the fruits of economic growth while sustaining a biosphere that not only sustains full ecological functions but retains its living diversity.[3, 34]

References and Notes

1   S.E. Sanderson, K.H. Redford, *Oryx* 37, 1 (2003).
2   S. Palumbi, *Science* 293, 1786 (2001).
3   W.M. Adams, *Against Extinction: The Story of Conservation* (Earthscan, London, 2004).
4   C.R. Margules, R.L. Pressey, *Nature* 405, 243 (2000).
5   A.S. Rodrigues et al., *Nature* 428, 640 (2004).
6   A.G. Brunner, R.E. Gullison, R.E. Rice, G.A.B. da Fonseca, *Science* 291, 125 (2001).
7   http://sea.unep-wcmc.org/wdbpa/ (accessed 27 November 2009).
8   www.biodiv.org (accessed 27 November 2009).
9   M. Norton-Griffiths, C. Southey, *Ecol. Econ.* 12, 125 (1995).
10   D. Brockington, *Fortress Conservation: The Preservation of the Mkomazi Game Reserve, Tanzania* (Currey, Oxford, 2002).
11   C.L. Fortwangler, in *Contested Nature: Promoting International Biodiversity with Social Justice in the Twenty-First Century*, S.R. Brechin, P.R. Wilshusen, C.L. Fortwangler, P.C. West (eds) (State Univ. of New York Press, Albany, NY, 2003), pp. 25–40.
12   M. Colchester, *Salvaging Nature: Indigenous Peoples, Protected Areas and Biodiversity Conservation* (World Rainforest Movement, Montevideo, 2002).

13 K. Ghimire, M. Pimbert, *Social Change and Conservation* (Earthscan, London, 1997).

14 C. Geisler, R. de Sousa, *Public Adm. Dev.* 21, 159 (2001).

15 M. Wells, *Ambio* 21, 237 (1992).

16 D. Roe, J. Elliott, *Oryx* 38, 137 (2004).

17 World Bank Poverty Net, www.worldbank.org/poverty (accessed 27 November 2009).

18 A. Sen, *Development as Freedom* (Oxford Univ. Press, Oxford, 2001).

19 www.chronicpoverty.org/chronic_poverty_report_2004.htm (7 July 2004).

20 www.developmentgoals.org (accessed 27 November 2009).

21 www.worldbank.org/poverty/strategies/index.htm (accessed 27 November 2009).

22 J. Bojo, R.C. Reddy, *Poverty Reduction Strategies and Environment* (World Bank Environment Department Paper 86, World Bank, Washington, DC, 2002).

23 www.un.org/esa/sustdev/natlinfo/nsds/map2002.htm (accessed 27 November 2009).

24 D. Roe, in *The Millennium Development Goals: Hitting the Target or Missing the Point?* (IIED, London, 2003), pp. 55–70.

25 A. Phillips, *George Wright Forum* 20, 8 (2002).

26 S. Ramphal, in *Parks for Life: Report of the IVth World Congress on National Parks and Protected Areas*, J. McNeely (ed) (IUCN, Gland, Switzerland, 1993), pp. 56–58.

27 A. Steiner, *New Sci.* 180, 21 (2003).

28 www.iucn.org/themes/wcpa/wpc2003/english/outputs/ recommendations.htm (10 March 2004).

29 D. Brockington, K. Schmidt-Soltau, *Oryx* 38, 140 (2004).

30 C. Geisler, in *Contested Nature: Promoting International Biodiversity Conservation with Social Justice in the Twenty-First Century*, S.R. Brechin, P.R. Wilshusen, C.L. Fortwangler, P.C. West (eds) (State Univ. of New York Press, Albany, NY), pp. 217–229.

31 World Bank, *World Development Report 1992: Development and the Environment*, (Oxford Univ. Press for the World Bank, New York, 1992).

32 R.F. Dasmann, J.P. Milton, P.H. Freeman, *Ecological Principles for Economic Development* (Wiley, Chichester, UK, 1973).

33 W.M. Adams, *Green Development: Environment and Sustainability in the Third World* (Routledge, London, 2001).

34 S.E. Sanderson, K.H. Redford, *Oryx* 38, 146 (2004).

35 Livestock and Wildlife Advisory Group, *Wildlife and Poverty Study* (Department for International Development, London, 2002).

36 F. Berkes, *Conserv. Biol.* 18, 621 (2004).

37 J. Terborgh, *Requiem for Nature* (Island Press, Washington, DC, 1999).

38 J.F. Oates, *Myth and Reality in the Rain Forest: How Conservation Strategies Are Failing in West Africa* (Univ. of California Press, Berkeley, CA, 1999).

39 IUCN, *Beyond Rhetoric: Putting Conservation to Work for the Poor* (IUCN, Gland, Switzerland, 2002).

40 D. Roe, J. Hutton, J. Elliott, K. Chitepo, M. Saruchera, *Policy Matters* 12, 52 (2003).

41 D. Hulme, M.W. Murphree (eds), *African Wildlife and Livelihoods: The Promise and Performance of Community Conservation* (Currey, Oxford, 2001).

42 J.S. Murombedzi, *J. Int. Dev.* 11, 287 (1999).

43 C.S. Barrett, P. Arcese, *World Dev.* 23, 1073 (1995).

44 M. Wells, K. Brandon, *People and Parks: Linking Protected Areas with Local Communities* (World Bank, Washington, DC, 1992).

45 T. Kepe, M. Saruchera, W. Whande, *Oryx* 38, 143 (2004).

46 P.J. Ferraro, *Science* 298, 1718 (2002).

47 A. Balmford et al., *Science* 297, 950 (2002).

48 G.C. Daily (ed) *Nature's Services: Societal Dependence on Natural Ecosystems* (Island Press, Washington, DC, 1997).

49 S. Gosling, *Ecol. Econ.* 29, 303 (1999).

50 A. Balmford, T. Whitten, *Oryx* 37, 238 (2003).
51 B.M. Campbell, M.K. Luckert, *Uncovering the Hidden Harvest: Valuation Methods for Woodland and Forest Resources* (Earthscan, London, 2002).
52 D.S. Wilkie, J. F. Carpenter, *Oryx* 3, 338 (1999).
53 D. Brockington, *Policy Matters* 12, 22 (2003).
54 J. Hutton, N. Leader-Williams, *Oryx* 37, 215 (2003).
55 T. Franks, *Issues Nat. Resour. Manage.* 1, 2 (2003).
56 I. Koziell, J. Saunders (eds), *Living Off Biodiversity: Exploring the Livelihoods and Biodiversity Issues in Natural Resources Management* (IIED, London, 2001).
57 www.biodiv.org/decisions/default.aspx?m0cop-05 (accessed 27 November 2009).
58 M.L. Imhoff et al., *Nature* 429, 870 (2004).
59 M. Wackernagel, W. Rees, *Our Ecological Footprint: Reducing Human Impact on Earth* (New Society Publishers, Gabriola Island, British Columbia, 1996).
60 P.R. Wilshusen, S.R. Brechin, C.L. Fortwangler, P.C. West, *Soc. Nat. Resources* 15, 17 (2002).

Chapter 3

Linking Conservation and Poverty Reduction: Landscapes, People and Power

Robert Fisher, Stewart Maginnis, William Jackson, Edmund
Barrow and Sally Jeanrenaud

The Challenge of Sustainable Development

There have been a number of major initiatives that attempt to address poverty
through conservation, including the People–Environment Partnership,[1] the Rights
and Resources Initiative (both coalitions of development and conservation agencies) and IUCN's 'Conservation for Poverty Reduction'.[2]

The Millennium Ecosystem Assessment was a major international initiative
that commenced in 2001 and involved over 1000 experts. The assessment led to
four main findings, all of which establish fundamental connections between
healthy ecosystems and human well-being. The outcomes were presented in a wide
variety of publications. Two of the findings are particularly relevant to a discussion
of conservation and poverty (Millennium Ecosystem Assessment, 2005, p. 1):

- *The changes that have been made to ecosystems have contributed to substantial net
  gains in human well-being and economic development, but these gains have been
  achieved at growing costs in the form of degradation of many ecosystem services,
  increased risks of nonlinear changes, and the exacerbation of poverty for some groups
  of people. These problems, unless addressed, will substantially diminish the benefits
  that future generations obtain from ecosystems.*
- *The degradation of ecosystem services could grow significantly worse during the first
  half of this century and is a barrier to achieving the Millennium Development
  Goals.*

In *Linking Conservation and Poverty Reduction*, we wish to reinvigorate sustainable development rather than suggest an entirely new approach. We believe this can be done by improving the linkages and balancing the impact of actions in each pillar of sustainable development, particularly on the poor.

The call to reinvigorate sustainable development presents major challenges to the development and conservation communities alike. The challenge to the development community is that, despite many years and large investments, rural poverty remains a major problem: 75 per cent of the poor are rural dwellers (IFAD, 2002). Many development activities have made many people worse off. Whatever the benefits at larger scales, development has often occurred at a cost to the poorest people and the environment. Indeed, the environment has been ignored as an opportunity for poverty reduction and the focus on short-term development at the cost of environmental damage has often undermined longer-term efforts at poverty reduction.

For conservationists, despite many years of effort and some important successes, a biodiversity crisis still exists. Conservationists have largely failed to convince economists and developmental practitioners of conservation's long-term importance to development. Further, in the process of promoting conservation, conservationists have, to a considerable extent, ignored its costs to poor peoples' livelihoods and the inequitable distribution of these costs. Conservationists face three challenges:

1. making a better case for the long-term economic and social benefits of conservation;
2. accounting for the real costs of some conservation activities to the poor; and
3. recognizing biodiversity as a livelihood resource as well as a global public good.

While *Linking Conservation and Poverty Reduction* calls for the reinvigoration of sustainable development, it focuses particularly on a subset of sustainable development issues: the links between poverty reduction, economic development and biodiversity conservation. The connections between poverty, the economy and the environment are complex and the extent to which conservation activities can and should address poverty issues is still being argued. This, however, does not negate the need for conservationists to do a better job at figuring out how to address poverty, for both ethical and practical reasons.[3]

Linking Conservation and Poverty Reduction highlights the importance of improving institutional arrangements in ways that build opportunities to reduce poverty and improve conservation. In particular it looks at the importance of creating institutional mechanisms for equitable negotiation about competing objectives for resource use and competing interests. It also argues that thinking of conservation and natural resource management on a landscape scale provides better opportunities to achieve diverse objectives than striving to meet multiple objectives in specific sites. This has particular relevance to protected areas. While protected areas are important to conservation, a more comprehensive package of tools and strategies must be applied, both inside and outside protected areas.

Livelihoods, Poverty and Conservation

Livelihoods can be thought of as the ways in which people make a living. This is not just a matter for the poor, although sometimes livelihoods are equated with subsistence. Livelihoods contribute to human well-being, which includes spiritual and aesthetic values. Poverty can be thought of as a state of reduced or limited livelihood opportunities. This obviously includes tangibles like assets and goods for consumption, but also involves vulnerability and powerlessness to make meaningful choices about livelihoods. Although poverty is often defined in absolute terms (people falling below a specified level of income, commonly US$2 per day), it can also be seen as having multiple dimensions. The World Bank (2001) refers to three dimensions of poverty: lack of assets, powerlessness and vulnerability. *Linking Conservation and Poverty Reduction* adopts the World Bank definition.

The term 'conservation' is used in its broadest sense, including management of natural resources sustainably as well as their protection and restoration, rather than in the narrow sense of maintaining an original state, or preservation. This is an important distinction. The term is often used by different people to mean quite different things, which creates considerable confusion.

Conserving natural resources can have important direct positive benefits on livelihoods, particularly those of rural people. Natural resources are used for direct consumption and for income generation. The economic value of wild resources is often ignored in quantifying rural economy and livelihoods, but it can have considerable importance (see Box 3.1).

Conservation is essential for livelihoods in a variety of ways. In developing countries, maintenance of diverse natural resources can be particularly important in providing livelihood security in times of seasonal shortage (by providing alternative foods and other resources) and in times of crisis, such as drought, crop failure or even market failure (see Box 3.2). Maintaining diverse livelihood options is essential for many of the rural poor. Conservation of natural resources is important in providing secure environmental services (such as water and clean air) to all humans, rural and urban, wealthy or poor. It also provides important insurance against risks, including crop failure, market failure and natural disasters.

While it is clear that species gathered from the wild can be important to poor people, especially in times of crisis, some economists point out that poorer households generally have no other livelihood options open to them, and that many would not choose to depend on wild resources for their survival if given a choice. It is precisely because they are so poor that they depend on such safety nets. Instead it is claimed that tying livelihoods and poverty reduction objectives to natural resource conservation creates a 'poverty-trap'. Wunder (2001), for example, argues that the potential of tropical forests to lift people out of poverty is very limited.[4] Dove (1993) argues that forest conservation is unlikely to lead to poverty reduction because the poor tend only to have the rights to low-value forest products. Whenever products become valuable, the poor lose access.

Box 3.1 *The value of wild resources*

The economic value of wild resources in Senegal

An analysis of the value of wild foods and other wild resources in Senegal focused on non-timber forest products, game and freshwater fisheries. It found that, in the surveyed areas, these products were mostly used to generate income. Small amounts were used for home consumption.

Although the value of these products is not included in national accounts, the study concluded that the annual value is between US$19 million and US$35 million. This does not include the value of plant resources such as 'fuelwood, charcoal and building materials, which are equally significant but largely accounted for in national economic statistics'. The study also noted that 'natural resources appear to be more important as a share of total cash income for poorer households'.

The study also presented some important findings on the impacts of gender and education:

> ... *female-headed households report less cash income from hunting but more from other wild products and artisanal mining, although the latter differences are not statistically significant. Women also report less cash income in total. Finally, household heads with little or no formal education reported more cash income from gathering wild resources (not hunting) on average, than those who had attended primary school or received [Quranic] instruction.*

Source: UDRSS/VALEURS (2002)

The economic value of wildlife

The Department for International Development's study of wildlife and poverty linkages found that poor people are significantly dependent 'on wildlife for livelihood and food security, particularly through bushmeat and tourism'. According to the study '[o]f the estimated 1.2 billion people who live on less than the equivalent of a dollar a day ... as many as 150 million people (one-eighth of the world's poorest) perceive wildlife to be an important livelihood asset'.

Source: DFID (2002)

Box 3.2 *Food security and diversity in Laotian forests*

In Salavan province, in Lao PDR, the rural diet is dominated by glutinous rice, which contributes 73 per cent of total dietary intake during the rainy seasons. Forest foods are essential components of the diet, accounting for an average of 19 per cent of total dietary intake in the rainy season. Excluding rice, forest foods amount to 70 per cent of dietary intake. As forest foods provide year-round diversity to otherwise bland and poorly balanced diets, they also ensure a regular source of nutrients. Approximately 44 per cent of the total calcium and vitamin A and C intake, 25 per cent of total iron intake and 27 per cent of daily protein requirements come from the forest.

Source: Dechaineux (2001)

We agree that such safety nets must never become poverty traps. However, especially in the absence of functioning social security systems and reliable market networks in rural areas, we maintain that the sustainable use of biological resources will remain crucial to the secure livelihoods of the poor in the foreseeable future. Further, we would stress poverty reduction involves empowerment in the form of altered access to valuable natural resources in order to allow benefits to flow to the poor. Poverty traps are not so much a result of dependence on natural resources as they are a result of lack of access to valuable natural resources.

It is important to note the emerging recognition of the complex connections between poverty and vulnerability to natural disasters: these present another angle on the importance of conservation for poverty reduction. It is increasingly clear that the poor tend to be particularly vulnerable to natural disasters (as the 2004 Asian tsunami made clear) and it is likely that they will be particularly vulnerable to the effects of climate change. Such vulnerability arises from a number of factors:

- The poor are often located in the areas vulnerable to natural disasters.
- The poor are usually not well endowed with economic assets (or insurance) and, in the case of disasters, often lose everything.
- As they depend heavily on natural resources, drastic changes to the environment also drastically affect their livelihood systems.
- Reconstruction efforts after natural disasters can also be a problem as the poor lose rights to land and resources, sometimes because they lack formal rights in the first place and sometimes because more powerful people take advantage of a situation, as happened in southern Thailand after the Asian tsunami when a 'private investor used police and soldiers to ... prevent people from accessing their devastated community' (Kaewkuntee, 2006).

The value of conservation to integrated risk management for natural disasters, and the associated need to consider the particular vulnerability of the poor are increasingly recognized (see, for example, Sudmeier-Rieux et al., 2006).

Threats to livelihoods from development

Clearly (as illustrated in Box 3.3) natural resources can be very important to livelihood security of rural people. Ineffective economic development policies and practices pursued by governments, sectoral development and large-scale infrastructure projects, and macroeconomic reform have all too often jeopardized poor peoples' livelihoods by destroying the resource base.

One example from the Northern Province of Cameroon shows how sectoral development planning can dramatically affect livelihoods and undermine the functions – and the economic value – of natural ecosystems (Box 3.3).

Box 3.3 *Effects of irrigation in Cameroon*

The Waza Logone floodplain (8000 square kilometres) is a critical area of biodiversity and high productivity in a dry area, where rainfall is uncertain and livelihoods are extremely insecure. The floodplain's natural goods and services provide income and subsistence for more than 85 per cent of the region's rural population, or 125,000 people. The biodiversity and high productivity of the floodplain depend to a large extent on the annual inundation of the Logone River. In 1979 the construction of a small irrigated rice scheme (40 square kilometres) reduced flooding by almost 1000 square kilometres. The socio-economic effects of this loss have been devastating, incurring livelihood costs of almost US$50 million over approximately 20 years. Up to 8000 households have suffered direct economic losses of more than US$2 million a year through reduction in dry-season grazing, fishing, natural resource harvesting and surface water supplies. The losses incurred are far in excess of the anticipated return from irrigation.

After 1994, pilot flood releases were made in the Waza Logone floodplain, unblocking watercourses that had been sealed off as a result of the irrigation scheme. Without altering the operations of the rice scheme, these led to demonstrable recoveries in floodplain flora and fauna over 1000 square kilometres, and have been welcomed by local people. The economic value of the floodplain restoration is immense. Improved planning at the regional scale will rehabilitate vital pasture, fisheries and farmland areas used by nearly a third of the population, with a value of almost US$250 per capita.

Source: Loth (2004)[5]

Large-scale infrastructure development often has negative impacts on the livelihoods of the poor, even though it may provide benefits at a wider scale or for a nation as a whole. The construction of large dams is one example of short-term regional or national economic benefits taking precedence over the rights and long-term livelihood security of the rural poor. As the World Commission on Dams (WCD, 2000, p. 7) concluded, large dams have often made an 'important and significant contribution to human development', but the costs of securing benefits have been very high and unevenly distributed, with poor and vulnerable groups 'likely to bear a disproportionate share of the social and environmental costs of large dam projects without gaining a commensurate share of the economic benefits' (p. 17). The WCD argues that a 'balance-sheet' approach to assessing costs and benefits (that is, adding up costs and benefits without looking at the way in which they are distributed) 'is increasingly seen as unacceptable on equity grounds and as a poor means of assessing the "best projects"' (p. 17).

Threats to livelihoods from conservation

While it is clear that development activities may have unintended negative impacts on the poor or may fail to include the poor as beneficiaries, conservation has sometimes had similar outcomes. Conservation practices can have serious negative effects on livelihoods by limiting access to the resources necessary for subsistence, livelihood security or income generation. One major way in which conservation has been detrimental to the poor is by excluding people from protected areas or limiting their access to resources within protected areas. Such exclusionary practices have serious and well-documented negative outcomes (Brockington, 2003; McLean and Straede, 2003; Brockington and Igoe, 2006), especially when resident people are resettled to other locations. There are very few documented cases where forced resettlement[6] provides adequate alternative livelihoods, and resettled people frequently place additional pressure on those already living in resettlement areas. This applies to forced resettlement resulting from both large-scale development projects (such as dams) and the creation of protected areas. In recent years many conservation projects and programmes have attempted to address some of the negative effects of exclusory practices on people with integrated conservation and development programmes. These initiatives essentially aim to provide alternatives to livelihood-related resources from protected areas. These projects have had limited success, but they are an important step forward.

It is not conservation itself that is the problem for poor rural people whose livelihoods depend on natural resources. Rather, conservation approaches often do not adequately take into account the adverse impacts of conservation activities on the rural poor. Conservation has often been narrowly interpreted as requiring exclusion of people from resource use. Protected areas provide an important alternative to destructive land uses such as large-scale forest plantations, mining projects and commercial agriculture, which not only have negative environmental impacts but can undermine poor people's livelihood security. Protected areas are not the only, and certainly not the worst, large-scale land use that affects the livelihoods of the rural poor. Nevertheless, it is not good enough to justify processes of exclusion and expropriation of resources on the grounds that others do it.[7] We recognize the need for 'trade-offs'. The point is that interventions often do not even recognize that the costs of these trade-offs are borne by the rural poor, leave alone dealing with the issue in an equitable way.

Causal linkages and their implications

This chapter does not provide a comprehensive review of the linkages between conservation, environmental degradation, poverty and wealth. Clearly these linkages are very complex, although people have a strong tendency to try and demonstrate one-way causal links between various factors. For example, the following often contradictory assertions are all made frequently and often backed up with good evidence (at least for a particular case):

- Poverty leads to increased environmental degradation, either because rural people don't know better or because they have no choice but to overexploit natural resources.
- Wealthy people have a severe impact on natural resources because they consume more. This often leads to environmental degradation.
- People who are dependent on resources for their livelihoods are likely to protect them more carefully.
- Conservation worsens poverty by excluding people from resources.
- Conservation contributes to better quality of livelihoods because it guarantees availability of resources.

All these assertions can be valid interpretations of specific cases, but none of them is true universally.[8] Attempts to understand causal linkages must be related to the contexts of specific situations. The specific factors that govern causes and effects need to be carefully identified and properly understood, a process that will often be quite complex. For example in the case of Shinyanga, a change in rights of access to forest resources changed the way people used forests, despite increasing population. There was no simple relationship between population increase and resource degradation. Further, in the absence of widely applicable causal patterns, addressing poverty and conservation linkages will inevitably be more of an art – requiring creativity and flexibility – than an exact science.

To some extent this view runs contrary to calls for an 'evidence-based approach' to conservation. Sutherland et al. (2004) argue that conservation practice is often 'based upon anecdote and myth rather than upon the systemic appraisal of the evidence'. They argue that conservation practitioners can learn from the results of applying the 'evidence-based approach' in medical practice. They make particular reference to work that attempts to link development with conservation:

.A major thrust of recent conservation work has been to incorporate socioeconomic development, but many of the practices seem based upon faith and a political agenda rather than on the benefits to biodiversity. As examples, does clarifying who owns the property rights to each area result in long-term sustainable development or overexploitation? Does providing alter-

native sources of income ... reduce the need to exploit natural resources, act as an additional activity with neutral effects, or provide the extra income that enables investment, such as purchasing a chainsaw or vehicle, that further accelerates resource loss? (Sutherland et al., 2004, p. 306)

Obviously any approach to conservation or development needs to be informed by evidence and, in that sense, the call for an evidence-based approach makes good sense. But there are difficulties inherent in assuming that there is a single clear and consistent answer to the question of whether 'clarifying who owns the property rights to each area results in long-term sustainable development or overexploitation'. The answer will almost certainly be 'yes' in some cases, 'no' in other cases and in most cases will depend on a whole range of additional situational and contextual factors. Causality can be highly complex and uncertain. Further, it is not predestined; a change in contextual factors (such as institutional arrangements at various levels) can lead to very different outcomes.[9]

It is also important to address the point that socio-economic approaches 'seem based upon faith and a political agenda rather than on the benefits to biodiversity'. This is not surprising. The rationale for addressing socio-economic factors is, at least to some extent, explicitly based on political (social justice) objectives. It is not based solely on assertions of benefits to biodiversity.

Linking Conservation and Poverty Reduction is based on the belief that conservation can do more to address poverty reduction and that poor ecosystem health will often undermine social and economic stability and the livelihoods of the poor. It should be clearly understood from the outset that this book is not advocating that poverty reduction is essential to biodiversity conservation.

Efforts at integrating conservation and development have sometimes been based on unrealistic assumptions about achieving win–win solutions. Obviously these are not always possible and it may be more realistic to look for trade-offs that may provide the best realistically possible outcomes. But, while assumptions about perfect solutions may be overly optimistic, it should not be thought that poverty reduction and conservation will always be in conflict. As the cases of Pred Nai and Shinyanga show, rural people, and especially the poor, may have very good reasons for supporting the restoration of biodiversity in areas where severe degradation has occurred, providing appropriate institutional arrangements can be established. Restoring degraded lands provides considerable opportunities for improving conservation and poverty reduction.

Addressing Poverty and Conservation

The discussion about the links between livelihoods, poverty and conservation is not particularly new. Many conservationists have expressed concern about the need to take livelihoods and poverty into account in conservation activities. Since the 1970s, the movements advocating integrated conservation and development projects (ICDPs) and community-based conservation and resource management have reflected these concerns. Despite innovative and exciting work, however, ICDPs have been criticized for a lack of a clear framework and for weak or piecemeal implementation (McShane and Wells, 2004). In recent years, with the development of the livelihoods framework by the UK governments' Department for International Development (DFID) and other agencies,[10] terms such as 'pro-poor wildlife conservation' and 'pro-poor conservation' have appeared in conservation literature (DFID, 2002).[11] *Linking Conservation and Poverty Reduction* is not an attempt to replace these earlier approaches. Instead we stress the importance of commitment to poverty reduction within conservation activities.

As part of the concern with poverty reduction in conservation, human rights and social justice have emerged as fundamental issues. The rights of indigenous peoples to natural resources, especially in protected areas, have been recognized for many years and are encapsulated in a number of publications and policy statements (WWF, 1996; MacKay, 2002).

Others have advocated a stronger 'rights-based approach' to conservation, arguing that all conservation should start with a concern for human rights and, by implication, that this should be a primary concern of conservation. This book does not assert that human rights should necessarily be the primary concern of conservation. It does assert that, while conservation is justifiable on its own account, conservation approaches should also be socially just in the sense that they avoid or mitigate the 'actual [i.e. financial] and opportunity costs' of conservation to the poor (Phil Franks, CARE, personal communication). Social justice can be used as an operating principle, a measure to assess a minimum standard for conservation in areas where high levels of poverty persist. This can be thought of as a 'do not harm principle'. The minimum standard should be combined with a strong ethical commitment to support poverty reduction as a fundamental human right and development goal.

Discussion of 'rights' in conservation often revolves around the concept of environmental rights, understood as the right to a safe and healthy environment. This is often limited, in practice, to a concern for rights such as the right to clean water and the right to enjoy an aesthetically pleasing environment. It is more relevant, in the context of poverty reduction, to think in terms of more fundamental rights, such as the right to food, the right to shelter, the right to health, the right to enjoy cultural identity (a right which is particularly relevant to many indigenous peoples) and even the 'right to development', which is recognized in several international legal documents (Scanlon et al., 2004).

Cultural and indigenous issues are important in discussions of poverty and environment, partly because indigenous peoples are often especially vulnerable to environmental change and loss of environmental rights, partly because cultural identity is itself often linked to particular environments and partly because people who lose cultural identity are more prone to fall into poverty.

The conservation approach advocated in *Linking Conservation and Poverty Reduction* does not attempt to limit conservation activities to cases where poverty can be directly addressed. We are not proposing that conservation agencies stop worrying about conservation or that they become development-focused agencies. Rather, this book provides a broad approach for exploring negotiated outcomes in different types of circumstances, so that both conservation and land-use-related development efforts are guided by social justice principles. Further, conservation should proactively look for opportunities to address poverty and livelihoods while development activities should actively support improved environmental management wherever possible. This is not about diluting the impact of conservation activities or shifting focus by stealth. Rather, it is about finding more appropriate, more equitable and more realistic ways of achieving conservation. We aim to augment the conservation toolkit by suggesting ways in which conservation can better address its associated social responsibilities.

Taking poverty reduction more seriously in conservation has a number of implications:

- All conservation initiatives should strive to ensure that they do not make the poor worse off. The costs of conservation should not be imposed on those least able to absorb them; they should be met by those groups – usually national governments and the international community – who regard conservation as a priority. This must go beyond narrow quid pro quo compensation. Best-practice measures designed to offset the impact of conservation activities should maintain, if not expand, development options, rather than leaving people in a poverty trap or a condition of 'sustainable poverty'.
- Conservation ought to contribute actively to poverty reduction more broadly where it can – as in the restoration of ecosystems – simply because it can.
- There is a pressing need to be more realistic. Integrated conservation and development may not result in perfect solutions, but an equitably balanced trade-off will still lead to better conservation outcomes than could have been achieved otherwise.
- Strengthening or guaranteeing access to natural resources will contribute to secure livelihoods for the people who depend on them. This implies that rural people will have more decentralized control over the resources that they have traditionally used and managed.

If conservationists and development specialists are serious about linking poverty reduction and conservation, then we must be able to show this in our performance. In other words, we must be accountable. This means that monitoring and evaluation of all conservation activities needs to take account of social impact assessment, particularly the impacts of activities on poor people. In cases where programmes or projects aim to maintain or improve livelihoods, or to increase income directly, methodologies must directly assess impacts in terms of costs and benefits to the poor.

Conclusions

There is an ethical imperative for conservation to take account of poverty issues. There are often good practical reasons for doing so. The issue is not promoting poverty reduction over conservation, but acknowledging that both poverty reduction and conservation are important objectives. It is often necessary to address both in order to achieve either. We want to avoid the stale argument about whether conservation is the means to achieve poverty reduction, or poverty reduction is the means to achieve conservation. Both are desirable objectives.

In practice, different actors will have different points of entry. Development practitioners may focus on reducing poverty, although conservation will often be necessary in order to achieve their objective. For conservationists, reducing threats to biodiversity may be paramount. Poverty reduction will be important as both an ethical prerequisite and as a practical requirement to achieve that objective.

Linking Conservation and Poverty Reduction is not offering a magic formula for conservation and development; on the contrary. Trade-offs will sometimes define the best possible (however imperfect) outcome. At the same time, attempts to balance economic development and conservation will often lead to better outcomes than would otherwise occur.

Linking Conservation and Poverty Reduction discusses several strategies for dealing jointly with poverty and conservation:

- focus on removing limitations (particularly institutional constraints) and building opportunities;
- identify causes of environmental degradation and poverty beyond the site level and address problems at appropriate levels, both geographically and institutionally;
- use landscape-based initiatives as well as – in many cases instead of – site-based solutions. This involves seeking ways to meet objectives in different parts of the wider landscape rather than trying to address all goals in a single site (such as a protected area).

Sustainable development needs negotiated outcomes that are equitable, economically viable and socially sustainable. It is easier to achieve this type of outcome at broader geographical scales rather than at the site level.

Notes

1 Editors' note: this group is actually called the Poverty Environment Partnership (PEP) not People Environment Partnership.

2 www.iucn.org/themes/spg/portal/policy/mdg/mdg.htm

3 The relationship between poverty reduction (or 'poverty alleviation') has been the subject of debate in the pages of the journal *Oryx* (2003 and 2004). Sanderson and Redford (2003) argued that the emphasis on 'poverty alleviation' has largely replaced biodiversity conservation, but they acknowledge the importance of conservation to poverty alleviation. They worry that the costs of development (in the form of poverty alleviation) will again be borne by conservation. Roe and Elliott (2004) respond that 'poor people should not pay the price for biodiversity conservation'.

4 For a detailed discussion of the question of whether forests are safety nets or poverty traps, see Angelsen and Wunder (2003).

5 The text for the case study on Waza Logone was provided by Jean-Yves Pirot (IUCN).

6 It is important to stress here that the problem is forced resettlement. Voluntary resettlement or migration can be options for poverty reduction and many people have voluntarily chosen relocation as a strategy for improving their livelihoods.

7 At the fifth IUCN World Parks Congress in Durban, 8–17 September 2003, there was a strong recognition that conservation needs to take much more notice of the negative impacts of protected areas on the poor, as well as their potential to make a real contribution to poverty reduction through conservation activities (WPC Recommendation 29). For a discussion of ways in which protected areas can address poverty, see Scherl et al. (2004).

8 We do not intend to discuss the literature on these asserted causal relationships in detail (we think our readers will recognize each of them). Examples in the following pages will illustrate the complexities of causal relationships in particular cases. For those who wish to explore the issue further, Angelsen and Kaimowitz (1999) review the literature about the causes of deforestation, finding that there are 'serious questions concerning the conventional wisdom, either ...[because of] contrary evidence or ... the weakness of the supporting evidence' (p. 91).

9 Applying adaptive management is one way to deal with complex management issues without being paralysed by uncertainty and complexity. This approach proposes that actions be performed in situations where results are uncertain and then be modified based on careful monitoring of outcomes. (For a discussion of adaptive management applied to conservation, see Buck et al., 2001. For adaptive management of forests, see Fisher et al., 2007.)

10 Oxfam, CARE and the United Nations Development Programme (UNDP) have all been actively involved in developing livelihoods-based approaches.

11 Although the term 'pro-poor' has frequently been applied to conservation approaches in the last few years, there are some serious difficulties with it. Perhaps the main concern is that it can sound paternalistic; it also has welfarist connotations (doing good for others). The intention has been to avoid using any particular new term to describe the approach. It seems desirable to avoid developing a new term anyhow, as approaches with new names quickly become reduced to acronyms and the point gets lost.

References

Angelsen, A. and Kaimowitz, D. (1999) 'Rethinking the causes of deforestation: Lessons from economic models', *World Bank Research Observer*, 14 (1): 73–98.

Angelsen, A. and Wunder, S. (2003) *Exploring the Forest-Poverty Link: Key Concepts, Issues and Research Implications*, Occasional Paper, No 40, CIFOR, Bogor, Indonesia.

Brockington, D. (2003) 'Injustice and conservation: Is local support necessary for sustainable protected areas?', *Policy Matters*, 12: 22–30.

Brockington, D. and Igoe, J. (2006) 'Eviction for conservation: A global overview', *Conservation and Society*, 4(3): 424–470.

Buck, L.B., Geisler, C.C., Schelhas, J. and Wollenberg, E. (eds) (2001) *Biological Diversity: Balancing Interests Through Adaptive Collaborative Management*, CRC Press, Boca Raton, Florida.

Dechaineux, R. (2001) *The Role of Forest Food Resources in Village Livelihood Systems: A Study of Three Villages in Salavan Province*, Lao PDR, Vientiane.

DFID (2002) *Wildlife and Poverty Study*, DFID, Rural Livelihoods Department, London.

Dove, M. (1993) 'A revisionist view of tropical forest deforestation and development', *Environmental Conservation*, 20(1): 17–24.

Fisher, R.J., Parbhu, R. and McDougall, C. (eds) (2007) *Adaptive Collaborative Management of Community Forests in Asia: Experiences from Nepal, Indonesia and the Philippines*, Center for International Forestry Research, Bogor, Indonesia.

IFAD (2002) *Enabling the Rural Poor to Overcome their Poverty. Strategic Framework for IFAD:2002–2006*, International Fund for Agricultural Development, Rome.

Kaewkuntee, D. (2006) 'Land tenure, land conflicts and post tsunami relocation in Thailand', *Mekong Update and Dialogue*, 9(2): 2–5.

Loth, P. (ed) (2004) *The Return of the Water: Restoring the Waza Logone Floodplain in Cameroon*, IUCN, Wetlands and Water Resources Program, Gland, Switzerland and Cambridge, UK.

MacKay, F. (2002) *Addressing Past Wrongs. Indigenous Peoples and Protected Areas: The Right to Restitution of Lands and Resources*, Occasional Paper, Forest Peoples Programme, Moreton-in-Marsh.

McLean, J. and Straede, S. (2003) 'Conservation, relocation, and the paradigms of park and people management: A case study of Padampur Villages and the Royal Chitwan National Park, Nepal', *Society and Natural Resources*, 16(6): 509–526.

McShane, T.O. and Wells, M.P. (2004) *Getting Biodiversity Projects to Work: Towards More Effective Conservation and Development*, Columbia University Press, New York.

Millennium Ecosystem Assessment (2005) *Ecosystems and Human Well-Being: Synthesis*, Island Press, Washington, DC.

Roe, D. and Elliott, J. (2004) 'Poverty reduction and biodiversity conservation: Rebuilding the bridges', *Oryx*, 38(2): 137–139.

Sanderson, S.E. and Redford, K.H. (2003) 'Contested relationships between biodiversity conservation and poverty alleviation', *Oryx*, 37 (4): 389–39.

Scanlon, J., Cassar, A. and Nemes, N. (2004) *Water as a Human Right?* Paper No. 51, IUCN Environmental Policy and Law, IUCN/UNDP.

Scherl, L.M., Wilson A., Wild, R., Blockhus, J., Franks, P., McNeely, J.A. and McShane, T.O. (2004) *Can Protected Areas Contribute to Poverty Reduction? Opportunities and Limitations*, IUCN, Gland.

Sudmeier-Rieux, K., Masundire, H., Rizvi, A. and Rietbergen, S. (eds) (2006) *Ecosystems, Livelihoods and Disasters: An Integrated Approach to Disaster Risk Management*, IUCN, Gland.

Sutherland, W.J., Pullin, A.S., Dolman, P.M. and Knight, T.M. (2004) 'The need for evidence-based conservation', *Trends in Ecology and Evolution*, 19: 305–308.

UDRSS/VALEURS (2002) *The Economic Value of Wild Resources in Senegal: A Preliminary Evaluation of Non-Timber Forest Products, Game and Freshwater Fisheries*, Synthesis Report.

WCD (World Commission on Dams) (2000) *Dams and Development: A New Framework for Decision-Making,* Earthscan, London.

World Bank (2001) *Attacking Poverty: Opportunity, Empowerment, and Security: Overview, World Development Report 2000/2001,* Oxford University Press, New York.

Wunder, S. (2001) 'Poverty alleviation and tropical forests: What scope for synergies?', *World Development,* 29 (11): 1817–1833.

WWF (1996) *WWF Statement of Principles on Indigenous Peoples and Conservation,* WWF International, Gland.

Chapter 4

Poverty, Development and Biodiversity Conservation: Shooting in the Dark?

Arun Agrawal and Kent Redford

Introduction

Poverty alleviation and biodiversity conservation are both fundamental to the policy agendas of post-colonial states even if they do not enjoy similar levels of commitment (Escobar, 1995; Rangan, 1997; Peluso and Vandergeest, 2001; Thies, 2004). The continued legitimacy of the developmental state rests on its willingness and ability to address poverty. Modern states have also created multiple agencies to conserve the natural resource environments such as forests, national parks, and water bodies where biodiversity exists.[1] Indeed, it is not just states that attempt to conserve biodiversity and alleviate poverty. Large numbers of non-government organizations operating at various scales of socio-spatial aggregation also consider one or both of these goals as prime reasons for their existence.

Because of the centrality of these two objectives to the rationale and continued existence of a variety of organizational actors, a number of different programmes to achieve them simultaneously are in existence (Schwartzman et al., 2000). However, there is a wide spectrum of views about whether and to what extent it may be possible to craft policies and interventions that can secure the two objectives jointly (Adams et al., 2004). Two broad sets of inferences summarize prevalent conclusions. One is that biodiversity conservation and poverty alleviation cannot be achieved together. This general inference has led into two distinct policy directions: either that poverty alleviation should be the preoccupation of states, or that hard-headed biodiversity conservation without much attention to poverty alleviation goals is the necessary task. The second set comes from those who see potential synergies between poverty alleviation and biodiversity conservation. Within this set, for some poverty alleviation will by itself lead to conservation since the poor degrade the

LEEDS METROPOLITAN UNIVERSITY LIBRARY

Reprinted from *Poverty, Development and Biodiversity Conservation: Shooting in the Dark?*, by Agrawal, A. and Redford, K., WCS Working Paper no 26, copyright © (2006) with permission from The Wildlife Conservation Society, New York. Extract or abridged version.

environment because of their poverty; for others, programmes to combine the two goals are the necessary means to achieve them jointly. Despite the lack of agreement on the appropriateness of policy directions in varied contexts, literally billions of international aid dollars are being spent on programmes that view a particular policy as the best solution.

The main goal of our paper is to show that widespread differences in how poverty and biodiversity are understood, and limited attention to contextual particularities of empirical interventions, mean that existing empirical studies are poor guides to policy and systematic theoretical insight into the conditions under which poverty alleviation and biodiversity conservation may be compatible goals. To achieve this we first review the extensive theoretical literature on poverty and biodiversity and demonstrate the nuanced treatment these two concepts have received in this literature. We then examine the empirical literature on programmes that seek simultaneously to alleviate poverty and conserve biodiversity. Our discussion shows that the literature on programmatic interventions depends on relatively simplified understandings of poverty and biodiversity in stark contrast to the theoretical literature on these two concepts. Additionally, the significant differences in ways of measuring poverty and biodiversity in existing studies mean that their results are not easily comparable, and conclusions not easily generalizable as a basis for sustainable development policies.

Our paper is based on 37 peer-reviewed empirical studies. We primarily cover policy-oriented scholarly writings that consider it possible to connect poverty alleviation with biodiversity conservation through specific programmatic interventions, and focus on three such interventions: community-based wildlife management, ecotourism and extractive reserves. The analysis in the paper shows that different empirical studies of poverty alleviation and biodiversity conservation focus on diverse measures of poverty and biodiversity. But within a study there is rarely much evidence on multiple measures of these two complex concepts. Hence, available evidence provides relatively little systematic knowledge about the nature of the relationship between biodiversity conservation and poverty alleviation. Indeed, the multiplicity of socio-political, spatial and ecological contexts of specific programmatic interventions means that conclusions of a given study cannot easily be generalized to other contexts.

Variations in contexts also mean that even if a programme is successful in one location, it needs careful adaptation to enjoy success in other contexts. But there is insufficient knowledge about what the nature of such adaptations should be. Conceptual simplification and lack of attention to contextual specificity makes it easier to design and implement specific interventions – programme managers can gloss over and ignore potential disagreements over the meanings of foundational terms such as poverty and biodiversity or how they should be translated into the goals of a given programme. But the absence of concrete, context-sensitive criteria to measure progress also makes it more difficult to know whether a given programme has achieved goals set out by its advocates, or how experiences gained in one context may be relevant to another. We conclude our paper by outlining a research agenda that should be based on explicit recognition of conceptual complexity, contextual variety and, over time, evidence on impacts of specific types of programmes. Such a research agenda is essential to satisfy scholarly curiosity about the relationship between poverty alleviation and biodiversity conservation, but, as importantly, meet the needs of the policy community that grapples daily with the challenge of combining these two social objectives.

Conclusion

The approaches discussed in this paper are all founded on the general assumption that it is possible simultaneously to achieve two seemingly incompatible goals – biodiversity conservation and poverty alleviation. Indeed, were it possible to identify a transcendent mechanism that could accomplish the integration of these two goals, one might speculate that it would be widely adopted. Such a magic bullet would unite diverse camps of social thinkers, environmentalists and dogmatic believers in development-at-any-cost, and permit the politics that bedevils all collective decision-making to be set aside. The evidence and discussion in the paper suggest, however, that optimism on the subject needs to be tempered with great caution and substantial new thinking. Indeed, the discussion is aimed at the inference that the knowledge base on which one might ground assumptions about the nature of the relationship between biodiversity and poverty is extremely shaky, if not almost unreliable.

The evidence from the examined case studies suggests that it may even be inappropriate to pose a question such as 'What is the relationship between biodiversity and poverty?' The theoretical literature on these two concepts demonstrates their multiple referents and meanings, and how attempts to alleviate one aspect of poverty may undermine efforts to alleviate another. For example, it may well be possible to reduce the headcount ratio on which most official measures of poverty are based, at the same time as the intensity and volatility of poverty increases. Similarly, genetic, species and ecosystem components of biodiversity bear no necessary, monolithic relationship to each other so that efforts to conserve one component may well hurt another. If one cannot make definitive statements about whether a particular policy measure can alleviate all aspects of poverty or conserve all components of biodiversity, surely it is foolhardy to hazard that a particular policy can simultaneously alleviate poverty per se *and* conserve biodiversity. We suggest that particular policy efforts and programmatic interventions, when they are successful, probably alleviate only some aspects of poverty even while they successfully maintain different components and attributes of biodiversity. The balance of such trade offs has been neither documented nor theorized in any general way. Such massive ignorance about trade-offs makes it all the more ironic that we inhabit a world where shaky assumptions about this trade-off are the grounding logic of most policies that aim at positive outcomes related to poverty and biodiversity. The question going forward is how to identify settings and create landscapes with diverse trade-offs so that even while some aspects of poverty are alleviated, different components and attributes of biodiversity can be conserved. Only through additional systematic investigation will we come to know which aspects of biodiversity can co-prosper with alleviation of different aspects of poverty.

Confusion about different aspects of poverty and biodiversity, and conflation of different measures of these two concepts, thrives in the empirical and applied literature as a result of well-meaning studies that present biodiversity and poverty as monolithic concepts that can easily be jointly addressed. Different studies identify different measures to assess the performance of interventions that seek to conserve biodiversity and alleviate poverty but there is little basis on which to compare the substantive results of these studies. We suggest that until analysts and policy-makers begin to think much more precisely about exactly which aspects of biodiversity and poverty are addressed by their favourite approaches, there will be little or no progress in understanding why people remain poor in certain ways (but perhaps not others), what makes (certain aspects of) biodiversity decline, and how to slow and even reverse such declines. Without greater nuance in thinking about poverty and biodiversity, future studies that take these terms to be their compass may provide greater understanding of specific programmes in specific places, but will not advance the agenda of a more general understanding or more effective policy.

What is even more troubling is that if the most widespread and frequently used analytical approaches to understand and document the relationship between poverty alleviation and biodiversity conservation continue to be used, it may not be possible to throw greater light on this relationship. Case study approaches based on evidence that is collected from a single time period and without careful and systematic consideration of the causal mechanisms at play are ill-suited to generate policy-relevant insights into the trade-offs between poverty alleviation and biodiversity conservation. But as we have noted, these approaches dominate the existing empirical work on the subject.

The point is also relevant and broadly applicable to research that seeks to illuminate the relationship between environment and development more generally. The specific meanings of environment and development are at least as encompassing as those of biodiversity conservation and poverty alleviation. In fact, considering that for many scholars, appropriate measures of environmental conservation can include improvements along such dimensions as indoor air quality or availability of clean drinking water, the ambit of environmental conservation is probably much larger. But it is still necessary to work with quite specific measures and dimensions of development in thinking about how to generate positive policy outcomes in a given location without adversely affecting particular measures of environmental conservation. To the extent specificity in measures used to assess changes in poverty and biodiversity improves our understanding of their relationship, the same logic also holds for the relationship between environment and development.

In light of the limited generalizability of findings from existing studies, it is clear that the future research agenda on the subject needs to be broadened in two key ways. The first concerns the specific questions that are being asked by those interested in understanding how changes in biodiversity and poverty are related. The second relates to the methods needed to gain a better and deeper understanding of these changes and their trade-offs.

Perhaps the most critical aspect of a new research agenda would be to explicitly document and test the likely trade-offs involved in pursuing specific poverty alleviation and biodiversity conservation goals. It is necessary to understand how efforts to conserve particular components and attributes of biodiversity affect different aspects of poverty in particular contexts, and vice versa. Research efforts, rather than trying to find the 'silver bullet' that will provide a quick and universal solution to problems of poverty and biodiversity loss, need to focus on the contextual details that make particular outcomes more or less likely. Further, for research to be policy-relevant, new studies need to focus on the dynamics of the relationship between various measures of poverty and biodiversity, and on how these dynamics are affected by macro-social and political variables such as education, demographic change, levels of unemployment, and technological change among others. Without greater attention to change over time, the goal of policy-relevant understanding of the relationship between biodiversity conservation and poverty alleviation is likely to remain chimerical.

If it is necessary to reconfigure the analytical lens to focus more insistently on trade-offs in the relationship between poverty alleviation and biodiversity conservation, it is equally important to rethink the methods that have hitherto been adopted to study this relationship. Better research design, based on careful specification of the relevant hypotheses, will probably require panel data from a suite of sites and households to allow systematic comparison across cases and regions. Where possible, researchers would need to collaborate with policy-makers to identify potential natural experiments so that the impacts of particular interventions can be studied more authoritatively. Such before and after studies are likely to prove invaluable in gaining a deeper understanding of the links between different measures of poverty and biodiversity.

Note

1   There are evident differences between the nature of biodiversity in national parks, forests and water bodies, and some of these differences are at play in the debates on what exactly it means to conserve biodiversity. We elaborate on how this chapter uses the terms biodiversity and poverty in due course.

References

Adams, W.K., Aveling, R., Brockington, D., Dickson, B., Elliot, J., Hutton, J., Roe, D., Vira, B. and Wolmer, W. (2004) 'Biodiversity conservation and the eradication of poverty', *Science,* 306: 1146–1148.

Escobar, A. (1995) *Encountering Development: The Making and Unmaking of the Third World*, Princeton Unversity Press, Princeton.

Peluso N.L. and Vandergeest, P. (2001) 'Genealogies of the political forest and customary rights in Indonesia, Malaysia, and Thailand', *Journal of Asian Studies,* 60(3): 761–812.

Rangan, H. (1997) 'Indian environmentalism and the question of the state: Problems and prospects for sustainable development', *Environment and Planning A*, 29(12): 2129–2143.

Schwartzman, S., Moreira, A. and Nepstad, D. (2000) 'Rethinking tropical forest conservation: Perils in parks', *Conservation Biology*, 14(5): 1351–1357.

Thies, C.G. (2004) 'State building, interstate and intrastate rivalry: A study of postcolonial developing country extractive efforts, 1975–2000', *International Studies Quarterly,* 48(1): 53–72.

Chapter 5

Livelihoods, Forests and Conservation in Developing Countries: An Overview

William D. Sunderlin, Arild Angelsen, Brian Belcher, Paul
Burgers, Robert Nasi, Levania Santoso and Sven Wunder

The Potential Role of Forests in Poverty Alleviation

In this section, we summarize information about the future potential for forest-based poverty alleviation (FBPA) considering the opportunities and obstacles in different kinds of forest use, and the enabling conditions that may increase possibilities for pro-poor outcomes. This section condenses and modifies information published elsewhere (Angelsen and Wunder, 2003; FAO, 2003). We emphasize that the list of principal forest uses given below is descriptive and not prescriptive.[1] It summarizes the past and present trends, examines some possible future uses, and is not meant to serve as a programme for FBPA.

(a) Principal forest uses

(i) Conversion of forests to agriculture

As in past millennia, natural forests will continue to be converted to agriculture in developing countries to enable livelihood support. Forests have (indirectly) had an important role in increased levels of consumption over time. In energetic terms, the transition from hunting and gathering to agriculture represents a change from per-capita appropriation of energy from 5000 to 26,000 kcal per day (Bennett, 1976, p. 42). Forests and other forms of vegetative matter, through photosynthesis and their role in soil formation and restoration, have been one important foundation for the establishment and maintenance of agriculture. Worldwide, incomes have increased dramatically in part because forest cover removal, on either a tempo-

Reprinted from *World Development*, vol 33, no 9, Angelsen, A., Belcher, B., Burgers, P., Nasi, R., Santoso, L., Sunderlin, W.D. and Wunder, S., 'Livelihoods, Forests, and Conservation in Developing Countries: An Overview', pp. 1383–1402, copyright © (2005) with permission from Elsevier, London. Extract or abridged version.

rary (swidden cultivation) or permanent (sedentary agriculture) basis, has allowed access to fertile soils.

In most developing countries, forests continue to be used for swidden cultivation, and forests continue to be converted to permanent agriculture. But natural forests will probably not continue to serve as an important driving force for improved average income worldwide in the way they have historically, for the following reasons. Although much land remains and much of it underlies forests, a lot of it cannot be converted to agriculture. This is because of its inaccessibility, relatively low quality, and vulnerability to erosion, among other reasons (Evans, 1998, pp. 2 and 200). Deforestation and 'soil mining' will continue in areas that one might deem not rationally appropriate for agriculture. Technological change will alter the panorama of possibilities for productive agriculture, but diminishing returns on the availability of agricultural lands are evident worldwide. Most future gains in agricultural productivity will have to come from improved efficiency on existing agricultural lands and not expansion (Dyson, 1996, p. 117). Nevertheless, in many areas, there will be a continuation of the historical role of forests in wealth creation through predatory forest-product harvesting and forest conversion, even if at a reduced scale compared to the past.

(ii) Timber

Historically, timber has served as an important catalyst to various kinds of economic activity. It is not only that timber has been used to build shipping fleets and railroads but also that wealth from massive timber extraction has been used as seed capital to establish economic enterprises and even empires outside the forest sector. For example, in Indonesia, Malaysia, and the Philippines, timber wealth served as a basis for political patronage systems linking heads of state, the military, and the private sector (Ross, 2001, pp. 191–192).

Timber is by far the most valuable commercial commodity in most forests. The value of international forest products exports from developing countries in 1998, excluding non-timber forest products (NTFP)s, was US$10.4 billion (FAO, 2001, pp. 122–135).[2] There are three reasons why very little of this wealth has gone to people living in forested areas.

First, the poor are often statutorily excluded from access to timber wealth because of its high value and because they lack power to compete for access to high-value natural resources. Although there have been some positive changes in recent years, forestry laws and regulations in many countries were written to assure privileged access to timber wealth and to prevent counter-appropriation by the poor.

Second, timber extraction and tree growing tend to be capital and skill intensive, and are sometimes aimed at specialized consumer markets. Tree growing for timber requires secure land tenure, which the poor often do not have (if they have access to land). It also represents a long-term, high-risk investment whereas low-income people need short-term income and want to avoid risk (Wunder, 2001).

Third, although 'trickle-down' effects of the conversion of forest capital have gone largely unmeasured over time, there is reason to believe little of this has reached the poor (see Section (vi) on 'indirect benefits').

Two models of timber production can potentially help alleviate poverty, but both have deficiencies. One option is management of natural forests by forest villagers. However, its poverty-alleviation potential is undermined by weak and slow-changing institutions, rent capture by local elites, inconsistent laws and regulations, cumbersome bureaucracy, and lack of control of downstream activities. The absence of real devolution of decision-making and real tenure rights are two reasons why community forestry has, by and large, performed poorly in providing livelihood benefits (Fisher, 2003, p. 18). Another option is tree growing by small-holders, which can produce substantial income. This activity requires land and tenure security, which some smallholders classified as poor do have, but that the poorest of the poor by definition tend not to have.

(iii) Non-timber forest products (NTFPs)

There is a wide variety of NTFPs that are used for fuel, food, medicine, forage, fibre, that have valuable chemical components or that are used for ritual purposes. The majority of NTFPs are consumed directly by collectors and their families. Some are important mainstays in the household economy. Others are used infrequently, but can be critically important as sources of food when other sources are unavailable. Such emergency foods can make a difference between life and death.

Many NTFPs are also produced for sale or barter. The extension of the market system to more remote areas has increased both the demand and the opportunity for increased cash incomes, and there is a growing international interest in various kinds of natural products, from herbal medicines to hand-crafted utensils and decorative items. Still, the majority of these products is sold in relatively small quantities (per producer, collective quantities can be very large), and for relatively low prices.

They are important for helping households meet current consumption needs, and are often relied on as the main or only source of cash income in a household to pay school fees, to purchase agricultural inputs, or to pay emergency medical costs, for example. Some NTFPs have large and reliable markets that are supplied by specialized producers (Belcher et al., 2005).

Discussions about NTFPs have been hampered by ambiguous and inconsistent definitions of the term, with debate about what kinds of products and what kinds of production environments to include (Belcher, 2003). But, no matter whether a narrow or wide definition is used,[3] there is strong evidence that the poorest of the poor around the world are those that use NTFPs the most (Neumann and Hirsch, 2000), that the poor frequently use NTFPs as an 'employment of last resort' (Angelsen and Wunder, 2003), and that they serve an important safety net function (e.g. McSweeney, 2004; Pandit and Thapa, 2004). This is because many wild NTFPs are available as common-property resources in traditional systems or as de facto open-access resources, in state forest lands for example. Many NTFPs are used with little processing, using low-cost (often traditional) technologies. As discussed earlier, areas of poverty and forest cover overlap, and so in certain places need and opportunity combine. Using the two-stage definition of 'poverty alleviation,' most of this kind of use would be classified as poverty mitigation or poverty avoidance.

The same factors that tend to make NTFPs important in the livelihoods of the poor also limit the scope for NTFPs to lift people out of poverty. Markets for many of these products are small. Naturally reproducing products tend to be dispersed, with seasonal and annual fluctuations in quantity and quality of production. NTFPs produced in open-access regimes are highly susceptible to overexploitation. Remote settings with poor market access put producers in a weak bargaining position relative to traders who typically provide transport, market connections, and credit to NTFP collectors in classic patron–client relationships.

As Dove (1993) noted, in those cases where NTFPs have a high value, they tend to be appropriated by people with more power, more assets, and better connections – that is, the non-poor. This is especially true when market forces lead to intensified and specialized production. Homma (1992) developed a simple economic model that shows how high demand for NTFPs can over time lead to collapse of the naturally regenerating resource base, production on plantations outside of forests, and increased competition from synthetic substitutes. There is strong supporting evidence for this in empirical studies such as that by Belcher et al. (2005). Intensified management of valuable products can create opportunities to increase earnings. Taking advantage of such opportunities, however, requires market access, secure tenure over the resource base, sufficient labour and capital to invest, the wherewithal to wait for that investment to mature (especially with slow-maturing species) and entrepreneurial skills.

(iv) Environmental services

The environmental services of forests can benefit the local poor either directly (internalized benefits) or indirectly through transfer payment arrangements (compensation to local people for externalized benefits). Examples of internalized benefits include safeguarding healthy forest ecosystems for the purpose of protecting the quantity and quality of local dwellers' water supplies (WRI, 2000, p. 101) or for maintaining or enhancing on-farm agricultural production by restoring fertility in agroforestry systems (Sanchez et al., 1997). These direct benefits are mostly linked to the poverty avoidance/mitigation function of forest-resource use.

Until now, four types of direct payments for forest environmental services have been dominant: carbon storage, hydrological protection, biodiversity conservation, and recreational values. To date, they have been implemented on a small scale tropics-wide, with most projects concentrated in Latin America. The external forest environmental benefits are being enjoyed by external users, yet usually they have not been paid for. Land-use change increasingly threatens the continuous provision of these benefits, since local land users have no incentive to take them into account. This provides the rationale for the incipient markets for environmental services.

Environmental service payments could become an important vehicle for poverty alleviation only if two conditions are met simultaneously. First, the markets would need to experience a take-off such that a significant number of poor people are made better off. There are factors working against such an expansion, including the fact that it takes time to change service-buyer attitudes and get people to pay for something they used to receive for free. The turnover in these markets is currently too limited to have an effect on poverty at the aggregate scale. Also, forests may not always be the most cost-effective way to provide a certain environmental service. For instance, it may be cheaper to address global warming by reducing emissions in sources outside the forest sector (Smith et al., 2000).

However, ongoing forest degradation and conversion in the tropics will continuously decrease the supply of 'free' forest environmental services. On balance, because the 'free' services are disappearing, it makes payments for those vanishing services more attractive. We would thus expect the expansion trend to dominate, creating a substantial market expansion over time. However, policies that hinder or over-regulate these markets will risk reducing their potential for poverty alleviation.

The second precondition is that potential service providers who are poor must be well equipped to compete in these expanding markets. Sceptics have pointed to the high transaction costs of working with many (poor) smallholders, compared to the economies of scale of working with a few large landholders (Bass et al., 2000; Smith et al., 2000). A second main obstacle is that poor people often do not have formal and secure land tenure. This may limit their de jure ability to sign service-provision contracts. Moreover, restrictions on actual control over land, that is, the right and ability to exclude external intruders, may also de facto limit poor people's prospects to be reliable service providers.

While we expect all these caveats to be valid, some options may exist to reduce transaction costs that impede the poor from participating in payments for environmental services. For instance, recent changes in the Costa Rican environmental service payment schemes introduce bundled 'group contracts' on an experimental basis, thus reducing enrolment transaction costs for small producers. It is possible that creative design and experimental applications can produce solutions that reduce obstacles to poor service producers' participation. Finally, one should remember that participation of the poor in environmental service markets that is limited in relative market-share terms can still be significant in its absolute contribution to income improvements. For instance, while forest-based tourism companies often gain disproportionately from benefit-sharing schemes with local communities, there is evidence that even small cash transfers can significantly raise incomes for local people in marginal areas with few alternative sources of monetary income (Gurung and Coursey, 1994; The Zimbabwe Trust et al., 1994; Wunder, 2000, 2003b).

(v) Employment

In the late 1990s, there were 17.4 million employees worldwide in the formal forestry sector and about 47 million altogether, including formal and informal employment (ILO, 2001, p. 39). The scope for poverty alleviation through increase of forest sector employment is unknown.

(vi) Indirect benefits

We define indirect benefits as those forestry activities that assist poverty alleviation through multiplier and trickle-down effects.

Local multiplier effects related to timber concessions include local demand for food, goods, and services created by the presence of a logging workforce; making of a logging road that opens remote forest dwellers' access to markets and improves possibilities for delivery of health services and education to them; and compensation to the community by the logging company for access to forest resources. But there are also possible associated negative consequences including destruction of natural forests and reduced availability of NTFPs; conflicts with logging companies; rising local prices associated with logging; and difficulties in adjusting to the collapse of the economic boom when the logging is done.

As stated in Section (ii), not much is known about the extent to which forestry contributes to poverty alleviation through trickle-down effects. Examples are the extent to which cheaper forest products make consumers better off, or how much the reinvestment of forest-derived economic rents (e.g. from timber) in other sectors benefits the poor. Timber in developing countries (measured in tens of billions of dollars) has clearly had an impact on economic growth, but this does not necessarily translate into a large contribution to poverty alleviation. The timber sector in many developing countries is often described as capital intensive, as having limited forward and backward linkages, as paying few taxes, and as repatriating its profits to other countries – suggesting low delivery of 'trickle-down' benefits.

(b) Enabling conditions

In the recent past, new conditions have emerged that may provide impetus to forest-based poverty alleviation. Here we identify policy-driven, market-driven and other conditions which – while in some cases two-edged – nonetheless provide some basis for assuming that a larger share of forest benefits may reach forest dwellers in the future.

(i) Policy factors

Decentralization of authority and resource control, now occurring in many developing countries, increases though by no means guarantees the possibility of greater local access to forest rents. Presumably, in the best of cases, greater local access to forest rents can assist poverty alleviation.

In the most forested developing countries, ownership or control of the forest estate by indigenous and rural communities has doubled in the last 15 years, and its share of the total is now approximately 25 per cent; it will probably double again in the next 15 years (Scherr et al. 2004, p. 11; White and Martin, 2002, p. 7). As with decentralization, this process does not guarantee poverty alleviation but may improve its chances.

The trend toward democratization in many developing countries potentially increases the bargaining power of rural communities vis-à-vis the state and large enterprises. For example, in Indonesia, rural villagers are now freer to stake a claim to forest lands and resources than they were during the 30-year authoritarian Suharto regime. In Brazil, the rubber tappers were persecuted under the military regimes. Now, the Minister of Environment comes from the rubber tappers union.

Corrupt practices in the forest sector tend to work against the interests of the poor (e.g. Hill, 2000). Campaigns against corruption are increasing in developing countries in association with the trend toward democratization. To the extent they are successful, they might boost opportunities for the rural poor to get a larger share of forest wealth.

(ii) Market factors

Rapidly growing urban markets for forest products in developing countries provide new opportunities for smallholders, especially those who live in peri-urban areas. This is because many forest products are shipped in a quantity that is too large or are too easily perishable to be profitably shipped long distances, and because small farmers own or occupy many peri-urban areas. Increased scarcity of forest products, such as fuelwood, makes it more profitable to grow forest products on-farm.

Market deregulation and liberalization can favour FBPA in two ways: First, it can be a force behind eliminating regulations that have prevented growing trees on farms. Trees on farms have been more controlled than the growing of annual crops. Second, it can lead to reform of forestry marketing regulations that have tended to discriminate against small producers. However, trade liberalization does not always favour the interests of the poor, and government monopolies can easily be replaced by private ones. Thus, there is still a need for government intervention to protect vulnerable people against these negative effects (Mayers and Vermeulen, 2002, p. 4).

(iii) Other factors

In many tropical countries, after overharvesting timber, concessionaires have not renewed their concessions. This presents an opportunity for forest communities to intercede and compete for access rights before the remaining timber stock matures and becomes marketable.

Small portable sawmills with lower capital requirements should favour a more decentralized production system for sawn wood. This should make it easier to involve local entrepreneurs. Technological changes in the plywood industry allow the use of smaller diameter trees and more species. Given that control over less valuable commercial forests has been granted to local communities, at least in the past, this technological change could increase the value of these forests. However, this also risks speeding up deforestation by making new areas and species commercially profitable for logging.

The growing threat of global warming and biodiversity loss increases the likelihood that developed countries will be willing to compensate forest dwellers in developing countries for environmental services through carbon sequestration and conservation concessions.

Poverty Alleviation and Forest Conservation

The challenge of reconciling livelihood improvement and forest conservation in developing countries is daunting and largely unmet. Some authors have argued that, due to a number of intrinsic characteristics of forests and forestry, the real scope for reconciling the two objectives is inevitably quite limited (Wunder, 2001; Levang et al., 2003). In the course of the last several decades, rural incomes have on average increased in developing countries, yet natural forests have been disappearing at a high rate. The various site-level solutions that have been tried have fallen well short of their goals. While there have been some positive outcomes in community and social forestry (Fomete and Vermaat, 2001; Antinori and Bray, 2005), there have been many failures (e.g. Malla, 2000; Mekonnen, 2000). As noted above, new creative approaches such as payments for environmental services are in their infancy and largely untested.

(a) What is to be done?

What is to be done? One possible interpretation of the environmental Kuznet's curve (EKC) and forest transition (FT) literature[4] is that it might be best to do nothing more than promote economic growth. The logic of such a position would be that reconciliation of poverty alleviation and forest conservation will take place, as a matter of course, in the process of socio-economic development, so no forest-specific intervention is necessary or desirable at the level of the site. There are some elements of truth to this argument. A remarkable degree of natural forest restoration has taken place in many rich countries in tandem with increased levels of per-capita income. Since 1950, agricultural intensification in Europe and North America has permitted the reconversion of 16 million ha of farmlands to forest, even as the population in those countries has increased by 170 million people (Grubler, 1994, p. 324). Case study research has been conducted on forest cover restoration in Denmark, France, Italy and Switzerland (Fairbairn and Needle, 1995; Mather et al., 1998, 1999; Mather and Fairbairn, 2000).

While recognizing that economic growth can potentially assist in reconciling poverty alleviation and forest protection, we reject this laissez-faire position for several reasons. First, forest cover restoration in rich countries is largely predicated on high per-capita consumption of fossil fuels which enables not just agricultural intensification, but also reduces dependence on agriculture, greater reliance on the urban sectors (service, manufacturing, industry), and wood fuel substitution, all of which reduce pressure on domestic forests in net terms. Because of risks posed by global warming, this level of fossil fuel consumption cannot be extended globally and is not tenable in the long term. Second, assumptions that developing countries can or should simply follow in the footsteps of the more 'advanced' countries have been flawed in the past. Blind faith in the implications of the forest transition might follow in this naive tradition. Third, even if forest cover does later increase, it will not be the same forest. A lot of diversity will undoubtedly be lost in the process. Fourth, even if the EKC or FT predictions hold true, the estimated EKC turning points occur at high GDP per capita levels (US$4000–6000) (Wunder, 2003a, p. 377), and therefore, most tropical countries are decades away from their turning points. Much more damage would happen before those turning points are reached.

So what should be done instead? We argue that attempts to reconcile poverty alleviation and forest conservation should be carried out deliberately and systematically both at the level of the site, with informed attention to endogenous dynamics, and also with due attention to international-, regional- and national-level exogenous factors.

In giving attention to site-level/endogenous factors, we propose that – in spite of project failures – it is necessary to persevere, not just learning from the mistakes of the past, but also making fundamental course corrections suggested by the enabling conditions described above. It is also important to distinguish what changes can and cannot be achieved through attention to problems at the level of the site alone. Giving attention to exogenous factors means research and policy attention to those macro-and meso-level causal factors that influence or may determine outcomes at the site level. The case of Gabon is instructive. The fact that incomes in Gabon are among the highest in all of Africa and Gabon's forests are among the best preserved in the world has almost nothing to do with deliberate planning of site-level outcomes. This convergence of poverty alleviation and forest conservation is mostly an accidental artefact of the country's high dependence on oil income, and low population (Wunder, 2003a, pp. 84–129).

(b) The need to conceptualize outcomes

To maximize the possibility that site-level programmes and projects will succeed, it is necessary to have a clear conceptual grasp of various positive and negative outcomes, and the reasons for them. Many plans of action aim for 'win–win' outcomes, where livelihood improvements are matched by gains in environmental protection. Yet these plans of action rarely define 'win–win' outcomes, nor those that fall short of 'win–win.' We propose a simple, fourfold typology for understanding outcomes, as described in Figure 5.1.[5]

Are there key socio-economic and biophysical characteristics associated with the four basic outcomes? Aggregation, comparison and contrast of case studies can serve to identify broad patterns which in turn can be used to inform the policy process. The following observations about the tendencies may be useful in guiding such an undertaking.

Win–win: The relative scarcity of such outcomes in developing countries and tendency toward forest cover stabilization and restoration in developed countries begs the question: 'Are high levels of per capita GDP at the national level, high levels of per capita consumption of fossil fuels, and high rates of urbanization the essential preconditions for systematic achievement of win–win outcomes in developing countries?' Perhaps not, because there are important exceptions to the rule, for example, the Yurimaguas multistrata agroforestry systems in Peru (ICRAF, 1997, pp. 39–69; Leakey, 2001, pp. 4–5); regrowth of trees in pastoral systems in Tanzania and Kenya (Barrow and Mlenge, 2003); and multistrata agroforestry systems in Sumatra, Indonesia based on the production of damar resins (Leakey, 2001, pp. 3–4; Michon et al., 2000).

Win–lose: At the risk of oversimplification, this category is roughly synonymous with the history of agricultural and rural development. The expansion of agricultural lands over time has often been at the expense of natural forest cover and biodiversity, and the transition from hunting and gathering, to swidden agriculture and then to sedentary agriculture and pastoralism has often meant an increased consumption of natural resources and level of income over time (Figure 5.1).

Figure 5.1 *Fourfold classification model of human well-being and forest cover.*

Lose–win: There are at least two circumstances that typify a lose–win outcome: (1) a situation in which communities have been forcibly excluded from access to forest resources they depend on, for conservation purposes, leading to deterioration of well-being; and (2) a situation in which war and conflict make farmers unable to maintain their farming practices for fear of victimization, resulting in declining well-being and natural restoration of forest cover.

Lose–lose: These outcomes are those variously described in the environmental literature as 'the downward spiral of poverty and environmental degradation', the 'vicious circle', or as 'desperate ecocide'. Under these circumstances, there is a causal, reciprocal relationship between worsening social and environmental conditions. Note that the temporal dimension is important: What begins as 'win-lose' may end up as 'lose–lose' because of loss of the resource base. A common formulation of 'lose–lose' involves outsiders exploiting and eliminating local forest resources, leading to livelihood decline. The classic case is large extensive cattle ranches in Latin America that produce little value per hectare, keep small farmers off the land, clear the forests, and often receive government subsidies. Poorly managed forestry concessions are another common example.

Although this model tends to be readily grasped by users and is attractive because of its simplicity, this simplicity incorporates ambiguities and shortcomings that must be well understood to avoid pitfalls in its use. The main problems are as follows:

- The real-life conditions described by this model are never as 'black and white' and rigidly categorical as the model implies. For example,

  a) In association with forest cover change, there can be considerable variability in win or lose livelihood outcomes from forest cover change, or no change at all, not just between groups within a given community, but also within households.
  b) The same person or household can both 'win' and also 'lose' in the livelihood sense from the same process of forest cover change. For example, deforestation can supply badly needed arable land at the same time that it can remove access to non-timber forest products and forest-based environmental services.
  c) Cashing in forest capital can give short-term gains and can imply long-term livelihood losses.

An assumed relationship between well-being and forest cover may conceivably have little or nothing to do with local resource management practices and may instead be attributable to economic factors in the wider national or regional economy (viz. the Gabon example above). Appropriate application of the model requires a capacity to differentiate what effects are endogenous or exogenous to the site being analysed.

(c) Improved policy solutions

The empirical characterization of the fourfold outcomes can be useful in efforts to improve policies designed to alleviate poverty and overcome forest management problems, in at least three ways.

Linking desired (win–win) and undesired (lose–lose) outcomes to policy change. Careful documentation and analysis of instances of win–win outcomes can serve to identify the necessary and sufficient preconditions for reproducing such outcomes. The same holds true in reverse for research and analysis of lose–lose outcomes. The more we know about the underlying causes of such cases, the greater our ability to design policies that either prevent or reverse such outcomes.

How to minimize trade-off (win–lose and lose–win). Useful applications of knowledge on win–lose and lose–win outcomes are more complex than the above, but potentially rewarding. The policy lessons would be guided by the analysis of these types of outcomes in terms of two principal types of solutions.

The first would involve reducing the trade-offs and, in essence, seeking outcomes of the type 'winning more and losing less' and 'losing less and winning more'. The problem is that these types of solutions are likely to be costly and therefore not necessarily justifiable. The second would involve identifying the appropriate point on the trade-off curve, for example, the optimal level of well-being, or the optimal level of forest cover. The challenge of specifying 'appropriate deforestation' according to biophysical, economic and political criteria (Kaimowitz et al., 1998, p. 304) is an example of the latter. We recognize the inherent difficulty, if not the impossibility, of having various stakeholders agree on optimal trade-offs, but believe clear information on the choices can help avoid needless conflict and lay the groundwork for consensual solutions.

Avoidance of the win–win and lose–lose fixation. In some environmental analysis and policy documents, there is a tendency to focus on win–win and lose–lose outcomes, almost as if these were the only outcomes that take place in the real world. This tunnel vision originates in part from simplistic elaborations of the concept of sustainable development which assume an indissoluble link between improved livelihoods and alleviation of environmental problems. A linked assumption is that failure of poverty alleviation efforts surely leads to worsening of environmental conditions. Neoliberal prescriptions often assume that economic growth will jointly alleviate poverty and redress environmental problems, and conversely, that insufficient economic growth can worsen both problems. These assumptions tend to render the win–lose and lose–win outcomes theoretically invisible. This is unfortunate because, as we have seen above, the challenge of linking science to effective policy is in many ways more demanding in this realm.

Summary and Conclusions

This chapter has summarized theory and knowledge with respect to two central questions at the interface of livelihoods and forests: To what extent can forests be relied on to support poverty alleviation in developing countries? Can the use of forests for poverty alleviation be compatible with efforts to conserve what remains of developing country natural forests? We recognize that we have just touched the surface of a vast topic, and that this chapter does not address all the important points that are relevant to this topic.

With respect to the first question, we emphasize three points in connection with improved strategic poverty alleviation planning. First, the location of chronic rural poverty and natural forests tend to overlap. To the extent that this knowledge can be elaborated through further research, and that this overlap signifies forest dependence, the relevance of forestry in broad strategic planning for poverty alleviation is strengthened. Second, it is crucial to distinguish between the use of forest resources to prevent rural people from falling into (deeper) poverty versus their role in lifting people out of poverty in a lasting way. Third, there are intrinsic qualities of forest resources and the context in which they are used that tend to run counter to the goal of poverty alleviation, but there are important new enabling trends that might compensate for these undesirable qualities.

Are Poverty Reduction Strategy Papers (PRSPs) justified in limiting their attention to forest resources? In a sense yes, and in a sense no. Limited attention to forest resources is partly justified in that many paths out of poverty do not involve continued use of forest resources. However, PRSPs and other anti-poverty policies can be greatly remiss in overlooking attention to forest resources, especially in areas where chronic poverty and forest cover tend to overlap. This is because forest resources are often important in poverty mitigation and avoidance, and there is often no substitute for these vital services, especially in remote areas. It is also because forest resources provide local environmental services for which there are often no substitutes, and because increasingly fewer remote areas overlie high-quality agricultural soils, so land uses there can be better suited to forestry or agro-forestry in perpetuity. Lastly, it is because some forest-conserving land uses may not only assist poverty mitigation and avoidance, but poverty elimination as well. It should be stressed that forest resources can be important for poverty alleviation even in places where forest cover is low, because they are vanishing. Scarcity produces higher economic returns. Marketing of wood products in peri-urban regions is a growing livelihood opportunity for this reason, and because of rapidly increasing demand.

With respect to the second key question, we conclude that efforts to reconcile FBPA and forest conservation should continue in the tradition of site-level research and development, but these efforts need to be integrated with an understanding of society-wide effects. It cannot be assumed that economic growth will, in and of itself, bring about the win–win solutions implied in the EKC and FT literatures. This site-specific work must give due attention to the distinction between endogenous and exogenous causal factors. Lastly, it is vital that this research and development distinguishes among various outcomes (win–win, win–lose, lose–win, lose–lose) and that it does so at sites where there has been little or no programmatic intervention. This will help assure the relevance of research and enable replicability of good results.

Notes

1   A descriptive list recognizes that many forest uses (e.g. permanent conversion of forests to agriculture) imply destruction of forests over the long term, whereas a prescriptive list might explicitly incorporate forest conservation goals.

2   The contribution of the forestry sector to gross domestic product (GDP) tends to be small in most developing countries. However, the value-added figure for the forestry sector significantly underestimates the total value since a large share of forest products is not registered. This is because forest resources are often used for subsistence and trade in local markets, or are harvested and traded illegally.

3   A narrow definition tends to focus on products extracted from natural forests, where the poor are clearly highly involved. A wider definition would also include cultivated, higher-value products, which tend to be produced by those relatively few NTFP producers who are better off.

4   The authors of EKC and FT literature do not make this argument. Moreover, they recognize that terminal forest cover is much smaller than initial forest cover, and has less biodiversity.

5   For useful elaborations of these kinds of typologies, see Prescott-Allen (2001), who provides a country-by-country index of data on well-being and the quality of the environment, and Bass et al. (2001, p. 54), who propose a nine cell model that includes a 'no change' option on each of the two axes.

References

Angelsen, A. and Wunder, S. (2003) *Exploring the Forest-Poverty Link: Key Concepts, Issues and Research Implications*, CIFOR Occasional Paper No. 40, Center for International Forestry Research, Bogor, Indonesia.

Antinori, C. and Bray, D.B. (2005) 'Community forest enterprises as entrepreneurial firms: Economic and institutional perspectives from Mexico', *World Development*, 33(9): 1529–1543.

Barrow, E. and Mlenge, W. (2003) *Trees as Key to Pastoralist Risk Management in Semi-arid Landscapes in Shinyanga, Tanzania, and Turkana, Kenya*, unpublished paper presented at the International Conference on Rural Livelihoods, Forests, and Biodiversity, Bonn, Germany, 19–23 May, 2003.

Bass, S., Dubois, O., Moura Costa, P., Pinard, M., Tipper, R. and Wilson, C. (2000) *Rural Livelihoods and Carbon Management*, IIED Natural Resources Issues Paper No. 1, International Institute for Environment and Development, London.

Bass, S., Hughes, C. and Hawthorne, W. (2001) 'Forest, biodiversity and livelihoods: Linking policy and practice', in Koziell, I. and Saunders, J. (eds), *Living Off Biodiversity: Exploring Livelihoods and Biodiversity Issues in Natural Resources Management*, International Institute for Environment and Development, London.

Belcher, B.M. (2003) 'Comment: What isn't an NTFP?', *International Forestry Review*, 5(2): 161–168.

Belcher, B., Ruiz Perez, M. and Achdiawan, R. (2005) 'Global patterns and trends in the use and management of commercial NTFPs: Implications for livelihoods and conservation', *World Development*, 33(9): 1435–1452.

Bennett, J.W. (1976) *The Ecological Transition: Cultural Anthropology and Human Adaptation*, Pergamon, Oxford.

Dove, M. (1993) 'A revisionist view of tropical deforestation and development', *Environmental Conservation*, 20(1): 17–24.

Dyson, T. (1996) *Population and Food: Global Trends and Future Prospects*, Routledge, London and New York.

Evans, L.T. (1998) *Feeding the Ten Billion: Plants and Population Growth*, Cambridge University Press, Cambridge.

Fairbairn, J. and Needle, C. (1995) *The Forest Transition in Italy*, Working Paper No. 2, Department of Geography, University of Aberdeen.

FAO (2001) *State of the World's Forests*, Food and Agriculture Organization of the United Nations, Rome.

FAO (2003) 'Forests and poverty alleviation', pp. 61–73, in Sunderlin, W.D., Angelsen, A. and Wunder, S., *State of the World's Forests 2003*, Food and Agriculture Organization of the United Nations, Rome.

Fisher, R.J. (2003) 'Innovations, persistence and change: Reflection on the state of community forestry', pp. 16– 29, in RECOFTC and FAO (eds), *Community Forestry: Current Innovations and Experiences*, CD-ROM. RECOFTC and FAO, Bangkok.

Fomete, T. and Vermaat, J. (2001) *Community Forestry and Poverty Alleviation in Cameroon*, Rural development forestry network, Network Paper No. 25h.

Grubler, A. (1994) 'Technology', pp. 287–328, in Meyer, W.B. and Turner, B.L. (eds), *Changes in Land Use and Land Cover: A Global Perspective*, Cambridge University Press, Cambridge, New York and Melbourne.

Gurung, C.P. and Coursey, M.D. (1994) *Nepal, Pioneering Sustainable Tourism. The Annapurna Conservation Area Project: An Applied Experiment in Integrated Conservation and Development*, The Rural Extension Bulletin, no. 5, August, University of Reading, UK.

Hill, I. (2000) 'Corruption in the forest sector in India: Impacts and implications for development assistance', *International Forestry Review*, 2(3): 200–207, 240, 242.

Homma, A.K.O. (1992) 'The dynamics of extraction in Amazonia: A historical perspective', *Advances in Economic Botany*, 9: 23–31.

ICRAF (1997) *International Centre for Research in Agroforestry Annual Report 1996*, International Centre for Research in Agroforestry, Nairobi.

ILO (2001) *Social and Labour Dimensions of the Forestry and Wood Industries on the Move*, International Labour Office, Geneva.

Kaimowitz, D., Byron, N. and Sunderlin, W. (1998) 'Public policies to reduce inappropriate deforestation', pp. 302–322, in Lutz, E. (ed), *Agriculture and the Environment: Perspectives on Sustainable Rural Development*, The World Bank, Washington, DC.

Leakey, R.R.B. (2001) 'Win–win land use strategies for Africa: Building on experience with agroforests in Asia and Latin America', *International Forestry Review*, 3(1): 1–10.

Levang, P., Dounias, E. and Sitorus, S. (2003) *Out of the Forest, Out of Poverty?* Paper presented at the international conference on 'Rural livelihoods, forests, and biodiversity' in Bonn, Germany, 19–23 May, 2003.

Malla, Y.B. (2000) 'Impact of community forestry policy on rural livelihoods and food security in Nepal', *Unasylva*, 51(202): 37–45.

Mather, A.S. and Fairbairn, J. (2000) 'From floods to reforestation: The forest transition in Switzerland', *Environment and History*, 6(4): 399–421.

Mather, A.S., Fairbairn, J. and Needle, C.L. (1999) 'The course and drivers of the forest transition: The case of France', *Journal of Rural Studies*, 15(1): 65–90.

Mather, A.S., Needle, C.L. and Coull, J.R. (1998) 'From resource crisis to sustainability: The forest transition in Denmark', *International Journal of Sustainable Development and World Ecology*, 5(3): 182–193.

Mayers, J. and Vermeulen, S. (2002) *Power from the Trees: How Good Forest Governance Can Help Reduce Poverty*, unpublished manuscript.

McSweeney, K. (2004) 'Forest product sale as natural insurance: The effects of household characteristics and the nature of shock in Eastern Honduras', *Society and Natural Resources*, 17: 39–56.

Mekonnen, A. (2000) 'Valuation of community forestry in Ethiopia: A contingent valuation study of rural households', *Environment and Development Economics*, 5(3): 289–308.

Michon, G., de Foresta, H., Kusworo and Levang, P. (2000) 'The damar agroforests of Krui: Justice for forest farmers', in Zerner, C. (ed), *People, Plants and Justice: The Politics of Nature Conservation*, Cambridge University Press, New York.

Neumann, R.P. and Hirsch, E. (2000) *Commercialisation of Non-timber Forest Products: Review and Analysis of Research*, Center for International Forestry Research, Bogor.

Pandit, B.H. and Thapa, G.B. (2004) 'Poverty and resource degradation under different common forest resource management systems in the mountains of Nepal', *Society and Natural Resources*, 17: 1–16.

Prescott-Allen, R. (2001) *The Well-being of Nations: A Country-by-Country Index of Quality of Life and the Environment*, Island Press, Washington, DC and International Development Research Centre, Ottawa.

Ross, M.L. (2001) *Timber Booms and Institutional Breakdown in Southeast Asia*, Cambridge University Press, Cambridge.

Sanchez, P.A., Buresh, R.J. and Leakey, R.R. (1997) 'Trees, soils, and food security', *Philosophical Transactions of the Royal Society of London*, 352(1356): 949–961.

Scherr, S., White, A. and Kaimowitz, D. (2004) 'A new agenda for forest conservation and poverty reduction: Making markets work for low-income producers', *Forest Trends*, CIFOR, and IUCN.

Smith, J., Mulongoy, K., Persson, R. and Sayer, J. (2000) 'Harnessing carbon markets for tropical forest conservation: Towards a more realistic assessment', *Environmental Conservation*, 27(3): 300–311.

White, A. and Martin, A. (2002) 'Who own the world's forests?: Forest tenure and public forests in transition', *Forest Trends*, Center for International Environmental Law, Washington, DC.

WRI (2000) *World Resources 2000–2001: People and Ecosystems: The Fraying Web of Life*, World Resources Institute, Washington, DC.

Wunder, S. (2000) 'Ecotourism and economic incentives: An empirical approach', *Ecological Economics*, 32(3): 465–479.

Wunder, S. (2001) 'Poverty alleviation and tropical forests: What scope for synergies?', *World Development*, 29(11): 1817–1833.

Wunder, S. (2003a) *Oil Wealth and the Fate of the Forest: A Comparative Study of Eight Tropical Countries*. Routledge, London and New York.

Wunder, S. (2003b) Native tourism, natural forests and local incomes on Ilha Grande, Brazil, pp. 148–177, in Gossling, S. (ed), *Tourism and Development in Tropical Islands: A Political Ecology Perspective*, Edward Elgar, Cheltenham (UK) and Northampton (US).

The Zimbabwe Trust, The Department of National Parks and Wildlife Management and The CAMPFIRE Association (1994) *Zimbabwe: Tourism, People and Wildlife*, The Rural Extension Bulletin, no. 5, August, University of Reading, UK.

Part 2

Conservation's Place in International Development

Editors' Introduction

International development policy has changed significantly over the last two decades, both in its focus and primary choice of delivery mechanism. In the late 1980s and early 1990s – as we noted in Chapter 1 – the focus was on sustainable development, including large-scale integrated conservation and development projects and community-based natural resource management programmes, with official development assistance agencies directly supporting project implementation through intermediaries including NGOs. In the late 1990s the focus switched to poverty reduction, with direct budget support the preferred delivery mechanism. Previously, conservation organizations had been recipients of substantial aid funds to implement practical projects in developing countries. This is still the case with some donor agencies – the US Agency for International Development (USAID) for example is an important donor to many of the US-based international conservation organizations. However, increasingly, and in response to the 2005 *Paris Declaration on Aid Effectiveness* which emphasized developing country ownership of the aid agenda and harmonized donor alignment behind that domestic agenda, direct budget support has taken over as the main aid delivery mechanism. As a result, over the past decade, donor agencies have become increasingly reluctant to provide direct support to NGOs or to fund conservation efforts unless they make a tangible contribution to poverty reduction.

Poverty reduction has always been a recurring theme within the international development agenda (Maxwell, 1999). However, it became the single defining focus of development assistance policy in the late 1990s, for two main reasons. First, the Development Assistance Committee of the Organisation for Economic Co-operation and Development published its report *Shaping the 21st Century* in 1996 (OECD, 1996). This included seven international development targets that reflected commitments made at various UN summits since the 1970s (Satterthwaite, 2003). Consequently, many bilateral aid agencies shifted their policies in line with these targets. For example, the UK Department for International Development (DFID) published a White Paper on poverty reduction (DFID, 1997). The United Nations repackaged these international development targets in 2000 as the MDGs, gaining an unprecedented level of international commitment to poverty reduction (Satterthwaite, 2003).

Second, the World Bank and International Monetary Fund initiated the development of country-level Poverty Reduction Strategy Papers in 1999 as the basis for concessional lending and debt relief to poor countries. These were underpinned by the Comprehensive Development Framework that emphasized developing country ownership and direction of the development agenda (Stiglitz, 1998). This had a significant impact on the delivery of development assistance funds, with many donor agencies moving away from project-based funding and towards direct budget support. Under this mechanism, aid money is paid to the recipient country treasury and the government decides on its allocation in line with the priorities identified in its poverty reduction strategy. Consequently, development assistance funding that had previously been made available for biodiversity conservation projects was significantly reduced, unless identified as a priority by recipient countries (Roe and Elliott, 2004).

This shift in aid policy and subsequent decline in funding available to conservation organizations stimulated a concern that biodiversity conservation had 'fallen off' the development agenda and that, simultaneously, the conservation agenda had been burdened with a responsibility for poverty reduction. This argument emerged at the 2002 meeting of the Society for Conservation Biology and was aggravated by a speech by the UK Minister for International Development, who highlighted the so-called 'bushmeat problem' in terms of its implications for poor peoples' livelihoods (Short, 2002). Consequently, the conservation literature soon carried articles critiquing the assumed links between bushmeat consumption and poverty (Robinson and Bennett, 2002), and the overall emphasis of development policy on poverty reduction, at the expense of attention to conservation objectives (Chapter 10).

The World Summit on Sustainable Development (WSSD) was held during 2002 in Johannesburg. Biodiversity was included as one of five priority issues for the summit, but its two main products, the Johannesburg Declaration on Sustainable Development (United Nations, 2002a) and the Johannesburg Plan of Implementation (United Nations, 2002b), both highlighted poverty reduction as the overarching priority for sustainable development. The Plan of Implementation states that reversing the trend in biodiversity loss will only be achieved if local people benefit from the conservation and sustainable use of biological diversity (United Nations, 2002b). The reaction to this from some conservationists was that the sustainable human–nature interactions proposed at the 1992 Earth Summit in Rio had been hijacked by the development agenda, abandoning any linkage between human concerns and nature conservation (Chapter 11).

Development agencies do continue to fund biodiversity, notably through their contributions to the Global Environment Facility (GEF) – whose budget (of which an estimated one third is regularly allocated to biodiversity) has increased in each replenishment to date – and also through their contributions to multilateral institutions that support biodiversity, for example the World Bank, the United Nations Environment Programme (UNEP) and, for European agencies, the European Commission. Nevertheless overall, official donor funding for biodiversity conservation has been steadily declining (Chapters 8 and 9) and where donor agencies do retain significant budgets for environmental issues these have become increasingly dominated by the climate change agenda. Furthermore, the volumes of both public and private sector funding have been severely hit by the global recession of 2008–2009.

Our selected readings illustrate the changes in donor policy and practice and the reactions to these changes from the environmental community.

Our first reading (Chapter 6) is an OECD-DAC policy statement on 'Integrating the Rio Conventions in Development Cooperation', made in 2002. This statement was remarkable at the time for maintaining a focus on poverty–conservation linkages, at a time when member governments had moved firmly towards a poverty reduction first agenda, and illustrates the gap that can occur between policy rhetoric and programme implementation.

Chapter 7 is a short extract from the UK Department for International Development (DFID) *Wildlife and Poverty Study* of the same year. This reflects the reality of changing donor priorities and practices. Wildlife conservation is seen as peripheral to DFID's core business of poverty reduction, and the parallel move towards budgetary support as a primary aid delivery mechanism, sounds the end of direct DFID funding for conservation projects. The extract also emphasizes the need for a 'joined-up approach' to international biodiversity conservation across individual donor governments, with the environment department – in the UK this is the Department for Environment, Food and Rural Affairs (DEFRA) – highlighted as the obvious lead agency.

In Chapter 8, Lapham and Livermore (2003) explore donor agency funding for biodiversity and confirm a downward trend that is widely apparent across development agencies – both bilateral and multilateral. They highlight the huge and growing shortfall in financial resources needed to run protected area networks in developing countries. They call on development agencies to better integrate conservation, and the seventh MDG, into their poverty reduction mandates and into their country-driven approaches. At the same time this paper acknowledges that it is the development agencies that have been at the forefront of efforts to investigate the links between biodiversity conservation and poverty, and calls on conservation organizations to step up to the mark in providing their perspectives. The report concludes that public donors have made significant progress toward acknowledging biodiversity conservation as a core component of sustainable development assistance and yet that they have decreased resources dedicated to proven conservation investments.

The Chapter 9 extract from the Secretariat of the CBD provides more up to date information on biodiversity funding trends, including regional analyses. It highlights that funding for biodiversity is delivered as much – or more so – through its integration into various development sectors (mainly forestry and fishing, but also agriculture and water supply) as through general environmental protection or conservation. As such, it also confirms Lapham and Livermore's conclusions that non-development as well as development actors have a major role to play in funding conservation. This theme of the different roles and responsibilities of different organizations in addressing each others' agendas is picked up again in *Part 4*.

Sanderson and Redford (2003) provide an alternative perspective on the issue of the respective roles of conservation and development agencies in Chapter 10. While the earlier chapters have emphasized that it is not just development agencies that should be providing funding for conservation, here the role of conservation organizations in addressing poverty reduction is queried. The authors note that the focus on poverty alleviation has virtually supplanted biodiversity in the sustainable development agenda and fear that the human 'subsidy from nature' will tax biodiversity to death. Sanderson (2005) takes this a stage further in Chapter 11 highlighting the past failures of rural development and the need for a 'new optic on rural development' to ensure that benefits accrue to the truly poor and to the future of wild nature: 'For all the papers and panels and centres and conferences, there is still too little understanding of the relationship among agricultural development, poverty alleviation and biodiversity conservation.'

In the final Chapter of **Part 2**, Chapter 12, Bass (2006) draws on the findings of the Millennium Ecosystem Assessment (MA) in an attempt to make the case to the development community that investing in the environment – including biodiversity – makes sense for development, particularly the development model of today that purports to be focused on the needs of the poorest.

References

Bass, S. (2006) *Making Poverty Reduction Irreversible: Development Implications of the Millennium Ecosystem Assessment*, Environment for the MDGs series, IIED, London.

DFID (1997) *Eliminating World Poverty: A Challenge for the 21st Century*, White Paper on International Development, HMSO, London.

Lapham, N.P. and Livermore, R.J. (2003) *Striking a Balance: Ensuring Conservation's Place on the International Biodiversity Assistance Agenda*, Conservation International, Washington, DC.

Maxwell, S. (1999) *The Meaning and Measurement of Poverty*, Poverty Briefing No. 3, Overseas Development Institute, London.

OECD (1996) *Shaping the 21st Century*, Organisation for Economic Co-operation and Development, Paris.

Robinson, J. and Bennett, E.L. (2002) 'Will alleviating poverty solve the bushmeat crisis?', *Oryx*, 36, 332.

Roe, D. and Elliott, J. (2004) 'Meeting the MDGs: Is conservation relevant?', pp 7–19, in Roe, D. (ed) *The Millennium Development Goals and Conservation: Managing Nature's Wealth for Society's Health*, International Institute for Environment and Development, London.

Sanderson, S. and Redford, K. (2003) 'Contested relationships between biodiversity conservation and poverty alleviation', *Oryx*, 37: 1–2.

Sanderson, S. (2005) 'Poverty and conservation: The new century's "peasant question?"', *World Development*, 33: 323–332.

Satterthwaite, D. (2003) *The Millennium Development Goals and Local Processes: Hitting the Target or Missing the Point?*, International Institute for Environment and Development, London.

Short, C. (2002) *Bushmeat and Poverty*, Speech by Clare Short, Secretary of State for International Development, at the UK Bushmeat Campaign Conference, Zoological Society of London, 28 May 2002, UK Department for International Development, London.

Stiglitz, J. (1998) *Towards a New Paradigm for Development: Strategies, Policies, and Processes*, 1998 Prebisch Lecture, UNCTAD, Geneva.

United Nations (2002a) *Johannesburg Declaration on Sustainable Development*, UN Department of Economic and Social Affairs, New York.

United Nations (2002b) *Johannesburg Plan of Implementation*, UN Department of Economic and Social Affairs, New York.

Chapter 6

Integrating the Rio Conventions into Development Cooperation

Organisation for Economic Co-operation and Development (OECD)

Nearly a billion households, particularly the rural poor, rely directly on natural resources for their livelihoods. But global environmental threats are undermining this resource base. Biodiversity loss is proceeding at a rapid rate in many countries, as is the build-up of toxic chemicals. Desertification and drought are problems of global dimensions, affecting all regions. Greenhouse gas emissions pose risks to the world's climate and developing countries are likely to be the most vulnerable to the impacts. Three UN Conventions, on Climate Change, Biological Diversity and Desertification – closely associated with the 'Earth Summit', held in Rio in 1992 – address these threats, which could undermine collective efforts to eradicate poverty and foster sustainable development worldwide.

We recognize that OECD countries bear a special responsibility for leadership on sustainable development worldwide, historically and because of the weight they continue to have in the global economy and environment. We also recognize the need to help developing countries address sustainable development issues as well as the need for further work on global and 'mixed' public goods. These issues include those related to a clean atmosphere and the control of infectious diseases such as malaria and HIV/AIDS. Tackling these complex challenges will require better coherence in a wide range of policy areas, such as energy, trade, health, agriculture, investment and development cooperation. These issues and responsibilities are addressed in the Report prepared by the OECD Secretariat for the World Summit on Sustainable Development.

This Statement, and the detailed Guidelines that underlie it, spell out the role of our agencies in integrating global environmental challenges in development cooperation.

Although all countries are affected, the poorest are the most threatened because they have fewer resources to address the root causes of environmental threats and adapt to their impacts, and because their populations are highly dependent on natural resources for their livelihoods. Sustainable poverty reduction, a central

Reprinted from the Policy Statement by the DAC High Level Meeting, 16 May 2002, The DAC Guidelines *Integrating the Rio Conventions into Development Co-operation*, copyright © OECD 2002. Extract or abridged version.

priority on the development agenda, is therefore closely linked to sound environmental management at the local, national, regional and global levels.

We are concerned about the high vulnerability of many of the poorest countries to desertification and biodiversity loss and to the impacts of climate change. These environmental threats impact on rural livelihoods, food security and health, while exacerbating natural disasters such as floods and droughts. This vulnerability risks intensifying competition and conflict over already strained land and water resources and undermining efforts to reduce poverty. For many countries, these represent near-term threats requiring urgent responses.

Integrating environmental concerns in poverty reduction strategies and other national planning processes is a priority. Global environmental threats, and issues of global importance such as desertification and drought, present us with particular challenges in this respect. Their causes and consequences respect no national boundaries, but they call for responses at the international, regional, national and local levels.

Addressing the causes and impacts of biodiversity loss, climate change and desertification require measures in sectors such as agriculture, forestry and energy. Development cooperation agencies, which provide assistance in many of these areas, can play an important role in assisting with capacity building in developing countries to improve the integration of these critical issues in national planning and policy-making mechanisms.

We are already working towards this objective in a number of forums, including through the Global Environment Facility, but this is not enough.

The 'Rio Conventions' reflect the commitment of all countries to preserve the global environment, on the basis of common but differentiated responsibilities and respective capabilities. They also clearly recognize that meeting national development needs and responding to global environmental threats must go hand in hand. Thus, they are about sustainable development, not just about the environment.

Too often, global environmental issues have been considered as a 'stand-alone agenda' of limited concern to national or local development priorities. In many countries, for example, environment ministries have been assigned the prime responsibility for implementing the Conventions, without coordination at a government-wide level to implement the necessary response measures in key sectors such as agriculture, energy, transport, and beyond.

It is urgent to recognize this shortcoming and take necessary corrective actions, focusing on national development strategies which respond simultaneously to social, economic and environmental concerns.

Tackling environmental degradation should go hand in hand with improving economic and social welfare. Improving food security and livelihoods for rural population requires combating desertification, conserving biodiversity and reducing vulnerability to climate change. Safeguarding the livelihoods of poor landless peasants, pastoralists or forest dwellers requires protecting the ecosystems on which they rely for food and shelter. Improving access to efficient fuels and cookstoves improves the health and safety of women and children, reduces the burden of fuelwood collection chores, and also helps reduce pressures on forests.

In our capitals:

- *We will develop our agencies' capacity to recognize critical poverty reduction–global environmental linkages and formulate appropriate responses.* A sound understanding of poverty–environment linkages, and the threats arising from global environmental degradation, is necessary for the formulation of sound policies. We are committed to integrate these issues in our policies and country support strategies. We will also work to ensure that understanding of these issues is shared throughout our agencies, and not confined to the environmental specialists.

- *We will intensify our relationships with other ministries and agencies involved in global environmental issues.* Intensifying our relationships with other ministries and agencies involved in global environmental issues will help to formulate coherent approaches. Our active participation in international negotiations on global environmental issues and in the formulation of national positions gives us direct opportunities to ensure that the agreements made, and the mechanisms established to support them, complement our efforts to sustainably reduce poverty and reflect our experience in the field.

With our developing country partners:

- *We will help our partners meet their commitments and take advantage of the new opportunities arising from global environmental agreements.* We will assist our partners to develop the policy and institutional framework necessary to meet their commitments under the conventions. This includes helping our partners avail themselves of incentives provided by emerging market-based mechanisms to achieve global environmental goals.

In this context, there will be a heavy focus on support for capacity development, in the public and private sectors and civil society, making full use of available capacity. The 'Rio Conventions' identify a wide variety of fields where capacity development is needed – for example, for compliance with reporting obligations; for scientific monitoring and technology assessment; for policy formulation; and for effective participation in international negotiations on environmental conventions. The GEF, the Global Mechanism of the Desertification Convention and, in the context of climate change, the new funds established in Marrakesh, are all valuable instruments in this connection. Additional support will be provided through our bilateral programmes and through multilateral development banks. We will also support pilot-scale projects in order to experiment with new emerging approaches, and to demonstrate their feasibility, thereby helping create a critical mass of concrete experience.

- *We will also help our partners to integrate global environmental issues in Poverty Reduction Strategies*

Country-led planning frameworks such as Poverty Reduction Strategies or National Agendas 21 provide unique opportunities to integrate issues of environmental sustainability in poverty reduction efforts.

This will imply integrating the national action plans formulated under the global environmental conventions in relevant national, or sub-national, or even regional-level planning processes.

We will also highlight the importance of global environmental issues, and their links with development objectives, by systematically putting these issues on the agenda of our regular dialogues with senior policy-makers from partner countries, in the context of aid programming. We are already supporting efforts in a number of areas which link closely with one or several issues addressed by the 'Rio Conventions'.

We will ensure that these ongoing initiatives recognize and take maximum advantage of opportunities for win–win approaches.

Among development cooperation agencies:

We will intensify our coordination among development cooperation agencies in support of the 'Rio Conventions', at the country level and globally, including on the implications for our efforts in related areas, such as sustainable poverty reduction, conflict prevention and gender equality.

Chapter 7

Wildlife and Poverty Study

Department For International Development (DFID)

Introduction

The DFID context

DFID policy has changed significantly over the past decade. This change in policy is captured in the government's first White Paper on International Development (1997), the New White Paper (2000), and the DFID Target Strategy Papers (TSPs) including *Halving World Poverty by 2015* and *Achieving Sustainability*. In these papers a clear mandate for DFID has been set – DFID is, above all, committed to helping achieve the UN Millennium Development Goals agreed in September 2000 (see Box 7.1).

Since the mid-1990s, wildlife-linked work has been receiving less attention within DFID. Until the mid- 1990s DFID was well known for funding conservation as well as development initiatives, including support for protected area systems throughout the developing world (e.g. Kenya, Botswana, Zimbabwe). Reasons for the reduced attention include:

- *Wildlife not seen as central to poverty reduction, particularly as compared with other key sectors such as health, education and agriculture.* DFID measures its impact in terms of poverty reduction and requires that all initiatives it supports directly can demonstrate a clear and direct impact on poverty, which many wildlife conservation projects are unable to do. Wildlife as a livelihood asset is seen as relevant to a small minority of poor people, and, through wildlife tourism, to be an asset that delivers only a small proportion of its value to poor people, with the bulk taken by the elite and the private sector. DFID does recognize that it has a commitment to environmental sustainability (see Box 7.1), and has actively pursued sustainable natural resource management, particularly of water, forests, fisheries and biodiversity, through international processes, such as the Global Environment Facility (GEF) and the recent World Summit on Sustainable Development (WSSD).

Box 7.1 *UN Millennium Development Goals (MDGs)*

The commitment: 'we will spare no effort to free our fellow men, women and children from the abject and dehumanizing conditions of extreme poverty to which more than a billion of them are currently subjected.'

The goals:

- Eradicate extreme poverty and hunger

- Achieve universal primary education

- Promote gender equity and empower women

- Reduce child mortality

- Improve maternal health

- Combat HIV/AIDS, malaria and other diseases

- Ensure environmental sustainability

- Develop a global partnership for development

Source: www.developmentgoals.org

- *Move from projects towards budgetary support.* To implement its new strategy DFID is placing a growing emphasis on providing aid through direct budgetary support to partner governments, which should help support the cost-effective provision of essential public services to the poor. Bilateral programme and sector support are likely to continue (e.g. DFID's bilateral forest programmes), as will selective investment in innovative and high-impact projects, but the number of field projects funded will be significantly smaller than in the past.

- *Growing questioning of the extent of conservation–development 'win–wins'.* From the optimism of the post-Rio drive for sustainable development, the past few years have seen a swing back to questioning the potential for 'win–wins' between conservation and development, in part due to the disappointing performance of flagship projects such as CAMPFIRE in Zimbabwe.

- *Concerns about the negative impact of conservation on poor people.* The conservation agenda is still perceived as being largely pro-wildlife and anti-people by development agencies.

- *High transaction costs of community-based projects.* One reason that DFID is less inclined to offer direct support to community-based wildlife projects is that they are perceived as having high cost per beneficiary and low replicability. High transaction costs are generally associated with efforts to reach poor people living in remote areas with low population densities. However, governments are committed to reaching and supporting these people. In terms of replicability, anthropologists tend to argue that there is no generic model for working at the local level. However, experience with supporting private sector–community joint ventures suggests that there are indeed 'economies of learning' for the private sector partners, for the intermediaries and for communities, and therefore, presumably for governments and donors, e.g. getting the strategy, culture and approach right the first time takes time, but is then transferable.

- *Joined-up government.* DEFRA now takes primary responsibility for UK government support for species conservation. Efforts within DFID and between DFID, DEFRA and the Foreign and Commonwealth Office (FCO), to pursue a 'joined-up' approach to wildlife conservation are ongoing, e.g. through the Inter-Departmental Consultative Group on Conservation.

DFID currently funds only two bilateral wildlife-linked projects (Mbomipa in Tanzania and WILD in Namibia) and a handful of wildlife-linked forestry projects, with no new projects in the pipeline. The Tourism Challenge Fund and the new Programme Partnership Agreement (PPA) with WWF-UK have provided the only sources of new DFID wildlife investment in the past three years.

Chapter 8

Striking a Balance: Ensuring Conservation's Place on the International Biodiversity Assistance Agenda

Nicholas P. Lapham and Rebecca J. Livermore

Introduction

Maintaining biodiversity – for both the benefits it provides to people and for its inherent value – is a massive, long-term and increasingly complex challenge for human society. In both developing and developed countries, it will require changes in development and consumption patterns and the integration of biodiversity concerns across a range of economic sectors by promoting, for instance, enlightened agricultural, forestry, fisheries and rural development practices that improve the status of biodiversity in multiple-use zones and sustain resources for human consumption.

Scientific research has demonstrated that the survival of many species will also require direct action in the short term to protect natural ecosystems. While some species are well adapted to and even benefit from human-modified systems, many more can only thrive in natural habitats. A comprehensive global network of protected areas where conservation is a priority over other forms of land use is thus a fundamental cornerstone of an effective strategy for protecting the Earth's biodiversity.[1]

Conservation, of course, costs money. A wide range of analysis indicates a significant gap between the current level of investment in the global system of protected areas and the level of investment needed. James et al. (2000) reviewed protected area budgets and found that a total of approximately US$6 billion is spent annually on the entire global system of protected areas, with over half of this amount spent in the US alone. James et al. further estimate that an additional $2.3 billion per year is required simply to make management adequate in the existing protected area network, with the majority of this need located in developing countries. Estimates of the financial resources necessary to create and manage a broadly representative and effective global system of protected areas are upwards of $20 billion annually (Balmford et al., 2002). A significant portion of the shortfall in protected areas funding is in developing countries, whose governments are generally unable to provide sufficient financial resources on their own. Where will the money come from?

Private donors, whether individuals or foundations, are clearly an important source of funds. Through their support, international non-governmental organizations (NGOs) have grown considerably as an influential force in conservation.[2] Corporations are also playing an increased role in conservation, whether by favouring business practices with a reduced environmental impact, taking actions to offset the environmental damage their activities cause, or contributing outright to conservation projects. An intriguing prospect is the potential for markets in ecosystem services, including carbon sequestration, watershed protection and even pollination. These markets could one day generate financial resources for conservation at a globally significant scale, yet today they are only in the nascent stages of development. Ultimately, though, as long as biodiversity remains a public good, undervalued in the marketplace, governments will continue to be primarily responsible for financing its protection.

In this report, we present the findings of our study of government resources targeted at reducing biodiversity loss in developing countries. While most developing country governments make domestic conservation investments – a funding source that is important both in real terms and as a demonstration of political commitment – they are largely incapable on their own of providing the resources needed to adequately support conservation. Rather, they depend on assistance from donors, both bilateral (single governments providing direct assistance) and multilateral (multiple governments working together to provide assistance). Virtually every country that belongs to the Organisation for Economic Co-operation and Development (OECD)[3] provides some level of bilateral biodiversity assistance to developing countries. Donor governments also provide assistance through multilateral institutions such as the World Bank, the United Nations (UN), and the Global Environment Facility (GEF), which has allocated over $1.7 billion toward biodiversity projects and programmes in developing nations since 1991 (GEF, 2003a). A recent survey of biodiversity investments in Latin America confirms the importance of donor government resources – it found that multilateral and bilateral assistance, totalling $2.5 billion, accounted for nearly 90 per cent of all biodiversity funding in the region from 1990 to 1997 (Castro and Locker, 2000).[4]

Donor government funds are important for other reasons beyond their aggregate total. For example, donor funds can target the poorest countries, where private investment tends to be scarce. Furthermore, 'official' funding from a donor government or a multilateral institution like the UN or the World Bank often fosters environmental policy dialogue and helps generate a political commitment to biodiversity by the recipient government. Government funding – particularly where it builds on historical relationships between countries or where economic and political interests are at stake – also tends to be more stable than other sources, which fluctuate based on the whims of the market or the shifting priorities of a particular donor or organization. Multilateral funding in particular gives donor governments the opportunity to coordinate their interests with regard to biodiversity. Finally, government funding plays a vital leveraging role because it often attracts co-financing from other sources.

Since the Convention on Biological Diversity(CBD) was established in 1992, governments have largely structured and described their biodiversity assistance based on its framework, and it remains an important instrument driving international biodiversity policy. However, it has not proven sufficiently strong to generate the resources or political will needed to slow biodiversity loss, and efforts to hold countries accountable for committing 'new and additional' funding have fallen short.

At the 2002 World Summit on Sustainable Development (WSSD), governments once again underscored the importance of donor country support for biodiversity in developing countries. The summit's final declaration stated, 'a more efficient and coherent implementation of the three objectives of the Convention and the achievement by 2010 of a significant reduction in the current rate of loss of biological diversity will require the provision of new and additional financial and technical resources to developing countries' (UN, 2002).

In some cases, government commitments at the international level are supported by specific national mechanisms that ensure certain levels of international biodiversity assistance. For example, in the wake of the Rio Earth Summit, France created the French Global Environment Facility (FFEM), a unique separate national fund established to target global environmental issues, including biodiversity and climate change. Similarly, the Netherlands, a rarity among donor countries, seeks to adhere to a Rio Earth Summit recommendation to target 0.1 per cent of gross national product to environmental initiatives (including biodiversity) in developing countries (Minbuza, 2003).[5]

Mechanisms have also been established to channel donor resources to particular countries or regions with high biodiversity value. Perhaps the most prominent example is the International Pilot Program to Conserve Brazilian Rainforest (PPG7), set up in 1992 to promote conservation and sustainable development in the tropical rainforests of the Brazilian Amazon and Atlantic coast. The PPG7 is a joint undertaking of the government of Brazil, Brazilian civil society, and the international donor community and is managed by the World Bank. The G-7 governments have pledged more than $340 million in biodiversity-related assistance to this programme since its inception, with nearly 80 per cent coming from Germany and the European Commission (World Bank, 2003a).[6]

Today, despite these and other commitments, public biodiversity funding falls well short of the need. Still, governments remain by far the most important source of biodiversity funding. With this in mind, our study aims to reveal important findings regarding the characteristics and direction of donor government biodiversity funding.

Findings

While the strategies of each country and donor institution vary considerably, we have identified four key trends in international biodiversity assistance that are significantly influencing the overall direction, delivery, effectiveness, and scale of funding for conservation. Each of these four trends is discussed separately in the sections below.

Finding 1: *As poverty has become the overarching focus of development assistance, biodiversity funding is increasingly framed in terms of its relation to poverty reduction. This has placed a growing emphasis on mainstreaming biodiversity into other development sectors and promoting sustainable use. At the same time, it appears to be diminishing support for shorter-term conservation investments.*

Over the past decade, poverty reduction has become an overriding priority of the World Bank, UN agencies delivering development assistance, and many other multilateral and bilateral aid agencies. As a consequence, international biodiversity assistance increasingly depends on the extent to which it can be justified within a poverty reduction context. The following examples illustrate this trend:

- Many donor institutions are structuring their development assistance around the UN Millennium Development Goals (MDGs), a set of eight objectives aimed at 'reducing poverty in all its forms' (UN, 2000; World Bank, 2002a).
- The World Bank's Environment Strategy, unveiled in 2001, pledges a 'poverty focused' environmental agenda in which the primary objectives are 'improving quality of life, improving the quality of growth, and protecting the quality of the regional and global commons' (World Bank, 2001). Subsequently, the Bank revised its forest policy to place increased emphasis on poverty reduction benefits arising from the sustainable management of forests and forest resources, with a major change being the removal of a 1991 ban on the financing of commercial logging in primary moist tropical forests (World Bank, 2002b).
- The Asian Development Bank's (ADB) new Environment Policy is grounded in its Poverty Reduction Strategy and emphasizes 'promoting environmental and natural resources interventions to reduce poverty directly' (ADB, 2002).
- The UK Department for International Development (DFID) now explains that its 'work on biodiversity is guided by three principles, the first of which is the overriding priority of poverty elimination' (DFID, 2001).
- The CBD (which plays a vital role in setting the parameters for GEF and other biodiversity funding) notes, 'The international community's approach to

biodiversity has changed over the past 10 years. Biological diversity is now considered as an essential part of efforts to eradicate poverty and achieve sustainable development' (CBD Secretariat, 2003).

Moreover, this evolving focus on poverty has influenced the restructuring of a number of development agency programmes. The following examples illustrate these structural changes:

- DFID's former Natural Resources Department is now the Rural Livelihoods Department, a change that mirrors DFID's 'sustainable livelihoods approach'. According to DFID staff, this reflects a more holistic method for addressing how people in developing countries realize livelihoods with a large diversity of strategies and resources (Brown, pers. comm., 2002). In the future, the ten policy departments at DFID headquarters, including the Environmental Policy Department, are to be streamlined. The three provisional budget streams are 'Pro-poor Sustainable Economic Growth,' 'Pro-poor Human Development,' and 'Pro-poor Social and Political Change' (DFID, 2002).
- The European Commission recently restructured its policy on development aid to prioritize six 'focal areas' aimed at reducing poverty. The environment is not one of these areas; instead the Commission aims to integrate environmental issues across all six areas (FERN, 2002; LeGrand, pers. comm., 2002). The European Commission's development agency, EuropeAid, is structured according to these six focal areas, and the environment is treated as a cross-cutting issue.

Mainstreaming biodiversity assistance

As the examples listed above show, biodiversity is increasingly treated as part of a broader strategy aimed at tackling poverty. Based on a growing recognition that biodiversity and well-functioning ecosystems are fundamental to both poverty reduction and sustainable development, biodiversity concerns are being mainstreamed into sectors such as agriculture, forestry, fisheries, and rural development.

The new tendency to mainstream biodiversity concerns derives in part from research on the intersection of biodiversity and poverty undertaken by the World Bank, UN and various development agencies, sometimes in cooperation with environmental organizations. For instance, the World Bank, UNDP, the European Commission and DFID produced a major paper for the 2002 World Summit on Sustainable Development (WSSD) entitled *Linking Poverty Reduction and Environmental Management: Policy Challenges and Opportunities*. The paper's central argument is that 'environmental management cannot be treated separately from other development concerns, but requires integration into poverty reduction and sustainable development efforts' (DFID et al., 2002). Other publications have drawn similar conclusions. A recently published position paper by the World Bank, for example, states that environmental issues must be addressed across all development sectors

(World Bank, 2002a). Similarly, the Biodiversity in Development Project, supported by DFID and the European Commission and co-sponsored by the World Conservation Union (IUCN), has produced a series of publications that discuss the value of biodiversity to poor people both as a resource and as a way of reducing exposure to risk and outline an approach for incorporating biodiversity into development and poverty reduction strategies (Biodiversity in Development Project, 2001a, 2001b).

While there is well-developed theory behind mainstreaming environment issues across development sectors, it remains to be seen whether the design and implementation of such development programmes will consider biodiversity adequately and leave room for conservation investments. In this respect, a critical audience includes development economists and ministers of finance who require compelling arguments and analysis on the linkages between biodiversity and poverty, hunger, human health and other development priorities. Dr Jeffrey Sachs, Director of the United Nations Millennium Project (tasked with developing a plan for implementing the MDGs) recently remarked that biodiversity issues are virtually absent from the key development community dialogues, including the discussions on how to achieve the MDGs (Sachs, 2003).

At the same time, the MDGs offer perhaps the best hope for effectively mainstreaming biodiversity into development activities and ensuring support for conservation. Described as mutually reinforcing, the MDGs provide a framework for donor institutions to integrate biodiversity concerns into efforts to achieve all eight goals. Further, the MDGs explicitly recognize the importance of development assistance aimed at managing natural resources and conserving biodiversity. Goal 7 deals explicitly with environmental sustainability and includes a target to 'integrate the principles of sustainable development into country policies and programmes and reverse the loss of environmental resources'. Specific indicators of success toward achieving Goal 7 include land protected to maintain biological diversity and the proportion of land area covered by forest (UN, 2000; World Bank, 2002a).[7]

Increased emphasis on sustainable use and benefit sharing

The new priority given to poverty reduction and the shift toward mainstreaming biodiversity assistance into various development sectors dovetail with a renewed emphasis on the CBD's sustainable use and equitable benefit-sharing objectives. Both donors and recipients of biodiversity assistance are highlighting these objectives, with the intention of ensuring that developing countries receive maximum economic benefits from and retain sovereign control over biodiversity resources and the products derived from them in both the short and long terms. For example, the 2002 *Cancun Declaration of Like-Minded Megadiverse Countries*, signed by Brazil, China, Colombia, Costa Rica, Ecuador, India, Indonesia, Kenya, Mexico, Peru, South Africa and Venezuela, emphasizes fair and equitable benefit sharing, the protection of traditional knowledge, and the protection of intellectual property rights related to biodiversity and genetic resources (Secretaría de Medio Ambiente y Recursos Naturales, México, 2002).

Similarly, a number of bilateral donors have raised the profile of sustainable use and benefit sharing in their biodiversity programmes, and the GEF is receiving guidance to better address these two CBD objectives. At its most recent Conference of the Parties, the CBD urged the GEF to broaden its emphasis from the Convention's conservation objective to increasingly target the treaty's sustainable use and equitable benefit-sharing components (CBD, 2002). The Second Overall Performance Study of the GEF provided similar guidance, suggesting that addressing the root causes of biodiversity loss will require 'GEF conservation objectives that are grounded more strongly in the sustainable development context' and 'stronger emphasis to initiatives that promote sustainable use and benefit sharing of biodiversity products and services' (GEF, 2002).

Diminished support for conservation investments

In a trend that reflects encouraging progress, development agencies are increasingly recognizing that maintaining ecosystem functions and biodiversity is vital to the long-term success of poverty reduction efforts. This has strengthened the substantive and political case for integrating biodiversity concerns into the broader development agenda. Unfortunately, an apparent side effect is diminished support for long-proven conservation actions that most scientists agree are fundamental to maintaining the full array of biodiversity. Biodiversity funding is now driven heavily by social and economic objectives, which are not necessarily synonymous with objectives such as avoiding extinctions or protecting unique and biologically diverse landscapes.

Several of the donor institutions examined here have endorsed the MDGs, which include a biodiversity indicator that assesses land area protected to maintain biological diversity. However, in our interviews, the representatives of many of these same institutions were careful to distance their programmes from the science-based agenda favoured by many conservation-oriented NGOs. Indeed, several influential members of the development community have criticized activities related to protected areas and species-specific conservation. Evelyn Herfkens, the former Netherlands Minister for Development Cooperation, has stated, '"Wildlife park. Keep out!" This type of approach doesn't work. People are beginning to see that it is misguided to try to keep the animals in and the people out, to build a fence between them, and post armed guards to protect nature' (Herfkens, 2002). Clare Short, former UK Minister for International Development, recently remarked:

Too often in the past environmentalists in developed countries, preoccupied with global rather than local values, have focused on the conservation of endangered animals, plants, and trees, taking little account of the needs of poor people. Time and again well-intentioned conservation efforts on protected area systems have been resisted by local people whose livelihoods have been jeopardized. Yet the poor could be allies of the conservationists. But for this to come about we need to focus much more on sustainable use rather than on conservation for its own sake. (Short, 2003)

Certain donors still play a leadership role in providing funding for conservation and protected area activities, including Germany and the United States.[8] Others, however, are clearly shifting their biodiversity investments to more closely fit a poverty-focused agenda. A recent DFID study highlights the institution's decreased funding for wildlife projects: 'Since the mid-1990s, wildlife-linked work has been receiving less attention within the UK Department for International Development (DFID). DFID now funds only two bilateral wildlife projects (Mbomipa in Tanzania, which finishes this year, and WILD in Namibia) and a handful of wildlife-linked forestry projects with none in the pipeline. … [T]he reasons for the decline in DFID wildlife investment include that wildlife is generally not seen as central to poverty reduction' (DFID, 2002). This shift in donor government biodiversity investments was confirmed by the CBD Secretariat, which noted that the activities reported by donor countries have moved away from the long-established focus on parks and protected areas and toward investments across all sectors, especially projects emphasizing the sustainable use and equitable benefit-sharing objectives of the CBD (Xiang, pers. comm., 2002). This trend is exacerbated by stagnant or declining foreign aid for all sectors, including those closely linked to biodiversity (FAO, 2003; OECD, 2003).[9]

Rather than matching the GEF's significant investments in protected areas and other conservation programmes, many donors are providing biodiversity assistance that is more closely tied to economic development. Development agency representatives often describe their biodiversity programmes, which tend to focus on rural livelihoods, productive sectors and other forms of poverty reduction, as complementary to GEF biodiversity investments. For instance, the European Commission's protected areas strategy 'aims to complement conservation-focused GEF investments' and encourages a 'participatory review of conflicts and opportunities' – particularly income generation opportunities – to support local livelihoods (European Commission, 2001). Similarly, the FFEM, while established as a mechanism to set aside funds for the global environment, including biodiversity, makes a clear distinction between its investments and those of the GEF: 'The FFEM intervenes exclusively in projects that are focused mainly on the economic and social development of the beneficiary countries. The GEF also works in the framework of projects that are aimed essentially at protecting the global environment' (FFEM, 2003).

At the same time, many of these same donors would like to see the GEF strengthen the links to poverty reduction in its projects and focus more on mainstreaming biodiversity into economic development. The GEF Business Plan for fiscal years 2004–2006 (FY04–06)[10] outlines the reasoning behind the increased financial resources for new strategic priorities, including 'mainstreaming biodiversity in production landscapes and sectors'.[11] It states:

During the last decade, the emphasis in the GEF biodiversity portfolio has been on financing protected areas with smaller, but growing, engagement with sustainable use, mainstreaming and other private sector initiatives. As the GEF moves into its second decade, and while recognizing that protected areas are the cornerstones of conservation, it is proposed that biodi-

versity conservation be mainstreamed increasingly by emphasizing growing support for conservation beyond protected areas. Such an approach would place greater emphasis on sustainability of results and the potential for replication, and move beyond a projects-based emphasis to approaches that systematically target country enabling environments and long-term institutional building. (GEF, 2003b)

The GEF's new strategic priorities will support actions that are necessary to achieve long-term, sustainable conservation. However, should other public donors continue to shift their resources away from crucial conservation activities, the GEF's niche as the foremost source of public funds for protected areas is likely to become even more important.

A final illustration of the trend away from conservation-focused investments is the World Bank's changing biodiversity portfolio, represented in Figure 8.1. The differences between the 1994–1999 period and the previous six-year period are telling: the percentage of protected areas projects has declined as the percentage of projects outside protected areas and in productive landscapes has increased. Indeed, the Bank states explicitly that 'the greatest growth in the [biodiversity] portfolio in [the] future will be through mainstreaming biodiversity, and especially the sustainable use and restoration of biodiversity, into regular sustainable development operations and policy reforms' (World Bank, 2000).

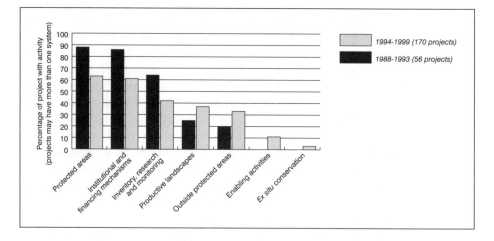

Source: Supporting the Web of Life: The World Bank and Biodiversity – A Portfolio Update 1988–1999 (World Bank, 2000). (

Note: Single projects typically include more than one biodiversity activity; therefore, these categories are not mutually exclusive, and totals exceed 100 per cent.

Figure 8.1 *Frequency of biodiversity activities in entire portfolio, FY 1988–99 (percentage of projects in which a given activity occurs)*

Finding 2: *As development institutions decentralize, development assistance frameworks negotiated at the country level will become more and more important. To date, such frameworks inconsistently reflect biodiversity concerns and seem to leave little room for conservation actions despite a proven demand for them.*

Bilateral and multilateral development institutions are becoming more decentralized, adopting a 'country-driven' approach in an effort to provide more durable development assistance driven by recipient country priorities. This decentralization has brought major structural and substantive change, with important implications for biodiversity assistance. As part of their structural decentralization, development institutions are delegating responsibility for designing and implementing projects, managing funds and setting strategic priorities to in-country missions, developing country governments, and civil society groups. For their part, development agency headquarters are focused increasingly on coordinating development efforts, tracking progress, and providing intra-sector and intra-regional strategic and technical support.

Country-driven development strategies

As part of the trend towards decentralized assistance, development institutions are relying increasingly on strategies negotiated at the country level. Country-driven development frameworks, such as the European Commission's Country Strategy Papers (CSPs) and the World Bank's Poverty Reduction Strategy Papers (PRSPs), are playing a central role in defining development assistance priorities.

Recent analyses suggest, however, that country-level development strategies negotiated by donor institutions and recipient governments are not adequately accounting for environmental considerations. For example, a study assessing CSPs in countries with significant forest cover found very little assistance dedicated to forests or the environment,[12] inadequate or non-existent analyses of the forest sector or the social and environmental value of forests, and a poor understanding of issues affecting indigenous people and forest-dependent communities (FERN, 2002). A similar study shows that environment and energy issues are integrated into PRSPs (including interim PRSPs) in a mixed fashion, with some country plans treating environment issues as important elements of a sustainable development strategy, some treating them sketchily, and others not mentioning them at all (Castro, 2002).

While these studies do not focus on biodiversity per se, they strongly suggest that significant progress remains to be achieved in adequately accounting for biodiversity considerations within development assistance frameworks. Certainly, this would seem an important step in the successful mainstreaming of biodiversity.

The demand for conservation investments

These studies also reveal a funding structure that appears to leave little room for conservation-specific investments. However, significant demand for such investments exists in many key countries. A first example of this demand is the growth in the GEF's biodiversity focal area[13] and its considerable investments in protected areas. The GEF reports spending $960 million over a ten-year period (FY91–01) to fund 894 protected areas covering 162 million hectares (GEF, 2003c). Currently, 95 full-sized biodiversity projects worth approximately $800 million sit in the GEF pipeline awaiting approval and funding.[14] Many of these are conservation-focused. A second illustration of the demand for financial resources targeting conservation objectives are the numerous recent commitments by developing countries to conservation, which will require significant donor support to ensure long-term success.[15] Examples of such commitments include the following:

- In July 2002, Cambodia created the 402,000 hectare Central Cardamoms Protected Forest, following a ban of all hunting and logging in the area 18 months earlier. The new protected area is the largest in Indochina and joins two other neighbouring wildlife sanctuaries, preserving 990,000 hectares of tropical forest.
- In August 2002, Brazil created the 3.9 million hectare Tumucumaque National Park, the world's largest tropical forest protected area.
- In September 2002, Gabon announced its intention to create a national park system comprised of 12 units covering more than five million hectares or approximately 10 per cent of the country's land area.
- In January 2003, Peru established three key protected areas within the biodiversity-rich Vilcabamba-Amboro Corridor, totalling more than 700,000 hectares.
- Myanmar has increased its coverage of protected areas from 0.5 per cent to 5 per cent in less than a decade. This includes a recent commitment to establishing the world's largest tiger reserve in Hukaung Valley, at about 1.4 million hectares. This will be added to pre-existing areas, creating the largest complex of contiguous protected areas in the region.

Finding 3: *While institutions with a development mandate provide the bulk of public biodiversity assistance, other government agencies fill important gaps, as do programmes executed directly by NGOs.*

A number of government agencies, including ministries of environment and natural resources, foreign affairs, and finance, as well as NGOs, manage international biodiversity assistance. These funding sources are an important complement to the biodiversity assistance provided by public donors with a development mandate.

Non-development government funding sources

While natural resource government agencies have a primary mandate to work domestically and regionally, they often manage a limited number of international conservation programmss. In the United States, for instance, the Department of Interior's Fish and Wildlife Service (USFWS) manages several species-specific funds dedicated to the conservation of elephants, great apes, tigers, rhinos and neotropical migratory birds. These programmes received $7.8 million cumulatively in fiscal year 2003. Similarly, the United Kingdom's Department of Environment, Food and Rural Affairs (DEFRA) manages the Darwin Initiative, a grants program focused on reducing habitat and species loss by supporting research, surveys and monitoring, capacity building, training, environmental education and awareness, and other activities aimed at implementing the CBD. DEFRA also supports the Flagship Species Fund, a partnership with the NGO Fauna & Flora International to fund conservation activities targeted at high-profile species in developing countries. The Netherlands Ministry of Agriculture, Nature Management and Fisheries (LNV) is yet another example of an agency that provides funding for international projects and programmes with a conservation focus. LNV spends approximately $7 million a year on conservation initiatives in developing countries and countries in Middle and Eastern Europe.

While generally limited in scale, these types of funding vehicles have significant conservation advantages. Because they are managed by institutions with conservation mandates and expertise, they tend to be more science-driven and are often able to fill gaps left by funding focused primarily on poverty reduction. For example, the international affairs programmes of the USFWS (including the Multinational Species Conservation Funds described above) support activities such as protected-area law enforcement, park management training, conservation education, facility maintenance and targeted research.

Natural resource agencies are not the only non-development agencies involved with biodiversity funding. Finance ministries within some governments play a role by overseeing the disbursement of biodiversity funds to multilateral institutions like the World Bank and the GEF. They are also responsible in certain cases for conservation finance arrangements such as debt-for-nature swaps. Perhaps the most active debt-for-nature programme is the US Tropical Forest Conservation Act (TFCA), managed by the Treasury Department. From 2001 to 2002, TFCA debt swaps have been concluded in Bangladesh, Belize, El Salvador, Peru and the Philippines. Collectively, these agreements will reduce $54 million in debt and generate $42 million for forest conservation activities. By linking conservation with debt relief (a top priority for many developing countries), these programmes serve an important political function and often engage counterpart finance ministries in developing nations.

Ministries of foreign affairs are another source of biodiversity assistance. Besides playing a key biodiversity policy role (e.g. often as the lead government departments for the CBD process), ministries of foreign affairs sometimes provide funding for conservation. For example, the UK's Foreign and Commonwealth Office, through its Environmental Policy Department, provides financial assistance for biodiversity projects within the UK's Overseas Territories. Like the funding provided by finance ministries, foreign-affairs funding often has an important political value because it allows conservation to be integrated with diplomatic efforts. This can be particularly effective when countries share historical ties and strong bilateral relations.

Conservation funding available from natural resource agencies, finance ministries, foreign affairs ministries, and other non-development agencies is important because it can be used to meet some of the demands not covered by financial resources from development agencies. Furthermore, the relatively small size and specific mandates of their biodiversity funding programmes allow non-development agencies to operate more efficiently, moving resources to the field with less bureaucracy and delay than their larger development-agency counterparts.

NGO execution of publicly funded projects

Another important dynamic in international biodiversity assistance is the extent to which bilateral and multilateral donors allow international NGOs to directly execute publicly funded programmes. Where this does occur, it is often through partnerships that combine government and private sector investments in conservation. NGO execution of biodiversity programmes offers the comparative advantages of administrative flexibility, greater accessibility and more direct delivery to civil society funding recipients. It also holds the promise of a science-based investment strategy. Key examples of public funding for NGO-executed biodiversity programmes include the following:

- The US Agency for International Development (USAID) supports the Parks in Peril Program (PiP), managed by The Nature Conservancy, with upwards of $7 million per year for site-based conservation in Latin America and the Caribbean. PiP has promoted the conservation of over 28 million hectares in biologically rich and threatened areas and has leveraged millions of dollars of investment from conservation and development institutions.
- Public investors in the Critical Ecosystems Partnership Fund (CEPF), managed by Conservation International (CI), include the World Bank, the GEF and the government of Japan. Each has contributed $25 million over five years (matched by equivalent commitments from the MacArthur Foundation and CI) to support conservation activities in biodiversity hotspots, which are the richest and most threatened reservoirs of biodiversity on Earth.[16] As fund manager, CI uses its scientific expertise and in-country presence to guide the deployment of funds. By retaining a seat on the board of CEPF, each donor is able to oversee its activities and influence its strategic direction.
- A number of donor governments provide biodiversity resources through NGOs for particular projects or initiatives. For example, German official

development assistance (ODA) includes 'funds in trust' for biodiversity projects and programmes carried out by NGOs, in particular World Wild Fund for Nature (WWF), IUCN and World Resources Institute (WRI). Similarly, USAID's Global Conservation Program will provide approximately $19 million from FY99 to FY03 to support the efforts of six partner NGOs to address threats to biodiversity at 18 sites worldwide.

Finding 4: Inconsistent reporting on and expanding definitions of biodiversity assistance prevent an accurate assessment of overall funding, impeding the creation of an effective system for collecting and sharing information, and hampering efforts to make informed investments.

Both bilateral and multilateral donors report their biodiversity assistance inconsistently. Moreover, biodiversity funding is often difficult to disaggregate from other types of funding because biodiversity activities are often components of broader development programmes, in particular with the recent trend towards mainstreaming biodiversity across various development sectors.[17] These factors prevent an accurate assessment of overall biodiversity assistance. More consistent and complete information on public biodiversity investments would allow for a more strategic use of limited financial resources.

Tracking bilateral biodiversity investments

Donor governments do not track and report on their bilateral biodiversity assistance in a standard fashion, making it difficult to accurately compile data on biodiversity spending from public sources. Data reported to the OECD's Creditor Reporting System (CRS) underscores this problem.[18] OECD member nations reporting to the CRS must assign their project-level assistance to sectors (e.g. education, agriculture and environment). Projects in each sector must then be assigned more specific 'purpose codes'. The 'biodiversity' purpose code within the environment sector is defined as 'including natural reserves and actions in the surrounding areas [and] other measures to protect endangered or vulnerable species and their habitats (e.g. wetlands preservation)' (OECD, 2003). Table 8.1, middle column, shows the average ODA amounts assigned the biodiversity purpose code, as reported by six donor governments during 1998–2000.

Separately, the OECD has also conducted a 'Rio Markers' study to assess total funding provided in 1998–2000 to support the CBD and the other Rio conventions (Table 8.1, right column).[19] As part of the Rio Markers study, donors reported the 'biodiversity-related aid' they had provided in a range of sectors, including general environmental protection, forestry, fishing, water supply and agriculture. Unlike the CRS, however, the reporting system for the Rio Markers study did not require donors to disaggregate specific, direct biodiversity spending. Rather, 'biodiversity-related aid' included the entire amount of funding for large projects where biodiversity was just one of many components as well as funding for projects where biodiversity was the central component.

Table 8.1 *Average annual bilateral biodiversity ODA reported to the OECD 1998–2000 ($ millions)*

Country	CRS 'biodiversity' purpose code	Aid targeting the CBD objectives (Rio Marker)
France	7.7	44.7
Germany	33.2	275.6
Japan	5.6	144.1
The Netherlands	20.3	146.9
United Kingdom	2.1	23.9
United States	44.7	84.2

Source: CRS database searched by donor country for 'biodiversity'-coded spending (OECD, 2003); *Aid Targeting the Objectives of the Rio Conventions 1998–2000* (Rio Markers Study), Table 3.1 (OECD, 2002).

Interviews with development officials and a careful review of other published materials on bilateral spending point to serious problems with both sets of numbers in Table 8.1. Responding to a conservation-oriented 'purpose-code' definition does not appear to be a priority for many development agencies, some of which oppose entirely the notion of reporting this type of aid. As a consequence, CRS reporting data appears to under-represent conservation investments. In contrast, reporting based on the 'Rio Markers' is highly unreliable because of its broad definition of biodiversity. Donors are allowed to count total project funding amounts, even funding outside the environment sector, as contributing to CBD objectives. 'Rio Markers' data are also likely to be inflated because donors are motivated to show significant financial support for the CBD. Moreover, in both the CRS and the 'Rio Markers' cases, the OECD has little capacity to verify the data provided to it.

A recent UNDP study on ODA financial flows in the forest sector came to similar conclusions about donor country reporting. It found that definitional issues and trends toward including forestry components in broader, multifaceted projects made the classification of funding difficult and caused figures representing flows to forestry to be defined in a very broad sense. With regard to OECD reporting in particular, the study found that (1) the data available on forestry were extremely incomplete, (2) the figures reported to the DAC and those reported to the more specific CRS database had significant discrepancies, (3) some donors were significantly under-reporting, while others were not reporting at all, and (4) the OECD system was unable to handle multifaceted projects (Madhvani, 1999).

Tracking multilateral biodiversity investments

By comparison, it is relatively easy to track the GEF's biodiversity assistance. Donor countries commit funds to the GEF for four-year periods. The amount of these commitments is determined in part by a burden-sharing formula based on the size of each donor country's economy. Donor government commitments to the GEF, made every four years since 1994, represent one clear measure of financial support for biodiversity and other global environment issues.[20] Besides providing estimates of biodiversity spending and regular programmatic reviews, the GEF has a publicly available database of descriptive and financial information about its projects. Because participating countries have agreed to standard definitions of activities eligible for GEF support, funding that has been approved for biodiversity projects is easily identified in the database. However, information on actual disbursements for biodiversity projects is not readily available.

Compared to GEF funding, assessing World Bank biodiversity funding is not as simple for many of the reasons noted above. It is difficult to accurately attribute the Bank's biodiversity funding because, with the exception of its GEF grants, many funds classified as 'targeted assistance for biodiversity' actually represent the biodiversity-related components of development projects whose scopes extend beyond biodiversity. The Bank's public project database identifies biodiversity as a 'targeted thematic outcome' in relevant projects, but does not separate out biodiversity spending because biodiversity, unlike agriculture, fishing, forestry, law and justice, and public administration, is not defined as a major sector. The most comprehensive publicly available figures on World Bank biodiversity funding come from assessments of the Bank's 'biodiversity portfolio', where biodiversity costs were determined by adding up biodiversity activity components (where they were clearly itemized) or estimating costs (where they were not itemized) using the best available information for each project (World Bank, 2000, 2002c).

Recommendations

This study's findings illustrate important changes in international public biodiversity assistance. Some are positive, such as donor governments' increased emphasis on cross-sectoral integration of biodiversity concerns. Others are not so positive, such as the apparent decrease in resources dedicated to long-proven and effective conservation investments. The consequences for global biodiversity, both positive and negative, of the four trends discussed lead us to make several recommendations to donor governments and NGOs.

Recommendations for governments

Donor governments should act to increase the conservation assistance they provide through multiple channels and apply existing biodiversity resources in a way that will effectively reduce global biodiversity loss and promote sustainable development. Specifically, we recommend that governments take the following four actions:

- Define a more secure and permanent place for conservation in the context of a poverty-focused development agenda.

  Poverty reduction is a noble cause and a legitimate priority. But unless the mechanisms of development in the twenty-first century incorporate a greater regard for conservation than did their predecessors, the habitability and natural variety of the world we live in will increasingly be put at risk. (Steven Sanderson, President & CEO, Wildlife Conservation Society, 'The future of conservation', *Foreign Affairs*, 2002)

As poverty reduction becomes the driving force behind development assistance across all sectors, conservation appears to be falling by the wayside. This report suggests that the ramifications may include a reduced role for science in shaping biodiversity assistance priorities, decreased funding for crucial conservation activities, fewer projects with clear conservation outcomes, diminished biodiversity expertise within funding agencies, and less political attention to conservation.

Donor governments must seize the opportunity provided by the MDGs to ensure a balanced approach to providing biodiversity assistance. While recognizing the connections between biodiversity and poverty, hunger, human health and other development priorities will lead to more effective development strategies, donors must also directly address the MDG target of reversing the loss of environmental resources. The MDG indicators explicitly acknowledge the importance of conserving biodiversity in situ through establishing protected areas and maintaining forest cover. Moreover, they acknowledge that 'reducing poverty in all its forms' requires that biodiversity be maintained. With the MDG framework in mind, the development portfolios of bilateral and multilateral donors should maintain a strong and consistent place for significant public investments targeted directly at the conservation of species and ecosystems.

- Integrate biodiversity concerns more effectively into development strategies.

Currently, the decentralized approach of development institutions and the country-driven strategies used to guide aid programmes do not sufficiently address biodiversity issues broadly, or conservation specifically. As a result, efforts to integrate biodiversity concerns across other sectors are hampered, and available funding for protected areas and other conservation-focused investments is greatly limited.

Development strategies such as the World Bank PRSPs and the European Commission CSPs must be based on careful analysis that takes into account the full value of biodiversity resources and also the impacts of specific development projects on important ecosystems. Consistent with the trend toward more country-driven assistance, such strategies must also acknowledge the significant demand for conservation resources in developing countries.

- Encourage the increased participation of a range of government institutions in providing biodiversity assistance, and support opportunities for direct NGO execution of publicly funded programmes.

Development agencies direct most bilateral biodiversity assistance. Yet other government agencies – including natural resource, finance and foreign affairs ministries – also play an important role both by providing resources that fill particular funding gaps and by building a broader political constituency for conservation activities in donor and recipient countries. International NGOs have also demonstrated their value as important and useful vehicles for channelling donor-government funding to field-based conservation activities. Governments should take further advantage of these alternative funding vehicles by increasing resources dedicated to them and capitalizing on synergies between them.

- Improve coordination and dissemination of measurable information about international biodiversity assistance.

Currently it is difficult to ascertain how much public funding is allocated for conservation, and where, how, by whom and how successfully it is being spent. This is a disadvantage to donors, developing country governments, NGOs and all other stakeholders interested in reducing biodiversity loss. In interviews conducted as part of this study, many donor agency representatives stated that they had limited information about the international biodiversity investments of their counterparts in other governments (and sometimes within their own governments). NGOs in developing countries seeking public funding support as well as those with resources of their own that are looking for investment partners also have a piecemeal vision of the biodiversity activities of the various bilateral and multilateral donors. Finally, almost all of the involved parties seem frustrated by the difficulty of compiling the data necessary to design integrated funding strategies for conserving biodiversity in priority regions.

Given the complications cited in this report, an accurate assessment of overall ODA related to biodiversity is currently an unrealistic goal. However, more could certainly be done to improve coordination and communication, especially regarding conservation investments targeted at specific landscapes. This suggests an increased role for the CBD Secretariat and also for public funding institutions, which should maintain more current and detailed information on their biodiversity investments and share it in publicly available forums.

Recommendations for NGOs

NGOs have a crucial role to play in engaging governments more comprehensively on the issues described above and in catalysing sustained public pressure on government leaders to create political will for conservation investments. Poverty-focused development agencies are mostly responsible for the many ongoing efforts to investigate the links between biodiversity and poverty. Not well represented in the debate is a strong and informed voice that advocates the conservation of unique and threatened species, habitats and ecosystems as a critical component of sustainable development and poverty reduction strategies. Unless the current dynamic changes, conservation will be robbed of a secure place within the overall development agenda.

Currently, the MDGs are perhaps the most important framework for international development assistance. NGOs should capitalize on this framework by supporting the integration of environment concerns in efforts to achieve all eight goals and making persuasive arguments for governments to increase their commitments to conservation.

NGOs should also support both donor and developing-country government institutions in their efforts to more effectively integrate biodiversity concerns into development assistance strategies. This would entail activating NGO offices in developing countries and making sure they are aware of the timing and process by which development frameworks are prepared, better articulating the benefits that conservation, and in particular protected areas, offer to national and local economies, challenging specific development initiatives that do unnecessary harm to biodiversity, ensuring the adequate use of environmental safeguards and environmental impact assessments, and proposing viable alternatives to national development models that rely heavily on resource extraction.

The inconsistent and incomplete reporting of biodiversity funding suggests that NGOs may have a role to play as part of a coordinated effort to maintain more current and detailed information on public conservation investments. NGOs could launch such an effort by improving the way information on their own conservation funding is shared. An important step in this regard is the recent initiative by leading conservation NGOs to map their conservation investments for selected priority regions.

Finally, the spotlight on international biodiversity issues has faded in the past decade, highlighting a major role for NGOs in generating the political will necessary to ensure that governments deliver on their commitments to provide international biodiversity resources. The period that preceded the 1992 Rio Earth Summit saw unprecedented international attention devoted to biodiversity loss, and the adoption of the CBD presented a tangible focal point for political action. However, the level of attention given to the global environment issues of the Rio Summit – including biodiversity, climate change and international waters – was considerably less at the WSSD in Johannesburg ten years later. Biodiversity was largely eclipsed at the WSSD by concerns about water, energy, health, agriculture and poverty, which was the WSSD's overriding focus. Furthermore, the WSSD itself, without the conventions or other clear outcomes to galvanize attention, attracted fewer heads of state and less media coverage. In this climate, donor governments are less likely to fulfil their commitments to biodiversity assistance.

Of particular concern is the current situation in the US, which is arguably the world's largest bilateral funder of conservation. Most US biodiversity funding flows through USAID, which afforded the environment a prominent place on its overall agenda during the 1990s. In a recent restructuring, however, environmental concerns, including biodiversity, were subsumed within the new Bureau of Economic Growth, Agriculture and Trade and consequently have assumed a much lower profile. A further potential sign of diminished US attention to environment and biodiversity issues is the Millennium Challenge Account (MCA), a new entity that could increase US development assistance by as much as $5 billion per year. To date, however, official documents on the MCA have included no reference to the environment, either as a criterion for country selection or as a potential priority for funding. The US commitment to the GEF is also a concern: current US GEF arrears total approximately $200 million. In the absence of a visible public profile for biodiversity issues, US decision-makers feel little pressure to address them. Furthermore, current biodiversity funding is maintained largely through earmarks inserted into annual appropriations bills, which are vulnerable to budget pressures or leadership changes within relevant congressional committees.[21]

NGOs can bring public attention to biodiversity issues and generate political will for increased international biodiversity assistance by doing the following:

- *Engaging government leaders.* A greater effort is needed in both donor and developing countries to engage political leaders as conservation champions. Few efforts currently exist to directly expose key decision-makers (especially ministers of finance and development) to conservation issues, challenges and opportunities.
- *Leveraging the private sector.* Government donors are increasingly focused on leveraging public investments by establishing partnerships with the private sector that aim to reduce the ecological footprint of business practices and provide direct support for conservation. Indeed, such partnerships were a central feature of the WSSD.
- *Educating the public.* Today the mainstream media pays less attention to biodiversity than it did ten years ago. New ways must be found to put the issue back on the public agenda and to engage supportive constituencies, including the foreign policy, faith-based, medical/pharmaceutical and sportsmen communities.
- *Capitalizing on upcoming events.* Two key forums are planned for the next year: the World Parks Congress in Durban, South Africa, in September 2003 and the Seventh Conference of the Parties to the CBD, focused on protected areas, in April 2004. These forums present opportunities for NGOs to make strong arguments for increased public investments in conservation.

This study shows that public donors have made significant progress toward establishing biodiversity as a core component of sustainable development assistance. However, this advance has come at some expense to the financial resources available for long-established conservation activities, which are essential for reducing biodiversity loss. The recommendations above suggest steps toward a more balanced approach to public biodiversity assistance and show that NGOs have an important role to play in maintaining a secure place for conservation on the international development agenda.

Notes

1   Ours is a human-dominated planet (Vitousek et al., 1997; Woodruff, 2001; Sanderson et al., 2002). More than a third of the Earth's land surface has already been transformed by human action, and projections suggest that an additional third could be converted within the next 100 years (WRI, 2000). The need for a network of protected areas and in situ conservation is widely recognized by biodiversity scientists (Noss, 1996; Terborgh, 1999; Oates, 1999; Bruner et al., 2001) and is a requirement of the Convention on Biological Diversity (CBD, 1992). Experts at a recent conference entitled 'Defying Nature's End' made the overarching recommendation that 'enforceable protection of remaining natural ecosystems' is essential for preventing extinctions (Pimm et al., 2001).

2   A notable example is the recently established Global Conservation Fund (GCF) at Conservation International, a $100 million initiative made possible through a grant from the Gordon and Betty Moore Foundation to finance the creation, expansion and long-term sustainability of protected areas. For more information on the GCF, see the Conservation International website: www.conservation.org.

3   The OECD Development Assistance Committee member countries include Australia, Austria, Belgium, Canada, Denmark, European Commission, Finland, France, Germany, Greece, Ireland, Italy, Japan, Luxembourg, the Netherlands, New Zealand, Norway, Portugal, Spain, Sweden, Switzerland, the United Kingdom, and the United States.

4   A study by the UN Food and Agriculture Organization (FAO) shows that foreign donors contribute about 40 per cent of the money African governments spend on forests. Moreover, in 10 of the 20 countries with available data, foreign donors provide more than 60 per cent of forest sector resources (FAO, 2003).

5   In recent development assistance negotiations, only 5 of the 21 countries prioritized by the Netherlands to receive development assistance elected to focus on the environment sector. Of these, several are characterized by arid landscapes – a poor match with Dutch expertise in the forest sector. In order to meet the 0.1 per cent target, the Netherlands chose 14 additional countries on which to spend environment/biodiversity funds (van Helden, pers. comm., 2002).

6   As of March 2002, Germany had committed $171.27 million and the European Commission had committed $64.34 million out of a total of $301.16 million committed by donor governments to the PPG7 (World Bank, 2003a).

7   See the UN Millennium Development Goals, www.un.org/millenniumgoals (UN, 2000), and the World Bank Development Goals, www.worldbank.org/data/dev/ devgoals.html (World Bank, 2003b).

8   For example, the US government recently announced the Congo Basin Initiative, which will provide $36 million in new USAID funding to 11 priority conservation landscapes in Gabon, Congo, Central African Republic, Cameroon, DR Congo, and Equatorial Guinea (United States Department of State, 2002). Germany's recent review of its biodiversity investments shows that 70 per cent of projects give priority to in situ conservation (BMZ and GTZ, 2002).

9   A recent FAO study found that foreign donor support to African governments for forest-sector spending is declining; it fell from $132 million in 1995 to $100 million in 1999 (FAO, 2003). Recognizing a downward trend in ODA, certain donor governments made significant new commitments to increasing aid at the International Conference on Financing for Development in Monterrey, Mexico, in March 2002 (UN, 2002). However, it remains to be seen whether these commitments will be realized.

10   A revised version of this draft Business Plan will be approved at the upcoming May 2003 GEF Council meeting.

11   According to the GEF's proposed financial allocation framework, during FY03–05 $207 million will be allocated to the strategic priority 'Mainstreaming Biodiversity Conservation in Production Systems,' representing approximately 37 per cent of total projected spending in the biodiversity focal area during that time period.

12   In the 16 countries reviewed, 21 to 85 per cent of land surface area is covered by forest. Of the $1.66 billion in development assistance allocated these countries, only $63.6 million (3.8 per cent) is forest-related (FERN, 2002).

13   The FY02–04 GEF Business Plan (2000) reported 'strongly positive' annualized growth for the biodiversity focal area in FY99 (29 per cent) and FY00 (18 per cent) as compared to FY98.

14   This estimate is based on a December 2002 review of the GEF pipeline and the average value of GEF full-sized biodiversity projects (about $8.3 million) in the approval period 1999–2002. The GEF pipeline is available online: www.gefweb.org/Projects/Pipeline/pipeline.html (accessed 28 November 2009).

15   Protected area designation is perhaps the clearest example of commitments by developing country governments to conservation. Governments have also made significant commitments to conservation by investing in scientific research, protected area management, community engagement and other important activities. Several NGO-run programmes provide further examples of these 'conservation commitments'. The WWF 'Gifts to the Earth' programme recognizes conservation actions by governments and other stakeholders. To date WWF has accepted 29 Forest Gifts from governments and individuals around the world who have pledged to create new forest protected areas or better protect existing ones. These Gifts amount to a total commitment of approximately 180 million hectares of forest; over 100 million hectares have been fully implemented (www.panda.org/about_wwf/how_we_work/gifts_to_the_earth/ forests/index.cfm). The Nature Conservancy's Parks in Peril programme has engaged governments, resulting in significant commitments to conservation (TNC, 2003).

16   For more information on biodiversity hotspots, visit www.biodiversityhotspots.org.

17   For example, in the Netherlands, over two-thirds of what the development agency counts as spending on the environment is bilateral and multilateral support in 'other development sectors with an orientation towards the environment', such as agriculture and rural development (vander Zon, pers. comm., 2002).

18   The OECD International Development Statistics online databases (IDS/o) include the Development Assistance Committee online (DAC/o) and the Creditor Reporting System online (CRS/o). The DAC/o distinguishes between broadly defined sectors and types of aid, whereas the CRS allows more detailed breakdowns. These databases can be accessed at www.oecd.org/dac/stats/.

19   This study, released at the WSSD, tracked funding for the UN conventions on biodiversity, climate change and desertification from 1998 to 2000. It responded to requests from the convention secretariats to determine if regular CRS reporting could accurately depict funding provided

for convention implementation. The DAC asked donor countries to use a 'marker' system to identify projects in all CRS sectors related to the implementation of each convention.
20 The GEF's largest contributors are the US, Japan, Germany, the UK and France.
For FY03, the foreign operations appropriations bill includes language directing USAID to spend 'not less than $145,000,000' on 'programs and activities which directly protect biodiversity, including forests, in developing countries'.

References

ADB (Asian Development Bank) (2002) *Environment Policy*, Available at: www.adb.org/Environment/envpol/default.asp (last accessed 30 May 2003).

Balmford, A., Bruner, A., Cooper, P., Costanza, R., Farber, S., Green, R.E., Jenkins, M., Jefferiss, P., Jessamy, V., Madden, J., Munro, K., Myers, N., Naeem, S., Paavola, J., Rayment, M., Rosendo, S., Roughgarden, J., Trumper, K. and Turner, R.K. (2002) 'Economic reasons for conserving wild nature', *Science*, 297: 950–953.

Biodiversity in Development Project (2001a) *Strategic Approach for Integrating Biodiversity in Development Cooperation*, European Commission, Brussels and IUCN, Gland, Switzerland.

Biodiversity in Development Project (2001b) *Biodiversity Briefs*, European Commission, Brussels and IUCN, Gland, Switzerland.

Brown, L. (2002) Personal Communication, Department for International Development, United Kingdom, 7 August.

Bruner, A., Gullison, R.E., Rice, R.E. and da Fonseca, G.A.B. (2001) 'Effectiveness of parks in protecting tropical biodiversity', *Science*, 291: 125–128.

BMZ and GTZ (German Federal Ministry for Economic Cooperation and Development & German Association for Technical Cooperation) (2002) *Biodiversity Conservation in German Development Cooperation*, 4th Revised Editions, GTZ, Berlin.

Castro, G. (2002) Personal Communication, Biodiversity Team Leader, Global Environment Facility, 15 October.

Castro, G. and Locker, I. (2000) *Mapping Conservation Investments: An Assessment of Biodiversity Funding in Latin America and the Caribbean*, Biodiversity Support Program, Washington, DC.

CBD (Convention on Biological Diversity) (1992) *Convention Text*. Available at: www.cbd.int/convention/convention.shtml (last accessed 28 November 2009).

CBD (2002) *COP 6 Decisions*. Available at: www.cbd.int/decisions (last accessed 28 November 2009).

CBD Secretariat (2003) *Convention on Biological Diversity*. Available at: www.cbd.int (last accessed 28 November 2009).

DFID (Department for International Development) (2001) *Biodiversity – A Crucial Issue for the World's Poorest*, DFID, London.

DFID (2002) *Wildlife and Poverty Study*. Available at: www.dfid.gov.uk/Pubs/files/wildlife_poverty_study.pdf (last accessed 30 May 2003).

DIFD, European Commission (EC), United Nations Development Program (UNDP), and World Bank (2002) *Linking Poverty Reduction and Environmental Management: Policy Challenges and Opportunities*, DFID, London.

European Commission (2001) *Biodiversity Action Plan for Economic and Development Cooperation*, Communication from the Commission to the Council and the European Parliament, COM(2001)162, Volume V, European Commission, Brussels.

FERN (The EC Forest Platform) (2002) *Forests at the Edge: A Review of EC Aid Spending.* Available at: www.fern.org (last accessed 28 November 2009).

FAO (UN Food and Agriculture Organization) (2003) *Forest Finance.* Available at: www.fao.org/forestry/finance (last accessed 28 November 2009).

FFEM (French Global Environment Facility/Fonds Francais pour l'Environnement Mondial) (2003) Available at: www.ffem.net (last accessed 28 November 2009).

GEF (Global Environment Facility) (2002) *Focusing on the Environment: The First Decade of the GEF,* Second Overall Performance Report (OPS2), GEF, Washington, DC.

GEF (2003a) *GEF Project Tracking System.* Available at: www.gefonline.org (last accessed 28 November 2009).

GEF (2003b) *GEF Business Plan FY04–06. GEF/C.21/9.* GEF Council Agenda Item 10, 14–16 May, 2003. Available at: www.gefweb.org/Documents/Council_Documents/GEF_C21/C.21.9_GEF_Business_Plan_FY04–06.pdf (last accessed 30 May 2003).

GEF (2003c) *Strategic Business Planning: Directions and Targets.* GEF/C.21/Inf.11. GEF Council, 14–16 May, 2003. Available at: www.gefweb.org/Documents/Council_Documents/GEF_C21/C21.Inf.11-_Strategic_Business_Planning.pdf (last accessed 30 May 2003).

Herfkens, E. (2002) Minister for Development Cooperation, The Netherlands, *Biodiversity and Poverty,* Speech in The Hague at a meeting organized by the World Wildlife Fund, 9 April.

James, A.N., Gaston, K.J. and Balmford, A. (2000) 'Balancing the Earth's accounts', *Nature,* 401: 323–324.

LeGrand, S. (2002) Personal Communication, Environment and Rural Development Unit, DG-Development, European Commission, 5 November.

Madhvani, A. (1999) *An Assessment of Data on ODA Financial Flows in the Forest Sector,* Forest Policy and Environment Group, Overseas Development Institute, Prepared for Forests Programme, Sustainable Energy and Environment Division, UNDP.

Minbuza (The Netherlands Ministry of Foreign Affairs) (2003) Available at: www.minbuza.nl (last accessed 28 November).

Noss, R.F. (1996) 'Protected areas: How much is enough?', pp. 91–118, in Wright, R.G. (ed) *National Parks and Protected Areas: Their Role in Environmental Protection,* Blackwell Science, Cambridge, MA.

Oates, J.F. (1999) *Myth and Reality: How Conservation Strategies are Failing in West Africa,* University of California Press, Berkeley.

OECD (Organisation for Economic Co-operation and Development) (2002) *Aid Targeting the Objectives of the Rio Conventions 1998–2000* (Rio Markers Study), Development Assistance Committee (DAC), Working Party on Statistics. A contribution by the DAC Secretariat for the information of participants at the World Summit on Sustainable Development in Johannesburg. OECD, Paris.

OECD (2003) Development Assistance Committee (DAC), Creditor Reporting System (CRS). Available at: www.oecd.org/dac/stats (last accessed 28 November 2009).

Pimm, S.L., Ayres, M., Balmford, A., Branch, G., Brandon, K., Brooks, T.M., Bustamante, R., Costanza, R., Cowling, R., Curran, L.M., Dobson, A., Farber, S., Fonseca, G.A.B. da, Gascon, C., Kitching, R., McNeely, J., Lovejoy, T., Mittermeier, R.A., Myers, N., Patz, J.A., Raffle, B., Rapport, D., Raven, P., Roberts, C., Rodriguez, J.P., Rylands, A.B., Tucker, C., Safina, C., Samper, C., Stiassny, M.L.J., Safina, C., Supriatna, J., Wall, D.H. and Wilcove, D. (2001) 'Can we defy nature's end?', *Science,* 293: 2207–2208.

Sachs, J. (2003) Director, Earth Institute at Columbia University and Special Advisor to UN Secretary General Kofi Annan. Keynote address and discussion on 'Achieving the Millennium Development Goals: The Role of the International Biodiversity Community'. At 'Biodiversity After Johannesburg: The Critical Role of Biodiversity and Ecosystem Services in Achieving the Millennium Development Goals,' London, 2 March.

Sanderson, S. (2002) 'The future of conservation', *Foreign Affairs,* 81(5): 162–173.

Sanderson, E.W., Jaiteh, M., Levy, M.A., Redford, K.H., Wannebo, A.V. and Woolmer, G. (2002) 'The human footprint and the last of the wild', *Bioscience,* 52: 891–904.

Secretaría de Medio Ambiente y Recursos Naturales, Mexico (2002) *Cancun Declaration of Like-Minded Megadiverse Countries.* Available at: www.semarnat.gob.mx/internacionales/reunion/convocatoria_ingles.shtml (last accessed 30 May 2003).

Short, C. (2003) Minister of International Development, Department for International Development (DFID), United Kingdom. Speech at 'Biodiversity After Johannesburg: The Critical Role of Biodiversity and Ecosystem Services in Achieving the UN Millennium Development Goals', London, 3 March.

TNC (The Nature Conservancy) (2003) *Parks in Peril.* Available at: www.nature.org/initiatives/programs/parks/index.html (last accessed 28 November 2009).

Terborgh, J. (1999) *Requiem for Nature,* Island Press, Washington, DC.

United States Department of State (2002) *Congo Basin Forest Partnership: US Contribution.* Available at: www.state.gov/g/oes/rls/fs/2002/15617.htm (last accessed 30 May 2003).

UN (United Nations) (2000) *Millennium Development Goals.* Available at: www.un.org/millenniumgoals (last accessed 28 November 2009).

UN (2002) *World Summit on Sustainable Development Plan of Implementation.* Available at: www.johannesburgsummit.org/html/documents/summit_docs/2309_planfinal.htm (last accessed 30 May 2003).

van Helden, F.W. (2002) Personal Communication, Senior Policy Advisor, International Biodiversity Unit, Department of Nature Management, Ministry of Agriculture, Nature Management, and Fisheries, The Netherlands, 9 September, 6 November.

vander Zon, T. (2002) Personal Communication, The Netherlands Ministry of Foreign Affairs, The Netherlands, 18 September.

Vitousek, P.M., Mooney, H.A., Lubchenco, J. and Melillo, J.M. (1997) 'Human domination of Earth's ecosystems', *Science,* 277: 494–499.

Woodruff, D.S. (2001) 'Declines of biomes and biotas and the future of evolution', *Proceedings of the National Academy of Sciences,* 98: 5471–5476.

World Bank (2000) *Supporting the Web of Life: The World Bank and Biodiversity – A Portfolio Update 1988–1999.* Available at: www-wds.worldbank.org/servlet/WDSServlet?pcont=details&eid=000094946_0010140549554 (last accessed 30 May 2003).

World Bank (2001) *Making Sustainable Commitments: An Environment Strategy for the World Bank.* Available at: lnweb18.worldbank.org/ESSD/essdext.nsf/41ByDocName/EnvironmentStrategy (last accessed 30 May 2003).

World Bank (2002a) *The Environment and the Millennium Development Goals.* Available at: lnweb18.worldbank.org/ESSD/essdext.nsf/44DocByUnid/DB84A62D45062B2585256C060077049D?Opendocument (last accessed 30 May 2003).

World Bank (2002b) *A Revised Forest Strategy for the World Bank Group.* Available at: lnweb18.worldbank.org/ESSD/essdext.nsf/14ByDocName/ForestPolicyandStrategy (last accessed 30 May 2003).

World Bank (2002c) *Biodiversity Conservation in Forest Ecosystems: World Bank Assistance 1992–2002.* Available at: www.worldbank.org/biodiversity (last accessed 28 November 2009).

World Bank (2003a) *Pilot program to Conserve the Brazilian Rainforest.* Available at: www.worldbank.org/rfpp (last accessed 28 November 2009).

World Bank (2003b) *World Bank Development Goals.* Available at: www.worldbank.org/data/dev/devgoals.html (last accessed 28 November 2009).

WRI (World Resources Institute) (2000) *World Resources 2000–2001,* World Resources Institute, New York.

Xiang, Y. (2002) Personal Communication, Program Officer, Financial Resource Analyst, Convention on Biological Diversity Secretariat, 14 August, 23 October, 31 October.

Chapter 9

Report of the Ad Hoc Open-ended Working Group of Review of Implementation of the Convention

Secretariat of the Convention on Biological Diversity (CBD)[1]

Review of Implementation of Articles 20 and 21

I. Estimates of funding needs of global biodiversity efforts

3. In its preamble, the Convention acknowledges that substantial investments are required to conserve biological diversity and that there is an expectation of a broad range of environmental, economic and social benefits from those investments. The Conference of the Parties has not so far undertaken any estimation of funding needs of the Convention and its decisions. However, other intergovernmental and major international processes have carried out such exercises as to determine the level of funding required for purposes of the Convention.

4. The United Nations Development Programme commissioned an International Conservation Financing Project to the World Resources Institute in late 1980s. The project examined the ongoing conservation financing mechanisms, assessed the prospects for expanding their scope, and proposed four additional initiatives based on the results of intensive study and consultation in Asia, Africa, Europe, and the Americas. The project report entitled 'Natural endowments: Financing Resource Conservation for Development' (1989) states: 'This study defines conservation as maintaining natural resources as the basis for meeting the needs of current and future generations. While unmet conservation financing needs in developing countries are difficult to gauge precisely,

indicators are that as much as $20–$50 billion per annum will be needed over the next decade.'

5. During the negotiations for the Convention on Biological Diversity, many estimates of funding needs were circulated. In its address to the negotiators at the first day of the fourth negotiating session in 1991, Dr Mostafa K. Tolba, the then Executive Director of the United Nations Environment Programme, informed the Intergovernmental Negotiating Committee (INC) that the World Bank had estimated that the cost of biodiversity conservation ranged from $500 million to $50 billion per year. These figures were based on the experience which the GEF had in biological diversity conservation projects. The GEF biological diversity conservation projects cost approximately $35,000 per square kilometre at that time.

6. Another estimate was proposed by the Secretariat of the United Nations Conference on Environment and Development (UNCED) (3–14 June 1992, Rio de Janeiro, Brazil). Agenda 21, Chapter 15, stated: 'The Conference secretariat has estimated the average total cost (1993–2000) of implementing the activities of this chapter to be about $3.5 billion, including about $1.75 billion from the international community on grant or concessional terms. These are indicative and order-of-magnitude estimates only, and have not been reviewed by Governments. Actual costs and financial terms, including any that are non-concessional, will depend on, inter alia, the specific strategies and programmes Governments decided upon for implementation.'

7. The Vth IUCN World Parks Congress (8–17 September 2003, Durban, South Africa) released a more recent estimate. Recommendation 5.07 (Financial Security for Protected Areas) adopted by the Congress noted a significant funding gap, and declared: 'As an indicator of this need, it is estimated that protected area budgets in the early 1990s totalled only about 20 per cent of the estimated US$20–30 billion annually over the next 30 years required to establish and maintain a comprehensive protected area system including terrestrial, wetland, and marine ecosystems.'

V. Resources available from integration of biological diversity into sectoral development and assistance programmes, policies and plans

23. In decision VI/16, paragraph 8, the Conference of the Parties 'Urges Parties and Governments, the World Bank, the International Monetary Fund, the United Nations Development Programme and other relevant institutions to take concrete action to review and further integrate biodiversity considerations in the development and implementation of major international development initiatives, such as the Highly Indebted Poor Countries (HIPC) Initiative,

Poverty Reduction Strategies (PRSs), and Comprehensive Development Frameworks (CDF), as well as in national sustainable development plans and relevant sectoral policies and plans'.

24. In a sample of 93 third national reports, only 9 per cent of the reporting countries report that they have not taken concrete actions to review and further integrate biodiversity in national plans and international development initiatives. Half the reporting countries indicated some initiatives, and a quarter of the reporting countries have undertaken major initiatives. Sixteen per cent report that the review is under way.

25. In decision VII/21, paragraph 7, the Conference of the Parties 'Invites Parties and Governments to enhance the integration of biological diversity into their sectoral development and assistance programmes.'

26. In a sample of 89 third reports, only 10 per cent of the reporting countries did not enhance biodiversity integration, and a few more were developing some programmes. More than half the reporting countries report that they have integrated biodiversity into some sectoral development and assistance programmes, and nearly a quarter of the reporting countries have integration into major programmes.

30. In general, there are four approaches used to integrate biodiversity into development cooperation:
   - Most countries have integrated environmental considerations, including biodiversity, into all aspects of development cooperation, in particular through mandatory environmental impact assessments;
   - Many countries have integrated biodiversity and environmental considerations in sectoral programmes and country strategy planning procedures, strategy for aid to developing countries or Chart on Sustainable Development;
   - A number of countries have pursued sectoral integration into, such as agriculture, forestry, fisheries sectors, sustainable resource management and rural development strategy; and
   - Certain countries have established specific policy instruments or programmes to promote integration of biodiversity, such as the French Global Environment Facility, and International Policy Programme on Biodiversity.

VIII.   Official development assistance to biodiversity

52. In decision VIII/13, paragraph 5, the Conference of the Parties requested the Executive Secretary and invited the Organisation for Economic Co-operation and Development (OECD) to further collaborate on data collection and to provide regular reports on the status and trends of biodiversity finance to the Conference of the Parties

53. The following synthesis is based on the OECD data extracted on 1 March 2007, which contains funding information from Australia, Austria, Belgium, Canada, Denmark, Finland, France, Germany, Greece, Ireland, Italy, Japan, Netherlands, New Zealand, Norway, Portugal, Spain, Sweden, Switzerland, United Kingdom, United States and European Commission. As biodiversity and other Rio issues are relatively new concepts within development statistical system, different understandings of their definitions and statistical attributes may have more impact on accuracy and consistency of applying the Rio markers across countries than over time. Figure 9.1 presents the results of applying the Rio markers in development cooperation data. The percentages of marked aids for the Rio conventions have varied significantly, providing a trend measurement of the extent to which the Rio conventions have been frequently integrated into development assistance programmes. The period between 2001 and 2003 appear to be relatively high, with nearly 6 per cent in 2003. There was a turning point in 2000, and also in 2004. The relatively low percentage in 2005 may be a reflection of time factor in data processing.

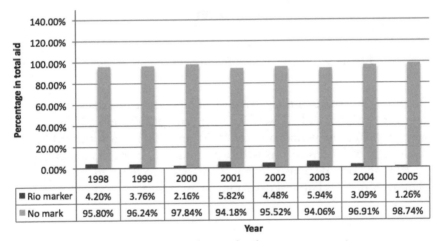

	1998	1999	2000	2001	2002	2003	2004	2005
■ Rio marker	4.20%	3.76%	2.16%	5.82%	4.48%	5.94%	3.09%	1.26%
■ No mark	95.80%	96.24%	97.84%	94.18%	95.52%	94.06%	96.91%	98.74%

Year

Figure 9.1 *Rio marker in development cooperation*

Historical trends in biodiversity finance

54. The data generate around US$6 billion for biodiversity-related assistance from 21 developed countries and the European Commission for the period between 1998 and 2005. Four countries (Japan, Germany, Netherlands and the United States) together provided 70 per cent of the marked total biodiversity-related assistance in this period. Other countries in the top ten supporting countries are Denmark, France, Norway, Canada, Sweden and Switzerland.

55. Since several countries and the European Commission were not involved in the pilot phase of the Rio markers, and certain countries may have not

completed the marking for the year 2005, Figure 9.2 presents the more representative trend based on 19 countries whose data are available for the whole
period between 1998 and 2004. There was generally an increasing trend of
biodiversity-related assistance from 1998 to 2003, but a downward trend
started in the year 2004.

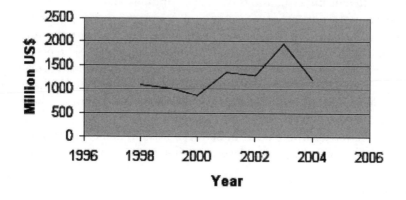

Figure 9.2 *Trend of total biodiversity aid of 19 countries*

56. According to Table 9.1, the percentage of biodiversity assistance in total development assistance had a low of 1.32 per cent in 2000 and a high of 2.94 per
cent in 2001. The period between 2001 and 2003 also witnessed high-level
percentage of biodiversity assistance in total official development assistance.
Overall, the data demonstrate that biodiversity accounts for around 2.10 per
cent of annual total official development assistance.

Table 9.1 *Biodiversity assistance as percentage of total ODA*

Year	Biodiversity assistance as percentage of total ODA
1998	2.13%
1999	1.71%
2000	1.32%
2001	2.94%
2002	2.39%
2003	2.55%
2004	1.63%
2005	0.55%
Average (1998–2004)	2.10%

Regional trends in biodiversity finance

57. *Least developed countries:* There are some US$1.6 billion marked for the least developed countries between 1998 and 2005. On average, about US$200 million have been invested in biodiversity-related development assistance in the least developed countries every year. Such assistance declined to around US$100 million in 2000, but has recovered since then. As shown in Figure 9.3, the overall trend in bilateral biodiversity assistance for the least developed countries is to increase positively. The top ten supporting countries are: Netherlands, Germany, Norway, Japan, Denmark, Canada, United States, Sweden, France, Belgium and European Commission.

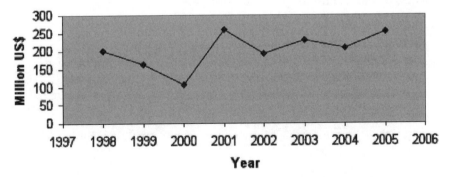

Figure 9.3 *Biodiversity marker for assistance to least developed countries*

58. *Small island developing States:* Among 22 developed countries, 14 countries marked over US$212 million for biodiversity assistance in their development assistance for the small island developing States. On average, development assistance has allocated some US$27 million to biodiversity activities in the small

island developing States every year, and there is a general trend of increasing biodiversity cooperation with small island developing States led by the European Commission, as shown in Figure 9.4. The top ten supporting countries: Netherlands, Switzerland, Canada, Japan, Australia, France, Germany, Spain, New Zealand, Norway and European Commission.

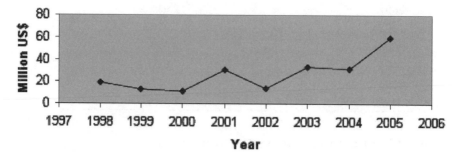

Figure 9.4 *Biodiversity marker for assistance to small island developing States*

59. *Africa:* A total of 19 developed countries and the European Commission marked US$2.5 billion for biodiversity in their development cooperation to Africa, implying that over US$3 million have been invested in African biodiversity on an annual basis. According to Figure 9.5, the overall trend of development assistance to African biodiversity is increasing significantly despite incomplete marking in 2005. The top ten supporting countries are Germany, Netherlands, Norway, Canada, Denmark, France, Japan, Sweden, United States, Belgium and European Commission.

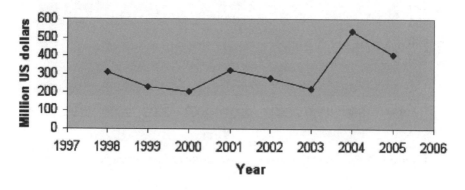

Figure 9.5 *Biodiversity marker for assistance to Africa*

60. *Asia and the Pacific:* More than US$4.35 billion are marked for biodiversity in Asia and the Pacific from 18 developed countries and European Commission, and Japan alone accounts for more than half of the marked assistance. On

average, over US$0.5 billion have been invested in biodiversity activities of Asia and the Pacific every year. Partly due to heavy reliance on a single donor, as shown in Figure 9.6, biodiversity assistance to Asia and the Pacific has varied dramatically in the observing period. Other top ten supporting countries are Netherlands, Germany, Denmark, France, Norway, Canada, Switzerland, Australia, Sweden and European Commission.

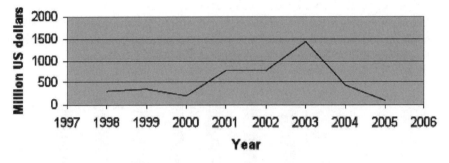

Figure 9.6 *Biodiversity marker for assistance to Asia and the Pacific*

61. *Latin America and the Caribbean:* Nineteen developed countries and European Commission have marked over US$1.1 billion for biodiversity in Latin America and the Caribbean, at an annual average of US$140 million. Considering incomplete marking for 2005, the overall trend in biodiversity assistance to Latin America and the Caribbean is generally going up, as shown in Figure 9.7. The top ten supporting countries are Germany, Netherlands, United States, Japan, Spain, Canada, Denmark, Switzerland, France, Norway and European Commission.

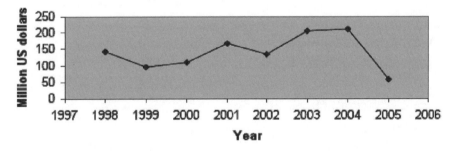

Figure 9.7 *Biodiversity marker for assistance to Latin America and the Caribbean*

Sectoral pattern of biodiversity finance

62. Figure 9.8 presents sectoral distribution of biodiversity assistance between 1998 and 2005. Multi-sector including general environmental protection and traditionally defined biodiversity projects accounts for 36 per cent of marked total biodiversity aid. Production sectors (agriculture, forestry, fishing, industry, mining, trade policy and regulation, tourism) and social infrastructure (education, health, water supply and sanitation, government and civil society) contain 33 per cent of marked biodiversity assistance and 27 per cent respectively. Economic infrastructure (transport and storage, communications, energy, banking and financial services) and other non-sectoral cooperation explain the remaining minor portion of total marked biodiversity assistance.

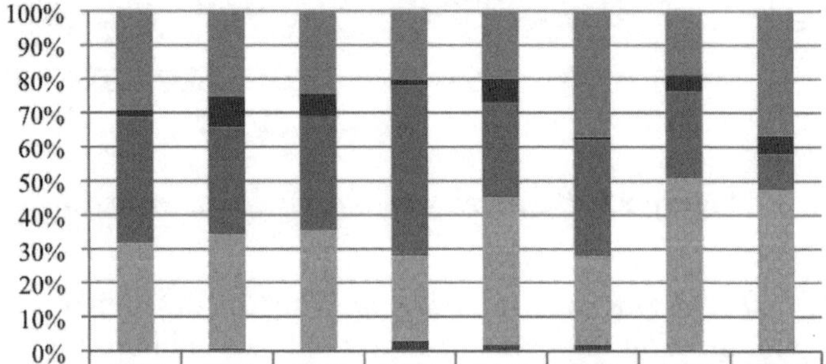

	1998	1999	2000	2001	2002	2003	2004	2005
■ I. Social infrastructure	242.9	201.00	151.90	276.30	277.60	751.50	248.80	216.40
■ II. Economic infrastructure	17.18	74.60	43.51	23.36	101.20	21.23	63.57	32.00
■ III. Production sectors	308.00	253.60	210.40	685.70	391.80	690.40	338.50	62.87
■ IV. Multisector	263.50	270.90	221.80	341.20	608.90	525.00	665.60	275.20
■ Sectors unallocable	0.03	6.35	1.83	40.78	24.60	40.50	5.83	4.51

Figure 9.8 *Broad sectoral categories of biodiversity assistance*

Table 9.2 *Sectoral distribution of biodiversity assistance (1998–2005)*

Sectors	Marked biodiversity aid between 1998–2005	Percentage in total marked biodiversity assistance
Water supply and sanitation	2296.52	25.83%
Agriculture	1450.08	16.31%
Forestry	1208.99	13.60%
Fishing	220.72	2.48%
Energy	144.34	1.62%
Transport and storage	127.04	1.43%
Government and civil society	39.79	0.45%
Industry	35.35	0.40%
Education	17.79	0.20%
Tourism	12.45	0.14%
Banking and financial services	9.75	0.11%
Mining	8.90	0.10%
Health	7.78	0.09%
Trade policy and regulation	5.11	0.06%
Communications	2.48	0.03%

63. General environmental protection, water supply and sanitation, agriculture, forestry, fishing, energy, transport and storage are the six largest sectors channelling biodiversity cooperation, together accounting for 97 per cent of all marked biodiversity assistances. As shown in Table 9.2, water supply and sanitation, agriculture and forestry have featured prominently in bilateral assistance to biodiversity, with 26 per cent, 16 per cent and 14 per cent in total marked biodiversity assistance respectively.

64. The major sectors important for biodiversity may broadly cover many elements of the programmes of work under the Convention. For instance, multi-sector assistance contains traditionally defined biodiversity activities, and water supply and sanitation as well as fishing may correspond to programmes of work on inland water ecosystems, marine and coastal biological diversity and also island biodiversity. Agriculture and forestry can be broadly captured in the programmes of work on agricultural biodiversity and on forest biological diversity.

Box 9.1 *Coverage of sectoral assistance marked for biodiversity*

Multi-sector: Environmental policy and administrative management, biosphere protection, biodiversity, site preservation, flood prevention/control, environmental education/ training, environmental research, urban development and management, rural development, non-agricultural alternative development, multi-sector education/training, research/scientific institutions

Water supply and sanitation: Water resources policy and administrative management, water resources protection, water supply and sanitation – large systems, basic drinking water supply and basic sanitation, river development, waste management/disposal, education and training in water supply and sanitation

Agriculture: Agricultural policy and administrative management, agricultural development, agricultural land resources, agricultural water resources, agricultural inputs, food crop production, industrial crops/export crops, livestock, agrarian reform, agricultural alternative development, agricultural extension, agricultural education/training, agricultural research, agricultural services, plant and post-harvest protection and pest control, agricultural financial services, agricultural co-operatives, livestock/veterinary services

Forestry: Forestry policy and administrative management, forestry development, fuelwood/charcoal, forestry education/training, forestry research, forestry services

Fishing: Fishing policy and administrative management, fishery development, fishery education/training, fishery research, fishery services

---

Table 9.3 *Biodiversity marker in sectoral assistance*
(percentage of biodiversity in sectoral total)

Year	Multi-sector	Water	Agriculture	Forestry	Fishing	Energy	Transport
1998	3.77%	5.81%	3.11%	25.43%	5.33%	0.24%	0.01%
1999	3.71%	5.41%	2.20%	48.37%	18.58%	1.90%	0.02%
2000	3.16%	3.10%	1.68%	22.76%	11.08%	0.36%	0.25%
2001	5.57%	6.40%	8.69%	51.78%	11.55%	0.13%	0.19%
2002	8.72%	10.15%	7.99%	26.23%	11.36%	0.16%	0.01%
2003	6.45%	15.67%	4.37%	75.34%	19.72%	0.30%	0.01%
2004	8.50%	3.76%	5.47%	18.72%	6.32%	0.13%	0.44%
2005	2.74%	2.78%	0.75%	1.73%	3.03%	0.01%	0.27%
Weighted average	5.25%	6.08%	3.98%	33.21%	9.98%	0.34%	0.17%
Simple average	6.64%	8.16%	5.27%	42.10%	13.36%	0.49%	0.19%

65. Although general environmental protection, water supply and sanitation and agriculture host the bulk of biodiversity-related bilateral assistance, the overall importance of biodiversity in these two sectors are a little below 10 per cent. Biodiversity-related assistance is more important to forestry and fishing. Over one third of forestry assistance come from biodiversity-related activities, and about 10 per cent of fishing assistance is related to biodiversity. Table 9.3 provides details of biodiversity marker in sectoral bilateral cooperation.

IX.   Resources available through bilateral channels

66. Article 20, paragraph 3, provides: 'The developed country Parties may also provide, and developing country Parties avail themselves of, financial resources related to the implementation of this Convention through bilateral, regional and other multilateral channels.' Bilateral channels together may have provided more than two-third of all finances related to biodiversity. A study shows that in Latin America and the Caribbean, more than 90 per cent of biodiversity-related finances originated from bilateral and multilateral institutions.

68. Several countries have established funding targets, though not specifically for biodiversity. In Sweden, the overall target for Swedish development cooperation disbursements was planned to reach the 1 per cent target by end of 2006, and the Environment, Peace and Stability Fund established in 1993 would reach 0.25 per cent of the Danish gross domestic product. The Netherlands is committed to provide 0.1 per cent of its gross national products annually for International Nature and Environment Issues in the context of ODA, and most of the activities financed under the 0.1 per cent allocation are related to CBD targets. Switzerland made available a credit line for the global environment in developing countries.

69. A number of developed countries' national biodiversity strategies and action plans set out strategic objectives for biodiversity-related development coopera-tion. Some examples are as follows:
    - To ensure continued and effective international cooperation in the conser-vation of biological diversity, directly between governments or through relevant international governmental and non-government organizations;
    - To ensure a coherent implementation of/and between biodiversity-related commitments and agreements; ensure continued and effective interna-tional cooperation for the protection of biodiversity; promote sustainable forest management in other countries; ensure the provision of adequate resources for biodiversity;
    - To work with other countries to conserve biodiversity, use biological resources in a sustainable manner and share equitably the benefits that arise from the utilization of genetic resources;
    - To help developing countries to include the environment issue in their development process, through the formulation of adapted public policies,

or by setting up showcase projects where the principles of sustainable development and of those of the Convention on Biodiversity (CBD) are raised to the status of a code of conduct;

- To cooperate with the developing countries for the conservation and sustainable use of biodiversity; strengthen participation in programmes of multilateral cooperation; adopt at national and international level codes of behaviour and other measures of protection against the negative environmental and socio-economic effects of biotechnologies;
- To have a visible and effective international role in seeking to ensure improved biodiversity management globally by participating in international forums, sharing information and expertise, and fostering bilateral and multilateral cooperation in biodiversity conservation efforts.

71. Biodiversity-targeted assistance programmes continue to play a valuable role in shaping international financial cooperation for biodiversity. Special programmes/initiatives targeted at biodiversity include:
- Australia's Pacific Governance Support Programme;
- Regional Natural Heritage Programme (RNHP);
- Austrian Global Environment Cooperation Trust Fund;
- Flemish Fund for Tropical Forests;
- Equator Initiative;
- IDRC's Sustainable Use of Biodiversity Program;
- Environment, Peace and Stability Fund;
- Trust Fund for Environmentally and Socially Sustainable Development;
- French Global Environment Facility;
- UNEP/Development Cooperation Ireland Multilateral Environmental Trust Fund for Africa;
- International Policy Programme on Biodiversity in the Netherlands;
- Spain's Azahar and Araucaria Programmes;
- Swedish International Biodiversity programme (SwedBio);
- Darwin Initiative;
- Flagship Species Fund;
- UK Foreign and Commonwealth Office Sustainable Development Global Opportunities Fund; and
- Overseas Territories Environment Programme (OTEP).

72. Most developed countries have adopted a policy to integrate environmental considerations into all aspects of development cooperation.

Policy orientation:
- The aim of policy integration is not simply to avoid 'doing harm' to the environment but to recognize that because poor people, in particular, are highly dependent on their natural resource base, that effective environmental management is a key to long-term poverty reduction;

- Mainstreaming not only refers to mitigating negative effects to the environment and biodiversity but also to contributing to positively enhance the state of the environment;
- Through EIA processes (EIA guidelines include biodiversity assessments), all programmes and projects are screened towards their compliance with and support to relevant national strategies and action plans, including the biodiversity plans;
- Strong focus is given on 'up-streaming' planning through including biodiversity aspects in policies and strategies. Special attention is given to addressing biological resources and their importance for poverty alleviation in development of country strategies.

Sectoral integration:
- In the agriculture, forestry and fisheries sectors, sustainable resource management is particularly critical where it intersects with rural livelihoods and particularly fragile or special places for biodiversity;
- Biodiversity-related measures play a vital role in most integrated rural development programmes;
- Biodiversity aspects are increasingly addressed in bilateral sectoral programmes (marine/coastal, agriculture, forestry, rural development etc.).

73. Many bilateral donors are able to track their assistance to biodiversity, often based on the 'Rio markers' in the ODA statistics, and a large number of recipient countries also have a record of external support to biodiversity by agency over time. In Cambodia, external donors make pledges at its Consultative Group Meetings. The aid of New Zealand is guided by the priorities established by the Pacific Round Table for Nature Conservation. Bilateral environmental agreements are widely used by donors to guide biodiversity cooperation. Non-governmental organizations or business from the respective donor country are often instrumental in facilitating bilateral funding agreements.

Note

1   Opened for signature at the Earth Summit in Rio de Janeiro in 1992, the Convention on Biological Diversity is an international treaty for the conservation and sustainable use of biodiversity and the equitable sharing of the benefits from utilization of genetic resources. With 191 Parties, the CBD has near-universal participation among countries committed to preserving life on Earth. The CBD seeks to address all threats to biodiversity and ecosystem services, including threats from climate change, through scientific assessments, the development of tools, incentives and processes, the transfer of technologies and good practices and the full and active involvement of relevant stakeholders including indigenous and local communities, youth, NGOs, women and the business community. The headquarters of the Secretariat of the Convention are located in Montreal.

Chapter 10

Contested Relationships between Biodiversity Conservation and Poverty Alleviation

Steven Sanderson and Kent Redford

The development assistance community has collectively identified poverty alleviation as one of the Millennium Development Goals. Ambitious, hopeful targets have been set to redress one of the most vexing problems of our time, and the United Nations General Assembly called on 18 September 2000 for a halving of the number of people living in extreme poverty by 2015. With this declaration of a new global war on poverty, the United Nations system challenges the human community on behalf of the world's poor. However, achieving the goal of liberating half the world's poor from their poverty by 2015 will either mark the true beginning of sustainability or the end of biodiversity at the hands of the best-intentioned policies. Without reshaping poverty alleviation strategies, biodiversity will pay the price for development yet again, and the human 'subsidy from nature' (Anderson et al., 1991) will tax biodiversity to death.

This far-reaching and laudable social goal for poverty reduction is being debated within the development community itself by development advocates, but missing in this dialogue are the implications of traditional poverty alleviation strategies for another millennial priority, the conservation of biodiversity. In fact, biodiversity has all but disappeared from the global dialogue on sustainable development. Even the most eminent spokesman of development and freedom, Amartya Sen, scarcely mentions biodiversity in his otherwise compelling proposals for the poor (Sen, 1999).

The renewed focus on poverty alleviation without biodiversity conservation is concomitant with a shift of interest and funding away from biodiversity conservation programmes and objectives. Compare the agenda and results of last year's World Summit on Sustainable Development in Johannesburg with the 1992 World Summit on Environment and Development in Rio de Janeiro. Prior to 1992, sustainable development married economic improvement to conservation practice, however imperfectly. Frustrated by the floundering Rio process during

Reprinted from *Oryx*, vol 37, Sanderson, S. and Redford, K., 'Contested relationships between biodiversity conservation and poverty alleviation', pp.1–2, copyright © Fauna & Flora International (2003), with permission from Cambridge University Press, Cambridge.

the 1990s, developmentalists shifted the sustainability argument to read that poverty alleviation will itself achieve many conservation goals. According to this view, poverty alleviation does not abandon conservation, but funds different means to achieve the same ends (Bojo et al., 2001). This perspective mirrors an earlier, equally flawed argument that clear property rights would produce conservation. In fact, both poverty alleviation and property rights only yield conservation when tied to an explicit conservation strategy (Naughton and Sanderson, 1995).

Current poverty alleviation perspectives resuscitate economic development strategies of the 1950s, in which the gains in development were explained by greater access to markets, infrastructure support, and economies of scale. In a world far more rural than today's, development emphasized significant increases in productivity of labour, land and capital. It meant agricultural credit, water, improved seed and inputs, and rationalization of labour and capital in primary commodities (Meier, 1984). Now, in an increasingly urban world, the bulk of the world's rural poor struggle to increase productivity, pushed by pressures from urban consumption. With the exception of the poorest rural countries of Equatorial Africa and South-east Asia, poverty alleviation today means access to the means of consumption in urban communities, with much greater demand on a reduced agriculture and a declining agricultural population. With a closed agricultural frontier in much of the world, minimal unclaimed fresh water, high levels of land degradation, and an increasingly skewed rural–urban income distribution, the world will demand that fewer and poorer agriculturalists produce more commodities with less inputs for a rapidly growing consumer population. To call this model sustainable requires great feats of imagination. In fact, the global community risks repeating the experience of the post-war developmentalists. It is no less true now than 50 years ago that 'There is a real danger of the macro-models of economic development "running on their own steam" without any reference to the fundamental human problems of backwardness' (Myint, 1954).

The tremendous gains in human welfare in the post-war decades cannot be undervalued. But neither can the huge environmental costs of this economic development. Accordingly, the sustainable development push of the 1980s and 1990s, with its explicit conservation objectives, had great potential to marry human possibilities to conservation needs (Lele, 1992; Redford and Sanderson, 1992). Without changing the economic premises of development, the global community risks travelling back to the future, by recycling strategies from a bygone era. The battlefields in this contested relationship between biodiversity and economic growth are the tropical forests of Equatorial Africa, Indonesia and Amazonia, where mining biodiversity means short-term gains in forestry sector growth but long-term detriment to the world's tropical biota. Likewise, the river basins of South-east Asia are now captured by giant multilateral schemes such as the Mekong River Basin development programme, charged with developing the region but burdened by massive ecological dislocation.

In its new incarnation, poverty alleviation has largely subsumed or supplanted biodiversity conservation. This trend has gone largely unnoticed, but poses a significant threat to conservation objectives. Yet conservation organizations could actually help poverty alleviation through conservation by working with small-scale, low-output producers on the ecological frontier. This prospect complements Millennium Goals and can be important to true long-term poverty alleviation. Human-oriented, small-scale conservation could be as important to poverty alleviation as micro-lending is to development finance: not readily scalable, not changing aggregate national income figures, but also not irresponsible in resource use, and extremely valuable to those who will not benefit from traditional development strategies.

What would a more successful poverty alleviation strategy look like, and how can conservation organizations help? Millennium Goals must include the complicated interactions between biodiversity and poor people. Far more attention needs to be paid to rural poverty (IFAD, 2001), with specific cautions. Much agricultural development can be consistent with both human sustainability and conservation of biodiversity – not requiring revolution, but rather careful attention to many ideas that receive more lip service than true devotion:

- freezing the expansion of the agricultural frontier and working to recover degraded lands. Much can be done to enhance the use of lands already converted for human use;
- scaling down rural development, emphasizing low-output producers;
- redesigning animal husbandry to emphasize indigenous breeds, low herd densities, and husbandry techniques most beneficial to the poor;
- sustaining fisheries through small-scale common property arrangements.

There is another, broader opportunity than refinements in primary commodity production. That is to think of conservation in the most remote and fragile ecosystems as partnership opportunities for poverty alleviation. Effective, long-term field conservation in small communities in fragile ecosystems can and does sustain biodiversity, as well as supporting vanishing folk ways, languages and communities (Redford and Padoch, 1991). But such complementarity can only be achieved if we respect the strengths and weaknesses of both conservation and poverty alleviation efforts and the trade-offs inherent in integrating them. Calls for 'pro-poor conservation' (DFID, 2002) that ignore these trade-offs will end up in failure, with both the poor and biodiversity suffering.

The millennial challenge is not to divert development and poverty alleviation from the needs of natural systems, nor to ratchet up the demand by human populations on primary commodity output. Even without bolder calls for changing income distribution to favour the poor, more creative and integrative poverty alleviation in the countryside could result from a more successful marriage of biodiversity conservation and rural development. The single requirement is a dedication

Reprinted from *World Development*, vol 33, Sanderson, S., 'Poverty and conservation: the new century's "peasant question?"', pp. 323–332, copyright © (2005) with permission from Elsevier, London. Extract or abridged version.

to creating the kinds of partnerships between conservationists and developmentalists that eluded the Rio process and virtually vanished in Johannesburg.

References

Anderson, A., May, P. and Balick, M. (1991) *The Subsidy from Nature*, Columbia University Press, New York.

Bojo, J., Bucknall, J., Hamilton, K. Ishor, N. Kraus, C. and Pillai, P. (2001) *Environment: Poverty Reduction Strategy Papers*, World Bank, Washington, DC.

DFID (2002) *Wildlife and Poverty Study*, Livestock and Wildlife Advisory Group, Department for International Development, UK.

IFAD (2001) *Rural Poverty Report*, International Fund for Agricultural Development, Rome.

Lele, S.M. (1992) 'Sustainable development: A critical review', *World Development*, 19: 607–621.

Meier, G.M. (1984) 'The formative period', pp. 3–22, in Meier, G.M. and Seers, D. (eds) *Pioneers in Development*, Oxford University Press, New York.

Myint, H. (1954) 'An interpretation of economic backwardness', *Oxford Economic Papers*, 6: 132–163.

Naughton, L. and Sanderson, S. (1995) 'Property, politics and wildlife conservation', *World Development*, 28: 1265–1275.

Redford, K. and Padoch, C. (1991) *Conservation of Neotropical Forests: Building from Traditional Resource Use*, Columbia University Press, New York.

Redford, K. and Sanderson, S. (1992) 'The brief barren narriage of biodiversity and sustainability', *Bulletin of the Ecological Society of America*, 73: 36–39.

Sen, A. (1999) *Development as Freedom*, Knopf, New York.

Chapter 11

Poverty and Conservation: The New Century's 'Peasant Question?'

Steven Sanderson

The relationship among economic growth, rural development, poverty alleviation and conservation of nature will influence the course of biodiversity in the coming decades. The intersection of growth, development, poverty and conservation defy single disciplines and invite an interdisciplinary approach, from social science to natural science and from academia to practice. The point of applied disciplines of managing natural resources for the sake of certain outcomes – 'sustainable development' or 'biodiversity conservation' – is not just to satisfy the curiosity of a single investigator or community of scholars. Certain kinds of scholarship can provide analytical power that will permit practitioners to progress against the twin challenges of human betterment and conservation of wild nature.

The search for such practical answers has been frustrated by the complications of rural life in an epoch of globalization. Even though individual countries have succeeded in some kinds of development, and certain approaches have yielded productivity results, the overall effort to create a more conservation-oriented or even a more poverty-oriented style of growth and development has fallen short of the mark. Could it be that conservation and development are not compatible, or that development is an economic aggregate without attention to the distribution of the gains from growth?

These questions and current sustainable development discourse have to be set in the context of the past half-century. Many scholars and development practitioners from the 1950s and 1960s studied the agrarian question (meaning agricultural development, land tenure, and peasant society) as fundamental to developing country interests. Agriculture and other primary sector activities focused economic attention because of the resource endowments, colonial experiences and capital shortcomings of the less-developed world. Agriculture was considered to be an engine of growth and generator of foreign exchange, as well as a sector appropriate for posing the timeless questions of equity, property rights, and poverty alleviation. Resource conservation was rarely mentioned in the literature, despite its importance to the primary sector and strategies of river basin development, irrigated agriculture, intensification of inputs for cropping, and mechanization. Sectoral shifts in favour of agriculturally based industries and processed primary sector goods were viewed as successes, notwithstanding their implications for labour markets and scarce resources. Energy scarcity was an infrastructure bottleneck, not a conservation issue. Biodiversity loss was absent from the equation until the late 1970s, as was attention to the negative impacts of large infrastructure projects on wild nature, important river courses, and the hydrology of natural landscapes.

Generalizations are usually more necessary than helpful, but rural development over the past 50 years can be said to have increased agricultural output, achieved huge gains in rural productivity, and delivered critical inputs to more agricultural producers than ever before in history.

Globally, the poorest people in the poorest countries have not benefited commensurately. The progress against poverty in some of the poorest countries of sub-Saharan Africa and South and South east Asia has been limited or negative. The indices of human development show a grim portrait of an Africa 'left behind' and an Indian and Chinese peasantry stagnating even when these two huge national economies are leading the world in growth (UNDP, 2003). The statistical litany is clear. More than 60 per cent of the 800 million hungry people in the world are in India, China and sub-Saharan Africa. More than three-quarters of the hungry are in rural areas of developing countries. Land assets per capita are declining in the poorest countries. The gap between the marginal rural person and the successful agriculturalist is growing, as is the gap between the countryside and the city (UNDP, 2003).

The strategies and patterns of rural development since World War II have also exacted a terrible toll on nature. The expansion of the agricultural frontier put humans in direct conflict with wild animals and uncultivated landscapes. Water, harnessed by dams and canals, came to serve human activities and not natural ecosystems and their processes. Forestry and fisheries, key parts of primary sector growth, suffered from rapacious practices and technologies designed for short-term output, not sustainability. The counterfactual world in the same period might have been worse in terms of land area in agriculture but less rapacious in the use of water and fisheries, limited by technologies and labour productivity (Evenson and Gollin, 2003). But the world that has resulted continues to abuse a declining rural resource base.

The 'Human Footprint' now extends to about 83 per cent of the terrestrial world, with the remaining tiny fraction left more or less without direct human impact. An estimated 60 per cent of freshwater runoff is taken for human use (Sanderson et al., 2002) or 70 per cent of developed freshwater resources (IWMI, 2004). According to the International Water Management Institute, freshwater use may increase by 62 per cent from 1995 to 2025, up to 90 per cent in some countries of the developing world. Irrigation water will be the limiting factor on food production increases in much of the world. Growth in water supply will lag agricultural demand. But according to the same agency, proper management of water resource use over that period could reduce the rate of increased demand in agriculture to zero. What policy choices will be made? What water will be used to feed the poor? What water will be left to wild nature?

The conversion of primary resources to higher-level animal protein has taken another toll on nature. The example of farmed salmon is only the most recent contributor to a global tendency to invest in agriculture for animal feed rather than human food, with attendant skew in benefits toward higher income strata. According to a recent study, one kilogram of farmed carnivorous fish typically uses about three kilograms of wild fish processed into fish-meal and fish oil. Farmed salmon in the North Atlantic require 40,000–50,000 times the surface area of production to be sustained. They rely on imports of fishmeal and oil from the Southeastern Pacific, because European salmon farms consume the equivalent of the entire primary production of the North Sea. They discharge levels of excretion comparable to a city of about 3.9 million people (Naylor et al., 1998). Globally, up to one quarter of total fishery production in a given year goes to livestock feed, not to humans. In 2001, 24 per cent of total fishery production was ground for use as meal and other non-food purposes (UNFAO, 2003).

Similarly, the bushmeat trade, a product of increased forest products exploitation, road development, and international trade, harvests an estimated 1–5 million metric tons of wild animal meat per year from Central African forests alone, the equivalent of 5–20 million cattle per year (Robinson, 2004). The costs to nature of the East Asian wildlife food markets are incalculable. These rapacious practices are hardly the incidentals of rural life or residuals of a successful development process.

Still, after half a century of rural development, in which both natural resource stewardship and rural poverty have proven terribly intractable in the face of primary sector growth, global policy leadership has once gain affirmed the poverty-alleviating aspects of rural growth. Strangely, in spite of the devastation of forests, arable land, water and fisheries, and despite the inability of primary sector growth to alleviate poverty, the international development community contends such poverty alleviation can be environmentally sustainable.

In view of this strong affirmation, it is all the more disturbing that the new millennial poverty alleviation strategy generally leaves biodiversity on the sidelines (Sanderson and Redford, 2003). It is a matter of great concern that large-scale wildlife conservation takes place mainly in heavily human-affected ecosystems, where much is to be gained or lost, and where a great deal of this world's rural poverty and its biodiversity can be found. An overlay of the map of the spatial distributions of biodiversity and rural poverty would show high threat and high potential in Equatorial Africa, East Africa, and South and South east Asia.

As ever, the rural poor are viewed as the problem – not productive enough, too fast to reproduce, too hard on fragile landscapes (though they have no others), too deprived of basic goods and services, and too slow to embrace modernity. Now they are the stalking horse for a new wave of rural economic change, but what is to ensure that they will be the beneficiaries of new poverty alleviation schemes? Even with such assurances, how can wild nature be protected in the process?

This set of puzzles is reminiscent of an old debate about the future of the peasantry, which took place in the 1960s agrarian reform movement and earned beatification in the 1970s as a new contribution to development thinking. The debate focused on what might be called 'the once and future agrarian question,' (Sanderson, 1983) which has been variously viewed in our time as the peasant question, the agricultural development question, the sectoral linkages question, the question of food production as part of a national incomes question, and of course the poverty question. Only recently has it been viewed in terms of sustainability or biodiversity – and then not very well. The sustainable part of the sustainable peasantry seems like a lead weight added to the burden of the rural poor.

The new version of the rural poverty problem restates an old predicament. Rio – meaning the United Nations Conference on Environment and Development (UNCED) process culminating in the 1992 Rio Conference – loaned its agenda of sustainable human–nature interaction to Johannesburg (the 2002 World Summit on Sustainable Development) where it was hijacked by 'the human question'. This does not diminish the human agenda. When 1.2 billion people are living on less than one dollar per day and 800 million are hungry, eliminating poverty is a clear moral and political mandate. But the disappearance of the biodiversity agenda favours an approach that recycles failed development thinking that led to the sorry state of rural affairs and the Rio 'propositions' in the first place. The Rio agenda was a response to the shortcomings of development the first time around; ironically, more than a decade after Rio, the new development agenda has abandoned the linkage between human concerns and nature conservation.

At small scales, new thinking on poverty, sustainability and development exists – the new pioneers in development, one hopes. New volumes such as *Ecoagriculture* (McNeely and Scherr, 2003) add substantially to the empirical literature. But why does their thinking not come through to policy more boldly?

By appearances, such new thinking does not have an impact on policy because development has been completely instrumentalized, and strong analytical thinking that would advance the field of development beyond its unsustainable past is not on the public agenda. The lack of theory is traceable in part to the lack of a viable road map for sustainability.

The stated new millennial goals still have to do with primary commodity production, consumption, exchange and distribution, but operate with many more important constraints. Those constraints require new analytical frameworks and new question-driven analysis rather than gross description.

The persistent lack of integration among agricultural development, rural poverty alleviation, international science, and conservation action is frustrating. Too often these literatures and their proponents talk about each other without adequate preparation. The predictable result is poor concept formation, in which such common terms as agriculture, biodiversity, the commons and farmers are all misused or overgeneralized. Agriculture is not distinguished from food, biodiversity from environment, commons from open access, and farmers from practically anybody residing in the countryside. For all the papers and panels and centres and conferences, there is still too little understanding of the relationship among agricultural development, poverty alleviation and biodiversity conservation. A case in point is the recent OECD (2000) report on *Domestic and International Impacts of Agricultural Trade Liberalization*, which simply refers to biodiversity as an 'option value' (OECD, 2000, p. 5) unrelated to production and apparently unworthy of analysis in the document. Even less documented is the spatial distribution of agricultural adjustment under different trade regimes. It is tempting to believe that this gap derives from doing such assessments or having such conversations at too general a scale of analysis. Hence, the invocation of the lamp of local knowledge.

More rural sociology and producer-based agricultural economics are needed, and especially with regard to the poverty agenda, both must be more oriented to the challenges of conservation. All of this work must be sensitive to local knowledge and built on painstaking empirical research, not recourse to aggregate data analysis. Robert Chambers pilloried what he called 'rural development tourism' 20 years ago, but it still goes on. Rural lives are lived in small places, not in sectoral strategies. Poverty alleviation needs to be individuated, not globalized. Analysis must not be simply curiosity driven, it must respond to problems and needs.

This raises an intriguing problem: how to sell poverty alleviation work that will not make the aggregate numbers move. The power of micro-banking for development and its insignificance in national finance are a good example. Such mechanisms require more sensitive measures than national accounts and gross sectoral output data to measure the impacts of poverty alleviation. Will the aid community or its national beneficiaries stand for such subtleties? Could they move money effectively at such small scales?

There is much more. How do incentives nest? Do targeted incentives and subsidies help or hurt, and at what scales of space and time? Can it really be true that a price signal in global commodities passes through uninterrupted and unchanged to a small-scale producer on fragile land (in other words, can getting international prices right help at the ecological frontier)? Can the Green Revolution become green? Will the next one be, based as it might be on biotechnology? Why are people leaving the countryside, not in general, but in specific places? Are they jumping or being pushed? How does tenure affect poverty in specific cases? Michael Lipton's work in Mexico from the mid-1980s was brilliant in dissecting rural employment and the fractal impact of land tenure on rural poverty, depending on microscale labour markets. Barrett and Swallow (2003) show similar attention to multiple equilibria and dense spatial dynamics. Alleviating poverty and conserving biodiversity will take place in the most difficult settings, places of extreme ecological vulnerability, very low population densities and no state presence.

In all these areas, policy recommendations must be informed by studies and field presence undertaken over the long haul. The temptations of the millennium or of ideological fads cannot divert attention from real poverty alleviation and biodiversity conservation. This chapter provides only a beginning list of priorities – extension, deep local knowledge, microscale support, concern for wild nature. This list must be accompanied by a new optic on rural development, not the tired brew of the past or the temptations to 'fix' events in the short term. Braudel (1980, pp. 10–11) was famous for his derisive comparison of event-based history to fireflies in the night, illuminating nothing. The quest for sustainable resource use and rural poverty alleviation should not fall prey to the same weakness.

References

Barrett, C.B. and Swallow, B. (2003) *Fractal Poverty Traps*, Manuscript.

Braudel, F. (1980) *On History*, University of Chicago Press, Chicago.

Evenson, R.E. and Gollin, D. (eds) (2003) *Crop Variety Improvement and its Effect on Productivity: The Impact of International Agricultural Research*, CABI Pub, Cambridge.

IWMI (International Water Management Institute) (2004) *More Nutrition per Drop: Towards More Sustainable Food Production and Consumption in a Rapidly Changing World*. Report of Stockholm International Water Institute (SIWI) and IWRI.

McNeely, J. and Scherr, S. (2003) *Ecoagriculture*, Island Press, Washington, DC.

Naylor, R., Goldburg, R., Mooney, H., Beveridge, M., Clay, J., Folke, C., Kautsky, N., Lubchenco, J., Primavera, M. and Williams, M. (1998) 'Nature's subsidies to shrimp and salmon farming', *Science*, 282(5390): 883–887.

OECD (2000) *Domestic and International Environmental Impacts of Agricultural Trade Liberalization*, OECD, Paris.

Robinson, J. (2004) Personal communication.

Sanderson, S.E. (1983) 'The once and future peasant question', *Inter-American Bibliographic Review/ Revista interamericana de bibliografía*, 33(4).

Sanderson, S. and Redford, K.H. (2003) 'Contested relationships between biodiversity conservation and poverty alleviation', *Oryx*, 37(4).

Sanderson, E., Jaiteh, M., Levy, M., Redford, K., Wannebo, A. and Woolmer, G. (2002) 'The human footprint and the last of the wild', *Bioscience*, 52(10): 891–904.

UNDP (2003) *Human Development Report 2003: MDGs: A Compact Among Nations to End Human Poverty*, UNDP, New York.

UNFAO (2003) *Overview of Fish Production, Utilization, Consumption and Trade, Based on 2001 Data*, UNFAO Fisheries Information, Data and Statistics Unit, Rome.

Chapter 12

Making Poverty Reduction Irreversible: Development Implications of the Millennium Ecosystem Assessment

Steve Bass

Why should development organizations respond to the Millennium Ecosystem Assessment?

The Millennium Ecosystem Assessment (MA) is 'a critical evaluation of information concerning the consequences of ecosystem changes for human wellbeing, for the purpose of guiding decisions on complex public issues' (Millennium Ecosystem Assessment, 2005a). The MA's credentials are impressive: called for by the UN Secretary General in 2000, it was authorized by UN member governments through four multilateral environmental conventions. It was prepared by 1360 experts from 95 countries. In addition to a global assessment, the MA includes information from 33 sub-global assessments. Its credibility and accuracy were assured through independent review by 850 experts and governments, and an 80-person board of review editors.

The MA's stocktake is far reaching, but this is also its major drawback. It comprises more than 3000 pages, in 81 chapters, addressing multiple questions, with a mandate to be 'policy-relevant, but not policy-prescriptive' – in all, quite a challenge to any reader. This might partly explain why the MA and the Millennium Development Goals (MDGs), despite their shared Millennial timing and multilateral mandates, and their analyses showing close links between poverty and environmental problems, are not closely aligned. This paper suggests how to improve that alignment. Four characteristics of the MA put this prospect within reach:

1   The MA assessed ecosystem-*people* links. This led it to conclude that drylands are a priority – since many poor people are vulnerable to the poor soils and limited water supply – rather than the coral reefs or tropical rainforests that one might expect to head a list of 'environment' priorities.

2   The assessment is organized in terms of *the services that people obtain* from ecosystems: 'provisioning' services like food, fresh water and fibre; 'regulating' services like climate and flood regulation; 'supporting' services like soil formation and nutrient cycling; and 'cultural' services like spirituality, aesthetics, education and recreation.

3   The MA offers a unique catalogue of *'response options'* proven to make better and more sustainable use of ecosystem services. Although the more dramatic MA messages are negative, it also offers many 'can-do' ideas and experiences.

4   Finally, the MA offers a conceptual – and potentially a political – *bridge* between the too separate worlds of environment and development. Although it was launched by environmental conventions, its dual focus on human and ecosystem well-being offers a real link to institutions concerned about the MDGs.

What do the MA's conclusions tell us about development?

The MA's main message is that we are spending the Earth's natural capital at excessive rates, straining its ability to support everybody in current and future generations, but particularly poor people. 15 of the 24 'ecosystem services' reviewed have been degraded or unsustainably used. This represents the loss of a capital asset and thus undermines human well-being and will prove to be a major barrier to achieving the MDGs. This degradation is not just a gradual, predictable problem that can be solved in due course: for some services there is increasing risk of non-linear system collapse – notably climate, water and disease regulation, and marine fisheries. Things will get worse before they improve – even more so with predicted growth in demand for food crops (70–85 per cent by 2050) and fresh water (30–85 per cent).

Most worryingly, the MA notes that while millions of people have benefited from ecosystem transformation and species exploitation (the increase in food production from modern agriculture has been a major societal benefit) the benefits have not been equitably distributed. The harmful effects of the degradation of ecosystem services are being borne disproportionately by the poor, are contributing to the growing inequities and disparities across groups of people, and are sometimes the principal factor causing poverty and social conflict. The problem is one of trade-offs. Modification of ecosystems to enhance one service generally comes at a cost to other services and these impacts affect different people in different ways. Poor people are more directly reliant on ecosystem services to support their day-to-day livelihoods and, with limited other resources, are more vulnerable to their degradation: 'people with low resilience to ecosystem changes – mainly the disadvantaged – have been the biggest losers and witnessed the biggest increase in not only monetary poverty but also relative, temporary poverty and the depth of poverty'. (MA, 2005b, p.40)

Whilst some 'response options' can help to reverse much of the degradation and to make sustainable use of environmental assets for development, the changes required in policy and practice are substantial. This is because the problems are partly due to richer people's greater access to environmental assets, and associated over-consumption and waste; and partly to the resource-intensive infrastructure systems and development patterns that prevail everywhere. This 'locking-in' is a stubborn legacy: the MA highlights the huge stresses it has placed on ecosystem services over the last 50 years, and presents worrying scenarios for the next fifty.

The MA confirms the finding of the UN Millennium Project that 'the environment is the foundation on which strategies for all MDGs must be built'. It implies that much more investment is needed to secure that foundation, but few details are offered. Now is the time to identify key investments, their costs, and the returns they can offer.

What is the case for investing in environmental assets?

Good development entails:

- increasing the asset base and its productivity per person;
- empowering poor people and marginalized communities;
- reducing and managing risks; and
- taking a long-term perspective including subsequent generations.

The environment is central to all four of these requirements. Here we discuss the particular importance of environmental assets and hazards to poor people, and the problems of under-investment in environmental management in developing countries. Whilst the MA highlights the many dangers that a continued lack of investment will bring, recent work from the World Bank and the Poverty Environment Partnership (PEP)[1] begins to lay out the case for investment.

Poor people are disproportionately dependent upon soils, water, wildlife and other environmental assets. At national level, these account for 26 per cent of the wealth of low-income countries – disproportionately higher than the 2 per cent they provide in OECD countries (World Bank, 2005). At household level, poor people with limited access to financial, human or physical assets often have only environmental assets on which to base their livelihoods. These assets can at the very minimum act as safety nets – preventing people slipping further into poverty – but sometimes offer 'stepping stones out of poverty' (WRI, 2005). Overall, environmental assets provide roughly two-thirds of household income for the rural poor (WRI, 2005) – thus environmental assets drive 'pro-poor' development – even if they are too often perceived by the development community as brakes on development. In spite of this role, environmental assets are under-supplied: OECD levels of environmental wealth per person are four times that of low-income countries (World Bank, 2005).

Poor people are also disproportionately vulnerable to environmental hazards: 97 per cent of the world's deaths from natural disasters are suffered in low-income countries (Abramovitz, 2001). Within those countries, the poorest people often have no choice but to live in the least desirable areas – those that suffer more land-slides, floods, poor sanitation, or pollution.

Finally, the sheer size of economic sectors that are environmentally sensitive is reason enough to warrant regular environmental accounting and investment in countries that depend upon them for development. The MA notes the market value of ecosystem-service industries:

- food production: US$980 billion per year;
- timber industry: $400 billion per year;
- marine fisheries: $80 billion per year;
- marine aquaculture: $57 billion per year;
- recreational hunting and fishing: >$75 billion per year in the US alone.

Such levels of dependency and vulnerability would suggest that returns to environmental investment could be high. The late David Pearce and colleagues from IUCN and IIED found this to be the case when they reviewed 400 separate economic assessments for the Poverty Environment Partnership (Pearce, 2005). Even with conservative assumptions, they identified promising rates of return:

- controlling air pollution <15:1;
- clean water and sanitation <14:1;
- natural disaster prevention <7:1;
- mangrove conservation <7:1;
- coral reef conservation <5:1;
- soil conservation <4:1.

These rates would be higher still if longer time frames were taken into account in the calculation, and the diverse needs of the poor were given due weighting. Furthermore, investment in social capital, such as common property regimes that improve the management of environmental assets, is also promising. However, a range of policy, institutional, market and information constraints tend to reduce the apparent rate of return and establish a bias against environmental investments. Clearly, several things need to change if under-investment in environmental assets is to be tackled: we propose the following agenda.

From asset stripping to environmental investment: A development agenda that responds to the MA's major conclusions

To secure the 'environmental foundation on which strategies for all MDGs must be built' (UN Millennium Project, 2005), we propose an agenda addressing the four 'Is' referred to in the summary: Information, Institutions, International cooperation and Investment. For each, three practical ideas are suggested as starting points. Some of them will be explored in future 'Environment for the MDGs' briefings.

Information – getting environmental information to the heart of development planning and action.

The MA framework, with its focus on the utility of environmental assets for people's well-being, is increasingly identified as an excellent way to keep track of key assets on which poor people depend. The challenge is both to generate demand for this information, and to structure information systems so that they inform policy and action. Ultimately, the preparation of new forms of national wealth accounts that take into account produced capital, natural resources, and human capabilities is desirable to identify the relative – and changing – status of national environmental assets. As steps in this direction, three useful starting points are suggested:

1. Including basic environmental information in *poverty monitoring systems*, initially for programmes and ultimately at national level. Environmental deprivations – dirty water, lack of access to fertile soils, and so on – are identified by the poorest people as being as significant a part of poverty as low 'dollars per day'. Poverty mapping is one way to do this – identifying where poor people live and the status of associated ecosystem services.
2. *Examining environmental expenditure within public expenditure reviews.* For environmentally sensitive sectors, it is helpful to know what has been spent on environmental management, and to ask what environmental expenditure can contribute to agreed outcomes such as the MDGs.
3. *Undertaking strategic environmental assessments (SEAs) of major policy initiatives* such as poverty reduction strategies (PRSs) and sector development plans. Recent guidance from the OECD-DAC on how to conduct SEAs is based on best practice in developing countries (OECD, 2006).

Institutions – capacity strengthening and reform to integrate environment and development

Although the MA was largely a technocratic process, and did not delve into issues of power and politics, it offers enough evidence to suggest that we are going to have to 'rewire' the institutional landscape if we are to secure the environmental foundations of development. Firstly, most of the effective 'response options' identified by the MA require multi-stakeholder or multi-level interactions. Secondly governments need to create incentives for poor people and businesses to invest in environmental assets, and then encourage them to use these assets wisely, thus creating a sustainable revenue and tax base. A large part of this conducive environment will comprise recognizing and supporting local groups' rights to environmental assets, their local environmental management knowledge, and their 'voice' on environmental values. Three starting points include:

1. Strengthening *national environmental authorities*, so that they are able to keep track of environmental assets, their use, and associated investments, revenues and rights – requiring improved ability to cooperate across sectors
2. Supporting *local organisations* that can balance environment and development needs, including community and common property regimes
3. Ensuring that major development initiatives (e.g. PRSs) are well-linked to effective *multi-stakeholder environment forums* and to civil society 'watchdogs', to improve transparency, accountability and interaction

International cooperation – improving international payments for ecosystem services and aid for pro-poor investments

In the medium term, there is much to be done to develop means to pay for global public goods, building on the very limited experience of the Clean Development Mechanism and the Global Environmental Facility. In the shorter term, there are several key starting points that international cooperation is well placed to tackle:

1. *Benchmarking aid against MDG7* and increasing support to those environmental investments that offer high returns for poverty reduction – given how far off-track progress is on MDG7.
2. *Including poverty–environment indicators in MDG7* and the other MDGs – notably indicators that are missing such as climate change vulnerability, learning from what countries are voluntarily reporting to the United Nations.
3. Encouraging use of the *MA framework in 'MDG based national strategies'* and other development plans – building on UNDP's lead in this area.

Investment – improved advice, budgeting and finance vehicles that support long-term environmental management

Severe under-investment in environmental assets needs to be tackled, especially in environmentally sensitive sectors and livelihoods. To increase market-led investment, the key issue is to support stable ecosystem service markets – requiring good science (for example to assure reliable production of the service in question) and equitable legal and policy regimes (including considering the needs of poor people as producers or consumers of environmental services). To increase governmental investment, innovative long-term finance models need to be developed, e.g. as suggested in the UN's *New Public Finance* (UNDP, 2005). Three starting points include:

1. Reviewing *the budgets and investment sources of major sectors that are environmentally sensitive*, such as health, infrastructure, energy, tourism and agriculture. Many will be 'feeling the burn' of current or approaching environmental problems, from the market, insurers, other stakeholders, and their operations. Many will also have significant investment budgets that could be influenced with better information on environmental benefits. Such sectors may be a more effective starting point than a fully comprehensive approach to 'environmental mainstreaming'.

2. *Identifying easy gains in environmental fiscal reform.* A recent review has revealed many ways in which tax reform can both protect key environmental assets and realize revenue for poverty reduction. National exploration of these win–win potentials is overdue (OECD, 2005).

3. *Constructing 'Millennium Ecosystem Budgets', globally and nationally.* The MA did not go as far as postulating a 'Millennium Ecosystem Budget' – and neither did the Millennium Project which 'costed' all MDGs comprehensively, with the exception of MDG7. Because of these oversights, the Poverty Environment Partnership offered an initial attempt. PEP suggests that US$60–90 billion are needed each year to meet MDG7 targets regarding water, sanitation, slums, clean air, land degradation, energy and protected areas (Pearce, 2005). To meet climate change targets, PEP suggests a wider range – from $80–1100 billion, depending upon assumptions[2]. All these figures compare rather well with the $1065 billion annual cost of subsidies to industry, energy, transport, agriculture and forestry. However, priority environmental investments will differ between countries. The key platform on which national budgets can be constructed should be national ecosystem assessments conducted along the lines of the MA. Sachs and Reid (2006) suggest that it will cost just $0.2 billion over five years to conduct national assessments in developing countries – an excellent initial investment.

Following its launch in 2005, it would be fair to ask how the MA's intensive efforts are being followed up. The MA closely follows the model used by the Intergovernmental Panel on Climate Change (IPCC) – a scientific assessment that has been critical to formulating climate change policy. It is hoped that the MA will be similarly influential in realizing a step change to ensure that development practice acts on environmental potentials and limits. But there is one difference. The IPCC's mandate continues, enabling policy and practice to adapt to new scientific findings. In contrast, the MA has already come to a close.

Like a one-off firework display for the Millennium, the MA revealed a great deal all in one go, but those who prepared it soon returned home. The spirit of the MA is being kept alight in some quarters concerned with development – notably by the Nordic Council of Ministers, which hopes to see the MA's findings influence development policy, and by UNDP, which is promoting use of the MA analytical framework in its support to 'MDG based national development strategies'. But far more needs to be done to continue the MA's work – at very least to illuminate more consistently and constantly our changing management of environmental assets, and preferably also to inspire improved institutions, international cooperation and investment.

Notes

1   The Poverty Environment Partnership is a network of bilateral aid agencies, multilateral development banks, UN agencies and international NGOs that aims to address key poverty–environment issues within the framework of international efforts to achieve the Millennium Development Goals.
2   To stabilize C at 550ppm – although it now looks as though 400ppm will be needed, requiring more investment.

References

Abramovitz, J. (2001) 'Unnatural disasters', *Worldwatch Paper*, 158, Worldwatch Institute.
Millennium Ecosystem Assessment (2005a) *Ecosystems and Human Well-being: Synthesis*, Island Press, Washington, DC.
Millennium Ecosystem Assessment (2005b) *Ecosystems and Human Well-being: Biodiversity Synthesis*, Island Press, Washington, DC.
OECD (2005) *Environmental Fiscal Reform for Poverty Reduction*, DAC Guidelines and Reference Series, OECD, Paris.
OECD (2006) *Strategic Environmental Assessment Guidelines*, DAC Guidelines and Reference Series, OECD, Paris.
Pearce, D.W. (2005) *Investing in Environmental Wealth for Poverty Reduction*, UNDP, New York.
Sachs, J.D. and Reid, W.V. (2006) 'Investments towards sustainable development', *Science*, 312: 1002.
UNDP (2005) *The New Public Finance: Responding to Global Challenges*, UNDP, New York.
UN Millennium Project (2005) *Investing in Development: A Practical Plan to Achieve the Millennium Development Goals: Overview*, United Nations, New York.
World Bank (2005) *Where is the Wealth of Nations? Measuring Capital for the 21st Century*, World Bank, Washington DC.
WRI (World Resources Institute) (2005) *The Wealth of the Poor: Managing Ecosystems to Fight Poverty*, World Resources Report.

Part 3

Conservation Policy and Protectionism

Editors' Introduction

Much of the conservation–poverty debate has been focused on the issue of protected areas and their impacts on local or resident communities. The debate focuses on rights (who really owns the right to the protected area?) and the distribution of costs and benefits (who bears the costs and how does this compare with who reaps the benefits?).

The colonization of the South by European powers in the 18th and 19th centuries, and the accompanying spread of conservation practice, tended to ignore traditional rights (Colchester, 1995). The model for wildlife conservation that was globally adopted was based on the American approach of pristine wild areas set aside for human enjoyment and fulfilment and was encouraged by concerns about the depletion of wildlife, timber and other valuable resources (Adams, 2004). In the post-colonial era, colonial land tenure arrangements and institutions were often retained, and in many instances central authority over lands and resources was extended and local rights further alienated (Alden Wily, 2008).

As we noted in Chapter 1, the debate about people and parks dates back over 50 years. In response to concerns raised about local peoples' rights, in 1975 the IUCN General Assembly adopted a Recommendation that indigenous people's rights should be taken into account in the definition and management of national parks and other protected areas (Holdgate, 1999). This Zaire Resolution was reaffirmed and strengthened at the third World Parks Congress in Bali in 1982, which advocated the implementation of joint management arrangements between societies that have traditionally managed resources and protected area authorities (Colchester, 2004). The Congress output – the Bali Action Plan – has been described as a 'revolutionary advance in linking the conservation of protected areas with social and economic development' (McNeely and Miller, 1982).

Despite the conceptual strides made over the 1980s and early 1990s in linking conservation and local benefits, especially with regard to protected areas, the people and parks debate had continued as an undercurrent and then took on a new dimension in the late 1990s, when it changed from simply arguing for and against protected areas to critiquing the success, or otherwise, of community-based or integrated approaches and advocating a return to more top-down approaches – described by Hutton et al. (2005) as 'Back to the barriers'.

The growing concerns about this apparent resurgence of protectionism are evident in the agenda and title (*Benefits Beyond Boundaries*) of the 2003 World Parks Congress which saw unprecedented attendance by indigenous and local community groups, social scientists and advocates of human rights. The congress produced a wealth of recommendations on indigenous rights, poverty and governance, and resulted in the Durban Accord, which announced a so-called 'new paradigm' for protected areas in which conservation goals were equitably integrated with the interests of all affected people (IUCN, 2003a). It also resulted in the Durban Action Plan, which included targets to ensure that protected areas strive to alleviate poverty and in no case exacerbate poverty, and that all existing and future protected areas should be managed and established in full compliance with the rights of indigenous and mobile peoples and local communities (IUCN, 2003b).

The following year, the 7th Conference of Parties to the CBD adopted an ambitious Programme of Work on Protected Areas, including a stream on equity, governance and benefit sharing. Coupled with the developments at the World Parks Congress, some celebrated this as heralding a new paradigm in participatory conservation (Phillips, 2003; Balasinorwala and Goyal, 2004). Equally, these developments added fuel to the fire of those commentators concerned that the conservation agenda was being hijacked (Terborgh, 2004; Oates, 2006).

Despite these new international policy initiatives, some observers continue to document negative impacts of protected areas while others challenge the broad applicability of these negative findings and make a case for livelihoods benefits from protected areas – particularly given the wide range of protected areas that exist. Notably a significant body of literature has focused on forced resettlement from protected areas (e.g. Chatty and Colchester, 2002; Brockington and Igoe, 2006 (Chapter 16); Rangarajan and Shahabuddin, 2006). Other commentators have highlighted cases where protected areas have succeeded in generating significant revenues for poor communities (e.g. Mulongoy and Gidda, 2008; BirdLife International, 2007), especially community conserved areas (Pathak et al., 2005) and co-managed protected areas (e.g. Borrini-Feyerabend et al., 2004).

The selected readings illustrate the two sides of the debate and the contexts in which negative and positive impacts seem most likely to occur. In Chapter 13, McShane (2003) indicates 'there is now an emerging recognition of both an ethical and practical imperative as to why we must consider the linkages between protected areas and poverty'. This reading affirms the recognition by conservationists of the need for conservation to take more of a rights-based approach. It looks to 'more inclusive approaches' for solutions to the gap between the interests of protected area authorities and those of poor people. However, in Chapter 14, Colchester (2004) is less optimistic. He challenges readers to review who, morally, has the rights to these spaces that we call protected areas. He documents the new principles that have been put into place for conservation practice, but finds that they are largely not yet being adequately implemented.

Naughton-Treves et al. (2005) highlight an important problem in Chapter 15 – the complexity of assessing effectiveness when different stakeholders have different goals and expectations from the same set of activities, recognizing that 'protected areas are now supposed to do far more than conservation of biological diversity ... [they] are charged with improving social welfare, guarding local security, and providing economic benefits across multiple scales'. This resonates with

Colchester's portrayal of a healthy level of agreement on new principles, but clear constraints in translating this into 'creative compromise' at site level.

Chapter 16 is taken from a ground-breaking global review of displacement from protected areas in which Brockington and Igoe (2006) document the body of knowledge pertaining to the scale and significance of evictions (a key focus of the people and parks debate) and trends in time and place. Capturing what they term the 'erosion of the moral high ground ... of conservation scientists', they provide, for the first time, aggregated quantitative evidence for the negative impacts of protected areas, demonstrating the substantial harm done but at the same time acknowledging the dearth of data and the fact that far more knowledge is needed across the whole theme of eviction and displacement.

Brockington and Igoe also highlight the growing importance of private protected areas, a theme picked up by Adams and Hutton (2007) in the opening of Chapter 17 describing the agreement between the government of Ethiopia and the private conservation organization African Parks Foundation to manage Nech Sar National Park and the subsequent implications for the resident community. Adams and Hutton explore the equity impacts of protected areas and their tendency to 'reproduce existing inequalities within local communities and local societies'. They identify 'wealthy wildlife lovers in developed countries' as disproportionate beneficiaries, who then choose to fund international conservation organizations that advocate the establishment of protected areas, thereby reinforcing these inequalities.

The people and parks debate has been very much focused on terrestrial protected areas – and in particular on those that fall within IUCN's classification as Category I or II in terms of the management approach (i.e. the most strictly protected). It is important to recognize that these are only a small proportion of all the protected areas that exist – of which there are a wide variety of types with widely varying management approaches and governance arrangements. In the final chapter of this section, Mascia and Claus (2008) use the example of marine protected areas to emphasize the need to disaggregate the numerous conceptually distinct and socially charged issues associated with the debate. They propose a property rights approach to understanding the substantive social impacts of protected areas, both positive and negative, concluding 'a critical next step in conservation social science research is to document and explain variation in the social impacts of protected areas. Such knowledge is the foundation of adaptive management that meets the needs of both people and nature.'

References

Adams, W.M. (2004) *Against Extinction. The Story of Conservation*, Earthscan, London.

Adams, W.M. and Hutton, J. (2007) 'People, parks and poverty: Political ecology and biodiversity conservation', *Conservation and Society*, 5(20): 147–183.

Alden Wily, E. (2008) 'Custom and commonage in Africa: Rethinking the orthodoxies', *Land Use Policy*, 25: 43–52.

Balasinorwala, T.K. and Goyal, M. (2004) *Participatory Conservation: Paradigm Shifts in International Policy*, IUCN, Gland.

BirdLife International (2007) *Livelihoods and the Environment at Important Bird Areas: Listening to Local Voices*, BirdLife International, Cambridge.

Borrini-Feyerabend, G., Pimbert, M., Farvar, M.T., Kothari, A. and Renard, Y. (2004) *Sharing Power: Learning by Doing in Co-management of Natural Resources throughout the World*, IIED, London.

Brockington, D. and Igoe, J. (2006) 'Eviction for conservation: A global overview', *Conservation and Society*, 4: 424–470.

Chatty, D. and Colchester, M. (2002) 'Introduction: Conservation and mobile indigenous people', pp. 1–20, in Chatty, D. and Colchester, M. (eds) *Conservation and Mobile Indigenous Peoples: Displacement. Forced Settlement and Sustainable Development*, Bergahn Books, New York and Oxford.

Colchester, M. (1995) *Salvaging Nature: Indigenous People, Protected Areas and Biodiversity Conservation*, UNRISD Discussion Paper no 55, UNRISD, Geneva.

Colchester, M. (2004) 'Conservation policy and indigenous peoples', *Cultural Survival Quarterly*, 28: 17–22.

Holdgate, M. (1999) *The Green Web: A Union for World Conservation*, Earthscan, London.

Hutton, J., Adams, W.M. and Murombedzi, J. (2005) 'Back to the barriers? Changing narratives in biodiversity conservation', *Forum for Development Studies*, 2: 341–370.

IUCN (2003a) *The Durban Accord*, IUCN, Gland.

IUCN (2003b) *The Durban Action Plan*, IUCN, Gland.

Mascia, M. and Claus, C.A. (2009) 'A property rights approach to understanding human displacement from protected areas: the case of marine protected areas,' *Conservation Biology*, 23(1): 16–23.

McNeely, J.A. and Miller, K.R. (eds) (1982) *National Parks, Conservation and Development: The Role of Protected Areas in Sustaining Society*, IUCN, Gland.

McShane, T.O. (2003) 'Protected areas and poverty – the linkages and how to address them', *Policy Matters*, 12: 52–53.

Mulongoy, K.J and Gidda, S.B (2008) *The Value of Nature: Ecological, Economic and Social Benefits of Protected Areas*, Secretariat of the Convention on Biological Diversity, Montreal.

Naughton-Treves, L., Buck Holland, M. and Brandon, K., (2005) 'The role of protected areas in conserving biodiversity and sustaining local livelihoods', *Annual Review of Environment and Resources*, 30: 219–52.

Oates, J.F. (2006) 'Conservation, development and poverty alleviation: Time for a change in attitudes', pp.277–284, in Lavigne, D. (ed), *Gaining Ground: In Pursuit of Ecological Sustainability*, International Fund for Animal Welfare, Guelph, Canada.

Pathak, N., Kothari, A. and Roe, D. (2005) 'Conservation with social justice? The role of community conserved areas in achieving the MDGs', in Bigg, T. and Satterthwaite, D. (eds), *How to Make Poverty History: The Central Role of Local Organisations in Meeting the MDGs*, IIED, London.

Phillips, A. (2003) 'A modern paradigm', *World Conservation Bulletin*, 2: 6–7.

Rangarajan, M. and Shahabuddin, G. (2006) 'Displacement and relocation from protected areas: Towards a biological and historical synthesis', *Conservation and Society*, 4: 359–378.

Terborgh, J. (2004) 'Reflections of a scientist on the World Parks Congress', *Conservation Biology*, 18: 619–620.

Chapter 13

Protected Areas and Poverty – The Linkages and How to Address Them

Thomas O. McShane

Protected areas are the cornerstone of the conservation movement. Almost all conservation organizations have targets for the amount of the Earth's surface that should be set aside as protected – both in terms of area and representation of biotic communities. This traditional approach to conservation, however, has often had a negative impact on the livelihoods of people – through forced displacement and/or denying access to natural resources that are vital to human needs. As a result, protected areas have often increased poverty amongst the poorest of the poor. While there has been a great deal of work undertaken recently on poverty–environment relationships, little has been done to better understand how protected areas both negatively and positively impact poverty.

Rural poverty has many causes, including inappropriate resource management, which in turn has its roots in the loss of rights to resources that rural communities have traditionally considered their own. It is these rights to timber, water, land and wildlife that are essential elements to sustainable rural development. The starting point in the protected area–poverty debate is to recognize that the cost of protected areas is often at the expense of the poor (e.g. through expropriation of their land or by having them deliver global public goods for free). Conservation organizations and governments seldom consider this equity dimension in the establishment and management of protected areas. As a result, the poor have been excluded from effectively participating in and influencing decisions about protected areas. Understanding of the costs and benefits of how local people are affected by these actions is weak, as is the institutional capacity of governments and resource management institutions to undertake socially responsible conservation.

There is now an emerging recognition of both an ethical and practical imperative as to why we must consider the linkages between protected areas and poverty. Ethically, Western environmentalists, no matter how well meaning, have no right to run roughshod over local needs and rights. Practically, protected area development has a chequered history that has often bred resentment in local communities and made people poorer. In practice this means that we have to balance the requirement of no net loss of biodiversity with no net negative impact on livelihoods

Reprinted from *Policy Matters*, vol 12, McShane, T.O., 'Protected areas and poverty – the linkages and how to address them', pp. 52–53, copyright © (2003) with permission from IUCN, Gland.

within protected areas – or at a minimum do no harm. Protected area establishment and management need to be assessed both on the basis of biodiversity conservation and how they impact opportunity, vulnerability and the voice of the poor. This is not to suggest that the rural poor should have exclusive veto over whether new protected areas are declared, but rather that more inclusive approaches are urgently required for the development and management of protected areas. Yet, we need to go beyond this and recognize biodiversity as part of the basis of local livelihoods as well as a global public good. The global values of protected areas present real opportunities for generating benefits for the rural poor in recognition of their stewardship role. The global community has a responsibility to identify, explore and support these possibilities.

Chapter 14

Conservation Policy and Indigenous Peoples

Marcus Colchester

The creation of protected areas has been a central element in conservation policy since its beginnings in the 19th century. From their inception, protected areas were conceived as areas of land alienated to the state and managed for the benefit of future generations but to the exclusion of residents. National parks, pioneered in the United States, denied indigenous peoples' rights, evicted them from their homelands, and provoked long-term social conflict. This model of conservation became central to conservation policy worldwide. But the emergence of indigenous peoples as a social movement and as a category in international human rights law has contributed to conservation agencies rethinking their approach to conservation. A new model of conservation can now be discerned based on a respect for the rights of indigenous peoples and other bearers of 'traditional knowledge'.

Conservation policies emerged at a time of fierce prejudice against indigenous peoples and led to the worldwide acceptance of a model of 'colonial conservation' which has caused, and continues to cause, widespread human suffering and resentment. Advances in human rights and in the thinking of conservationists have led to an acceptance that conservation can and must be achieved in collaboration with indigenous peoples and based on respect for their internationally recognized rights. However, on the ground, protected areas continue to be imposed according to the colonial model, calling into question the extent to which there is a real commitment to giving conservation a human face.

The first national parks

The idea that certain areas of land valued for the natural species that live there should be set aside for recreation and protected from other uses can be traced back to Mesopotamia in the first millennium BC. From there it spread east and west, into India and Europe (Colchester, 1994). The first national parks were established at the same time as a tumultuous rush of land-grabbing during the American conquest of the Wild West, when covered wagons, the US cavalry, gold miners,

Reprinted from *Cultural Survival Quarterly*, vol 28, Colchester, M., 'Conservation policy and indigenous peoples', pp. 17–22, copyright © (2004), with permission from Cultural Survival (www.cs.org), Cambridge, MA.

cowboys and Indians struggled to impose their different visions of life and land use on the continent.

The first such park, established in Yosemite in California in 1864, followed a bloody war of extermination of the Miwok people, and involved the repeated, forced eviction of remnant Miwok settlements over the following 105 years (Keller and Turek, 1998). The Yellowstone National Park, established 34 years later in what is now Wyoming, also involved the denial of indigenous peoples' rights. The Yellowstone National Park was created at a time when a devastating series of 'Indian Wars' was being waged to subdue Indian autonomy and realize the United States' 'manifest destiny'. The indigenous peoples who lived in and made use of the extensive woods, plains and waters of Yellowstone – the Shoshone, Lakota, Crow, Bannock, Nez Perce, Flathead and Blackfeet peoples – were thus excluded, leading to resistance and the subsequent killing of hundreds of Indians (Keller and Turek, 1998).

Underpinning this approach to conservation lay the idea that nature could only be preserved as 'wilderness', areas conceived as 'primitive and natural' and which must be kept uninhabited – set aside for recreation and science but otherwise left untouched. John Muir, one of the main forces in the national parks movement in the United States, argued vehemently and successfully that wilderness areas should be set aside for recreation to fulfil an emotional need for wild places (Colchester, 1994). Most protected areas established in the United States followed this approach although the great majority of these areas overlap lands owned and claimed by indigenous peoples (Keller and Turek, 1998). In the following century, the US model of nature conservation was to be exported worldwide and strongly influenced conservation policy in many countries.

Summarizing the recent history of conservation, the former chairman of the World Commission on Protected Areas has noted, 'The opinions and rights of indigenous peoples were of little concern to any government before about 1970; they were not organized as a political force as they are now in many countries' (Phillips, 2003).

Social impacts of protected areas

It has been estimated that, as a result of these policies, some 1 million square kilometres of forests, pasture and farmlands were expropriated in Africa to make way for conservation, but equivalent statistics are lacking of the number of people displaced as a consequence (Nelson and Hossack, 2003). An all-too-common testimony of such forced relocation comes from a Twa who was expelled from the Kahuzi-Biega National Park in the Democratic Republic of Congo in the 1960s (Kwokwo Barume, 2000):

> *We did not know they were coming. It was early in the morning. I heard people around my*
> *house. I looked through the door and saw people in uniforms with guns. Then one of them*
> *forced the door of our house and started shouting that we had to leave immediately because*

the park is not our land. I first did not understand what he was talking about because all my ancestors have lived on these lands. They were so violent that I left with my children.

Denied their traditional lands and livelihoods, these Twa – traditional hunting and gathering 'Pygmies' – now exist in a number of squatter camps on the fringes of their once extensive forest territory. They suffer extreme malnutrition, landlessness, demoralization, and despair. As another Twa explains: 'Since we were expelled from our lands, death is following us. The village is becoming empty. We are heading toward extinction. Now the old people have died. Our culture is dying too.'

Accurate statistics about just how many people have been displaced to make way for protected areas in Asia are also lacking. One estimate suggests that as many as 600,000 tribal people have been displaced by protected areas in India alone (PRIA, 1993). The statistics in Latin America are equally unavailable. Sources suggest that as many as 85 percent of the protected areas in Latin America are in fact inhabited (Amend and Amend, 1992).

However, though we lack overall numbers, the local consequences of these impositions of protected areas on the lives of indigenous peoples have been better documented. Summarizing the extensive literature and field studies,[1] indigenous peoples commonly experience:

- denial of rights to land;
- denial of use of and access to natural resources;
- denial of political rights and the validity of customary institutions;
- disrupted kinship systems;
- disorganized settlement patterns;
- loss of informal social networks, fundamental to the local economy;
- undermining of livelihoods, loss of property, no compensation;
- poverty;
- disruption of customary systems of environment management;
- enforced illegality – people become 'poachers', 'encroachers,' and 'squatters' on their own land and are subject to petty tyrannies by park guards;
- forced resettlement;
- leadership systems destroyed, for if the community leaders accept the relocation they are accused of betraying their people, but if they resist they are proved powerless – forced resettlement presents a no-win situation to community leaders;
- symbolic ties to environment broken;
- cultural identity weakened;
- intensified pressure on natural resources outside the protected areas;
- popular unrest, resistance, incendiarism, social conflict, and ensuing repression;

It is now widely recognized that the exclusion of indigenous peoples and other local communities from protected areas can also undermine their conservation objectives by creating conflict between local communities and parks managers. As a World Wide Fund for Nature–International (WWF) report notes (Carey et al., 2000):

> *Loss of traditional rights can reduce peoples' interest in long-term stewardship of the land and therefore the creation of a protected area can in some cases increase the rate of damage to the very values that the protected area was originally created to preserve ... Putting a fence around a protected area seldom creates a long term solution to problems of disaffected local communities, whether or not it is ethically justified.*

New principles of conservation

Since 1975, the World Conservation Union (IUCN) and World Parks Congress (WPC) have been making important statements implying recognition of the rights of indigenous peoples and the need to accommodate these rights in protected areas. The Kinshasa Resolution of 1975 recognized the importance of traditional ways of life and landownership, and called on governments to maintain and encourage customary ways of living. It urged governments to devise means by which indigenous peoples could bring their lands into conservation areas without relinquishing their ownership, use and tenure rights. It also noted that indigenous peoples should not normally be displaced from their traditional lands by protected areas, nor should protected areas be established without adequate consultation with the peoples to be directly affected. The same resolution was recalled in 1982 at the World National Parks Congress in Bali, Indonesia, which affirmed the rights of traditional societies to 'social, economic, cultural, and spiritual self-determination' and 'to participate in decisions affecting the land and natural resources on which they depend'. The resolution advocated 'the implementation of joint management arrangements between societies which have traditionally managed resources and protected area authorities'.[2]

At the World Congress on Protected Areas held in Caracas in 1992, a central issue addressed by the participants was the fact that the great majority of protected areas are in fact inhabited, notably by indigenous peoples. The congress recognized that the denial of the existence and rights of residents was not only unrealistic but counterproductive. At that time the IUCN defined a 'national park' in terms of state ownership or control: 'Where the highest competent authority of the country has taken steps to prevent or eliminate as soon as possible exploitation or occupation of the whole area.'[3]

In 1996, following several years of intensive engagement with indigenous peoples' organizations, the WWF adopted a Statement of Principles on Indigenous Peoples and Conservation, which endorses the Draft UN Declaration on the Rights of Indigenous Peoples; accepts that constructive engagement with indigenous peoples must start with a recognition of their rights; and upholds the rights of indigenous peoples to own, manage and control their lands and territories, and benefit from the application of their knowledge. That same year the World Conservation Congress, the paramount body of the IUCN, adopted seven resolutions on indigenous peoples, including one that recognizes indigenous peoples' rights to their lands and territories – particularly in forests, marine and coastal ecosystems, and protected areas – and a resolution that recognizes indigenous peoples' rights to manage their natural resources in protected areas either on their own or jointly with others. A third resolution endorses the principles enshrined in International Labour Organization's Convention 169 and the UN Draft Declaration on the Rights of Indigenous Peoples.

In 1997, the IUCN published a two-volume resource guide, *Beyond Fences*, which makes suggestions about how conservation objectives can be achieved through greater collaboration with local communities. The guide notes that the collaborative approach is not only justifiable in terms of conservation effectiveness but is also required if conservation is to be morally and ethically responsible.

In 1999, the World Commission on Protected Areas adopted guidelines for putting the principles contained in one of these seven resolutions into practice. These guidelines emphasize the co-management of protected areas, agreements between indigenous peoples and conservation bodies, indigenous participation in protected areas, and recognition of indigenous peoples' rights to 'sustainable, traditional use' of their lands and territories. The link between sustainability and secure tenure has also been clearly recognized. As the 1999 IUCN study *Global Tenure and Sustainable Use* (Borrini-Feyerabend, 1997) concluded:

> *Co-management is often hailed as the appropriate middle ground, within which the needs of all stakeholders can be negotiated and acceptable compromises achieved [but] ... this would seem to be only part of the solution. Co-management strategies can only be effective if they are accompanied by parallel efforts to address issues of tenure in the related territory. If tenure arrangements do not secure the interests of local users, there is no incentive to practice sustainable use.*

Obstacles to implementation

Putting these new principles into practice is easier said than done. Conservation initiatives take place within the same constraints as other 'development' activities. They must deal with the same competing enterprises and vested interests that confront local communities everywhere. In particular they have to confront the all-too-common ingrained prejudices against indigenous peoples, held by both the general public and personnel in government agencies.

A review carried out by the Forest Peoples Programme (FPP) over the past seven years, which has included an examination of the experiences of indigenous peoples with 36 protected areas in Latin America, Africa and Asia, has found that the new principles of conservation are not yet being widely applied in developing countries. The three regional conferences at which these case studies were presented and discussed concurred that, in general, protected areas continue to be established and administered in violation of indigenous peoples' rights and in ignorance of the new standards. In Central Africa, protected areas continue to oblige the forced relocation of indigenous peoples, often without any plans for resettlement or compensation (Nelson and Hossack, 2003). Serious impoverishment is widely reported and participation is at the most elementary level. Only in southern Africa have participatory wildlife management systems gained currency (Duffy, 2000). The San peoples have experienced uneven treatment: being evicted from reserves in Botswana,[4] while enjoying the restitution of some of their lands in South Africa (Chennells, 2003).

In Asia, while the overall pattern of denial of rights remains clear, reform efforts are under way in some areas. Overall national laws and policies continue to be framed by the colonial model of conservation, but benefit sharing through integrated conservation and development projects have a wider currency and in some areas sincere efforts have been made to involve local communities in decision-making and to accommodate (if not legally recognize) indigenous peoples' land rights.

In Latin America, the picture is more mixed. Most national constitutions now recognize indigenous peoples and the legislatures have enacted laws that recognize indigenous peoples' rights. Although implementation of these laws still leaves a lot to be desired, significant progress has been made. But corresponding reforms of conservation laws and policies lag behind these changes and most examples of indigenous-owned and run protected areas have been achieved outside the official protected area systems (Gray et al., 1997). Parallel studies suggest that conservationists in Latin America are only in the first phases of incorporating local communities into protected area management. Typically these measures include employing local people in such jobs as park guards, rangers, cooks and secretaries. Community development projects are then the next stage of participation, after which involving communities in natural resource management is attempted. Actual recognition of rights in protected areas is, often, not yet even on the national agenda (Dugelby and Libby, 1998).

These findings echo studies made in the United States, where the gradual move toward an accommodation of indigenous peoples' rights in protected areas took over half a century. As Robert Keller and Michael Turek note in *American Indians and National Parks*:

> *To begin, park/Indian relations seem to fall into four phases: (1) unilateral appropriation of recreation land by the government; (2) an end to land-taking but a continued federal neglect of tribal needs, cultures and treaties; (3) Indian resistance, leading to aggressive pursuit of tribal interests; (4) a new National Parks Service commitment to cross-cultural integrity and cooperation.*

The Forest Peoples Programme review finds that, in all three of the regions examined, examples can be found of protected areas where sincere efforts to apply these new standards are being made. These examples demonstrate that it is possible to recognize the rights of indigenous peoples and achieve conservation goals in the same areas. The case studies also show that a number of serious obstacles stand in the way of an effective recognition of indigenous rights in conservation practice. These include:

- Entrenched discrimination in national societies' attitudes toward indigenous peoples such that indigenous peoples' ways of life are seen as backward, dirty or subhuman. In the context of conservation initiatives, the result may be a denial of rights and a feeling among affected peoples that they are treated as worse than animals.
- Absence of reform of government policies and laws regarding indigenous peoples. Many governments, especially in Asia and Africa, pursue integrationist or assimilationist social policies toward indigenous peoples, designed to elevate them from backward ways into the national mainstream while ignoring or denying their cultural traditions, customary institutions, rights and preferences.
- National laws and policies with respect to land which deny indigenous peoples' rights to own and manage their lands.
- National conservation policies and laws still based on the old exclusionary model of conservation. Few of the countries studied have adopted legislation that would encourage community-owned protected areas in line with the revised IUCN protected area category system, which would allow communities and indigenous peoples to own and control protected areas.
- Conservation agencies and NGOs lack appropriate training, staff and capacity to work with communities. In many cases, national chapters of the large conservation organizations have not been informed about the new policies and principles which have been adopted at the international level.

A new paradigm

In September 2003, some 150 persons representing indigenous peoples and loosely coordinated through an Ad Hoc Indigenous Peoples Working Group for the WPC attended the Fifth WPC, held in Durban, South Africa. They called on the 3000 conservationists present at the meeting to respect their rights and to develop a work programme to give such declarations real effect. Support organizations such as the Forest Peoples Programme, which had helped raise funds for this mobilization, also issued a series of publications (MacKay, 2002) that called on conservationists to:

- reaffirm their commitment to respect and uphold indigenous peoples' internationally recognized rights in all their protected area programmes;

- give priority to reforming national laws, policies, and conservation programmes so that they respect indigenous peoples' rights and allow protected areas to be owned and managed by indigenous peoples;
- ensure that sufficient funds are allocated to national conservation programmes, and to the regional and international programmes that support them, to carry out these legal and policy reforms;
- retrain conservation personnel in both national and international bureaus so that they understand and know how to apply these new principles;
- establish effective mechanisms for open dialogue, the redress of grievances, and the transparent exchange of information between conservationists and indigenous peoples;
- encourage other major international conservation agencies to adopt clear policies on indigenous peoples and protected areas in conformity with their internationally recognized rights and these new conservation principles;
- combat entrenched discrimination in national and international conservation programmes and offices and, where necessary, adopt affirmative social policies that recognize and respect cultural diversity;
- support the consolidation of indigenous peoples' organizations as independent, representative institutions;
- support initiatives by indigenous peoples to secure their territorial rights ; and
- initiate transparent, participatory, and effective procedures for the restitution of indigenous peoples' lands, territories, and resources incorporated into protected areas and compensate them for all material and immaterial damages in accordance with international law.

The strong presence of indigenous peoples in Durban was successful in getting conservationists to accept a new approach to protected areas. The Durban Accord, the consensus document of the whole congress, announces that the WPC has accepted a new paradigm for protected areas, 'integrating them equitably with the interests of all affected people'. The accord celebrates the conservation successes of indigenous peoples. It expresses concern at the lack of recognition, protection, and respect given to these efforts. It notes that the costs of protected areas are often borne by local communities. It urges commitment to involve indigenous peoples in establishing and managing protected areas and to participate in decision-making on a fair and equitable basis in full respect of their human and social rights.

To implement this new vision, the Durban Accord Action Plan notes that the costs of past successes in establishing a global protected area system have been inequitably borne by local communities. To rectify this disparity, the congress now seeks as a major outcome that that the rights of indigenous peoples be recognized and guaranteed in relation to natural resources and biodiversity conservation. There are currently some 100,000 officially recognized protected areas worldwide covering as much as 12 per cent of the land surface of the planet. The great majority of these areas are owned or claimed by indigenous peoples. Reforming these in conformity with international law and in line with the new commitments made in

Durban is now going to require a major effort from policymakers and development agencies.

From stakeholders to rights-holders

The history of indigenous peoples' relations to protected areas can be seen as one of social exclusion and marginalization. Having once been independent nations within their own territories, many indigenous peoples have been pushed off their lands, which have been expropriated by government agencies in the name of conservation. This has facilitated the entry of a number of interests into these areas, ranging from the private sector to academia. Current development discourse, insofar as it recognizes indigenous peoples at all, tends to characterize them now as stakeholders who must compete with other interest groups to get their voices heard. This recognition is not enough. International law recognizes that indigenous peoples have rights to own, manage and control their lands, and conservationists have now accepted this as the basis for a new paradigm of conservation. The challenge is to allow indigenous peoples to move back into control of their lands.

Notes

1 For detailed reviews see: West and Brechin, 1991; Kemf, 1993; Colchester, 1994; Ghimire and Pimbert, 1996; Gray et al., 1997; Colchester and Erni, 1999; Chatty and Colchester, 2002; Nelson and Hossack, 2003; Cernea and Schmidt-Soltau, 2003.
2 See www.iucn.org
3 Cited in West and Brechin, 1991.
4 See www.survivalinternational.org

References and Further Reading

Amend, S. and Amend, T. (eds) (1992) *Espacios sin habitantes? Parques Nacionales de America del Sur*, IUCN, Gland.
Borrini-Feyerabend, G. (ed) (1997) *Beyond Fences: Seeking Social Sustainability in Conservation*, 2 Volumes, IUCN, Gland.
Carey, C., Dudley, N. and Stolton, S. (2000) *Squandering Paradise? The Importance and Vulnerability of the World's Protected Areas*, World Wide Fund for Nature–International, Gland, Switzerland.
Cernea, M. and Schmidt-Soltau, K. (2003) *Biodiversity Conservation versus Population Resettlement: Risks to Nature and Risks to People*, Paper presented to the International Conference on Rural Livelihoods, Forests and Biodiversity, Bonn.
Chatty, D. and Colchester, M. (eds) (2002) *Conservation and Mobile Indigenous Peoples: Displacement, Forced Settlement and Sustainable Development*, Berghahn, Oxford.

Chennells, R. (2003) 'The Khomani San of South Africa', pp. 269–289, in Nelson, J. and Hossack, L. (eds) *From Principles to Practice: Indigenous Peoples and Protected Areas in Africa*, Forest Peoples Programme, Moreton-in-Marsh.

Colchester, M. (1994) *Salvaging Nature: Indigenous Peoples, Protected Areas and Biodiversity Conservation*, UNRISD Discussion Paper 55, Geneva (and 2003, Revised Second edition, World Rainforest Movement, Montevideo).

Colchester, M. and Erni, C. (eds) (1999) *Indigenous Peoples and Protected Areas in South and Southeast Asia: from Principles to Practice*, Forest Peoples Programme and the International Work Group for Indigenous Affairs, Copenhagen.

Duffy, R. (2000) *Killing for Conservation: Wildlife Policy in Zimbabwe*, James Currie, Oxford.

Dugelby, B. and Libby, M. (1998) 'Analyzing the social context at PiP sites', pp. 63–75, in Brandon, K., Redford, K. and Sanderson, S., *Parks in Peril: People, Politics and Protected Areas*, Island Press Washington, DC.

Forrest, S. (1999) *Global Tenure and Sustainable Use*, IUCN Sustainable Use Initiative, Washington, DC.

Ghimire, K. and Pimbert, M. (eds) (1996) *Social Change and Conservation: Environmental Politics and Impacts of National Parks and Protected Areas*, Earthscan, London.

Gray, A., Newing, H. and Padellada, A. (eds) (1997) *Indigenous Peoples and Biodiversity Conservation in Latin America: From Principles to Practice*, International Work Group for Indigenous Affairs and Forest Peoples Programme, Copenhagen.

IUCN (1996) *World Conservation Congress: Resolutions and Recommendations*, IUCN, Gland.

Keller, R. and Turek, M. (1998) *American Indians and National Parks*, University of Arizona Press, Tucson.

Kwokwo Barume, A. (2000) *Heading Towards Extinction: Indigenous Rights in Africa – the Case of the Twa of the Kahuzi-Biega National Park, Democratic Republic of Congo*, Forest Peoples Programme and International Work Group for Indigenous Affairs, Copenhagen.

MacKay, F. (2002) *Addressing Past Wrongs: Indigenous Peoples and Protected Areas: The right to Restitution of Lands and Resouces*, Forest Peoples Programme, Moreton-in-Marsh, UK.

Nelson, J. and Hossack, L. (eds) (2003) *From Principles to Practice: Indigenous Peoples and Protected Areas in Africa*, Forest Peoples Programme, Moreton-in-Marsh.

PRIA (Society for Participatory Research in Asia) (1993) *Doon Declaration on People and Parks. Resolution of the National Workshop on Declining Access to and Control over Natural Resources in National Parks and Sanctuaries*, Forest Research Institute, Dehradun.

WCPA and IUCN (2000) *Indigenous and Traditional Peoples and Protected Areas: Principles, Guidelines and Case Studies*, edited by J. Beltran, IUCN, Gland.

West, P. and Brechin, S. (eds) (1991) *Resident Peoples and National Parks: Social Dilemmas in International Conservation*, University of Arizona Press, Tucson.

World Wide Fund for Nature-International (1996) *WWF Statement of Principles: Indigenous Peoples and Conservation*, WWF, Gland, Switzerland.

Chapter 15

The Role of Protected Areas in Conserving Biodiversity and Sustaining Local Livelihoods

Lisa Naughton-Treves, Margaret Buck Holland and
Katrina Brandon

Measuring Park Effectiveness

Evaluating the effectiveness of protected areas is difficult, especially given the poor availability of data on ecological and social conditions and their change over time. Evaluating park effectiveness is also a politically fraught endeavour given the ambitious and disparate agendas imposed on protected areas. For example, a conservation biologist may label a protected area as a conservation success only if the full suite of native wildlife species is present in viable populations, including large and rare carnivores. An anthropologist viewing the same protected area may deem it a failure if local citizens' rights or livelihoods were undermined when the park was established. Thus, public discussions regarding the effectiveness of protected areas sometimes resemble the familiar blind-men-observing-an-elephant parable. For example, recently the manager of Machalilla National Park in Ecuador publicly promised that this 39,000ha protected area would serve as a *maquina de dinero* (money machine) for the surrounding province. In the same meeting, indigenous leaders testified that Machalilla was above all else a cultural homeland and 'source of life' for the Agua Blanca people. Then an Ecuadorian botanist explained that the park represented the last hope for sustaining endemic species found in coastal dry forests.[3]

Recognizing the lack of a unified measure of protected area effectiveness, we offer two different analyses: (a) an empirical assessment of the ability of protected areas to prevent forest conversion and (b) a broader discussion of the progress

Reprinted from *Annual Review of Environment and Resources*, vol 30, Naughton-Treves, L., Buck Holland, M. and Brandon, K., 'The role of protected areas in conserving biodiversity and sustaining local livelihoods', pp. 219–252, copyright © (2005) with permission from Annual Review (www.annualreviews.org), Palo Alto. Extract or abridged version.

made thus far in integrating local economic development with protected area management.

Effectiveness of protected areas in sustaining local livelihoods: the experience of integrated conservation and development projects

By global mandates, protected areas are now supposed to do far more than conserve biological diversity. These areas are charged with improving social welfare, guarding local security, and providing economic benefits across multiple scales, objectives traditionally relegated to the development sector. These goals are vitally important and are founded on the truth that amidst desperate poverty the long-term prospect for biodiversity conservation is poor. But as expectations for protected areas have multiplied, confusion has ensued about what makes an effective park and how to operationalize the plurality of objectives.

Conservationists, although often accused of being unconcerned with social issues, have significantly altered their approach in an attempt to meet the new mandate for protected areas. In many cases, conservation organizations formed new partnerships with development agencies and institutions, as well as citizens' groups. Together they have pursued an array of strategies linking conservation with development that generally fall into three broad groups: community-based natural resource management, community-based conservation, and integrated conservation and development projects (ICDPs). Unlike community-based conservation or community-based natural resource management, ICDPs focus primarily on protected areas and thus deserve special attention in this review.

The term ICDP was introduced in a study of 23 projects linking development activities to conservation at 18 parks in 14 countries.[4] Since then ICDPs have proliferated around parks scattered throughout developing countries, and they have captured a sizeable portion of support for conservation.[5] ICDPs vary considerably in form and size between sites, but the underlying model throughout is to establish 'core' protected areas in which uses are restricted and, in the surrounding areas (often labelled 'buffer zones'), promote socio-economic development and income generation compatible with park management objectives. Specific economic activities promoted in ICDPs range from ecotourism to agroforestry to sustainable harvest of biological resources. Some ICDPs have made notable achievements in improving forest management outside parks and raising support for conservation among specific communities.[6] However, reviews of ICDPs consistently have found that despite their appeal, it is hard to identify substantial achievements either in improving social welfare or in protecting biodiversity.[7] Explanations for the limited success of these projects vary considerably. Political ecologists have harshly criticized these projects on the grounds that ICDPs do not invite true local participation in environmental management, but rather constitute coercive forms of conservation practice, which resemble 'ill-fated colonial efforts to convert shifting cultivators into progressive farmers'.[8] By this view, to succeed, ICDPs need to truly devolve authority to communities over biological resources so that they have a vested interest in protecting them. Political ecologists also call for more open, fair negotiation regarding the placement of less rigid and more 'dynamic' protected area boundaries.[9] By contrast, some conservation biologists argue that development and conservation are ultimately incongruent goals.[10] On a more encouraging note, other conservation biologists believe that development and conservation are intertwined goals, but their scale of integration is inappropriate in ICDPs.[11] Robinson and Redford[11] explain that the concept of scale involves two dimensions, extent and grain. In the context of ICDPs, extent refers to the total area to be considered for the integration of conservation and development (e.g. a bioregion), whereas grain is a smaller unit of analysis in which certain activities will be implemented. Instead of attempting to promote integrated conservation and development throughout the total area under consideration, success is more likely if smaller units of land are devoted primarily to conservation aims or economic activities, depending on the productive capacity of the soil and ecosystem. For example, in Zambia, commercial trophy hunting appeared to be more sustainable and profitable in community-managed areas that were located adjacent to national parks. These national parks served as 'sources' (sensu)[12] that replenished game populations when harvest rates in community areas were not sustainable.[13]

Recent reviews of ICDPs have found that although there has been an evolution in the scale of projects and how they are conceptualized, most of the projects are still hampered by implementation problems similar to those associated with rural development projects.[2, 14, 15] ICDPs have 'become all things to all people',[14] and what is now called an ICDP is often any conservation project that deals with people. A recent book on ICDPs found that both conservation organizations and funding agencies are identifying serious problems with the ICDP approach.[5] Some are turning toward more direct strategies, such as conservation concessions, whereby donors pay to have land managed for biodiversity.[16] But most conservation agencies remain broadly committed to ICDP approaches, with some attempting to shift both the focus and scale of these efforts, described below.

Biodiversity conservation and poverty alleviation

The fact that many parks today retain higher levels of biological resources than surrounding areas has led some prominent development groups to call on these areas to contribute substantially, and directly, to rural poverty alleviation (e.g. the UK Department for International Development[17]). These arguments gain greater significance as the area under protection expands. Yet some conservationists fear this will lead to cashing in on park resources, and they believe there should be more attention toward effective management outside of parks by communities, indigenous peoples, private sector or other interests. If parks are viewed as part of a broader landscape of initiatives that work with one another, such as corridor, ecoregional and landscape scales, then they can be viewed as an 'intact' area that can provide vital ecosystem services and help contribute to the quality and restoration of surrounding areas. In other words, it is equally urgent to promote the environmental agenda beyond protected area boundaries as it is to promote economic development inside parks.[18, 19]

Even conservation actions that may not appear to be directly linked to poverty alleviation may contribute because the poor are most reliant on natural and wild resources. If the ecological base upon which the rural poor depend becomes seriously degraded, then their livelihoods are likely to diminish as well. Only recently have studies emerged showing the tangible economic benefits of protected areas. One study of 41 reserves, covering approximately 1.5 million ha in Madagascar, found that the economic rate of return of the protected area system was 54 per cent.[20] The main benefits were from watershed protection, although ecotourism benefits were significant and expected to increase over time, providing greater returns to surrounding communities. The study also confirmed other findings, for example there are often winners and losers from conservation, even among groups of poor. In this example, 265,000 poor rice-farming households (average of 1.5ha per household) benefited, as did the 25,000 urban households receiving potable water. But 50,000 shifting agriculturalists (also known as 'slash-and-burn' farmers) were deprived of the land within the parks.

Challenges and opportunities for future protected area management

The remarkable physical expansion of protected areas during the past 25 years is a notable success for conservation, and it signals an international commitment to protecting biological diversity. Similarly, the group of advocates for protected areas has grown far beyond ecologists, foresters and recreational land-use planners to include development agencies, indigenous people's leaders, rural union leaders, water managers, and advocates for the poor. This groundswell of support has led to an ever more ambitious agenda for protected areas. By global mandate, in addition to conserving biological diversity, protected areas are to provide economic benefits at multiple scales, alleviate poverty, protect threatened cultures, and promote peace. The challenge for protected area management over the next 25 years will be to implement these multiple and often ambiguous aims as conservation strategies in the face of population growth, ever-increasing resource demands by northern and southern countries, and political instability.

The expansion of the protected area system has outpaced institutional and financial capacity for actual management,[21] and even if there were a tremendous infusion of financial resources toward protected areas, managing protected areas would still be profoundly difficult, given the multiple and at times ambiguous mandates for parks and reserves. Fortunately, there are energetic and committed scholars and activists working to improve protected area management, not only by appealing for more funds, but also by experimenting with new forms of protected areas and institutional arrangements for governing protected areas. It is also encouraging to note that international discussions and deliberations regarding protected areas are moving beyond divisive pro- or anti-park debates. Rather, there is an active exploration of how to design protected areas and park governance regimes to better reflect the local context. To conclude, we highlight two key efforts in this regard.

Land-use zoning and the creation of ecological corridors around protected areas

Faced with an overwhelming challenge to promote environmental protection while improving local lives and livelihoods across large or newly expanded protected areas, managers and agencies are increasingly turning to land-use zoning. Ideally, these zoning projects provide a means to balance conservation aims with economic development goals across large areas and among diverse stakeholders. Many of these projects centre on creating buffer or multiple-use zones to soften the line between nature preservation and resource extraction.[9] Others seek to establish ecological corridors or no-take zones amidst areas of resource extraction, so that biodiversity can be sustained in these zones and can replenish surrounding areas.[22] These landscape-level initiatives represent a more appropriate scale for reconciling biodiversity conservation and rural development.

Zoning represents an advance for high-conflict situations or cases where actual land use differs significantly from legal conservation mandates. But the bland terms used in project documents (e.g. buffer zones and stakeholder analysis) belie the intensely political nature of demarcating territories for conservation and/or resource exploitation. Not surprisingly, zoning projects have stirred criticisms from various perspectives.

Some conservation biologists fear that land-use zoning projects will compromise ecosystem integrity if parkland is rezoned for multiple use. Accordingly, because many parks are already small and poorly protected, conservation biologists call on park managers to 'draw a line in the sand' and 'hold ground' against powerful economic interests.[1, 23, 24] Meanwhile, political ecologists generally view many rezoning efforts as but a new incarnation of coercive conservation in which the state expands its authority and further displaces local people from vital resources.[8, 9] These critics doubt project leaders' claims of community participation, and assert that as long as state agencies or externally funded conservation NGOs direct rezoning projects, local citizens will lose out. Aside from political dilemmas, zoning exercises have suffered from problems of implementation. Considerable time and money have been invested in overly elaborate plans (e.g. laying out 20 or more categories of land use) that are far beyond the local managerial capacity. Other times, zoning only perpetuates ambiguity in protected area objectives. For example, a Peruvian manager explained that she was unsure how to enforce a large zone designated in her protected area for 'economic development harmonious with biodiversity conservation'. Such vague designations reflect the political advantages of avoiding difficult decisions about priority land uses; public consensus on zoning plans is more feasible when the management objectives for contested zones remain vague.

Zoning efforts are most likely to be effective if they are scaled to managerial capacity and are viewed as legitimate by local citizens and key stakeholder groups (note that not all stakeholders will be winners). Research in Latin America has shown that the very notion of park zoning and management can be co-opted by local elites or outside interest groups, who can wrap themselves in the cloak of conservation and manoeuvre both zoning and enforcement to limit access to other groups, especially when the actions of other groups may restrict or diminish their livelihood resources.[25] Given the expansion of biosphere reserves and other categories that allow for complex zoning, it is likely that what is contested will shift from 'people versus parks' to 'park insiders versus outsiders'.[18] In many places, both participatory legislation and participatory zoning allow needed flexibility in drawing boundaries that are more realistic given the current socio-political and ecological landscape surrounding each protected area.

Protected area governance and the importance of strengthening institutions

An important trend in protected area policy circles is greater attention to environmental governance.[26] Beyond elaborating what type of protected area is appropriate for a given place (e.g. type Ia, III or VI), conservationists are addressing who should have responsibility for management of individual protected areas. Barrett et al.[27] noted that local communities have become the 'default locus of most tropical conservation activity', owing in large part to recognized failures with the 'fences and fines' approach to conservation management from centralized institutions, as well as pressure to integrate community development and poverty reduction with conservation action.[27] The difficulty here is that, in this shift to community-based management of the area and natural resources, the bulk of the economic burden and responsibility of management has fallen to the community itself, and other institutions and stakeholder groups have either disappeared or maintained minimal roles. Although this may offer validation to the local community of the importance of its direct and present relationship with the protected area, the management arrangement as such fails to recognize the complex web of relationships that connect other groups with the protected landscape and resources.

This web of connections to the area and the resources can be mapped across spatial and temporal scales. These scales can include not only local communities that directly depend on the area for sustaining household livelihoods, but these can also aid regional and national constituencies, such as, for example, effectively managing resources to provide clean water to larger portions of the population. The connection then extends even further to international institutions and treaties, including those focused on mitigating the effects of global warming to provide a better outlook for future generations.

When considering the web of institutional and group connections to a protected area, it becomes imperative to look through an economic lens and define the costs and benefits, both direct and passive, that each group maintains with the landscape and resources of the area.[28] This type of analysis is challenging, but many argue that the exercise is a necessary step in the development of a more complex and integrated management order. In failing to do so, either local communities or weakened state institutions will continue to bear the brunt of the economic burden of maintaining these areas when international institutions and donors in particular could do much to alleviate it.

Finally, recent publications have illustrated that too little is known about national and regional institutional landscapes and that this research is imperative before conservation managers can effectively create a management 'menu,' which assigns responsibility to an array of stakeholder groups at varying levels.[27] Furthermore, practitioners must not impose uniform conservation strategies across the developing world. Rather, they must recognize the substantial and complex differences in institutional roles and power between Latin America, Africa and Asia or their subregions.

Environmentalists now face a time of 'tragic choices and creative compromises' (W. Cronon, personal communication). Protected areas on their own are unlikely to lift millions of people out of poverty in developing countries. And biodiversity will probably continue to be compromised in many protected areas that remain vulnerable to local, national and international economic forces. Just as is the case for sustainable development (a mission with 'broad appeal and plurality of purpose'),[29] greater clarity is needed on the mission of parks, with corresponding support to manage them so that they can effectively meet their assigned mission. At broad scales, it is possible for protected areas to maintain both biological diversity and to set the stage for better environmental stewardship in surrounding lands, a necessity if lasting poverty reduction is to be achieved.

Notes

1   Terborgh, J. and van Schaik, C. (1997) 'Minimizing species loss: The imperative of protection', pp. 15–35, in Kramer, R., van Schaik, C. and Johnson, J. (eds) (1997) *Last Stand: Protected Areas and the Defense of Tropical Biodiversity*, Oxford University Press, New York.

2   Brandon, K., Redford, K.H. and Sanderson, S.E. (eds) (1998) *Parks in Peril: People, Politics and Protected Area*, Island Press, Washington, DC.

3   Fiallo, E. and Naughton-Treves, L. (1998) 'Ecuador: Machalilla National Park', pp. 249–287, in Brandon, K., Redford, K.H. and Sanderson, S.E. (eds) (1998) *Parks in Peril: People, Politics and Protected Area*, Island Press, Washington, DC.

4   Wells, M. and Brandon, K. (1992) *People and Parks: Linking Protected Area Management with Local Communities*, World Bank, Washington, DC.

5   McShane, T. and Wells, M. (2004) *Getting Biodiversity Projects to Work: Towards More Effective Conservation and Development*, Columbia University Press, New York.

6   Chicchon, A. (2000) 'Conservation theory meets practice', *Conservation Biology*, 14: 138–139.

7   Kiss, A. (2004) 'Making biodiversity conservation a land use priority', pp. 98–123, in McShane, T. and Wells, M., *Getting Biodiversity Projects to Work: Towards More Effective Conservation and Development*, Columbia University Press, New York.

8   Neumann, R. (1997) 'Primitive ideas: Protected area buffer zones and the politics of land in Africa', *Dev. Change*, 28: 579–582.

9   Zimmerer, K. (2000) 'The reworking of conservation geographies: Nonequilibrium landscapes and nature-society hybrids', *Annals of the Association of American Geographers*, 90: 356–369.

10 Oates J. (1999) *Myth and Reality in the Rain Forest: How Conservation Strategies Are Failing in West Africa*, University of California Press, Berkeley.

11 Robinson, J.R. and Redford, K.H. (2004) 'Jack of all trades, master of none', pp. 10–34, in McShane, T. and Wells, M., *Getting Biodiversity Projects to Work: Towards More Effective Conservation and Development*, Columbia University Press, New York.

12 Novaro, A., Redford, K. and Bodmer, R. (2000) 'Effect of hunting in source-sink systems in the neotropics', *Conservation Biology*, 14: 713–721.

13 Lewis, D.M. and Alpert, P. (1997) 'Trophy hunting and wildlife conservation in Zambia', *Conservation Biology*, 11: 59–68.

14 Sanjayan, M., Shen, S. and Jansen, M. (1997) *Experiences with Integrated-Conservation Development Projects in Asia*, World Bank Tech. Pap. 388, World Bank, Washington, DC.

15 Larson, P., Freudenberger, M. and Wyckoff-Baird, B. (1998) *WWF Integrated Conservation and Development Projects: Ten Lessons from the Field 1985–1996*, World Wildlife Fund, Washington, DC.

16 Ferraro, P. and Kramer, R. (1997) 'Compensation and economic incentives: Reducing pressure on protected areas', pp. 187–211, in Kramer, R., van Schaik, C. and Johnson, J. (eds), *Last Stand: Protected Areas and the Defense of Tropical Biodiversity*, Oxford University Press, New York.

17 Department of International Development (2002) *Wildlife and Poverty Study*, DFID, London.

18 Brandon, K. (1994) 'Perils to parks: The social context of threats', pp. 415–440, in Brandon, K., Redford, K.H. and Sanderson, S.E. (eds), *Parks in Peril: People, Politics and Protected Area*, Island Press, Washington, DC.

19 Brandon, K. (1997) 'Policy and practical considerations in land-use strategies for biodiversity conservation', pp. 90–111, in Kramer, R., van Schaik, C. and Johnson, J. (eds) (1997) *Last Stand: Protected Areas and the Defense of Tropical Biodiversity*, Oxford University Press, New York.

20 Carret, J.-C. and Loyer, D. (2003) *Madagascar Protected Area Network Sustainable Financing, Economic Analysis Perspective*, Presented at 5th World Parks Congress, Durban South Africa.

21 Bruner, A., Gullison, R. and Balmford, A. (2004) 'Financial costs and shortfalls of managing and expanding protected-area systems in developing countries', *BioScience*, 54: 1119–1126.

22 Peres, C. (2005) 'Why we need megareserves in Amazonia', *Conservation Biology*, 19: 728–733.

23 Redford, K.H., Brandon, K. and Sanderson, S.E. (1998) 'Holding ground', pp. 455–463, in Brandon, K., Redford, K.H. and Sanderson, S.E. (eds), *Parks in Peril: People, Politics and Protected Area*, Island Press, Washington, DC.

24 Terborgh, J. and van Schaik, C. (1997) 'Minimizing species loss: The imperative of protection', pp. 15–35, in Kramer, R., van Schaik, C. and Johnson, J. (eds), *Last Stand: Protected Areas and the Defense of Tropical Biodiversity*, Oxford University Press, New York.

25 Fiallo, E. and Naughton-Treves, L. (1998) Ecuador: Machalilla National Park, pp. 249–287, in Brandon, K., Redford, K.H. and Sanderson, S.E. (eds), *Parks in Peril: People, Politics and Protected Area*, Island Press, Washington, DC.

26 Borrini-Feyerabend, G. (1996) *Collaborative Management of Protected Areas: Tailoring the Approach to the Context*, IUCN, Gland, Switzerland.

27 Barrett, C.B., Brandon, K., Gibson, C. and Gjertsen, H. (2001) 'Conserving tropical biodiversity amid weak institutions', *Bio-Science*, 51: 497–502.

28 Balmford, A. and Whitten, T. (2003) 'Who should pay for tropical conservation and how could the costs be met?', *Oryx*, 37: 238–250.

29 Parris, T.M. and Kates, R.W. (2003) 'Characterizing and measuring sustainable development', *Annual Review of Environment and Resources*, 28: 559–586.

Chapter 16

Eviction for Conservation: A Global Overview

Dan Brockington and Jim Igoe

Introduction

Protest against the experience of displacement and marginalization by protected areas, against impoverishment and injustice, against disempowerment and disenfranchisement, has become one of the defining features of the politics of protected areas in the last two decades. The World Parks Congress in Durban in 2003 was marked by strong and diverse protest against the disruptions of conservation to society and livelihoods (Brosius, 2004). The voices were coolly received by a faction of 'conservation scientists', who felt the meeting was being hijacked by unwelcome influences.[1] Terborgh noted: 'Countless workshops, lectures, and discussions delved into topics such as poverty alleviation, social injustice, indigenous peoples' rights, community management of protected areas, and gender equity in conservation. All these issues have their place in a global agenda but for me they dominated and drowned out the discussion of themes more directly related to conserving nonhuman life on this planet' (2004, p. 619).

The growing unpopularity of protected areas has come as an unwelcome shock for many conservationists. For years conservation has enjoyed the moral high ground. It was saving the planet, rescuing species from extinction, and taking a stand against the rapacious consumption of resources by one virulent species. This image of 'global good guys' is not only an important part of conservationists' own self-perceptions, it is also essential to the image of large conservation organizations in their fundraising appeals. Now these same organizations find themselves engaged in publicity battles, the negative consequences of which could be particularly damaging to their institutional well-being. This situation has provoked a great deal of anguish. But what is the nature of this anguish? 'Conservation scientists' are anguished over the perceived 'hijacking' of their agendas. Those who would hijack

Reprinted from *Conservation and Society*, vol 4, Brockington, D. and Igoe, J., 'Eviction for conservation: A global overview', pp. 424–470, copyright © (2006) with permission from Dan Brockington and James Igoe. Extract or abridged version.

those agendas are in turn anguished by conservation displacements. In order to better address both types of anguish, it will be necessary to arrive at a better understanding of these displacements and how best to address them.

Conservation displacement, like other forms of displacement, compromises two processes (Cernea, 2005): (1) the forced removal of people from their homes; and (2) economic displacement, the exclusion of people from particular areas in their pursuit of a livelihood (e.g. Horowitz, 1998). People dwelling on the edge of a park but unable to gather firewood or wild foods, to hunt, or fish, or unable to walk to their farms on the other side of the park, would be unable to live as they were before. Exclusion of economic activity which does not lead to moving house still displaces that activity elsewhere.

Beyond material loss to livelihoods or dwellings, protesters are fighting their symbolic obliteration from the landscape – their removal from its history, memory and representation (Schama, 1996). Other groups were protesting their loss of power and control over their environments, the interference of the conservation regulations into their lives in ways over which they had little control (Theodossopoulos, 2002; Novellino, 2003). Else they were protesting the interference of different value systems into local economies, the commodification of wildlife and nature into things which tourists can purchase, but which locals can then no longer afford (MacDonald, 2004, 2005).

Of course these consequences of protected areas are part of a whole variety of social, economic and political consequences many of which are more positive. Protected areas provide employment and income nationally and locally, they safeguard ecosystem services sustaining agriculture, they provide the symbols to unite and forge nations. Indeed their effects are too diverse merely to be categorized as 'good' or 'bad' (West et al., 2006).

If conservation provoked no protest then it would be unlikely to be doing its job properly. Providing more space for nature often requires constraining people's lives and activities. Few surrender willingly to such controls. Protest is likely to be loud when those affected are wealthy and powerful and are not able to become richer and more powerful as a result of the restrictions of conservation. More immediately, from the perspective of this paper, it is likely to be loud where people are highly dependent on natural resources for their livelihoods and risk facing impoverishment because of those regulations. Moreover, there is a growing sense that much protest is due to poor, clumsy or callous practice on the part of conservationists. Strident criticisms have been published in popular presses (Chapin, 2004; Dowie, 2005). There are strong calls for better forms of governance, which would facilitate people's participation in, and ownership of, conservation (Borrini -Feyerabend et al., 2002, 2004).

It is therefore important to take most seriously the anger and protest against the conservation movement and examine its material and political basis. What has happened to whom? Where has it happened, and as a result of whose actions? Who has borne the costs of conservation and who has realized its benefits in specific contexts? Of which groups and which parts of the world is the anger representative? Is the protest the result of deep-seated objections, which have long simmered but which are only now becoming visible? Has resistance long been occurring but only recently become visible (Holmes, forthcoming)? Or has there been some sort of recent change in conservation practice or rural politics? To what extent is the dissatisfaction the result of conservation alone, and to what extent the conjunction of several forces?

Answering these types of questions will require quite specific assessments of the trends, and marshalling of the evidence, of the different patterns of marginalization, impoverishment and displacement due to protected areas. This chapter looks specifically at global trends in relocation and eviction. It is essential to underline that this is therefore not about displacement more generally (by definition), nor about the diverse forms of marginalisation and disenfranchisement which conservation can cause. Our survey is a work in progress. Our conclusions are therefore speculative, suggesting hypotheses to refute rather than delineating patterns. We list these hypotheses in Box 16.1.

We proceed by first discussing our method. Then we examine the state of knowledge about relocation from protected areas. We move through a series of questions which consider how other authors have evaluated this literature, what the literature actually consists of, and what patterns are visible in it, both geographically and historically. Finally we consider what the better studies about relocation from protected areas have actually reported. In our conclusion we examine the case for further research.

The State of the Literature

What opinions exist about the state of knowledge concerning eviction from protected areas?

While we have been conducting the survey, two quite divergent opinions of the quality of knowledge about relocation have been published.[2] Borgerhoff-Mulder and Coppolillo recently published an important work, called simply *Conservation* (2005), which provided a magnificent overview of changing conservation practice and a detailed analysis of different means of strengthening the work of protected areas (for a review, see Brockington, 2005). The book was devoted to making conservation practice more just and effective. It was frank about conservation's problems, stating that the literature on evictions from protected areas offers 'a massive cataloguing of past, recent and ongoing abuses' (p. 36).

Wilkie and his colleagues offer quite a different assessment. They have recently begun an investigation into the consequences of new protected areas in Gabon, which will include quantitative surveys of the livelihoods and economic activity before and after their establishment. They asserted, contra Borgerhoff-Mulder and

Coppolillo, that 'to date little empirical evidence exists to substantiate the contention that parks are bad for local people' (Wilkie et al., 2006, p. 247). This is a bold, indeed, remarkable claim, covering all forms of displacement, not merely the aspects of relocation we cover here.

Which of these contrasting assessments is correct? We believe that neither is. Wilkie and colleagues are ignoring, or worse, dismissing numerous cases, which indicate considerable cause for concern. There is substantial evidence of the harm done by eviction and much more about the more general problems of displacement.[3] On the other hand, Borgerhoff-Mulder and Coppolillo are exaggerating the quality, extent and order of knowledge. Our grasp of the subject is simply not as good as they claim.

Conclusion

As we stated at the start of this discussion, all the patterns drawn out above are based on a patchy and parlous literature. Some of the patterns above are likely to prove robust descriptions of the state of eviction and displacement from protected areas, but clearly they require further scrutiny. There is an important research agenda here. Notwithstanding the number of peoples affected and the extent of the territories involved, these are questions which are fundamentally important to the success and prosperity of both conservation and local communities. We have summarized the most important of these questions in Box 16.1.

Some hypotheses require elaboration. With the exception of some regions (hypothesis 1), we believe that there have been substantially more evictions in the past than have currently been recorded (hypotheses 2-6). Currently, although protected areas have expanded remarkably, there does not appear to be a corresponding rise in evictions (hypothesis 7). We believe this because the protected area growth has occurred after social scientists became alert to the evictions protected areas can entail, yet there are relatively few reports. There are correspondingly numerous complaints from biologists about the problem of paper parks.

We recognize that there is a danger that hypothesis 7 will be quoted out of context. This would be unfortunate because we do not believe at all that the problem of protected area evictions has subsided. We would not have written this paper otherwise. Many people still reside illegally in protected areas. If conservation legislation is enforced in the future the problem will become prevalent again, indeed more serious than before (hypothesis 8). Poorer parts of the world have continued to create large strictly protected areas which could have significant impacts on large numbers of people (West et al., 2006). Furthermore a new wave of displacements and evictions is beginning to occur from community-based conservation schemes (Dzingirai, 2003). While each of these is small, they are numerous, insidious and difficult to document. Their aggregate impacts could be significant.

Box 16.1 *Hypotheses about eviction and conservation*

1 South America, the Pacific, Caribbean and Australia have experienced relatively few incidents of eviction from protected areas compared to the rest of the world.

2 The countries of the former Soviet Union have a long history of displacement from strictly protected areas.

3 Most protected areas from which evictions have occurred were established before 1980.

4 Eviction from protected areas did not occasion significant public debate before the 1980s.

5 There were many more evictions from protected areas in all regions before 1980 than are currently reported in the literature.

6 Complex nationally based environmental movements are driving current evictions from protected areas.

7 Large-scale evictions from large protected areas are currently less prevalent than they once were.

8 Evictions will become more common if existing conservation legislation in Africa and South Asia is enforced.

9 Economic displacement and exclusion from protected areas is more significant in people's lives and complaints about protected areas than physical eviction.

Finally we must reiterate that in dwelling on eviction in the paper we have only focused on one aspect of displacement (hypothesis 9). Time and again in the literature it was clear that the act of eviction alone was but one part of a whole series of marginalizations, inconveniences and impoverishments that merely addressing relocation will miss. Indeed all these are possible without physical eviction occurring at all. Important as understanding eviction trends is, it is more important to comprehend the bigger displacement picture.

In addition to the patterns we have documented, it is equally important to notice and attend to the silences of the conservation literature apparent in Box 16.1. For while the questions above indicate at least some attention to these issues, albeit scanty in places, there are clearly other important questions which have not been broached. The first is the growing importance of private protected areas. There are some countries where conservation is dominated by these. Large parts of Scotland, the private hunting estates of wealthy landlords, are effectively private conservation areas. In South Africa private game ranches occupy twice the area of state protected areas, a full 11 per cent of the country, and the area of land devoted to wildlife is growing rapidly. In Tanzania wealthy individuals such as Paul Tudor Jones, an American billionaire, are invigorating the protection and conservation status of vast tracts of land, and are trying to persuade more villagers to leave their lands in the interests of conservation. There are challenges of eviction and displacement from private protected areas as much as from state protected areas (Langholz, 2003). We know that the vast areas of Scottish wildness were created through mass evictions of crofters in the notorious Highland clearances (Pringle, 1988) (www.theclearances.org). In South Africa the expansion of public protected areas is often being pursued by the purchase of private farmland – from which farm labourers, often resident there for generations, have first to be removed (Goenewald and Macleod, 2004; Luck, 2003). Alienation from place, nature and home, which is, at bottom, the root objection to the dislocation-caused eminent domain, are just as easily inflicted by laws of property and the behaviour of the market.

The second is to emphasize the point made by Rangarajan and Shahabuddin (2006) about the general silence on the ecology of eviction. We have seen that few studies of the impacts of eviction offer good quality information on the social impacts of removal. Fewer still examine what has happened with their ecology. This is a vital point, for evictions are carried out in Nature's name, but often also in surprising ignorance of Nature's processes.

We need to qualify this point. There are well-documented examinations of how natural wildernesses in the US created by the removal of indigenous inhabitants were then carefully managed by the Parks Services to control fire and remove predators, often, it has later been realized, to the detriment of the ecosystem (Chase, 1987; Leopold, 1989 (1949)). We know that ring-fencing black and white rhinoceros and ensuring that no illicit human contact is allowed cause their populations to recover. We know that forest cover within protected areas tends to be better, richer and more continuous than without, and that trends of forest decline tend to be slower, or reversed, within protected areas than without (Bruner et al., 2001; DeFries et al., 2005; Naughton-Treves et al., 2005) – although we know less about the impacts on the larger ecosystems of which protected areas are part. We know that human hunting pressure within forests will locally decrease the abundance of some species (Alvard et al., 1997).

But these apparent successes resulting from the removal of people from landscapes and ecosystems are not a sufficient endorsement of the policy. The extreme measures of rhino enclosures can be deemed a success only when the fences have come down. Indeed the fact that it is now possible to shoot black and white rhinoceros in the wild in Africa is the best measure of the success of this policy. Borgerhoff-Mulder and Coppollilo (2005) have observed that the comparison made between protected and unprotected forests that Bruner and others reported is simply not a good measure of the consequences of protection with resident peoples. That category of conservation protection was not examined. Only by examining the ecologies of coexistence, of residence and eviction, can we know how or when eviction needs to be used. Given that strictly protected areas will never be sufficiently extensive and that space for nature has to be found outside them this is a vital task (Rosenweig, 2003).

Forced removals are drastic. Eviction is the most violent act a law-abiding state can inflict on its law-abiding citizens. Ultimately it is inimical to conservation's cause. There can only be successes when the fences are down. For if we love nature because of our early encounters with it, and cling to that love despite the diverse alienations and pressures modern life throws at it (Milton, 2002), as Bill Adams has observed:

> *'The challenge is not to preserve (or restore) 'the wild', but peoples'* relationships *with the wild ... [W]ithout contact with nature, people's capacity to understand it and engage with it withers. The future of conservation will turn on the extent to which a strong individual connection to nature and natural processes is maintained.'* (2004, p. 235–236, emphasis in the original)

Notes

1   The label is interesting, it recalls Foucault's observations that claiming the label 'science' is an attempt to acquire power and prestige to suppress opposition. Perhaps here it was chosen as an attempt to acquire authority, distance and some form of objectivity, as well as appealing to the perceived core values and practices of conservation.
2   Both come from authors close to, or working with, the Wildlife Conservation Society.
3   Indeed the best marshalling of the relocation data (by Kai Schmidt-Soltau, with assistance from Michael Cernea: Cernea and Schmidt-Soltau, 2003, 2006; Schmidt-Soltau, 2003, 2005) of which we are aware comes precisely from where Wilkie and his team are working.

References

Adams, W.M. (2004) *Against Extinction: The Story of Conservation*, Earthscan, London.

Alvard, M.S., Robinson, J.G., Redford, K.H. and Kaplan, H. (1997) 'The sustainability of subsistence hunting in the neotropics', *Conservation Biology*, 11: 977–982.

Borgerhoff-Mulder, M. and Coppolillo, P. (2005) *Conservation: Linking Ecology, Economics and Culture*, Princeton University Press, Princeton.

Borrini-Feyerabend, G., Banuri, T., Farvar, T., Miller, K. and Phillips, A. (2002) 'Indigenous and local communities and protected areas: Rethinking the relationship', *Parks*, 12: 5–15.

Borrini-Feyerabend, G., Pimbert, M., Farvar, T., Kothari, A. and Renard, Y. (2004) *Sharing Power: Learning by Doing in Co-management of Natural Resources Throughout the World*, IIED, London.

Brockington, D. (2005) 'Book Review of *Conservation: Linking Ecology, Economics and Culture*', *Journal of Ecological Anthropology*, 9: 82–83.

Brosius, J.P. (2004) 'Indigenous peoples and protected areas at the World Parks Congress', *Conservation Biology*, 18: 609–612.

Bruner, A.G., Gullison R.E., Rice, R.E. and da Fonseca, G.A.B. (2001) 'Effectiveness of parks in protecting tropical biodiversity', *Science*, 291: 125–128.

Cernea, M.M. (2005) '"Restriction of access" is displacement: A broader concept and policy', *Forced Migration Review*, 23: 48–9.

Cernea, M. and Schmidt-Soltau, K. (2003) 'The end of forcible displacements? Making conservation and impoverishment incompatible', *Policy Matters*, 12: 42–51.

Cernea, M.M. and Schmidt-Soltau, K. (2006) 'Poverty risks and national parks: Policy issues in conservation and resettlement', *World Development*, 34: 1808–1830.

Chapin, M. (2004) 'A Challenge to Conservationists', *World Watch Magazine*, Nov/Dec: 17–31.

Chase, A. (1987) *Playing God in Yellowstone: The Destruction of America's First National Park*, Harcourt Brace, Orlando.

DeFries, R., Hansen, A., Newton, A.C. and Hansen, M.C. (2005) 'Increasing isolation of protected areas in tropical forests over the past twenty years', *Ecological Applications*, 15: 19–26.

Dowie, M. (2005) 'Conservation refugees: When protecting nature means kicking people out', *Orion*, Nov/Dec.

Dzingirai, V. (2003) 'The new scramble for the African countryside', *Development and Change*, 34: 243–263.

Goenewald, Y. and Macleod, F. (2004) 'Park plans bring "grief"', in *Weekly Mail and Guardian*.

Holmes, G. (forthcoming) 'Cultivation, conservation and confrontation: The use of forest fire as a political tool in the Dominican Republic', *Area*.

Horowitz, L.S. (1998) 'Integrating indigenous resource management with wildlife conservation: A case study of Batang Ai National Park, Sarawak, Malaysia', *Human Ecology*, 26: 371–403.

Langholz, J. (2003) 'Privatizing conservation', pp. 117–135, in Brechin, S.R., Wilchusen, P.R., Fortwrangler, C.L. and West, P.C. (eds), *Contested Nature: Promoting International Biodiversity Conservaton with Social Justice in the Twenty-First Century*, State University of New York Press, New York.

Leopold, A. 1989 (1949) *A Sand County Almanac. And sketches Here and There*, OUP, Oxford.

Luck, K. (2003) *Contested Rights: The Impact of Game Farming on Farm Workers in the Bushman's River Area*, Rhodes University, MA.

MacDonald, K. (2004) 'Developing "Nature": Global ecology and the politics of conservation in Northern Pakistan', in Carrier, J. (ed), *Confronting Environments: Local Environmental Understanding in a Globalising World*, AltaMira Press, Lantham.

MacDonald, K. (2005) 'Global hunting grounds: Power, scale and ecology in the negotiation of conservation', *Cultural Geographies*, 12: 259–91.

Milton, K. (2002) *Loving Nature: Towards an Ecology of Emotion*, Routledge, London.

Naughton-Treves, L., Buck Holland, M. and Brandon, K. (2005) 'The role of protected areas in conserving biodiversity and sustaining local livelihoods', *Annual Review of Environment and Resources*, 30: 219–252.

Novellino, D. (2003) 'Contrasting landscapes, conflicting ontologies: Assessing environmental conservation on Palawan Island', pp. 171–188, in Anderson, D.G. and Berglund, E. (eds) *Ethnographies of Conservation: Environmentalism and the Distribution of Privilege*, Bergahn Books, New York.

Pringle, T.R. (1988) 'The privation of history: Landseer, Victoria and the Highland myth', in Cosgrove, D. and Daniels, S. (ed) *The Iconography of Landscape: Essays on the Symbolic Representation, Design and Use of Past Environments*, Cambridge University Press, Cambridge.

Rangarajan, M. and Shahabuddin, G. (2006) 'Displacement and relocation from protected areas: Towards a biological and historical synthesis', *Conservation and Society*, 4: 359–378

Rosenweig, M.L. (2003) 'Reconciliation ecology and the future of species diversity', *Oryx*, 37: 194–205.

Schama, S. (1996) *Landscape and Memory*, Fontana Press, London.

Schmidt-Soltau, K. (2003) Conservation-related resettlement in Central Africa: Environmental and social risks, *Development and Change*, 34: 525–551

Schmidt-Soltau, K. (2005) 'The environmental risks of conservation related displacements in Central Africa', pp. 282–311, in Ohta, I. and Gebre, Y.D. (eds) *Displacement Risks in Central Africa: Refugees, Resettlers and their Host Population,* , Kyoto University Press, Kyoto.

Terborgh, J. (2004) 'Reflections of a scientist on the World Parks Congress', *Conservation Biology,* 18: 619–620.

Theodossopoulos, D. (2002) 'Environmental conservation and indigenous culture in a Greek island community: The dispute over the sea turtles', pp. 244–260, in Chatty, D. and Colchester, M. (eds) *Conservation and Mobile Indigenous Peoples. Displacement, Forced Settlement and Sustainable Development,* Berghahn Books, New York.

West, P., Brockington, D. and Igoe, J. (2006) 'Parks and peoples: The social effects of protected areas', *Annual Review of Anthropology,* 20(3): 609–616.

Wilkie, D.S., Morelli, G.A., Demmer, J., Starkey, M., Telfer, P. and Steil, M. (2006) 'Parks and people: assessing the human welfare effects of establishing protected areas for biodiversity conservation', *Conservation Biology,* 20: 247–249.

Chapter 17

Political Ecology and the Costs and Benefits of Protected Areas

William M. Adams and Jon Hutton

Introduction

In 2004, 500 people were removed from the Nech Sar National Park in southern Ethiopia, and resettled outside its borders (Pearce, 2005). This forced displacement was undertaken by the government of Ethiopia, in order to clear the park of encumbrances before handing it over to a private Dutch-based organization awarded a contract to manage it, the African Parks Foundation (APF).[1]

This, and related displacements in Omo National Park, were swiftly condemned by international human rights NGOs.[2] Two years later, on 13 December 2006, the Botswana High Court ruled that the Botswana government's eviction of Bushmen from the Central Kalahari Game Reserve was 'unlawful and unconstitutional', and that they had the right to live on their ancestral land inside the designated area.[3]

These cases illustrate the contemporary importance of debates about the place of people on land set aside for the conservation of nature.[4] These have received increasing attention from academic researchers and human rights activists (e.g. Fairhead and Leach, 2000; Colchester, 2002; Chapin, 2004; Dowie, 2005). The stated aim of the APF, which also runs parks in Zambia, Malawi and South Africa, is 'to restore, manage and maintain the natural resources of the parks to ensure long-term ecological and financial sustainability'.[5] This framing of protected areas (PAs) in ecological and financial terms excludes any consideration of the social and political context of the establishment and management of PAs, despite the obvious importance of such issues. For whom are such areas set aside? On whose authority? At whose cost?

These issues are central to the growing public and policy debate about the social impacts of conservation. That debate, however, is much broader than just the question of the displacement of people from parks. It embraces the whole rela-tion between biodiversity conservation and human welfare, especially the compat-ibility of conservation and poverty alleviation and the feasibility of 'win–win' policy strategies (Adams et al., 2004; Agrawal and Redford, 2006).

There is growing policy literature about conservation and poverty in general, and the specific issue of the social impacts of PAs. This draws to only a limited extent on an explicit understanding of the political and economic dimensions of conservation policy. One important reason for this is the disciplinary gulf that exists between predominantly natural science-trained conservation planners and predominantly social science-trained critics of conservation. This gulf is profound and long-standing, but the need and opportunity for creative approaches to bridge it are being addressed from both sides (e.g. Brosius, 1999a, 2006; Mascia et al., 2003; Thornhill, 2003; Campbell, 2005).[6] One particular feature of this divide is the different capacity of natural and social scientists to engage with the politics of conservation action as a subject for analysis. Social science integrates politics centrally within its analysis of conservation; natural science typically places it outside, as a constraint on practical action. The field of political ecology offers productive possibilities for developing understanding of political dimensions of conservation (Stott and Sullivan, 2000; Zimmerer and Bassett, 2003; Peet and Watts, 2004; Robbins, 2004).

The transdisciplinary field of political ecology is increasingly important in the analysis of social dimensions of conservation. Key issues include the politics and economy of the spatial strategy of PA declaration in colonial and post-colonial contexts (e.g. Neumann, 1992, 2004b; Schroeder, 1999; Brockington, 2002), the role of the state as the central agent in the direction, legitimisation and exercise of power and control in the name of conservation (Peluso, 1993; Neumann, 2004a) and the role of non-governmental conservation actors (Brosius, 1999b; Bryant, 2002; Hecht et al., 2006). There is particular interest in the way conservation poli-cies on the ground reflect wider and more general ideas about nature, particularly through the development and application of scientific knowledge (e.g. Fairhead and Leach, 2003; Stott and Sullivan, 2000). This paper engages with work on the problematic relationship between conservation and human communities brought about by the designation of PAs. Wider dimensions of the political ecology of conservation are discussed in Adams and Hutton (2007).

The Social Impacts of Parks

The spatial strategy of setting aside PAs for conservation has inevitable social and economic impacts. These have long been acknowledged (McNeely and Miller, 1984; McNeely, 1993; Adams and Hulme, 2001) and are relatively well understood and widely reported (Emerton, 2001; O'Riordan and Stoll-Kleeman, 2002; Igoe, 2006). Direct costs to neighbours include hazards from crop-raiding wild animals such as elephants, buffalo, primates and a host of smaller species (Naughton-Treves, 1997; Sekhar, 1998; Woodroffe et al., 2005). Problems include crop damage, the labour and opportunity costs of crop defence (e.g. impacts on children who do not attend school), physical hazard (and fear of hazard) and death. Park neighbours can also be exposed to corrupt rent-seeking behaviour by PA staff, particularly linked to minor infringements of park boundaries (e.g. impoundment of stock alleged to be grazing illegally), or of regulations (e.g. informal charges to avoid arrest or fines for cutting fuelwood, or collecting medicinal plants).

The greatest social impacts of PAs, however, relate to population displacement. The issue of resident people in PAs is widely recognized (West and Brechin, 1991), especially in the case of indigenous people (Colchester, 2002; Chatty and Colchester, 2002). There have been a number of reviews of the problem (e.g. Geisler, 2003; Rangarajan and Shahabuddin, 2006; Agrawal and Redford, 2007). The complexity and enduring nature of post-resettlement impacts is known from research on the short- and long-term impacts of forced displacement in contexts such as dam construction (e.g. Scudder, 1993, 2005; Cernea and McDowell, 2000).

Displacement from PAs needs to be understood in a broad context. In 2004, the World Bank changed its guidelines on resettlement, extending the definition of 'involuntary displacement' to include the restriction of access to resources in PAs, even where no physical removal occurs (Cernea, 2006).[7] The phrase 'involuntary restriction of access' covers restrictions on the use of resources imposed on people living outside a PA as well as those living inside it. In the context of PAs, displacement includes loss of rights to residence, loss of rights to use land and resources, foreclosure of rights to future use and loss of non-consumptive use values, for example access to places of religious or cultural value. The economic cost to local or national economies of PAs can be considerable. Agricultural benefits forgone can be significant (e.g. Norton-Griffiths and Southey, 1995), even if offset by factors such as carbon storage in protected forest vegetation (e.g. Kremen et al., 2000).

Population displacement from PAs has a direct impact on livelihoods (e.g. Brechin et al., 2003; Chatty and Colchester, 2002; McElwee, 2006). Forced resettlement exposes displaced people and those in receiving communities to a wide range of risks of impoverishment (Scudder, 1993; Cernea and McDowell, 2000). These include landlessness, joblessness, homelessness, economic marginalization, food insecurity, increased morbidity and mortality, loss of access to common property and services, and social disarticulation (Cernea, 1997).

There is no accepted estimate of the total numbers of people displaced from PAs across the globe. Most published studies focus on particular cases, for example in Nicaragua (Kaimowitz et al., 2003), Tanzania (Neumann, 1998; Brockington, 2002), Uganda (Feeny, 1999) or Zimbabwe (Ranger, 1999). Some widely quoted cases of eviction, notably Turnbull's account of the plight of the Ik people following removal from Kidepo National Park, have subsequently been judged inaccurate

(Turnbull, 1974; Heine, 1985). Others are still inadequately documented (Colchester, 2002).

Attempts to establish the scale of evictions quantitatively are still experimental. Some estimates, derived by multiplying average population densities and the area of PAs, lead to surprisingly high figures. Geisler and de Sousa (2001) suggested there may be 14 million to 24 million 'environmental refugees' as a result of exclusionary conservation in Africa alone. Cernea and Schmidt-Soltau (2003) estimated that 40,000 to 45,000 people had been displaced or directly affected economically by displacement from nine PAs in central Africa. They subsequently argue that 120,000–150,000 people have been displaced or impoverished by 12 parks in six central African countries (Cernea and Schmidt-Soltau, 2006). The analysis on which these figures are based has been challenged, and they clearly need to be treated with considerable scepticism (Maisels et al., 2007). However, the currently published evidence base does indicate that population displacement is a real, and in many instances a significant, problem associated with PA establishment in a number of contexts (Brockington and Igoe, 2006; Agrawal and Redford, 2006).

A number of commentators have drawn attention to the use of force in programmes of involuntary population displacement. States claim legitimate power to enforce socially desirable outcomes, and on this ground, the protection of nature as state policy has often involved coercion, particularly where it has involved the displacement of human communities from PAs (Peluso, 1993). The military-style control of PAs that arose from the model of US National Parks has been maintained and developed in many countries, most prominently perhaps in Kenya (Leakey and Morell, 2001). Parker (2004) graphically describes the bombing of fleeing Somali poachers in Tsavo National Park in the 1950s with hand grenades. Neumann (2004a) analyses the moral context for the use of extreme force in conservation, drawing attention to the bizarre existence of 'shoot-to-kill' policies against poachers in countries where poaching is not a capital offence. As Peluso (1993) observes, in this militaristic worldview conservationists are constructed as heroes, literally fighting to protect nature against humankind. Military action is legitimized by the ontological separation between people and nature, and the construction of nature's value and threatened state.

Population displacements for one purpose can often end up serving another. Thus in colonial Tanganyika, the attempt to separate nature and people in Liwale District was driven in part by the sanitary objective of reducing sleeping sickness, concentrating people in agricultural districts, and leaving land further from the coast, deemed both wild and unhealthy, for nature (Neumann, 2001). Similarly, the Parc National Albert expanded onto land cleared in 1933 by the colonial state as part of its drastic sleeping sickness campaign in the Belgian Congo (Fairhead and Leach, 2000; cf. Lyons, 1985). Conservation planners have often been entrepreneurial in this way in recognizing the value of 'created wilderness:' the land lost by the Meru Mbise people to the Arusha National Park in Tanzania was initially taken for white settler farms and forest reserves, only subsequently being purchased by the state and conservation NGOs to extend the park (Neumann, 1998). Similarly, the violent forced resettlement of Tonga people from their land along the River Zambezi before the flooding of the reservoir behind the Kariba Dam in the 1950s (Howarth, 1961) preceded the creation of new 'wilderness' PAs in Zimbabwe (McGregor, 2005).

Attitudes to human presence in PAs have of course varied, even in colonial Africa. 'Squatters' were evicted from the Pongola Game Reserve in the 19th century, and its successor the Sabi Game Reserve, but were later (after 1905) tolerated because they provided a source of labour and rent, although the administration continued to complain of their resistance to discipline and their poaching (Carruthers, 1995). The more common historical pattern is for initial acceptance of human presence in a park to give way to intolerance either as ideas about the need to protect 'pristine' nature change or as human populations grow, or both. Thus, Brooks (2005) reports a measure of tolerance of people in and adjacent to the Hluhlue Game Reserve in Zululand in the 1930s, prior to fencing and eventual eviction in the 1940s. Brockington (2002) describes the eventually successful attempt to evict Parakuyo and Maasai pastoralists from the Mkomazi Game Reserve in Tanzania, in 1988, a full four decades after it was first designated.

Ironically, too, the displacement of people from PAs has long been dependent on identity. Tourists and scientists have conventionally been tolerated in PAs even where local resource users have been excluded. It is easy to imagine why conservationists might think that the work of scientists should be dealt with differently from other human activities, because of the role of natural science in conservation planning. However, it is more surprising that tourism (whose impacts were recognized early in the 20th century, and whose depredations strengthened the case for Federal involvement in national parks in the US in the first place) has been so widely treated differently to other kinds of human activity. As discussed in the next section, tourists were on balance thought useful, and their impacts judged a price worth paying. Tourism was tolerated; hunting and other forms of resource use by local people mostly were not.

The use of force by the state in the defence of PAs is but one example of the wider issue of governance and conservation. Where conservation organizations work in countries with poor human rights and governance records (such as Burma, Graham-Rowe, 2005) there are major ethical issues for conservationists to face: as the journal *Nature* observed, 'a true believer in any cause can ignore uncomfortable facts that conflict with its goals' (*Nature*, 2005, pp. 855). While the importance of issues of governance and corruption is beginning to be acknowledged by conservation practitioners (Smith et al., 2003), interest so far is as much in the ways these limit the effectiveness of conservation as wider issues of rights and justice (Zerner, 2000).

Terborgh (1999) suggests that 'order and discipline' is needed to preserve biodiversity in the 'dysfunctional societies' of many developing countries (p. 192). He extends his argument for stronger governance to call for internationally financed elite forces legally authorized to carry arms and make arrests (Terborgh, 1999). Such forces already exist, outside the control of any state. Clynes (2002) describes the work of non-governmental para-military 'counterpoaching' activities in the Central African Republic, organized by Africa Rainforest and River Conservation specifically to combat commercial Sudanese poaching gangs.[8] Neumann (2004a) argues that there has been a systematic qualitative shift in the level of violence with which biodiversity protection strategies are pursued in Africa, as the moral tension between fear of extinction and respect for human rights tightens. Whatever the balance of rights and wrongs in particular cases, it is clear that, as Brockington (2004) cynically notes, coercion has apparently become a feasible long-term conservation strategy where conservation interests are powerful and local opposition is weak.

The Political Economy of Conservation Benefits

Of course, PAs also bring benefits. Most fundamentally, perhaps, people locally and regionally can benefit through ecosystem services. The Millennium Ecosystem Assessment identified four kinds of service, provisioning services such as food, water, timber and genetic resources; regulating services such as waste treatment or the regulation of climate or flooding; cultural services such as recreation and aesthetic enjoyment; and supporting services such as soil formation, nutrient cycling and plant pollination (World Resources Institute, 2005). It is widely recognized that the presence of habitat in PAs reflects a real, and potentially measurable, contribution to human welfare. The idea of payments for ecosystem services provides a possible mechanism for the conversion if these values into streams of revenue.

The biodiversity and landscape of PAs can also provide the resource for a tourist industry. Local people can receive a share of revenues from tourist fees and from related economic activities (e.g. tourist facilities). Arrangements can include direct employment, land leasing or licensing arrangements, community equity or profit-share schemes, or independent locally owned commercial activities (such as selling curios, food or cultural performances to tourists; McNeely and Miller, 1984; Wells and Brandon, 1992; World Conservation Union, 2005). The idea of parks as the foundation for the development of a tourist industry is long established. In Africa at least, national park advocates pragmatically turned a blind eye to such impacts. They proposed national parks to provide protection from development that might otherwise attract a short-sighted government, for example mining or agriculture (Hingston, 1932). However, by a neat twist of logic, they also argued that national parks provided the basis for economic development, in the form of the tourist industry (Adams, 2004). Tourism, by train and later by motor car, was central to arguments for the development of national parks in the US and Canada (Runte, 1987; Wilson, 1992; McNamee, 1993), and a little later in South Africa (Carruthers, 1995; Brooks, 2005).

Economic benefits are also available to park neighbours if development investment is targeted on 'support zones' around a PA (e.g. Archabald and Naughton-Treves, 2001). However, such benefits are often much smaller than planners predict (Walpole and Thouless, 2005), and many actors in addition to local people demand a share of available funds, including local and national government agencies and departments (Adams and Infield, 2003).

Access to benefits from conservation (such as social investment or development funds, or profit sharing from tourist enterprise) is typically in the hands of employees of the state national park authority. It is subject to rules of eligibility (e.g. formalized membership of a selected community in immediate proximity to the park border) and compliance with a range of regulations. In such arrangements, there is ample room for elite capture of revenues. Paudel (2006) analyses the distributional inequities of conservation programmes in Nepal, even those intended to benefit local people. PA staff such as low-paid manual workers employed in and around PAs may themselves face economic hardships (Sodikoff, 2007).

The illegal extraction of economic benefits from PAs can also be significant. Direct illegal benefits for local communities (or others) come from practices such as hunting, grazing, collecting food or making charcoal. Indirectly, benefits come from corrupt practices associated with the licensing of use or access by state agencies and their employees, or the extraction of illegal rents through granting or overlooking illegal access, or threatening local people with punishment for real or imagined trespass (Brandon et al., 1998; Smith et al., 2003). The conventional strategies to counter such illegal activities are revenue sharing (discussed above), 'community outreach' activities such as education (e.g. Infield and Namara, 2001; Holmes, 2003), and more intense and effective policing. However, outreach activities are notoriously difficult to focus on those who break the law, and rhetoric is a poor counter to hunger and grievance against injustice. Persuasion of itself does little to outweigh economic incentives to break the law: poaching clearly often pays (Milner-Gulland and Leader-Williams, 1992). The cost of intense policing can be large (Leader-Williams and Albon, 1988), and the exercise of arbitrary power by conservation agencies is deeply problematic (Neumann, 2004a).

The creation of PAs generates a stream of legal and illegal benefits but both tend to reproduce existing economic inequalities within local communities and wider society (Paudel, 2006). There is no reason to expect illegal revenues to be any more equitably distributed than those that are legal, since capacity to hunt and willingness to bear risks vary between and within households. There is also inequality in the less tangible benefits of the existence value of the species and habitats preserved in PAs. A crude distributional logic applies to these benefits, for while in theory they are available to local people, in practice they are chiefly appropriated by remote and relatively wealthy wildlife lovers in developed countries (and to a lesser extent local urban elites), both through surrogate knowledge about species survival and through direct tourist experiences. These beneficiaries provide, of course, the funding for international conservation organizations that advocate the establishment of PAs. Thus the costs of PAs are mostly borne locally, while benefits accrue globally (Balmford and Whitten, 2003). It is widely argued within conservation that where people living with PAs face economic costs due to the park, they should clearly be fully compensated (Adams and McShane, 1992; Tacconi and Bennett, 1995; James et al., 1999). Logically, revenue for this purpose needs to be derived in some way from those who enjoy the wider global benefits of parks (Balmford and Whitten, 2003). Some argue that payments for ecosystem services may provide a mechanism for such funding, but the necessary institutions have not yet been developed on anything but an experimental scale.

Despite the hopeful rhetoric of the 2003 World Parks Congress in Durban about new ways of understanding and managing national parks, for example its recommendation that all involuntary resettlement and expulsions of indigenous peoples from their lands for protected areas cease, population displacement and injustice are still a feature of many protected areas in the developing world (Dowie, 2005).[9] The emphasis of political ecology on the links between political economy and the actual state of the environment offers some potential to open dialogue between social science-trained critics of conservation and natural science-trained advocates. Communication across that divide is critical if policy is to be made equitable and effective, and if conservationists and their critics are ever to join forces to address, explain and engage the structures and processes driving the social and environmental changes they regard as deleterious. Conservation biologists are being urged to seek to break down their traditional conceptual distinctions between humans and nature (Folke, 2006). Such ideas offer some promise of a future for conservation planning that moves beyond exclusion to imagine a conceptual and material place for human society within, and not outside, nature.

Notes

1 www.africanparks-conservation.com (accessed 30 November 2009). The African Parks Network is registered as a not-for-profit organization in terms of Section 21 of the Companies Act of South Africa. It was founded in 2000 in South Africa, and shifted its legislative base and Head Office to the Netherlands in 2004, and back to South Africa in 2007. The Board of The African Parks Network is supported by affiliate organizations, Stichting African Parks Foundation, Netherlands, African Parks Foundation of America and African Parks Foundation (UK); www.african-parks.org/apffoundation/index.php?option=com_content&task=view&id=37&Itemid=75 (accessed 30 November 2009). The African Parks Network withdrew from management of Nech Sar National Park in October 2008.

2 Refugees International; www.refugeesinternational.org, and Survival International; http://survival-international.org, see also www.iucn.org/themes/ceesp/alert.htm (29 November 2005).

3 www.survival-international.org/news.php?id=2128, accessed 14 December 2006. The identity 'bushmen' is highly complex (Suzman, 2000).

4 There is no universal term for the things that conservationists wish to protect. In this paper 'nature' is used to refer to all non-human life and the physical contexts in which they exist. The term 'biodiversity' is widely used but problematic (Takacs, 1996), as is the term 'wildlife'.

5   www.africanparks-conservation.com/peopleparks_localprotect.html (31 October 2005).
6   Leading this exploration is the Social Science Working Group of the Society for Conservation Biology, www.conbio.org/workinggroups/SSWG/Activities.CFM (accessed 30 November 2009).
7   See the World Bank's 2004 Operation Policy 4.12: http://wbln0018.worldbank.org/Institutional/Manuals/OpManual.nsf/0/CA2D01A4D1BDF58085256B19008197F6?OpenDocument #foot (2 November 2005).
8   www.africa-rainforest.org/expeditions.html, 24 October 2004.
9   IUCN's 'Theme on Indigenous and Local Communities, Equity, and Protected Areas' (TILCEPA), led discussion of communities, equity and protected areas at the Durban Congress in 2003, and continues to seek to open up debate on these issues, www.tilcepa.org/ (accessed 30 November 2009).

References

Adams, J.S. and McShane, T.O. (1992) *The Myth of Wild Africa: Conservation Without Illusion*, W.W. Norton and Co., New York.

Adams, W.M. (2004) *Against Extinction: The Story of Conservation*, Earthscan, London.

Adams, W.M. and Hulme, D. (2001) Conservation and communities: Changing narratives, policies and practices in African conservation, pp. 9–23, in Hulme, D. and Murphree, M. (eds) *African Wildlife and Livelihoods: The Promise and Performance of Community Conservation,* James Currey, London.

Adams, W.M. and Hutton, J. (2007) 'People, parks and poverty: Political ecology and biodiversity conservation', *Conservation and Society,* 5(2): 147–183.

Adams, W.M. and Infield, M. (2003) 'Who is on the gorilla's payroll? Claims on tourist revenue from a Ugandan National Park', *World Development,* 31: 177–190.

Adams, W.M., Aveling, R., Brockington, D., Dickson, B., Elliott, J., Hutton, J., Roe, D., Vira, B. and Wolmer, W. (2004) 'Biodiversity conservation and the eradication of poverty', *Science,* 306: 1146–1149

Agrawal, A. and Redford, K. (2006) *Poverty, Development, and Biodiversity Conservation: Shooting in the Dark?,* Wildlife Conservation Society, New York (WCS Working Paper 26).

Agrawal, A. and Redford, K. (2007) Conservation and displacement: An overview, pp. 4–15, in Redford, K.H. and Fearn, E. (eds) *Protected Areas and Human Displacement: A Conservation Perspective,* Wildlife Conservation Society, New York (Working Paper No. 29).

Archabald, K. and Naughton-Treves, L. (2001) 'Tourism revenue-sharing around national parks in Western Uganda: Early efforts to identify and reward local communities', *Environmental Conservation,* 28: 135–149.

Balmford, A. and Whitten, T. (2003) 'Who should pay for tropical conservation, and how could the costs be met?', *Oryx,* 37: 238–250.

Brandon, K., Redford, K.H. and Sanderson, S.E. (1998) *Parks in Peril: People, Politics and Protected Areas*, Island Press, for the Nature Conservancy, Washington, DC.

Brechin S.R., Wilhusen, P.R., Fortwangler, C.L. and West, P.C. (eds) (2003) *Contested Nature: Promoting International Biodiversity with Social Justice in the Twenty-First Century*, State University of New York Press, New York.

Brockington, D. (2002) *Fortress Conservation: The Preservation of the Mkomazi Game Reserve, Tanzania,* James Currey, Oxford.

Brockington, D. (2004) 'Community conservation, inequality and injustice: Myths of power in protected area management', *Conservation and Society,* 2: 411–432.

Brockington, D. and Igoe, J. (2006) 'Eviction for conservation: A global overview', *Conservation and Society*, 4: 424–470.

Brooks, S. (2005) 'Images of 'Wild Africa': Nature tourism and the (re)creation of Hluhluwe Game Reserve, 1930–1945', *Journal of Historical Geography*, 31: 220–249.

Brosius, J.P. (1999a) 'Anthropological engagements with environmentalism', *Current Anthropology*, 40: 27–309.

Brosius, J.P. (1999b) 'Green dots, pink hearts: displacing politics from the Malaysian rain forest', *American Anthropologist*, 101: 36–57.

Brosius, J.P. (2006) 'Common ground between anthropology and conservation biology', *Conservation Biology*, 20: 683–685.

Bryant, R.L. (2002) 'Non-governmental organizations and governmentality: 'Consuming' biodiversity and indigenous people in the Philippines', *Political Studies*, 50: 268–292.

Campbell, L.M. (2005) 'Overcoming obstacles to interdisciplinary research', *Conservation Biology*, 19: 574–577.

Carruthers, J. (1995) *The Kruger National Park: A Social and Political History*, Natal University Press, Durban.

Cernea, M.M. (1997) 'The risks and reconstruction model for resettling displaced populations', *World Development*, 25: 1569–1589.

Cernea, M.M. (2006) 'Population displacement inside protected areas: A redefinition of concepts in conservation politics', *Policy Matters*, 14: 8–26.

Cernea, M.M. and McDowell, C. (eds) (2000) *Risks and Reconstruction Experiences of Resettlers and Refugees*, World Bank, Washington, DC.

Cernea, M.M. and Schmidt-Soltau, K. (2003) 'The end of forcible displacement? Conservation must not impoverish people', *Policy Matters*, 12: 42–51.

Cernea, M.M. and Schmidt-Soltau, K. (2006) 'Poverty risks and national parks: Policy issues in conservation and resettlement', *World Development*, 34: 1808–1830.

Chapin, M. (2004) 'A challenge to conservationists', *World Watch*, 17(6): 17–31.

Chatty, D. and M. Colchester (eds) (2002) *Conservation and Mobile Indigenous Peoples: Displacement, Forced Resettlement and Sustainable Development*, Berghahn Press, New York.

Clynes, T. (2002) 'They shoot poachers, don't they?', *Observer Magazine*, 24 November, pp. 34–47.

Colchester, M. (2002) *Salvaging Nature: Indigenous Peoples, Protected Areas and Biodiversity Conservation*, World Rainforest Movement, Montevideo.

Dowie, M. (2005) 'Conservation refugees: When protecting nature means kicking people out', *Orion* November/December, www.orionmagazine.org/index.php/articles/article/161/ (accessed 30 November 2009)

Emerton, L. (2001) 'The nature of benefits and the benefits of nature: Why wildlife conservation has not economically benefited communities in Africa', pp. 208–226, in Hulme, D. and Murphree, M. (eds) *African Wildlife and Livelihoods: The Promise and Performance of Community Conservation*, James Currey, London.

Fairhead, J. and Leach, M. (2000) 'The nature lords', *Times Literary Supplement*, 5 May, pp. 3–4.

Fairhead, J. and Leach M. (2003) *Science, Society and Power: Environmental Knowledge and Policy in West Africa and the Caribbean*, Cambridge University Press, Cambridge.

Feeny, P. (1999) *Accountable Aid: Local Participation in Major Projects*, Oxfam, Oxford.

Folke, C. (2006) 'The economic perspective; conservation against development versus conservation for development', *Conservation Biology*, 20: 686–688

Geisler, C. (2003) 'A new kind of trouble: Evictions in Eden', *International Social Science Journal*, 55: 67–78.

Geisler, C. and de Sousa, R. (2001) 'From refuge to refugee: The African case', *Public Administration and Development*, 21: 159–170.

Graham-Rowe, D. (2005) 'Under the gun', *Nature*, 435: 870–872.

Hecht, S.B., Kandel, S., Gomes, I., Cuellar, N. and Rosa, H. (2006) 'Globalization, forest resurgence and environmental politics in El Salvador', *World Development,* 34: 308–323.

Heine, B. (1985) 'The mountain people: The Ik of north-eastern Uganda', *Africa,* 55: 3–16.

Hingston, R.W.G. (1932) 'Proposed British national parks for Africa', *Geographical Journal,* 76: 1–24.

Holmes, C.M. (2003) 'The influence of protected area outreach on conservation attitudes and resource use patterns: A case study from western Tanzania', *Oryx,* 37: 305–315.

Howarth, D. (1961) *The Shadow of the Dam,* Collins, London.

Igoe, J. (2006) 'Measuring the costs and benefits of conservation to local communities', *Journal of Ecological Anthropology,* 10: 72–77.

Infield, M. and Namara, A. (2001) 'Community attitudes and behaviour towards conservation: An assessment of a community conservation programme around Lake Mburo National Park, Uganda', *Oryx,* 35: 48–60.

James, A.N., Gaston, K.J. and Balmford, A. (1999) 'Balancing the Earth's accounts', *Nature,* 401, 323–324.

Kaimowitz, D., Faure, A. and Mendoza, R. (2003) 'Your biosphere is my backyard: The story of Bosowas in Nicaragua', *Policy Matters,* 12: 6–15.

Kremen, C., Niles, J.O., Dalton, M.G., et al. (2000) 'Economic incentives for rain forest conservation across scales', *Science,* 288: 1828–1832.

Leader-Williams, N. and Albon, S.D. (1988) 'Allocation of resources for conservation', *Nature,* 336: 533–535.

Leakey, R. and Morell, V. (2001) *Wildlife Wars: My Battle to Save Kenya's Elephants,* MacMillan, London.

Lyons, M. (1985) 'From "death camps" to *cordon sanitaire*: The development of sleeping sickness policy in the Uele District of the Belgian Congo, 1903–1914', *Journal of African History,* 26: 69–91.

Maisels, F., Sunderland, T., Curran, B., et al. (2007) 'Central Africa's protected areas and the purported displacement of people: A first critical review of existing data', pp. 75–89, in Redford, K.H. and Fearn, E. (eds) *Protected Areas and Human Displacement: A Conservation Perspective,* Wildlife Conservation Society, New York (Working Paper No. 29).

Mascia, M.B., Brosius, J.P., Dobson, T., Forbes, B.C., Horowitz, L., McKean, M.A. and Turner, N.J. (2003) 'Conservation and the social sciences', *Conservation Biology,* 17: 649–650.

McElwee, P.D. (2006) 'Displacement and relocation redux: Stories from southeast Asia', *Conservation and Society,* 4: 396–403.

McGregor, J. (2005) 'Living with the river: Landscape and memory in the Zambezi Valley, Northwest Zimbabwe', pp. 87–105, in Beinart, W. and McGregor, J. (eds), *Social History and African Environments,* James Currey, Oxford.

McNamee, K. (1993) 'From wild places to endangered spaces: A history of Canadian national parks', pp. 17–44, Dearden, P. and Rollins, R. (eds) *Parks and Protected Areas in Canada: Planning and Management* Oxford University Press, Toronto.

McNeeley, J.A. (1993) 'Economic incentives for conserving biodiversity: Lessons for Africa', *Ambio,* 22: 144–150.

McNeely, J.A. and Miller, K.R. (eds) (1984) *National Parks, Conservation and Development: The Role of Protected Areas in Sustaining Society,* Smithsonian Institute Press, Washington, DC.

Milner-Gulland, E.J. and Leader-Williams, N. (1992) 'A model of incentives for the illegal exploitation of black rhinos and elephants: Poaching pays in Luangwa Valley, Zambia', *Journal of Applied Ecology,* 29: 388–401.

Nature (2005) 'Save the people too: Conservationists must pay attention to the needs of local human, as well as animal, populations', *Nature,* 435: 855–856.

Naughton-Treves, L. (1997) 'Farming the forest edge: Vulnerable places and people around Kibale National Park, Uganda', *The Geographical Review,* 87: 27–46.

Neumann, R.P. (1992) 'The political ecology of wildlife conservation in the Mount Meru area, north-east Tanzania', *Land Degradation and Rehabilitation*, 3: 85–98.

Neumann, R.P. (1998) *Imposing Wilderness: Struggles Over Livelihood and Nature Preservation in Africa*, University of California Press, Berkeley.

Neumann, R.P. (2001) 'Africa's "last wilderness": Reordering space for political and economic control in colonial Tanzania', *Africa*, 71: 641–665.

Neumann, R.P. (2004a) 'Moral and discursive geographies in the war for biodiversity in Africa', *Political Geography*, 23: 813–37.

Neumann, R.P. (2004b) *Making Political Ecology*, Hodder Arnold, London.

Norton-Griffiths, M. and Southey, C. (1995) 'The opportunity costs of biodiversity conservation in Kenya', *Ecological Economics*, 12: 125–139.

O'Riordan, T. and Stoll-Kleeman, S. (eds) (2002) *Biodiversity, Sustainability and Human Communities: Protecting Beyond the Protected*, Cambridge University Press, Cambridge.

Parker, I. (2004) *What I Tell You Three Times Is True: Conservation, Ivory, History and Politics*, Librario, Elgin.

Paudel, N.S. (2006) 'Protected areas and the reproduction of social inequality', *Policy Matters*, 14: 155–169.

Pearce, F. (2005) 'Humans losing out to Africa's big game industry', *New Scientist*, 2495, 21.

Peet, R. and Watts, M. (eds) (2004) *Liberation Ecologies: Environment, Development, Social Movements*, Routledge, London.

Peluso, N. (1993) 'Coercing conservation: The politics of state resource control', *Global Environmental Change*, 3: 199–217.

Rangarajan, M. and Shahabuddin, G. (2006) 'Displacement and relocation from protected areas: Towards a biological and historical synthesis', *Conservation and Society*, 4: 359–378.

Ranger, T. (1999) *Voices from the Rocks: Nature, Culture and History in the Matopos Hills of Zimbabwe*, James Currey, Oxford.

Robbins, P. (2004) *Political Ecology: A Critical Introduction*, Blackwell, Oxford.

Runte, A. (1987) *National Parks: The American Experience*, University of Nebraska Press, Lincoln.

Schroeder, R.A. (1999) 'Geographies of environmental intervention in Africa', *Progress in Human Geography*, 23: 359–378.

Scudder, T. (1993) 'Development-induced relocation and refugee studies: 37 years of continuity among Zambia's Gwembe Tonga', *Journal of Refugee Studies*, 6: 123–152.

Scudder, T. (2005) *The Future of Large dams: Dealing with the Social, Environmental and Political Costs*, Earthscan, London.

Sekhar, N.U. (1998) 'Crop and livestock depredation caused by wild animals in protected areas: The case of Sariska Tiger Reserve, Rajasthan, India', *Environmental Conservation*, 25: 160–171.

Smith, R., Muir, R., Walpole, M., Balmford, A. and Leader-Williams, N. (2003) 'Governance and the loss of biodiversity', *Nature*, 426: 67–70.

Sodikoff, G. (2007) 'An exceptional strike: A micro-history of "people versus park" in Madagascar', *Journal of Political Ecology*, 14: 10–33.

Stott, P. and Sullivan, S. (eds) (2000) *Political Ecology: Science, Myth and Power*, Arnold, London.

Tacconi, L. and Bennett, J. (1995) 'Biodiversity conservation: The process of economic assessment and establishment of a protected area in Vanuatu', *Development and Change*, 26: 89–110.

Terborgh, J. (1999) *Requiem for Nature*, Island Press, Washington, DC.

Thornhill, A. (2003) 'Social scientists and conservation biologists join forces', *Conservation Biology*, 17: 1476.

Turnbull, C. (1974) *The Mountain People*, Pan Books, London.

Walpole, M.J. and Thouless, C.R. (2005) 'Increasing the value of wildlife though nonconsumptive use: Deconstructing the myths of ecotourism and community-based tourism in the tropics', pp. 122–139, in Woodroffe, R., Thirgood, S. and Rabinowitz, A. (eds) *People and Wildlife: Conflict or Coexistence?* Cambridge University Press, Cambridge.

Wells, M. and Brandon, K. (1992) *People and Parks: Linking Protected Areas with Local Communities*, World Bank, Washington, DC.

West, P. and Brechin, S.R. (1991) *Resident People and National Parks: Social Dimensions in International Conservation*, University of Arizona Press, Tucson.

Wilson, A. (1992) *The Culture of Nature: North American Landscape from Disney to Exxon Valdez*, Blackwell, Oxford.

Woodroffe, R., Thirgood, S. and Rabinowitz, A. (eds) (2005) *People and Wildlife: Conflict or Coexistence?* Cambridge University Press, Cambridge.

World Conservation Union – IUCN (2005) *Benefits Beyond Boundaries. Proceedings of the Fifth World Parks Congress*, World Conservation Union, Cambridge, UK.

World Resources Institute (ed) (2005) *Ecosystems and Human Well-being: Synthesis Report* (Millennium Ecosystem Assessment), Island Press, Washington, DC.

Zerner, C. (2000) 'Toward a broader vision of justice and nature conservation', pp. 3–20, in Zerner, C. (ed) *People, Plants and Justice: The Politics of Nature Conservation*, Columbia University Press, New York.

Zimmerer, K.S. and Bassett, T.J. (eds) (2003) *Political Ecology: An Integrative Approach to Geography and Environment-Development Studies*, Guilford, New York.

Chapter 18

A Property Rights Approach to Understanding Human Displacement from Protected Areas: The Case of Marine Protected Areas

Michael B. Mascia and C. Anne Claus

Introduction

In recent years scholars have increasingly examined conservation interventions as both a vehicle for sustainable social development and as a source of social costs (e.g. Newing and Wahl, 2004; Agrawal and Redford, 2006; Wilkie et al., 2006). Of particular interest are the positive and negative social impacts of national parks and other types of protected areas (PAs), the cornerstone of most biodiversity conservation strategies (Colchester, 1997; Stevens, 1997; Brechin et al., 2003). The physical, economic and sociocultural displacement of local peoples from PAs has generated especially intense discussion in the academic literature (e.g. Brechin et al., 2003; Brosius, 2004; Agrawal and Redford, 2007) and popular press (Chapin, 2004; Dowie, 2005; Paddock, 2006), as scholars and others have debated the concept of 'displacement' (Cernea and Schmidt-Soltau, 2006; Schmidt-Soltau and Brockington, 2007), its extent and magnitude (Cernea, 2000; Schmidt-Soltau, 2005; Cernea and Schmidt-Soltau, 2006), and its moral or ethical appropriateness (West and Brechin, 1991; Brockington, 1999).

Differing in size, scope and objectives, PAs are socially constructed sets of rules that collectively govern human interactions within a specified area and, thus, allocate access to and use of natural resources among stakeholders (Mascia, 2004). Because PAs allocate access to natural resources – and the economic wealth associated with these resources – it is not surprising that PA development, management and reform are politically and socially contentious (Blaustien, 2007). To foster greater precision and clarity in academic discussions and public policy-making, we used a conceptual framework from the political economy literature (Schlager and Ostrom, 1992) to examine different forms of human displacement from PAs. Using marine protected areas (MPAs) as an example, we explored the impact of PA establishment on resource rights and discuss how the reallocation of rights to PA resources directly and indirectly manifests itself in different social domains, across time, in space, and among groups.

Conceptualizing Displacement

Displacement has been defined in various ways by different authors. For some authors, displacement includes physical, economic and social exclusion (Cernea, 2000), whereas others view displacement as the product of physical exclusion, a phenomenon conceptually and morally distinct from the loss of economic or resource use rights (Agrawal and Redford, 2007). The concept of 'displacement', however, focuses on just one side of the coin (the excluded). To understand the full empirical and ethical dimensions of PA displacement, it is critical to consider the disempowered who lose rights and the empowered who gain rights. Examining the empowered and the disempowered provides insights into issues of power, equity and justice. Are the powerful gaining additional rights? Are empowered actors more marginal or impoverished than disempowered actors? Through the loss of some rights, are others gained?

Focusing on rights reallocation, rather than displacement, also allows one to differentiate between the process through which PA rights are reallocated and the substantive impacts of this reallocation. The structure of decision-making processes has a major impact on how rights are reallocated – and to whom (Ostrom, 1990). Focusing on the process through which protected-area rights are reallocated allows one to better identify illegitimate decision-making processes (which may have either positive or negative substantive impacts) and to design appropriate procedural reforms. Discussion of procedural aspects of PA decision-making processes has focused on stakeholder participation and free, prior informed consent (McNeely, 1999; Dearden et al., 2005; Lepp and Holland, 2006). Procedural justice, however, is distinct from substantive justice (Stone, 1988). Accordingly, we focused on the substantive impacts of MPA rights reallocation, which enabled us to characterize the types of social impacts that follow the emergence and evolution of MPAs (which may be the product of either legitimate or illegitimate decision-making processes). Rigorous study of the substantive social impacts of PA rights reallocation provides the basis for decision-makers to develop appropriate policy responses to these complex issues.

MPA Establishment and Rights Reallocation

Property rights are 'social institutions that define or delimit the range of privileges granted to individuals' regarding specific assets or resources (Libecap, 1989, p. 1). Like all PAs, MPAs reallocate pre-existing rights governing resource access and use. Singly or in bundles, these rights may be held by a lone individual, shared by a group, or held collectively by multiple groups (e.g. user groups, communities, government agencies, and non-governmental organizations). Rights may occur at any spatial scale, from local to global, and may have a mix of formal and informal components with written and unwritten origins (e.g. legal statutes, policy statements, organizational practices, social norms, cultural traditions; Libecap, 1989). As a result, the de facto rights that are actually affected by MPA establishment often differ from the pre-existing de jure rights outlined in formal legal documents (Mascia, 2004). Legally designated MPAs may formalize or invalidate pre-existing de facto rights, thus reinforcing or undermining pre-existing privileges. The social impacts of MPA establishment are mediated by this pre-existing structure of resource rights, as well as other pre-existing social and ecological conditions.

All forms of 'displacement' involve reallocation of property rights, but the specific types of rights created, lost, secured and gained dramatically shape the magnitude, extent and distribution of social impacts. (Hereafter, we use the term reallocation to encompass the formation of entirely new rights; the reaffirmation or securing of existing rights; and the restructuring of existing rights.) The most basic property rights that an individual may hold are the rights of access (Schlager and Ostrom, 1992). *Access rights* determine who may enter a defined area and who is eligible to exploit a specific resource. Access rights may be conferred by birth (e.g. citizenship), social relations (e.g. family member), geography (e.g. local resident), or contract (e.g. fishing licence). In Bonaire, Netherlands Antilles, for example, only those scuba divers and scuba tourism companies who pay an access fee are permitted to enter the Bonaire Marine Park (Dixon et al., 1993). Reallocation of rights regarding who may enter an MPA and exploit its resources may have significant social impacts, particularly for individuals living in or adjacent to MPAs. Loss of access rights may disrupt livelihood strategies, weaken social relationships among communities, and diminish sense of place (i.e. memory, history and myth associated with location; Fortwangler and Stern, 2004, p. 158). Conversely, restricting access to a certain number or type of individuals (e.g. local residents) may sustain cultural traditions or enhance subsistence or other forms of resource use and exploitation.

Withdrawal rights govern the appropriation of goods or resources generated by a natural or human-made resource system (Schlager and Ostrom, 1992). Withdrawal rights, therefore, define what resources may be exploited, and when, where and how individuals with access rights may exercise these rights and engage in consumptive (e.g. fishing) and non-consumptive (e.g. scuba diving) forms of resource use. In MPAs and other natural resource systems, reallocation of withdrawal rights may have significant economic and social ramifications – particularly in resource-dependent communities. In the Philippines, for example, establishment of an MPA in Mabini created economic opportunities for tourist boat operators and restricted fishing to designated zones (Oracion et al., 2005). Researchers have documented both positive and negative impacts of MPA reallocation of withdrawal rights on patterns of subsistence and commercial resource use (Ngugi, 2001; Hoffman, 2002), traditional lifestyles (Fortwangler and Stern, 2004; Gelcich et al., 2005), and cultural identity (Oracion et al., 2005). Collectively, access and withdrawal rights are known as *use rights*.

Management rights are the rights to regulate resource withdrawal and to 'transform the resource by making improvements' (Schlager and Ostrom, 1992, p. 251). Thus, management rights confer the authority to determine what MPA resources may be exploited and when, where, and how such exploitation may occur. In countries with state-managed marine resources, the establishment of collaboratively managed and community-based MPAs, for example, represents the partial (collaboratively managed) or complete (community-based) transfer of state-held management rights to local resource users. Devolution of management rights in the Moheli Marine Park (Comoros Islands), for example, led the local community to restrict certain types of fishing gear (Granek and Brown, 2005). Significantly, management rights also include the rights to control resource transformation and improvement. In the case of MPAs, this includes, for example, installing mooring buoys to prevent boat anchor damage (e.g. US Virgin Islands National Park; Marion and Rogers, 1994) and adding fish-aggregating devices to enhance fish catches (e.g. Kakuma, 2004). Recent trends toward decentralization and devolution of marine-resource management rights, often in the form of MPAs (Johannes, 2002), have reversed a centuries-old pattern of state appropriation of marine resource management rights from resource users (Johannes, 1978; Ruddle, 1996).

Exclusion rights, as the name suggests, confer the authority to exclude individuals from entering a defined space or exploiting a specific resource (i.e. restrict access rights, Schlager and Ostrom, 1992). Thus, although MPA management rights confer the ability to shape what MPA resources are exploited when, where and how, exclusion rights confer the ability to determine who may engage in consumptive and non-consumptive resource exploitation. In community-based and co-managed MPAs, local resource users ('insiders') with exclusion rights may prevent 'outsiders' (e.g. non-local fishers) from entering the MPA for any kind of resource use (e.g. Apo Islands and Philippines; Russ and Alcala, 1999) or require non-locals to obtain a licence or permit for entry (for which a fee is often required, e.g. Hol Chan Marine Reserve; Mascia, 2000). These preferential resource use rights grant local users a greater share of MPA benefits and may reduce local rates of resource exploitation and create incentives for more sustainable patterns of resource withdrawal. Loss of exclusion rights, by contrast, transfers significant aspects of control over resource use to new rights-holders; the resultant impacts on

MPA resources and resource users depend on how these new rights-holders exercise their authority.

Alienation rights are the rights to transfer resource management and exclusion rights to another actor (Schlager and Ostrom, 1992). The state generally holds alienation rights to MPA resources, but alienation rights may be held by other actors or transferred as part of MPA establishment. In MPAs with terrestrial components, for example, local residents may hold rights of alienation to the land on which they live, enabling them to sell or lease it to others. Similarly, fishers and other resource users may be entitled to transfer the right to manage resources and exclude others from marine territories or other marine resources. In Melanesia and elsewhere, communities or kin-based groups often hold alienation rights over specific coral reefs or other defined features of the marine environment, which they may sell, lease or rent to others (Akimichi and Ruddle, 1984; Ruddle, 1996). In Belize, establishment of the Hol Chan Marine Reserve resulted in the reconfiguration of alienation rights; the authority to transfer lagoon fishing rights shifted from local fishers ('owners' of fishing territory) to the co-managed MPA authority, which subsequently restricted the transfer of fishing rights to intra-familial transfers only (Mascia, 2000).

Marine protected areas often reallocate bundles of these five types of rights. In Australia, for example, establishment of the Lord Howe Island Marine Park reallocated access and withdrawal rights: who could enter (residents), the type of gear that entrants could use (drop lines), and what entrants could do with their catch (consumption allowed only on the island, Bishop et al., 2004). In the Philippines, MPAs reallocated management, withdrawal and use rights by involving local stakeholders in some management decisions (i.e. how the MPA would be used) and subsequently reshaping rules governing consumptive (seasonal restrictions on shellfish gathering) and non-consumptive (dive operations) activities (Oracion et al., 2005). Establishment of the Moheli Marine Park in the Comoros Islands led to significant reallocation of management rights; local guards now monitor and enforce the decisions of local communities regarding withdrawal rights (e.g. location and method of extraction) and access rights (no motorized boats; Granek and Brown, 2005). The reinstitution of Ra'ui on Rarotonga similarly reallocated some management rights (community meetings determined what uses would be allowed) and withdrawal rights (all consumptive uses banned for months to years, particular recreation uses allowed; Hoffman, 2002). In some cases, reallocation of exclusion and management rights does not affect withdrawal or access rights. Establishment of the Marine Extractive Reserve of Arraial do Cabo, Brazil, led to reconfiguration of decision-making arrangements without substantively changing resource use (Pinto da Silva, 2004). By contrast, establishment of the Hol Chan Marine Reserve restructured the full set of property rights (alienation to access) governing local marine resources (Mascia, 2000).

Ripple Effects of MPA Rights Reallocation

Marine protected areas rights reallocation may affect the governance, economic well-being, health, education, social capital, and culture of resource users, local communities, and other social groups (Table 18.1; Mascia, 2004). As many have noted, MPA establishment may have negative impacts on those individuals and groups losing ownership and use rights, whereas those gaining corresponding rights may benefit accordingly (Mascia, 2004). By reallocating rights to land, water and living resources, MPAs may affect resource control and other elements of governance (e.g. conflict-resolution mechanisms, gender roles in decision making,

Table 18.1 *Potential direct and indirect social costs and benefits of MPA rights reallocation*

Governance
- decreased/increased resource control
- property lost*/gained
- use rights lost/gained
- conflict resolution mechanisms weakened/strengthened

Economic well-being
- employment lost*/gained
- income lost*/gained
- assets lost*/gained
- consumption reduced/increased

Health
- health diminished*/enhanced
- food availability reduced*/increased
- nutritional status diminished/enhanced
- psychological well-being diminished/enhanced
- health services reduced/increased

Education
- public services lost*/gained
- human capital lost*/gained
- education opportunities lost/gained

Social capital
- social networks degraded*/increased
- social status lost*/gained
- partnerships/alliances lost/increased
- trust lost/gained

Culture
- cultural space lost*/gained
- local knowledge lost/gained
- sense of place diminished/enhanced
- norms and values undermined/reinforced

Note: * Highlighted by Cernea's (2000) framework of physical displacement risks.
Source: M.B.M. and A. Khurshid, unpublished data

and engagement in broader political processes). Reallocation of resource rights may also affect aspects of economic well-being, including employment, income, consumption, and natural and material assets (Ngugi, 2001). Changes in food security may be considered either a wealth or a health effect of MPAs. Other health effects may include shifts in nutrition, morbidity and mortality (Gjertsen, 2005). These economic and health effects may, in turn, shape rates of school enrolment and other educational variables. Less tangible (but no less important) effects of MPAs on social capital and culture may include shifts in trust, partnerships and alliances, identity, and sense of place.

The impacts of reallocating rights to MPA resources vary within and among social groups, often creating winners and losers. Actors engaged in extraction of non-renewable marine resources, such as coral mining, often see these rights severely restricted within the MPA. Land-based activities that affect the adjacent marine environment, such as farming and forestry (through runoff of sediment and other pollutants), are sometimes also restricted as part of MPA establishment. The benefits of these restrictions accrue to actors engaged in other MPA activities, such as fishing, scuba diving, scientific research, and other commercial and recreational activities (Mascia, 2000). No-take MPAs prohibit all forms of fishing, often creating new economic opportunities for individuals engaged in dive tourism and other forms of non-extractive resource use (Vogt, 1997). Marine protected areas sometimes also limit non-consumptive uses, such as dive tourism and research, which transfers benefits to fishers and other extractive users (Roberts et al., 2001). These changes in use rights and patterns of resource use among groups are shaped by the reconfiguration of ownership rights associated with MPA establishment.

Establishment of MPAs also commonly results in the reallocation of use rights among subgroups. In some instances MPAs limit certain modes of resource use (e.g. fishing), which transfers the benefits of resource extraction from one specialist group to another (e.g. fishers using nets vs. spear guns) (Goodridge et al., 1996). In other cases, rights are transferred from one community to another (e.g. local fishers often establish MPAs to exclude non-locals from fishing in their waters) (Russ and Alcala, 1999). Spatial zoning is used in MPAs to restructure patterns of resource use, often as a means of reducing conflict among groups and subgroups of resource users (Pomeroy et al., 2007). This reallocation of resource rights and benefits may induce broader positive and negative shifts in economic well-being, health, education and culture, which often vary in accordance with not only specific modes of resource use (e.g. occupation) and community of residence but also with gender, class, religion, and age (Mascia, 2004). In many instances MPA establishment will have mixed impacts on a particular group or subgroup (e.g. net fishers experience both increased income and loss of cultural identity).

Rights reallocation in MPAs may also have secondary social impacts, although these are even more poorly understood and documented than the most immediate social impacts of MPAs. Users whose rights are restricted within an MPA may migrate to exploit natural resources in adjacent areas, creating new social challenges (e.g. resource conflict) and opportunities (e.g. novel management practices) for existing resource users and others in these new host communities. Simultaneous with this out-migration, those who gain rights may physically migrate to an MPA to take advantage of new opportunities, which induces change in their communities of origin and creates new challenges and opportunities in the MPA community. Successive ripple effects, presumably weaker and more diffuse, play out in successive resource-user groups and associated communities. The social impact of these ripple effects depends on the diversity, complexity and dynamics of the social and ecological systems and vulnerability of these systems (Jentoft et al., 2007).

Marine protected areas not only reshape resource governance and patterns of resource use but, through these processes, they also induce changes in the resource system itself. Limiting consumptive resource use within MPAs generally leads to increases in the populations of fish and other species targeted by fishers (Halpern and Warner, 2002; Halpern, 2003). As these target populations increase within the MPA, adult organisms and their offspring may spill over into adjacent waters outside the MPA. Such an export of fishery resources may compensate for the loss of fishing access within the MPA through increased catches in adjacent waters (Alcala and Russ, 1990; Russ et al., 2004; but see McClanahan and Kaunda-Arara, 1996). These ecological dynamics occur across oceanographically connected seascapes tens to hundreds of kilometres wide, but become more diffuse at increasing distances from the MPA (Sala et al., 2002; Shanks et al., 2003). The positive externalities generated through this MPA dynamic may create incentives for resource users to restrict their own behavior. (Although MPA biological success and subsequent spill-over may create incentives for resource users to restrict use and to comply with rules, the biological success of terrestrial PAs may create negative externalities [e.g. spill-over of crop-raiding wildlife] that encourage exploitation within the PA and, thus, limit spill-over and conservation effectiveness.) Research suggests that the initial biological benefits of MPAs appear within several months after MPA establishment (Halpern and Warner, 2002), although it may take several years or longer for the full benefits to accrue (Roberts et al., 2001; Ward et al., 2001; Galal et al., 2002).

Management Implications

The rights reallocation framework outlined here provides scholars and practitioners with the starting point for rigorously assessing and addressing the substantive social impacts of PA establishment. Such a process might include the following steps:

- identify discrete groups and subgroups whose resource rights are affected by PA establishment (e.g. non-local net fishers);

- characterize the reallocation of resource rights associated with PA establishment for each of these groups and subgroups (e.g. gain or loss of management and withdrawal rights to pelagic fish);
- assess the impact of PA-induced rights reallocation on specific elements of governance, economic well-being, health, education, social capital, and culture for each of these distinct groups and subgroups (e.g. increased or decreased resource control, food security, and viability of traditional way of life);
- examine trade-offs and synergies among social impacts for any single subgroup or group and the distributive impact of PA establishment among subgroups and groups;
- identify and implement contextually appropriate actions to address the social impacts on the basis of management goals, social norms, legal standards, and available policy instruments.

This assessment process can be conducted prior to PA establishment (as part of a traditional pre-project environmental- or social-impact assessment process) or at any time after establishment (as part of a monitoring and evaluation programme).

Conclusion

Human displacement from PAs touches on numerous conceptually distinct and socially charged issues. Effective resolution of legitimate procedural and substantive concerns requires one to disaggregate these issues, so that each of them and the collective relationships among them may be better understood. A property rights approach to understanding the substantive social impacts of PA emergence and evolution provides one with a fine-grained analytic lens through which to examine not only displacement but the full range of positive and negative social impacts. As we have shown with MPAs, PAs have varied impacts on local people and communities, depending on local environmental, economic and social conditions and on how the PA is designed and implemented (West and Brockington, 2006). To date, however, scientific discussion of these impacts has focused on only a few variables, and the spatial, temporal and cross-PA variation in the magnitude and extent of social impacts remains largely unexamined and unexplained. To create more environmentally sustainable and socially just conservation practice, a critical next step in conservation social science research is to document and explain variation in the social impacts of protected areas. Such knowledge is the foundation of adaptive management that meets the needs of both people and nature.

References

Agrawal, A. and Redford, K.H. (2006) *Poverty, Development, and Biodiversity Conservation: Shooting in the Dark?* Working paper 26, Wildlife Conservation Society, New York.

Agrawal, A. and Redford, K.H. (2007) 'Conservation and displacement', pp. 4–15, in Redford, K.H. and Fearn, E. (eds) *Protected Areas and Human Displacement: A Conservation Perspective*, Working paper 29, Wildlife Conservation Society, New York.

Akimichi, T. and Ruddle, K. (1984) 'The historical development of territorial rights and fishery regulations in Okinawan inshore waters', *Senri Ethnological Studies*, 17: 37–86.

Alcala, A.C. and Russ, G.R. (1990) 'A direct test of the effects of protective management on the abundance and yield of tropical marine resources', *Journal du Conseil*, 46: 40–47.

Bishop, K., Dudley, N., Phillips, A. and Stolton, S. (2004) *Speaking a Common Language: The Uses and Performance of the IUCN System of Management Categories for Protected Areas*, Cardiff University, Cardiff, United Kingdom, IUCN, Gland, Switzerland, and Cambridge, United Kingdom.

Blaustien, R. J. (2007) 'Protected areas and equity concerns', *BioScience*, 57: 216–221.

Brechin, S., Wilshusen, P., Fortwangler, C. and West, P. (eds) (2003) *Contested Nature: Promoting International Biodiversity and Social Justice in the Twenty-First Century*, State University of New York Press, Albany.

Brockington, D. (1999) 'Conservation, displacement and livelihoods: The consequences of the eviction for pastoralists moved from the Mkomazi Game Reserve, Tanzania', *Nomadic Peoples*, 3: 74–96.

Brosius, J.P. (2004) 'Indigenous peoples and protected areas at the World Parks Congress', *Conservation Biology*, 18: 609–612.

Cernea, M.M. (2000) 'Risk, safeguards and reconstruction: A model for population displacement and resettlement', pp. 11–55, in Cernea, M.M. and McDowell, C. (eds) *Risk and Reconstruction: Experiences of Resettlers and Refugees*, World Bank, Washington, DC.

Cernea, M.M. and Schmidt-Soltau, K. (2006) 'Poverty risks in national parks: Policy issues in conservation and resettlement', *World Development*, 34: 1808–1830.

Chapin, M. (2004) 'A challenge to conservationists', *World Watch* 17(6): 17–31.

Colchester, M. (1997) 'Salvaging nature: Indigenous peoples and protected areas', pp. 97–130 in Ghimire, K.B. and Pimbert, M.P. (eds) *Social Change and Conservation*, Earthscan, London.

Dearden, P., Bennett, M. and Johnston, J. (2005) 'Trends in global protected area governance, 1992–2002', *Environmental Management*, 36: 89–100.

Dixon, J.A., Scura, L.F. and van't Hof, T. (1993) 'Meeting ecological and economic goals: Marine parks in the Caribbean', *Ambio*, 22: 117–125.

Dowie, M. (2005) 'Conservation refugees: When protecting nature means kicking people out', *Orion*, 24: 16–27.

Fortwangler, C. and Stern, M. (2004) 'Why history and culture matter – a case study from the Virgin Islands National Park', *Policy Matters*, 13: 148–161.

Galal, N., Ormond, R.F.G. and Hassan, O. (2002) 'Effect of a network of no-take reserves in increasing catch per unit effort and stocks of exploited reef fish at Nabq, South Sinai, Egypt', *Marine and Freshwater Research*, 53: 199–205.

Gelcich, S., Edwards-Jones, G. and Kaiser, M.J. (2005) 'Importance of attitudinal differences among artisanal fishers toward comanagement and conservation of marine resources', *Conservation Biology*, 19: 865–875.

Gjertsen, H. (2005) 'Can habitat protection lead to improvements in human well-being? Evidence from marine protected areas in the Philippines', *World Development*, 33: 199–217.

Goodridge, R., Oxenford, H.A., Hatcher, B.G. and Narcisse, F. (1996) *Changes in the Shallow Reef Fishery Associated with Implementation of a System of Fishing Priority and Marine Reserve Areas in*

Soufriere, St Lucia, Proceedings of the 49th Gulf and Caribbean Fisheries Institute, Gulf and Caribbean Fisheries Institute, Ft. Pierce, Florida.

Granek, E.F. and Brown, M.A. (2005) 'Co-management approach to marine conservation in Moheli, Comoros Islands', *Conservation Biology,* 19: 1724–1732.

Halpern, B. (2003) 'The impact of marine reserves: Do reserves work and does reserve size matter?', *Ecological Applications,* 13: S117–S137.

Halpern, B.S. and Warner, R.R. (2002) 'Marine reserves have rapid and lasting effects', *Ecology Letters,* 5: 361–366.

Hoffman, T.C. (2002) 'The reimplementation of the Raui: Coral reef management in Rarotonga, Cook Islands', *Coastal Management,* 30: 401–418.

Jentoft, S., van Son, T.C. and Bjorkan, M. (2007) 'Marine protected areas: A governance system analysis', *Human Ecology,* 35: 611–622.

Johannes, R.E. (1978) 'Traditional marine conservation methods in Oceania and their demise', *Annual Review of Ecology and Systematics,* 9: 349–364.

Johannes, R.E. (2002) 'The renaissance of community-based marine resource management in Oceania', *Annual Review of Ecology and Systematics,* 33: 317–340.

Kakuma, S. (2004) 'Reef fisheries co-management in Okinawa', pp. 1407–1415, in Suzuki, Y., Nakamori, T., Hadaka, M., Kayanne, H., Casareto, B.E., Nadaoke, K., Yamano, H. and Tsuchiya M. (eds) *Proceedings of the 10th International Coral Reef Symposium,* 10: 1407–1415.

Lepp, A. and Holland, S. (2006) 'A comparison of attitudes toward state-led conservation and community-based conservation in the village of Bigodi, Uganda', *Society and Natural Resources,* 19: 609–623.

Libecap, G.D. (1989) *Contracting for Property Rights,* Cambridge University Press, Cambridge, UK.

McClanahan, T.R. and Kaunda-Arara, B. (1996) 'Fishery recovery in a coral-reef marine park and its effect on the adjacent fishery', *Conservation Biology,* 10: 1187–1199.

McNeely, J.A. (1999) 'Protected area institutions', pp. 195–204, in Stolton, S. (ed) *Partnerships for Protection: New Strategies for Planning and Management for Protected Areas,* Earthscan, London.

Marion, J.L. and Rogers, C.S. (1994) 'The applicability of terrestrial visitor impact management strategies to the protection of coral reefs', *Ocean and Coastal Management,* 22: 153–163.

Mascia, M.B. (2000) *Institutional Emergence, Evolution, and Performance in Complex Common Pool Resource Systems: Marine Protected Areas in the Wider Caribbean,* Department of the Environment, Duke University, Durham, North Carolina.

Mascia, M.B. (2004) 'Social dimensions of marine reserves', pp. 164–186, in Dahlgren, C. and Sobel, J. (eds) *Marine Reserves: A Guide to Science, Design, and Use,* Island Press, Washington, DC.

Newing, H. and Wahl, L. (2004) 'Benefiting local populations? Communal reserves in Peru', *Cultural Survival Quarterly,* 28: 38–41.

Ngugi, I. (2001) 'Economic impacts of marine protected areas: A case study of the Mombasa Marine Park (Kenya)', in Francis, R. (ed) *Marine Science Development in Tanzania and Eastern Africa,* WIOMSA Book Series, Zanzibar, Tanzania.

Oracion, E.G., Miller, M.L. and Christie, P. (2005) 'Marine protected areas for whom? Fisheries, tourism, and solidarity in a Philippine community', *Ocean and Coastal Management,* 48: 393–410.

Ostrom, E. (1990) *Governing the Commons: The Evolution of Institutions for Collective Action,* Cambridge University Press, Cambridge, UK.

Paddock, R.C. (2006) 'Forked tongues rule', *Los Angeles Times,* 5 July: A1.

Pinto da Silva, P. (2004) 'From common property to co-management: Lessons from Brazil's first maritime extractive reserve', *Marine Policy,* 28: 419–428.

Pomeroy, R., Parks, J., Pollnac, R., Campson, T., Genio, E., Marlessy, C., Holle, E., Pido, M., Nissapa, A., Boromthanarat, S. and Thu Hue, N. (2007) 'Fish wars: Conflict and collaboration in fisheries management in Southeast Asia', *Marine Policy,* 31: 645–656.

Roberts, C.M., Bohnsack, J.A., Gell, F., Hawkins, J.P. and Goodridge, R. (2001) 'Effects of marine reserves on adjacent fisheries', *Science*, 294: 1920–1923.

Ruddle, K. (1996) 'Traditional management of reef fishing', pp. 315–335 in Polunin, N.V.C. and Roberts, C.M. (eds) *Reef Fisheries*, Chapman and Hall, New York.

Russ, G.R. and Alcala, A.C. (1999) 'Management histories of Sumilon and Apo Marine Reserves, Philippines, and their influence on national marine resource policy', *Coral Reefs*, 18: 307–319.

Russ, G.R., Alcala, A.C., Maypa, A.P., Calumpong, H.P. and White, A.T. (2004) 'Marine reserve benefits local fisheries', *Ecological Applications*, 14: 597–606.

Sala, E., Aburto-Oropeza, O., Paredes, G., Parra, I., Barrera, J.C. and Dayton, P.K. (2002) 'A general model for designing networks of marine reserves', *Science*, 298: 1991–1993.

Schlager, E. and Ostrom, E. (1992) 'Property rights regimes and natural resources: A conceptual analysis', *Land Economics*, 68: 249–262.

Schmidt-Soltau, K. (2005) 'The environmental risks of conservation related displacements in central Africa', pp. 282–311, in Ohta, I. and Gebre, Y.D. (eds) *Displacement Risks in Africa*, Trans Pacific Press, Melbourne.

Schmidt-Soltau, K. and Brockington, D. (2007) 'Protected areas and resettlement: What scope for voluntary relocation?', *World Development*, 35: 2182–2202.

Shanks, A.L., Grantham, B.A. and Carr, M.H. (2003) 'Propagule dispersal distance and the size and spacing of marine reserves', *Ecological Applications*, 13: S159–S169.

Stevens, S. (ed) (1997) *Conservation Through Cultural Survival: Indigenous People and Protected Areas*, Island Press, Washington, DC.

Stone, D. (1988) *Policy Paradox and Political Reason*, Scott Foresman, Glenview, Illinois.

Vogt, H.P. (1997) 'The economic benefits of tourism in the marine reserve of Apo Island, Philippines', in Lessios, H.A. and Macintyre, I.G. (eds) *Proceedings of the 8th International Coral Reef Symposium*, 8: 2101–2106.

Ward, T.J., Heinemann, D. and Evans, N. (2001) *The Role of Marine Reserves as Fisheries Management Tools: A Review of Concepts, Evidence and International Experience*, Bureau of Rural Sciences, Canberra, Australia.

West, P.C. and Brechin, S.R. (eds) (1991) *Resident Peoples and National Parks: Social Dilemmas in International Conservation*, University of Arizona Press, Tucson.

West, P. and Brockington, D. (2006) 'An anthropological perspective on some unexpected consequences of protected areas', *Conservation Biology*, 20: 609–616.

Wilkie, D.S., Morelli, G.A., Demmer, J., Starkey, M., Telfer, P. and Steil, M. (2006) 'Parks and people: Assessing the human welfare effects of establishing protected areas for biodiversity conservation', *Conservation Biology*, 20: 247–249.

Part 4

Conservation NGOs
and Poor People

Editors' Introduction

Of all international debates about conservation policy and practice, the controversies about conservation NGOs have probably aroused the most passion. ... Conservation NGOs are the means by which people can make a difference in a world that does not seem to care nearly enough about wildlife and the damage we do to it, yet conservation NGOs can also be harsh bureaucracies and callous in their imposition of alien policies. (Brockington et al. 2008)

A vociferous element of the conservation–poverty debate centres on the modus operandi of international conservation organizations and, in particular, their relationships with, and responsibilities towards local people. This has included critiques by anthropologists and indigenous peoples' advocates of conservation organisations' poor attendance to local people's rights – particularly indigenous rights and questioning by conservation scientists of the role of conservation organizations in directly addressing poverty reduction, noting the difficulty that even specialized and well-funded development organizations have in ensuring poverty reduction.

The issue of NGO accountability is a central one – and conservation organizations are not alone in grappling with issues of balancing the needs and concerns of widely different stakeholder groups – partners, members, affected communities, staff, trustees and so on. The issue of who holds NGOs to account was brought to public attention in an article in *The Economist* following the emergence of the anti-globalization movement in Seattle in 1999 (*The Economist*, 2000). Analysis by One World Trust, a UK charity, concluded that some NGOs, including the World Wide Fund for Nature (WWF), CARE International and Oxfam, ranked lower in terms of accountability than widely criticized institutions such as the World Trade Organization, or corporate entities such as Rio Tinto (Kovach et al., 2003). However, we have found that there is surprisingly little written about governance and accountability mechanisms, global or local, for the work of international NGOs.

Within the conservation sector, concern has focused on the increasing concentration of wealth within a handful of international NGOs, and the corresponding power and leverage over conservation decision-making in developing countries that this affords them (Chapter 21; Bray and Anderson, 2005); the real or perceived lack of attention they pay to human rights issues, and the absence of any mechanism to address this (e.g. see numerous papers in CEESP, 2007); and the specific role of conservation organizations in dealing with social issues. Chapin (2004) (Chapter 21) notes for example:

In the last year or so, the large conservation NGOs have come to claim that what they do is conservation, not 'poverty alleviation', which they seem to equate with any sort of work with indigenous or traditional peoples. ... In part, the NGOs have felt pressured by the bilateral and multilateral donors to include poverty alleviation in their conservation programmes, and some have tried to accommodate the donors with retooled language in their mission statements; yet the tendency among the large NGOs has been to set up a false dichotomy between poverty alleviation and conservation and say that they are not in the business of 'social welfare'.

While many international conservation NGOs have much in common with one another, it is important and useful to disaggregate them. They often hold goals and values in common and often work in partnership, yet have very different ways of working. Three UK-headquartered NGOs – Fauna & Flora International (FFI), WWF-UK, BirdLife International – were some of the first to articulate conservation—poverty linkages and to try to integrate these in their work, with WWF-UK winning substantial core funding from DFID for its work on livelihoods linkages. The US-based 'big international conservation NGOs' (often referred to as the BINGOs – a term generally used to refer to The Nature Conservancy, WWF-US, Conservation International and the Wildlife Conservation Society), have been the focus of a number of critics about conservation NGO work. On one hand they channel large volumes of private and public US funding to conservation work in developing countries, usually designed in close coordination with local governments and civil society organizations, yet on the other hand they are often seen to use their financial muscle to drive the conservation agenda without transparency or local accountability (Chapter 21).

The major international conservation NGOs are pursuing internal, and sometimes public, deliberations as to their accountability to local communities and their role in addressing socio-economic issues (Walpole, 2006; Redford and Fearn, 2007; Roe et al., 2009) but there continues to be much questioning of the extent of their responsibility, their specific role in pursuing a social agenda and the impacts this should have on local poverty and livelihoods.

Our selected readings seek to illustrate these different strands to the debate about the roles and responsibilities of conservation organizations. Chapter 19 is an extract from a key text of the late 1980s on indigenous rights and the links with both conservation and development, *Two Agendas on Amazon Development*. This was issued by the Coordinating Body for the Indigenous Organizations of the Amazon Basin (COICA), and addresses both conservation and development practitioners. Part Two, reproduced here, acknowledges the role of the international conservation community in rainforest conservation but expresses concern over their preoccupation with wildlife over and above the concerns of local communities, and calls for a closer working relationship between conservation organizations and indigenous groups. Shortly after this was published, COICA invited 12 environmental groups to the First Summit Between Indigenous Peoples and Environmentalists in Iquitos, Peru, in 1990. The resulting Iquitos Declaration confirmed the importance of recognizing indigenous land rights and proposed an alliance that was subsequently established as the Coalition in Support of Amazonian Peoples and Their Environment (Amazon Alliance). Nevertheless, the conservation literature of the period continued to debate the role of indigenous people in conservation and the apparent contradictions between indigenous values and international conservation priorities (Redford, 1990; Alcorn, 1993; Redford and Stearman, 1993).

Chapter 20 illustrates the level of concern about the impact of conservation NGOs on local people (and possibly a lack of acceptance of the indigenous people-led agenda laid out in Chapter 19). Romero and Andrade (2004) critique the NGO strategy of buying up large tracts of land in developing countries for strict biodiversity protection. They identify the danger of treating societal assets, specifically tropical forests, as private assets, and therefore distorting the values of these resources. They make a plea to the NGOs to 'assist less-developed countries in the process of building policies affecting tropical forests that consider the full range of options for forest conservation rather than implementing conservation initiatives that disregard local stakeholders'.

If the 2003 World Parks Congress was the point at which the conservation–poverty debate hit mainstream policy-making, it was the following year that it really went public with the publication of *A Challenge to Conservationists* by anthropologist Mac Chapin (Chapter 21). This expands on Romero and Andrade's critiques, looking beyond the 'buy it and then preserve it' strategy to the activities of conservation NGOs more broadly, and their impact on indigenous communities. Chapin critiques the activities of three of the US-based NGOs (WWF-US, The Nature Conservancy and Conservation International) for their attitudes to, and impacts on, indigenous people, notably in Latin America. He concludes that in the 1990s 'indigenous peoples were never given the chance to design and run their own projects, and with conservationists at the helm the failures mounted' and highlights the very different agendas of conservationists and indigenous people. Chapin also identifies the rapid growth in financial resources available to the three NGOs and the imbalance in power this implies for their relationships with indigenous peoples' organizations. When published by WorldWatch, this paper quickly became a seminal piece in broadening the debate beyond the academic literature to the popular press and was quickly followed by a similarly styled article in *Orion Magazine* (Dowie, 2005). Both these articles have been criticized for factual inaccuracies but have certainly served a purpose in terms of raising public awareness of the issues and popularizing the debate. The volume of letters sent to WorldWatch in response to Chapin's article is in itself evidence that this made a real impact (WorldWatch, 2005a, b).

Chapter 22 illustrates a different angle to the debate – this one written from a conservation perspective, questioning the role of conservation organizations in poverty alleviation and lamenting the continued quest to integrate conservation and development. The author, John Oates, reviews earlier work critiquing community conservation and ICDPs (discussed in Chapter 1) and lists 'increasing emphasis on relationships between poverty alleviation and conservation' and 'calls for greater rights for indigenous people' as examples of continuing negative trends since then. He concludes that there is an urgent need to change attitudes as to what conservation is about, and notes that, while poverty reduction is an important objective, it has become too closely entangled with conservation. He concludes that NGO conservation projects are not an efficient mechanism for tackling the governance improvements that are necessary for effective poverty reduction.

In Chapter 23 Kaimowitz and Sheil (2007) disagree with this perspective and explore the question of 'conservation for whom?' They pick up on the 'pro-poor conservation' theme first put forward at the 2003 World Parks Congress (Roe et al., 2003) and argue that a pro-poor approach to conservation can complement 'conventional' conservation, offering new opportunities to attract new supporters and to access new resources. They acknowledge that a pro-poor approach will not conserve everything and that conventional habitat and species conservation will need to continue alongside, but suggest that conservation 'can and should address broader, more diversified, and more democratically defined goals, and should recognize and address the needs and aspirations of local people: especially the poor and vulnerable'. They conclude: 'Clearly it is not a question of "either/or," but rather of finding a better balance.'

The final Chapter in Part 4 describes the experience of an international conservation NGO in linking its conservation activities directly with poverty reduction. Walpole and Wilder (2008) review the portfolio of Fauna & Flora International (FFI) and conclude that while the activities of international conservation organizations are unlikely to make a significant impact on global poverty, this does not mean that conservation is irrelevant to poor people: 'At a local scale, conservation activities have the potential to make a difference where local poverty (i.e. a lack of choice) threatens biodiversity.' They recommend that conservation organizations do more to promote the wider societal benefits of their activities and really make the most of the potential impact they can have in those specific situations where conservation and poverty coincide.

References

Alcorn, J.B. (1993) 'Indigenous peoples and conservation', *Conservation Biology*, 7: 424–427.
Bray, D.B. and Anderson, A.B. (2005) *Global Conservation, Non-governmental Organizations, and Local Communities: Perspectives on Programs and Project Implementation in Latin America*, Working Paper 1, Florida International University Institute for Sustainability Science in Latin America and the Caribbean, Miami.
Brockington, D., Duffy, R. and Igoe, J. (2008) *Nature Unbound: Conservation, Capitalism and the Future of Protected Areas*, Earthscan, London.
CEESP (2007) 'Conservation and human rights', *Policy Matters*, Vol 15, CENESTA, Tehran.
Chapin, M. (2004) 'A challenge to conservationists', *World Watch*, Nov/Dec: 17–31.
Dowie, M. (2005) 'Conservation refugees: When protecting nature means kicking people out', *Orion Magazine*, November/December, 16–27.

The Economist (2000) *Who Guards the Guardians?*, *The Economist*, 23 September, p. 129.

Kaimowitz, D. and Sheil, D. (2007) 'Conserving what and for whom? Why conservation should hep meet basic needs in the tropics', *Biotropica* 39(5): 567–574.

Kovach, H., Neligan, C. and Burall, S. (2003) *The Global Accountability Report: Power Without Accountability?*, One World Trust, London.

Redford, K.H. (1990) 'The ecologically noble savage', *Orion Nature Quarterly*, 9: 24–29.

Redford, K.H. and Fearn, E. (eds) (2007) *Protected Areas and Human Displacement: A Conservation Perspective*, Working Paper No. 29, Wildlife Conservation Society, New York.

Redford, K.H. and Stearman, A.M. (1993) 'On common ground? Response to Alcorn', *Conservation Biology*, 7: 427–428.

Roe, D., Hutton, J., Elliott, J., Saruchera, M. and Chitepo, K. (2003) 'In pursuit of pro-poor conservation: Changing narratives ... or more?', *Policy Matters* 12: 87–91.

Roe, D., Oviedo, G., Pabon, L., Painter, M., Redford, K., Siegele, L., Springer, J., Thomas, D. and Walker-Painemilla, K. (2009) *Conservation and Human Rights: The Need for Common Standards in International Conservation Practice*, IIED Briefing, IIED, London.

Romero, C. and Andrade, G.J. (2004) 'International conservation organisations and the fate of local tropical forest conservation initiatives', *Conservation Biology*, 18(2): 578–580.

Walpole, M. (2006) *The Case for Integrating Conservation and Human Needs*, Fauna & Flora International, Cambridge.

Walpole, M. and Wilder, L. (2008) 'Disentangling the links between conservation and poverty reduction in practice', *Oryx* 42(4): 539–547.

WorldWatch Institute (2005a) 'Readers' responses to "A challenge to conservationists"', *World Watch Magazine*, 18(1): 5–20.

WorldWatch Institute (2005b) 'Readers' responses to "A challenge to conservationists" – additions', WorldWatch Institute, Washington, DC.

Chapter 19

Two Agendas on Amazon Development

Coordinating Body for the Indigenous Organizations of the Amazon Basin (COICA)

To the Community of Concerned Environmentalists

We, the Indigenous Peoples, have been an integral part of the Amazonian Biosphere for millennia. We use and care for the resources of that biosphere with respect, because it is our home, and because we know that our survival and that of our future generations depend on it. Our accumulated knowledge about the ecology of our forest home, our models for living within the Amazonian Biosphere, our reverence and respect for the tropical forest and its other inhabitants, both plant and animal, are the keys to guaranteeing the future of the Amazon Basin. A guarantee not only for our peoples, but also for all of humanity. Our experience, especially during the past 100 years, has taught us that when politicians and developers take charge of our Amazon, they are capable of destroying it because of their shortsightedness, their ignorance and their greed.

We are pleased and encouraged to see the interest and concern expressed by the environmentalist community for the future of our homeland. We are gratified by the efforts you have made in your country to educate your peoples about our homeland and the threat it now faces as well as the efforts you have made in South America to defend the Amazonian rainforests and to encourage proper management of their resources. We greatly appreciate and fully support the efforts some of you are making to lobby the US Congress, the World Bank, USAID and the Inter-American Development Bank on behalf of the Amazonian Biosphere and its inhabitants. We recognize that through these efforts, the community of environmentalists has become an important political actor in determining the future of the Amazon Basin.

We are keenly aware that you share with us a common perception of the dangers which face our homeland. While we may differ about the methods to be used, we do share a fundamental concern for encouraging the long-term conserva-

Reprinted from *Cultural Survival Quarterly*, vol 13, no 4, COICA, 'Two agendas on Amazon development', pp. 75–78, copyright © (1989) with permission from Cultural Survival (www.cs.org), Cambridge, MA. Extract or abridged version.

tion and the intelligent use of the Amazonian rainforest. We have the same conservation goals.

Our Concerns

We are concerned that you have left us, the Indigenous Peoples, out of your vision of the Amazonian Biosphere. The focus of concern of the environmental community has typically been the preservation of the tropical forest and its plant and animal inhabitants. You have shown little interest in its human inhabitants who are also part of that biosphere.

We are concerned about the 'debt for nature swaps' which put your organizations in a position of negotiating with our governments for the future of our homelands. We know of specific examples of such swaps which have shown the most brazen disregard for the rights of the indigenous inhabitants and which are resulting in the ultimate destruction of the very forests which they were meant to preserve.

We are concerned that you have left us Indigenous Peoples and our organizations out of the political process which is determining the future of our homeland. While we appreciate your efforts on our behalf, we want to make it clear that we never delegated any power of representation to the environmentalist community nor to any individual or organization within that community.

We are concerned about the violence and ecological destruction of our homeland caused by the increasing production and trafficking of cocaine, most of which is consumed here in the US.

What We Want

We want you, the environmental community, to recognize that the most effective defence of the Amazonian Biosphere is the recognition of our ownership rights over our territories and the promotion of our models for living within that biosphere.

We want you, the environmental community, to recognize that we Indigenous Peoples are an important and integral part of the Amazonian Biosphere.

We want you, the environmental community, to recognize and promote our rights as Indigenous Peoples as we have been defining those rights within the UN Working Group for Indigenous Peoples.

We want to represent ourselves and our interests directly in all negotiations concerning the future of our Amazonian homeland.

What We Propose

We propose that you work directly with our organizations on all your programmes and campaigns which affect our homelands.

We propose that you swap 'debt for indigenous stewardship' which would allow your organizations to help return areas of the Amazonian rainforest to our care and control.

We propose establishing a permanent dialogue with you to develop and implement new models for using the rainforest based on the list of alternatives presented with this document.

We propose joining hands with those members of the worldwide environmentalist community who:

- recognize our historical role as caretakers of the Amazon Basin;
- support our efforts to reclaim and defend our traditional territories;
- accept our organizations as legitimate and equal partners.

We propose reaching out to other Amazonian peoples such as the rubber tappers, the Brazil-nut gatherers, and others whose livelihood depends on the non-destructive extractive activities, many of whom are of indigenous origin.

We propose that you consider allying yourselves with us, the Indigenous Peoples of the Amazon, in defence of our Amazonian homeland.

Chapter 20

International Conservation Organizations and the Fate of Local Tropical Forest Conservation Initiatives

Claudia Romero and German I. Andrade

If biologists want a tropics in which to biologize, they are going to have to buy it with care, energy, effort, strategy, tactics, time and cash. (Janzen, 1986)

Had the millions of dollars that have gone into unsuccessful International Conservation and Development Projects instead been invested in lands acquisition, the donor nations would now have title to huge tracts of tropical forests. (Terborgh, 1999)

Several international conservation organizations (ICOs) created in the developed world to promote conservation in the tropics are now extremely outspoken and powerful, due in large measure to their access to capital. We acknowledge that ICOs have been critical stakeholders in shaping international environmental policies. We also recognize that there have been successful collaborations between ICOs, governments of less-developed countries, and local and regional non-governmental organizations (NGOs). Our principal concern is that, given the asymmetric relationships that characterize most of the partnerships between ICOs and local institutions in less-developed countries, particularly in relation to their differential access to funds, there is a danger of treating societal assets in less-developed countries, more specifically tropical forests, as private assets, and therefore distorting the values of these resources. Furthermore, we believe that the preservationist agenda pushed by some ICOs and the associated processes through which decisions on tropical forests are made will abort local social processes that could contribute to conservation. We make a plea to ICOs to assist less-developed countries in the process of building policies affecting tropical forests that consider the full range of options for forest conservation rather than implementing conservation initiatives that disregard local stakeholders and possibilities for their involve-

Reprinted from *Conservation Biology*, vol 18, no 2, Romero, C. and Andrade, G.I., 'International Conservation Organisations and the Fate of Local Tropical Forest Conservation Initiatives', pp. 578–580, copyright © (2004) with permission of Blackwell Publishing Ltd, Oxford.

ment in the negotiation of policy frameworks for resource use. International support needs to be provided in ways that respect the rights of local people to make choices that are socially just and that assign stakeholders both rights and responsibilities (Brechin et al., 2002; but see Wollenberg et al., 2002).

The challenge that emerges for ICOs is to find a balance between preservationists, concerned solely with biodiversity preservation without consideration of the welfare of local communities (Janzen, 1986; Terborgh, 1999), and devolutionists, focused exclusively on empowering local people with control of forest resources. There will be difficulties in finding this balance, but we urge continued efforts at reconciling biodiversity conservation and the real economic and societal needs of less-developed countries. Without tipping the power balance from ICOs to one exclusively dictated by the desires of local communities, we advocate the creative search for negotiated solutions.

E.R. Rice and colleagues based at Conservation International are among the most vehement proponents of forest conservation exclusively through acquisition of land and resource-use rights (Rice et al., 1997; Bowles et al., 1998). They base their proposal on their assumption that sustainable management of forest resources, specifically timber, is financially less profitable than conventional logging and other land uses, which will hinder adoption of the best management practices by industry (Rice et al., 2001; Hardner and Rice, 2002; but see Boltz et al., 2001; Holmes et al., 2002). Instead of considering a variety of options for tropical forest conservation, they suggest that once forests have been logged they should be purchased at bargain prices by ICOs and set aside for preservation. Alternatively, they propose that ICOs 'retire' concessions by making annual payments equivalent to the revenues forgone by forest owners from timber extraction and then create parks (Gullison et al., 2001). A proposed variation on this theme involves direct negotiations between ICOs and timber concessionaires to allow logging of entire concessions over very short time periods, thereby ending exploitation and commencing preservation rapidly, without any effort to sustain timber yields (Rice et al., 2001).

In the best of possible worlds, most of the remaining tropical forests might be excluded from logging, not converted to legal or illegal crops (Cavelier and Etter, 1995; Alvarez, 2002), 'preserved' as a collateral benefit of armed conflicts (Dávalos, 2001; but see Dudley et al., 2002), or purchased to establish nature preserves. But instead of dwelling in the best of possible worlds, we occupy this one.

From our point of view, several issues need to be addressed with respect to the 'log-then-preserve' proposal and other such approaches to tropical forest conservation. Preservationist proposals fail to recognize that most tropical forests are inhabited (Schwartzman et al., 2000). In countries such as Colombia, Ecuador and Bolivia, millions of hectares of tropical forests have been recognized by governments as the common property of indigenous people. Exclusionist approaches are usually detrimental to rural people already suffering from low living standards and therefore exacerbate social conflicts (Ferraro, 2002). Preservationist initiatives also preclude local people from learning about conservation in practice, which, unfortunately, sometimes includes failing at it. In forests that are too biologically precious to risk with sustainable-use attempts at conservation, creative strategies are needed that consider the welfare of neighbouring communities without compromising preservation goals (Ferraro, 2002; Ferraro and Kiss, 2002).

For most of the remaining forests in the tropics, the best hope for conservation is through sustainable use. In vast portions of the Amazon forest, for example, the Brazilian government and collaborating institutions are in the process of defining territorial management categories and concomitant policies for promoting sustainable forest management, as part of a spectacular move to curb illegal logging, capture revenues, and contribute to the welfare of rural communities through improved local and regional governance (Carvalho et al., 2001; Nepstad et al., 2002; Verissimo et al., 2002). Such initiatives and others to come, which consider the structural changes needed for creating more reflective individuals and institutions capable of deciding the fates of tropical forests, are the sorts of options that the 'buying-tropical-forest' solution might preclude.

The proposal to buy tropical-forest logging concessions also evokes a series of concerns that are unlikely to diminish, even if an ICO 'buys' the forest and all rights to its resources. Who are the ICOs paying for those 'purchases'? We doubt that these funds will compensate the host government and local people for all the lost revenues down both the processing and market chains. Will the nature preserves created by ICOs serve as loci for regional development, or will they thwart the hopes of local people for improved access to jobs and markets and to social services such as schools and hospitals? We fear that the meagre financial benefits of ICO forest purchases will not accrue to local communities and that enforcement of preservation in a context of social mistrust and poverty will be impossible. Additionally, what will effectively prevent timber companies from obtaining other concessions and doing more (and usually bad) logging? Will their employees remain in the forest as colonists? These 'purchases' might promote what they are trying to mend: in short, more forest mismanagement and destruction and ultimately sustained underdevelopment.

We must address the ultimate reasons that governments in tropical countries have not, on their own initiative, declared former logging areas national parks. We suggest that there are complex interacting factors, ranging from short-term interests of powerful stakeholders seeking personal benefits to the more reasonable goals of growing food and contributing critical revenues to local, regional and national development. We contend that the creation of new protected areas by re-gazetting existing logging areas is generally beyond the capacity of most tropical governments.

More profoundly, we do not believe that it is legitimate and ethical for ICOs and the timber industry to decide the fates of societal assets. We fear that in the rush to save the tropics, social and private assets and social and private discount rates are getting dangerously confused. In the case of environmental damage, in particular, social discount rates can even be negative, whereas private discount rates are positive (Solov, 1974; Dasgupta et al., 1999). Furthermore, although tropical forests are considered by some people to be global assets, recognition of the global character of such assets by institutions and national governments through international agreements is still pending. Even if global resources are recognized as such, they should not be bought and sold without due consideration for the aspirations of the people that live nearby and of the institutions and governments that should control these assets.

Tropical forests need advocates to defend their value as a collective good for collective wealth. These novel stakeholders are in a position that is neither private nor public but that results from negotiation between the two (Eder, 1996). This negotiation can be understood as the social and political processes necessary for development of a diverse portfolio of options to promote sustainable management (i.e. local institution building and mechanisms for improving institutional frameworks to protect social assets) and preservation (Wilshusen et al., 2002). In short, we must strive to make forests sustainable sources of prosperity instead of poverty traps (Wunder, 2001).

If humility and respect characterize the interactions between wealthy countries and less-developed countries, and if all sorts of equity and ethical issues are considered, tropical forests and their people will genuinely benefit.

In the meantime, and until we realize this dream, tropical forests and their resources, including the people who most depend on them, will continue to vanish.

References

Alvarez, M.D. (2002) 'Illicit crops and bird conservation priorities in Colombia', *Conservation Biology*, 16: 1086–1096.

Boltz, F., Carter, D.R., Holmes, T.P. and Pereira, R. (2001) 'Financial returns under uncertainty for conventional and reduced-impact logging in permanent production forests of the Brazilian Amazon', *Ecological Economics*, 39: 387–398.

Bowles, I., Rice, E.R., Mittermeier, R. and da Fonseca, G.A.B. (1998) 'Logging and tropical forest conservation', *Science*, 280: 1899–1900.

Brechin, S.R., Wilshusen, P.R., Fortwangler, C.L. and West, P.C. (2002) 'Beyond the square wheel: Toward a more comprehensive understanding of biodiversity conservation as social and political process', *Society and Natural Resources*, 15: 41–65.

Carvalho, G., Barros, A.C., Moutinho, P. and Nepstad, D. (2001) 'Sensitive development could protect Amazonia instead of destroying it', *Nature*, 409: 131.

Cavelier, J. and Etter, A. (1995) 'Deforestation of montane forests in Colombia as a result of illegal plantation of opium (*Papaver somniferum*)', pp. 541–549, in Churchill, S.P., Balslev, H., Forero, E. and Luteyn, J.L. (eds) *Biodiversity and Conservation of Neotropical Montane Forests*, The New York Botanical Garden, Bronx, New York.

Dasgupta, P., Mäler, K. and Barrett, S. (1999) 'Intergenerational equity, social discount rates, and global warming', pp. 71–89, in Portney, P.R. and Weyant, J.P. (eds) *Discounting and Intergenerational Equity, Resources for the Future*, Washington, DC.

Dávalos, L. (2001) 'The San Lucas Mountain Range in Colombia: How much conservation is owed to the violence?', *Biodiversity and Conservation*, 10: 69–78.

Dudley, J.P., Ginsberg, J.R., Plumptre, A.J., Hart, J.A. and Campos, L.C. (2002) 'Effects of war and civil strife on wildlife and wildlife habitats', *Conservation Biology*, 16: 319–329.

Eder, K. (1996) *The Social Construction of Nature: A Sociology of Ecological Enlightenment*, Sage Publications, London.

Ferraro, P. (2002) 'The local costs of establishing protected areas in low-income nations: Ranomafana National Park, Madagascar', *Ecological Economics*, 43: 261–275.

Ferraro, P. and Kiss, A. (2002) 'Direct payments to conserve biodiversity', *Science*, 298: 1718–1719.

Gullison, T., Melnyk, M. and Wong. C. (2001) *Logging Off: Mechanisms to Stop or Prevent Industrial Logging in Forests of High Conservation Value*, Union of Concerned Scientists – Center for Tropical Forest Science, Smithsonian Institution, Washington, DC.

Hardner, J. and Rice, R. (2002) 'Rethinking green consumerism', *Scientific American*, 286: 89–95.

Holmes, T.P., Blate, G.M., Zweede, J.C. Pereira, R., Barreto, P., Boltz, F. and Bauch, R. (2002) 'Financial and ecological indicators of reduced impact logging performance in the eastern Amazon', *Forest Ecology and Management*, 163: 93–98.

Janzen, D. (1986) 'The future of tropical ecology', *Annual Review of Ecology and Systematics*, 17: 305–324.

Nepstad, D., McGrath, D., Alencar, A., Barros, A.C., Carvalho, G., Santilli, M. and del Vera Diaz, M.C. (2002) 'Frontier governance in Amazonia', *Science*, 295: 629–631.

Rice, E.R., Gullison, R.E. and Reid, J.W. (1997) 'Can sustainable management save tropical forests?', *Scientific American*, 276: 44–49.

Rice, E.R., Sugal, C.A, Ratay, S.M. and da Fonseca, G.A.B. (2001) *Sustainable Forest Management: A Review of Conventional Wisdom*, Center for Applied Biodiversity Science 3, Conservation International, Washington, DC.

Schwartzman, S., Moreira, A. and Nepstad, D. (2000) 'Rethinking tropical forest conservation: Perils in parks', *Conservation Biology*, 14: 1351–1358.

Solov, R.M. (1974) 'The economics of resources or the resources of economics', *American Economic Review*, 64: 1–14.

Terborgh, J. (1999) *Requiem for Nature*, Island Press, Washington, DC.

Verissimo, A., Cochrane, M.A. and Souza, C. (2002) 'National forests in the Amazon', *Science*, 297: 1478.

Wilshusen, P.R., Brechin, S.R., Fortwangler, C.L. and West, P.C. (2002) 'Reinventing a square wheel: Critique of a resurgent "protection paradigm" in international biodiversity conservation', *Society and Natural Resources*, 15: 17–40.

Wollenberg, E., Anau, N., Iwan, R., van Heist, M., Limberg, G. and Sudana, M. (2002) 'Building agreements among stakeholders', *International Tropical Timber Organization, Tropical Forest Update*, 12: 6–8.

Wunder, S. (2001) 'Poverty alleviation and tropical forests: What scope for synergies?', *World Development*, 29: 1817–1833.

Chapter 21

A Challenge to Conservationists

Mac Chapin

As corporate and government money flow into the three big international organizations that dominate the world's conservation agenda, their programmes have been marked by growing conflicts of interest – and by a disturbing neglect of the indigenous peoples whose land they are in business to protect.

A Wake-Up Call

In June 2003, representatives of major foundations concerned with the planet's threatened biodiversity[1] gathered in South Dakota for a meeting of the Consultative Group on Biodiversity. On the second evening, after dinner, several of the attendees met to discuss a problem about which they had become increasingly disturbed. In recent years, their foundations had given millions of dollars of support to non-profit conservation organizations, and had even helped some of those groups get launched. Now, however, there were indications that three of the largest of these organizations – World Wildlife Fund (WWF), Conservation International (CI) and The Nature Conservancy (TNC) – were increasingly excluding, from full involvement in their programmes, the indigenous and traditional peoples living in territories the conservationists were trying to protect.[2] In some cases, there were complaints that the conservationists were being abusive.

The meeting led to a series of soul-searching discussions, led by Jeff Campbell of the Ford Foundation, who initiated two studies – one to assess what was really happening between the indigenous communities and conservationists, and the other to look into the financial situation of each of these three big groups.

The work plan (or 'terms of reference') given to the investigators contained two key observations about the three conservation giants: they had become extremely large and wealthy in a short period of time; and they were promoting global approaches to conservation 'that have evoked a number of questions – and complaints – from local communities, national NGOs and human rights activists'.

Reprinted from *World Watch*, Nov/Dec 2004, Chapin, M., 'A challenge to conservationists', pp. 17–31, copyright © (2004) with permission from *Worldwatch Institute* (www.worldwatch.org), Washington, DC. Extract or abridged version.

Because the two studies provided only a quick first foray into terrain that is undeniably complex, geographically extensive, and diverse (WWF, for example, works in more than 90 countries around the world), they were understood to be just rough sketches that could help orient discussions among the concerned foundations. The findings were not intended – initially, at least – for publication.

There were many people working either in the field (as I was) or in the foundations sponsoring field projects in biodiversity and cultural diversity, who wanted to see these findings aired. As an anthropologist who had been working with indigenous peoples for more than 35 years (most recently as director of the Center for Native Lands), I was acutely familiar – and increasingly uneasy – with the conditions that had precipitated the two Ford investigations.

Historical Context

Complaints had been building for more than a decade, and they paralleled the extraordinary growth of the major conservation organizations. WWF, for example, was founded in 1961 with a small office in Switzerland. Its programme was limited to coordination and fundraising activities for the International Union for the Conservation of Nature (IUCN), which implemented programmes in the field. WWF grew slowly over the ensuing years, spawning country and regional offices in various countries of the industrial north. Third World countries weren't included until later. During the first two decades, despite its expansion, the WWF family remained small. In the late 1970s, for example, the US branch of WWF fit on one floor of a relatively small building on Dupont Circle in Washington, DC, staffed by 25 people. In the early 1980s, it began to grow rapidly – and today fills up four floors of a luxurious building nearby. Worldwide, the US and international branches of WWF now employ close to 4000 people.

The Nature Conservancy started up in the mid-1940s, when a small group of scientists joined forces to save natural areas in the United States. In 1965 TNC used a grant from the Ford Foundation to pay the salary of its first full-time president. In the 1970s, it grew to cover all 50 states and expanded into Latin America. Fuelled by fresh injections of bilateral and multilateral money, as well as corporate support, it began a vertiginous growth spurt in the 1990s – and spread into new regions of the globe; yet the bulk of TNC's work is carried out domestically. It is now the largest conservation organization in the world, with assets in excess of US$3 billion.

Conservation International began in dramatic fashion in 1986. During the previous several years, TNC's international programme had grown rapidly, and tension with its other programmes had mounted. When TNC's central management tried to rein it in, virtually the entire international staff bolted and transformed itself into CI. From the start, the new organization was well equipped with staff, contacts, and money it had assembled beforehand. In 1989, it brought in yet another group of defectors – this time from WWF – and began expanding with the help of an aggressive fundraising machine that has become the envy of all of its competitors. However, a substantial portion of its funding comes from just four organizations: the Gordon and Betty Moore Foundation, the MacArthur Foundation, the World Bank and the Global Environment Facility (GEF). TNC and WWF, in contrast, have far more diverse funding bases.

Discussion of 'natural' alliances between conservationists and indigenous peoples and the need to work closely with local communities, common just a few years ago, has largely disappeared. It has been displaced, in the biggest conservationist NGOs, by talk of changed priorities, with a new focus on large-scale conservation strategies and the importance of science, rather than social realities, in determining their agendas. At the same time, there has been an undercurrent of talk about how 'difficult' indigenous peoples can be, how hard they are to work with, and, in places such as Ecuador, Bolivia and the Chiapas region of Mexico, how some have moved in the direction of civil disruption and even violence. Then there have been cautions from various quarters of the conservation movement that indigenous peoples are not – contrary to what many of them have been advertising – suitable allies because they, like most other people, are not even good conservationists, sometimes choosing their economic well-being over preservation of natural resources. Examples of the Kayapó in Brazil logging their forests and Mayans slashing and burning the forests of the Petén of Guatemala are often trotted out as examples of the destructive tendencies of indigenous peoples.

Indigenous peoples, on whose land the three conservation groups have launched a plethora of programmes, have for their part become increasingly hostile. One of their primary disagreements is over the establishment of protected natural areas, which, according to the human inhabitants of those areas, often infringe on their rights. Sometimes the indigenous people are evicted, and the conservationists frequently seem to be behind the evictions. On other occasions, traditional uses of the land have been declared 'illegal', resulting in prosecution of the inhabitants by government authorities. Coupled to all of this has been the partnering of conservationist organizations with multinational corporations – particularly in the businesses of gas and oil, pharmaceuticals and mining – that are directly involved in pillaging and destroying forest areas owned by indigenous peoples.

How did relations deteriorate so rapidly and so drastically? In the 1970s and through much of the 1980s, conservationists and indigenous peoples had little to do with each other. In Latin America, for example, the large conservation NGOs tended to work through urban-based local groups and there was little awareness of who the indigenous peoples in the various countries were. By the mid-1980s, however, the wall was breached within WWF by a programme called Wildlands and Human Needs, a community-based conservation effort, with financing from the US Agency for International Development (USAID). This was seen as something of a distraction by many within WWF, who were mainly biologists lacking experience working with communities. They viewed the new programme as an unwanted diversion from strict conservation, which they saw as their mission. It was seen as an imposition by USAID, which was pushing for a more grassroots approach.

In 1989, the Coordinating Body of Indigenous Organizations of the Amazon Basin (COICA) made an appeal directly to 'the community of concerned environmentalists' at the international level, proposing that they form an alliance 'in defence of our Amazonian homeland'.[3] COICA's call for collaborative action came at a time when the Amazonian ecosystem was being threatened as never before by heavily funded and ill-conceived development and colonization projects, cattle ranching, and unregulated logging and mining operations. The appeal noted that the conservationists 'have left us, the Indigenous Peoples, out of your vision of the Amazonian Biosphere'. That omission, they claimed, was the primary reason the conservationists' programmes were ineffectual.

COICA's appeal presented *Two Agendas* – one for conservationists, the other for the multilateral banks. It included this declaration:

> *We, the Indigenous Peoples, have been an integral part of the Amazon Biosphere for millennia. We have used and cared for the resources of that biosphere with a great deal of respect, because it is our home, and because we know that our survival and that of our future generations depends on it. Our accumulated knowledge about the ecology of our home, our models for living with the peculiarities of the Amazon Biosphere, our reverence and respect for the tropical forest and its other inhabitants, both plant and animal, are the keys to guaranteeing the future of the Amazon Basin, not only for our peoples, but also for all humanity.*[4]

COICA's arguments combined human rights considerations with practical suggestions for action in the areas of sustainable development, territorial defence, conservation and research, all reflecting indigenous priorities. It proposed that the conservation and development organizations 'work directly with our organizations on all your programmes and campaigns which affect our homelands'. At the time, this suggestion came as a revelation to many conservationists – an alternative approach that just might work!

Some of them wondered why such an obvious connection had not occurred to them earlier.

Two Agendas had great impact around the world and generated much discussion about partnerships, alliances, co-management of protected areas, participatory management, and a variety of other working relationships.

In the late 1980s and early 1990s, the conservation groups began designing programmes to work with communities. Donors, too – both private foundations and multilateral and bilateral donor agencies – strongly supported this approach to what was then in vogue: the concept of sustainable development. It soon became a bandwagon onto which many organizations jumped.[5] The initiatives that appeared were variously called 'community-based natural resource management', 'community-based conservation', 'sustainable development and use', 'grassroots conservation', 'devolution of resource rights to local communities' and – perhaps most commonly – 'integrated conservation and development programmes'

(ICDPs). It is important to note that all of these terms were generated by the conservation organizations, not by the indigenous peoples; and the programmes were designed and run by the conservationists, not the indigenous peoples. Funders provided money to the conservation organizations to develop programmes for indigenous communities, and small units were formed in-house to carry out this mandate.

Emerging Difficulties

The outcome of these attempts to work with indigenous communities was, with a few exceptions, a string of failures. On the ground, ICDPs were generally paternalistic, lacking in expertise, and one-sided – driven largely by the agendas of the conservationists, with little indigenous input. As a consequence, few partnerships were formed in the wake of COICA's proposal, and few of those that were formed functioned very well. According to Thomas McShane of WWF International, 'Encouraged by the frantic quest for examples of sustainable development, ICDPs exploded in popularity, rapidly advancing from an untested idea attracting seed money to "best practice" for biodiversity conservation.' The fact that conservation organizations were perhaps not suited to work in the social and economic realms was missed in all the excitement. Successes have been few and far between, and today an expanding barrage of mostly critical literature has fuelled concern among organizations implementing and financing ICDPs.[6]

Others, however, have claimed that community-based conservation schemes are inherently contrary to the goals of biodiversity conservation, which should be based on rigorous biological science. For this reason, it is said, they are doomed to failure, regardless of who runs them or how they are run. TNC's Katrina Brandon and her colleagues Kent H. Redford and Steven E. Sanderson wrote, 'The trend to promote sustainable use of resources as a means to protect these resources, while politically expedient and intellectually appealing, is not well grounded in biological and ecological knowledge. Not all things can be preserved through use. Not all places should be open to use. Without an understanding of broader ecosystem dynamics at specific sites, strategies promoting sustainable use will lead to substantial losses of biodiversity.'[7]

In their discussion of TNC's Parks in Peril (PiP) programme, financed by USAID during the 1990s, Brandon, Redford and Sanderson repeatedly call community-based conservation approaches 'catchy phrases' and 'slogans' based on 'stereotypes'. These slogans and catchy phrases, they say, mislead by promising that 'conflicts over resources can be resolved with relative ease' (ibid) and divert us from the true task of protecting biodiversity, which has to be an enterprise based on sound science. Redford, in particular, has sought over the years to debunk the stereotype of the 'noble ecological savage',[8] which he claims has been cynically used by indigenous peoples and their advocates ... because they recognize the power of this concept in rallying support for their struggle for land rights, particularly from important international conservation organizations'.[9]

Be this as it may, the core fact remains that indigenous peoples were never given the chance to design and run their own projects, and with conservationists at the helm the failures mounted. Many projects were ill-conceived by the conservationists. Projects dealing with agroforestry and organic gardening fell apart because no one had figured out how to market what was grown. Local ecological conditions were often wrong for the crops introduced. Local people were not interested in setting up parks and doing management plans, which was what the conservationists proposed. Environmental education projects in indigenous areas were modelled on urban programmes. In short, the conservationists had little experience working with community groups.

Funders grew impatient, and relations between conservationists and indigenous peoples became increasingly tense – and, in some respects, intransigent. In its official policies, WWF-US has continued to voice respect for indigenous peoples, yet in many of its pronouncements it displays a studied lack of interest toward partnerships with indigenous or local communities of any stripe.[10] In broad strategy statements about its ecoregional approach, WWF simply avoids talk of involvement with indigenous peoples at all.[11] In late 2002, the director of the WWF Latin America programme told me flatly, in reference to the Amazon Basin, 'We don't work with indigenous people. We don't have the capacity to work with indigenous people.' Around this time, a CI biologist who works with the Kayapó in the Lower Xingu region of Brazil told me: 'Quite frankly, I don't care what the Indians want. We have to work to conserve the biodiversity.'

This last comment may sound crass, but I believe that it accurately represents the prevalent way of thinking within the large conservation organizations. Although they won't say it openly, the attitude of many conservationists is that they have the money and they are going to call the shots. They have cordoned off certain areas for conservation, and in their own minds they have a clear idea of what should be done. 'They see themselves as scientists doing God's work', says one critic, pointing out the conservationists' sense of 'a divine mission to save the Earth'. Armed with science, they define the terms of engagement. Then they invite the indigenous residents to participate in the agenda that they have laid out. If the indigenous peoples don't like the agenda, they will simply be ignored. 'I think there's been a shift', says a key official at one of the major foundations that have supported the conservationist NGOs – 'a shift away from building local capacity [by helping to launch local NGOs that can then work with the indigenous communities in their own countries]. These groups now see themselves as semi-permanent international organizations, that are not working themselves out of a job.'

The fact is that indigenous peoples and conservationists have very different agendas. Indigenous agendas almost invariably begin with the need to protect and legalize their lands for their own use. They emphasize the importance of finding ways to make a living on the land without destroying those resources. And they give high priority to documenting their people's history, traditions and cultural identity.

Conservationist agendas, by contrast, often begin with the need to establish protected areas that are off-limits to people, and to develop management plans. If they include indigenous peoples in their plans, they tend to see those people more as a possible means to an end rather than as ends in themselves. They are seldom willing to support legal battles over land tenure and the strengthening of indigenous organizations; they consider these actions 'too political' and outside their conservationist mandate. They have been reluctant to support indigenous peoples in their struggles against oil, mining and logging companies that are destroying vast swaths of rainforest throughout the world. Again, the excuse is that such interventions would be 'too political', and the conservationists often defer to national governments to handle those matters.

Beyond this pervasive reluctance, there is the difficulty of reconciling cultural differences between industrialized and indigenous ways of viewing the world, deliberating, negotiating and making decisions. Andrew Chapeskie notes the difficulties faced by those seeking co-management schemes in the Canadian context:

> How should co-management arrangements be established for lands and waters where one set of relationships to land – the aboriginal – have been built around the normative values of equity, cooperation and reciprocity that is expressed in terms of local authority and common property access arrangements while the other set of relationships to land – those regulated by the state – have been built around the normative values of competition, exclusive rights to property/resources, and centralized management authority? These are challenging questions as much for aboriginal communities as they are for their non-aboriginal counterparts in Northwestern Ontario.[12]

Establishing a relationship of trust across cultures, when people come to the table carrying different agendas and worldviews, requires patience and respect – qualities that are hard to muster even in normal circumstances. The challenge grows exponentially more difficult when money intervenes and the relationship becomes glaringly asymmetrical, with virtually all of the money and power held by one side.

The Money

Since 1990, there has been a sharp decline in the amount of money available for conservation programmes overall. According to a recent assessment of the finances of the conservation sector, 'between the mid-nineties and the turn of the century, the amount of funds available for conservation [has] declined almost by 50 percent'. At the same time, 'the funding made available to the large NGOs [WWF, TNC and CI] has increased in both relative and absolute terms'.[13]

Against the overall decline in conservation funding, the growth of the big NGOs has been accomplished in large part through an expansion of their fund-raising reach into new areas, with a wide array of tactics. One recent estimate notes that the combined revenues of WWF, TNC and CI in 2002 for work in the developing countries amounted to more than half of the approximately US$1.5 billion available for conservation in 2002; and the Big Three's investments in conservation in the developing world grew from roughly $240 million in 1998 to close to $490 million in 2002.[14]

This attraction of strong financial support in a weak economic environment has been accomplished in several ways. First, starting in the mid to late 1990s, WWF, CI and TNC all reformulated their mission statements to focus on what they term 'large-scale conservation' approaches.

If the first means of increasing the flow of cash was to wow foundations with large-scale goals, a second tactic was to go after the bilateral and multilateral agencies. The Big Three eased slowly into these arrangements, often amid internal discussion and debate. WWF's relationship with USAID, which began in the early 1980s, is illustrative. In the late 1970s, as USAID was becoming increasingly interested in the environment, the conservationist NGOs realized that this could be a lucrative new source of support for their work. At first, WWF took relatively small amounts, never more than 50 per cent of any project budget, and supplemented the new money with privately raised funds. It did not want to be caught up in USAID's political agendas or in the instability that comes with them. Yet gradually, according to a senior WWF official who was in the middle of these transactions at that time, the 50 per cent rule began to erode. As budgets from other, privately funded, projects dried up, WWF started shifting funds from the USAID-supported projects to keep those projects alive. Larger amounts of USAID money flowed in to fill the hole left by the shifted funds, and before long there was a string of projects in which 80 to 90 per cent of the budget was funded by USAID. 'Then somewhere along the line we stopped asking questions', the official said. 'We just eased into it. It's not clear where or when, but at some point we crossed the line and having entire projects and programs funded with government money was OK.' Not to be outdone, the other large NGOs eagerly followed suit.

A third strategy, which at first seemed fairly innocent, was to reach out more to the corporate sector. TNC and WWF have long been involved with private corporations, but by the mid-1990s the pace began increasing.

The Consequences

All told, the new mixture of fundraising strategies, coupled with the intensity of the hunt for money, has made the largest conservation NGOs both rich and powerful. In the 1980s, many of us thought that this was an important goal. Conservation requires money, and it seemed clear to environmentalists that the leading environmental organizations needed far better funding to carry out the huge mission of saving the planet from ecological calamity. There may still be truth in this belief – the conservation groups have developed admirably ambitious plans – but their growth has also brought unforeseen complexities and contradictions.

One problem is that the larger the three NGOs have grown, the more dependent on large amounts of cash they have become. This has created a climate of intense – and not always beneficial – competition among them. The result has been a strong reluctance to partner with each other, or with anyone else. In dealings with smaller organizations, either they tend to use their sheer heft to press their agendas unilaterally or they exclude the smaller groups altogether. A common tactic is to create new organizations out of whole cloth in foreign countries, implanting local bodies as extensions of themselves. In dealings with each other, the large conservationist NGOs enter into contractual arrangements when they must – USAID's Central America programme, for example, has a custom of setting up consortia of several organizations – yet in most cases they assiduously keep their distance and show great reluctance to share information.

It should be acknowledged that territoriality of this sort does serve the function of diminishing conflict. Were a number of competing NGOs to be given access to a single area, bidding wars for the favours of local groups and the bounty of donors could rapidly get out of hand, creating chaos. This occasionally happens, and the outcome is invariably disastrous for all unlucky enough to be involved.

On the other hand, cooperation is rare even when the groups share common goals. According to McShane, 'Biodiversity conservation's devil is the competition for donor funding. We all know that successful biodiversity conservation requires money. Unfortunately, in the pursuit of funds, conservation organizations find themselves making claims based on little more than theory. This marketing of conservation approaches has resulted in a dogmatic debate, outwardly over how best to conserve the world's biodiversity, which is a necessary question, but behind the scenes over how to get the funds before someone else does, which is not.'[15]

Another consequence of the recent bulking up of conservationist NGOs stems from the sources of their funding, and the conditions attached to it. The movement from dependence on private money to an income stream from bilateral and multilateral donors and corporations has meant that new interests – and restrictions – come into play. USAID, the World Bank and the Global Environment Facility, for example, are diplomatic agencies that work closely with national governments. The conservationist NGOs are no longer able to openly oppose government corruption or inaction, which is often the primary cause of environmental degradation in countries of the Third World; government backing of extractive industries in fragile forest areas is one of the most common outcomes.[16]

Yet another consequence of increased funding from bilateral and multilateral donors is that the NGOs have become 'gatekeepers' of external resources. The strategy of passing money through NGOs gives the donors considerable influence over the programmes of the large NGOs, and this in turn gives the large NGOs influence over local NGOs, who must rely on regranting through the large international NGOs. This results in two layers of controls: first those from the bilateral and multilateral donors, and second those from the international NGOs that do the regranting. When funds finally trickle down to the local NGOs, they are often so tangled in strings that the locals have little room to carry out their own programmes. In any case, these funds tend to be minimal; most stay with the large NGOs, never making it past the gate.[17]

The situation is far worse for indigenous peoples, who are frequently in an adversarial relationship with their national governments over their lands and natural resources. National governments – and the US government – have supported oil companies, miners, loggers and pharmaceutical companies on indigenous lands, and in many of those countries (Bolivia, Peru, Ecuador, Guyana, Indonesia and Papua New Guinea, among others) private concessions sanctioned by governments have provoked considerable violence. Each of the large conservation NGOs has close financial and political ties to the governments, bilateral and multilateral agencies, and multinational corporations operating throughout the Third World, and is reluctant to oppose them. This has given rise to the ironic observation that the large international NGOs are allying themselves with forces that are destroying the world's remaining ecosystems, while ignoring or even opposing those forces that are attempting to save them from destruction. Isn't it a bit odd that in 2003 Oxfam America supported an indigenous group in the Amazon Basin in its battle against the depredations of Chevron Texaco, while the large conservationist NGOs were providing this same company with a green fig leaf in exchange for financial aid? In last year's highly publicized series of articles about The Nature Conservancy, for example, *Washington Post* reporters Joe Stephens and David Ottaway note:

> *The Conservancy's mission makes it reluctant to take positions on some leading environmental issues, including global warming and drilling in Alaska's Arctic National Wildlife Refuge. Corporations represented on the Conservancy's board and advisory council have lobbied nationally on the corporate side of the issues. A Conservancy official said the group avoids criticizing the environmental records of its corporate board members.*[18]

Reluctance to oppose harmful practices in foreign countries is even greater where the NGOs are largely out of sight of First World eyes and under the protection of governments that are unconcerned with protection of the environment. And here we have a contradiction. Since the mid and late 1980s, indigenous peoples have received a good deal of support for a variety of causes, primarily from private foundations and a variety of European agencies. The Inter-American Foundation, a US government agency, gave hundreds of grants to indigenous organizations during this period and gave a significant boost to the indigenous movement in Latin America. Conservation organizations and foundations with conservationist agendas supported indigenous peoples all through the 1990s for work on conservation and sustainable economic development. One result was that indigenous organizations became more empowered. But when they began using their newfound strength to defend their lands and resources, they ran head-on into private companies, governments, bilateral and multilateral agencies, and conservationists all standing shoulder to shoulder. Not only did the conservationist NGOs turn away from indigenous peoples; so did many of the private foundations, to avoid getting caught in the crossfire.

As the major conservationist NGOs have distanced themselves from indigenous and traditional peoples in recent years, the causes of this separation can be tracked to two particularly sticky problems. First, there is the problem of indigenous resistance, which sometimes takes a violent turn, to the activities of many of the NGOs' funding partners. For the NGOs, siding with indigenous peoples in their struggles or uprisings against those partners might seem financially unwise.

Second, there is the presumption that biological science should be the sole guiding principle for biodiversity conservation in protected natural areas. This notion has produced a running debate between those who do not see human inhabitants as a part of the ecological equation,[19] and those who argue for partnerships and the inclusion of indigenous and traditional peoples in protected area plans, both on human rights grounds and for pragmatic ecological reasons.[20]

The Big Three NGOs are currently dominated, at least in their upper circles, by the second view. According to their critics, they have increasingly come to 'view rural people as the enemies of nature, rather than as political actors who can form an environmental constituency. By identifying indigenous and traditional peoples as obstacles to effective conservation, or by concluding that indigenous and other inhabited reserves are incompatible with "real" conservation, the people-free park school impugns the critical conservation value of inhabited forest areas and ignores the role of forest peoples as constituencies for forest conservation'.[21]

A suspicion often voiced by the conservationists is that once indigenous peoples are given tenure to their lands, there is no assurance that they will work to conserve their biodiversity. 'What if, after we have helped them out, they suddenly decide to log their forests?' is a standard question.

Just as the once widely recognized possibilities for native stewardship have been largely dismissed, the terms 'indigenous' and 'traditional' have largely dropped out of the discourse of the large conservationist NGOs – replaced mainly by 'marginalized' or 'poor'.[22] (The more neutral terms 'rural' and 'local' have also spread more widely in the literature and are commonly used by both sides.) This linguistic shift robs the dignity of indigenous peoples. Who is interested in saving the culture of marginalized people? What is the value of the traditional ecological knowledge of the poor? People who are viewed as having no distinctive culture, assets, or historic claims to the land they occupy end up being, in a very real sense, a people with no value.

In the last year or so, the large conservation NGOs have come to claim that what they do is conservation, not 'poverty alleviation', which they seem to equate with any sort of work with indigenous or traditional peoples. Ever since their work with grassroots conservation and integrated conservation and development projects fell on the rocks, they have avoided involvements along these lines, including talk of co-management of protected areas and sustainable development or alternative livelihoods with indigenous peoples. In part, the NGOs have felt pressured by the bi-lateral and multilateral donors to include poverty alleviation in their conservation programmes, and some have tried to accommodate the donors with retooled language in their mission statements; yet the tendency among the large NGOs has been to set up a false dichotomy between poverty alleviation and conservation and say that they are not in the business of 'social welfare'.[23]

To be sure, the views of the large NGOs are not monolithic. While some of those at the top may dismiss work at the community level as scattershot and inconsequential, or even contrary to the goal of large-scale biodiversity conservation, the picture at the field level is often quite different. WWF, for example, has a vigorous community forestry programme that works on forest management, certification and marketing in Mexico, the Guatemalan Petén, the Honduran Mosquitia, the Atlantic Coast region of Nicaragua, and Madre de Dios in Peru. TNC field offices work with communities in Mexico, Guatemala, and indigenous regions of Brazil. CI is less engaged at this level, although it does have a small project with organic coffee farmers in Chiapas, Mexico. WCS's South American programme is perhaps the best of the lot, with a strong focus on community-level conservation, co-management of protected areas with indigenous peoples, and sustainable community development. Its work with the Izoceño Guaraní in the Gran Chaco region of Bolivia is an exemplary example of mutual respect and smooth co-management of a protected area.

Unlike the brain trusts in the main offices, representatives in the field are not dealing with abstractions. Some have realized that they can accomplish little of value if they don't work in partnership with local people. Some have commented that they see their community work as their focus of attention and pay little heed to the global pronouncements coming from on high. Unfortunately, these field efforts are given little support in the home office, and as the drift from high-level support for indigenous peoples continues, future financial backing may prove hard to find.

What can be said about the 'increasing number of serious complaints' from the field reported in the Ford Foundation's internal investigation? Complaints against the activities of the Big Three conservation NGOs have now been heard from Mexico, Guatemala, Peru, Ecuador, Venezuela, Guyana, Suriname, Papua New Guinea and the Congo Basin, among others. In one case, CI has been accused of bullying and riding roughshod over local NGOs and indigenous organizations in the Vilcabamba region of Peru. In another, its work in the Laguna del Tigre area of the Guatemalan Petén ended in a bitter fight over resources with the local NGO it had created – and with angry villagers setting the CI research station on fire. Yet, relatively little is yet known about whether such abuses are pervasive or aberrations. No thorough, independent evaluation of these situations has as yet been carried out, and it is often difficult to distinguish fact from fiction. But in any case, perhaps the most central investigation should focus not so much on particular failures in the field as on the large NGOs' recent inclination to withdraw from working with indigenous and traditional peoples at all.

Where is All This Headed?

Shortly after the Ford Foundation's 'Study of Critical New Conservation Issues in the Global South' got under way, two board members – Yolanda Kakabadse, president of the IUCN, and Kathryn Fuller, president of WWF – reviewed the study's work plan. They concluded that the studies of the two consultants, which no one at Ford had yet seen, should not become public – and, in fact, should not even be officially turned in to the Ford Foundation. They recommended that the studies be embargoed, and this indeed happened, at least for a time. Ford officials received a verbal briefing, and finally saw the full studies, but the studies were never made public. News of this chain of events rapidly leaked out and was widely disseminated among foundations and NGOs – causing a furor about which the larger public heard very little.

On 20 April 2004, WWF convened a meeting of representatives from the big international NGOs – WWF, TNC, CI, IUCN and WCS – for a full-day session with the foundation representatives who had brought the issue to the fore in South Dakota, 10 months earlier. The Big Three presidents – Kathryn Fuller of WWF, Peter Seligman of CI, and Steven McCormick of TNC – all came, together with some of their technical people. No indigenous representatives were present.[24]

Beyond a bland summary document, nothing has been shared publicly from this gathering, but it is possible to piece together impressions from several accounts. Initially, the NGO people were somewhat defensive, but were unapologetic. The foundation representatives spent the morning voicing their concerns, and the NGOs responded that their primary mission was conservation, not 'poverty alleviation' – which in many minds is equated with working with local communities. They denied insensitivity to traditional or indigenous peoples and cited their programmes in 'capacity building'. But for the most part, the NGOs gave little ground.

One foundation representative brought up the fact that multinational companies were extracting natural resources and destroying ecosystems in fragile forest areas, and that indigenous peoples were fighting these companies while the conservationists who were working there stood by in silence. This representative noted that the NGOs usually sided with the companies, especially when the companies were corporate sponsors to the NGOs. The NGOs responded that they didn't want to intervene – that they wanted to remain apolitical. In any case, they said, these were matters for national governments to handle.

Conclusion

The challenges of biodiversity conservation are among the world's most difficult, especially in the southern latitudes. Alien languages and cultures, impenetrable political systems, and high-stakes greed and corruption converge with the rising pressures of population growth and development to create situations that often seem insurmountable. Project work in the field is arduous – marked by progress one day and setbacks the next. Misunderstandings and conflicts of interest – and long periods of stagnation – seem to be the rule. Often, it is difficult to know whether one is making real progress or not.

Take the case of Chiapas, Mexico. Here, CI has a strong presence and has been accused in the local press of trying to enlist the Mexican military to expel peasant families from the Lacandon Forest, of bioprospecting for international corporations, and of flying planes over the Mayan Forest region with USAID support and giving the information thus obtained to the US and Mexican governments. Pieces of this picture – such as the fact that CI has corporate ties – are well substantiated. Others – such as CI buying up land for bioprospecting – appear to be greatly exaggerated. Still others – such as the overflights, which are indeed taking place – would be acceptable in most areas of the world other than Chiapas, where an active guerrilla movement is ensconced and the Mexican military has a strong presence. David Bray, one of the people originally enlisted by the Ford Foundation to investigate the alleged abuses, notes that this region 'is probably the most politicized and difficult working environment for conservation and development in Mexico'.[25] Precisely what is going on in Chiapas is difficult to sort out, and CI's role in the drama, whether positive, negative or otherwise, is far from clear.

None of this is easy, but one thing that seems clear to many of us who have worked in the field is that if we are to make any headway, cooperation among groups and sectors is crucial. There are still some among us who strongly believe that conservation cannot be effective unless the residents of the area to be conserved are thoroughly involved. This is not solely a matter of social justice, which must in any case be a strong component of all conservation work. It is also a matter of pragmatism. Indigenous peoples live in most of the ecosystems that conservationists are so anxious to preserve. Often they are responsible for the relatively intact state of those ecosystems, and they are without doubt preferable to the most common alternatives – logging, oil drilling, cattle ranching, and large-scale industrial agriculture – that are destroying ever larger tracts of forest throughout the tropical latitudes. Forming partnerships and collaborative alliances between indigenous and traditional peoples and conservationists is no easy task, but it would seem to be one of the most effective ways to save the increasingly threadbare ecosystems that still exist.

Yet, cooperation by the large conservationist NGOs, both among themselves and with other, smaller groups, including indigenous and traditional peoples, has lost ground over the past decade, only to be replaced by often intense competition, largely over money. NGOs entrusted with the enormous responsibility of defending the planet's natural ecosystems against the encroachment of the modern world in its most destructive manifestations have increasingly partnered with – and become dependent on – many of the corporations and governments that are most aggressively making this encroachment.

I fully agree that more study of conservation programmes in the field is needed. It has been the case for some time that the large conservationists are not accountable to anyone, and that far too little is known about what is really happening in the field. In particular, we don't know whether the large-scale, science-based programmes that appeal so much to funders are really achieving conservation goals. We also have little sense of what works and what doesn't work in what circumstances. And we don't know what to make of the charges and counter-charges – the claims of success and rumours of abuse – that emanate from the backlands on a regular basis. One reason for the lack of clear information is the role of the Big Three's marketing and fundraising arms in 'packaging' field reports and data, a tactic that encourages the exaggeration of successes and downplaying or non-recognition of questionable results. The suggestion that the IUCN and WWF – or any of the other large conservation NGOs, for that matter – should now lead a search for reliable new information strikes some as a fox-guarding-the-henhouse solution.

What's needed now is a series of independent, non-partisan, thorough and fairly objective evaluations that answer key questions the NGOs can't credibly answer. These evaluations should be undertaken by non-hierarchical teams representing the various sectors – indigenous peoples, local communities, national NGOs, government agencies, and donors, including bilateral and multilateral donors (whose influence is enormous) and private corporations (which have been largely silent) – and should be prosecuted in the spirit of seeking information and insights, not justifying existing programmes. Together, these stakeholders need to pursue the kind of open, public discussion that can lead towards the creation of conservation programmes that are responsive to the needs of *both* biological and human diversity worldwide.

Notes

1   Among those foundations represented were Ford, MacArthur, Moriah, Wallace Global, C.S. Mott and Oak.
2   'Indigenous and traditional peoples' is a more inclusive category than simply 'indigenous peoples'. 'Traditional peoples' includes non-indigenous groups that are long-standing residents of wilderness areas, such as the rubber tappers of Brazil and long-term Latino and Creole residents of the Caribbean coastal region of Central America.
3   Coordinadora de Organizaciones Indígenas de la Cuenca Amazónica (COICA) (1989) 'Two Agendas for Amazonian Development', *Cultural Survival Quarterly*, 13(4): 75–78.
4   Ibid.

5   See: McNeely, J. (1989) 'Protected areas and human ecology: How national parks can contribute to sustaining societies to the Twenty-Frst Century', in *Conservation for the Twentyfirst Century*, Western, D. and Pearl, M. (eds), Oxford University Press, Oxford; Western, D. and Wright, M. (eds), 1994, *Natural Connections: Perspectives in Community-Based Conservation*, Island Press, Washington, DC; Western, D. and Pearl, M. (eds) (1989) *Conservation for the Twenty-Frst Century*, Oxford University Press, Oxford; Wells, M. and Brandon, K. (1992) *People and Parks: Linking Protected Area Management with Local Communities*, The World Bank, Washington, DC; and Barzetti, V. (ed) (1993) *Parks and Progress: Protected Areas and Economic Development in Latin America and the Caribbean*, International Union for the Conservation of Nature, Washington, DC.

6   McShane, T.O. (2003) 'The devil in the detail of biodiversity conservation', *Conservation Biology*, 17(1): 1–3.

7   Brandon, K., Redford, K.H. and Sanderson, S.E. (eds) (1998) *Parks in Peril: People, Politics, and Protected Areas*, The Nature Conservancy and Island Press, Washington, DC.

8   Redford, K.H. (1991) 'The ecologically noble savage', *Cultural Survival Quarterly*, 15(1): 46–48.

9   Redford, K.H. and Sanderson, S.E. (2000) 'Extracting humans from nature', *Conservation Biology*, 14(5): 1362–1364; and Redford, K.H. and Stearman, A.M. (1993) 'Forest-dwelling native Amazonians and the conservation of biodiversity: Interests in common or in collision?', *Conservation Biology*, 7(2): 248–255.

10 In 2000, WWF International, in collaboration with a group called Terralingua, produced a report entitled *Indigenous and Traditional Peoples of the World and Ecoregion Conservation: An Integrated Approach to Conserving the World's Biological and Cultural Diversity*. This was an attempt to bring together the earlier policy statements and the ecoregional approach; yet it appears to have had little effect on WWF's programme, and in any case the major author, Gonzalo Oviedo, departed from WWF International shortly after.

11 A WWF document titled *A Guide to Socioeconomic Assessments for Ecoregion Conservation*, published in 2000, talks about potential collaborators and partners ("partnership" implies a closer working relationship'). It notes that 'reversing biodiversity loss at the scales required by ecoregion conservation may require close collaboration or partnerships with and among industry, the private sector, resource owners and harvesters, government development agencies, foreign affairs departments, policy fora, and others' (WWF US Ecoregional Conservation Strategies Unit, 2000: 56). Indigenous peoples are not included as potential collaborators or partners. Also notable is the absence of mention of local NGOs.

12 Chapeski, A. (1995) *Land, Landscape, Culturescape: Aboriginal Relationships to Land and the Co-Management of Natural Resources*, Ottawa: Report to the Royal Commission on Aboriginal Peoples, p. 46.

13 Khare, A. and Bray, D.B. (2004) *Study of Critical New Forest Conservation Issues in the Global South*. Final Report Submitted to the Ford Foundation, June 2004.

14 Ibid.

15 McShane, T.O. (2003) 'The devil in the detail of biodiversity conservation', *Conservation Biology*, 17(1): 1–3.

16 Chicchón, A. (2000) 'Conservation theory meets practice', *Conservation Biology*, 14(5): 1368–1369.

17 Perhaps the most blatant example of this is with CI's Critical Ecosystems Partnership Fund (CEPF), which was set up to reach local NGOs. According to programme guidelines, 'only' 50 per cent of CEPF's money is supposed to be granted directly to CI. Yet during the first two years of its Latin American programme, CEPF granted $6,915,865 out of a total of $$8,919,221 – 78 per cent – to CI. Other groups, several of them CI clones, received a total of $2,003,356, or 22 per cent of the available money (CEPF Annual Reports).

18   Stephens, J. and Ottaway, D. (2003) 'Nonprofit land bank amasses billions', *Washington Post*, 4 May.

19   Stevens, S. (ed) (1997) *Conservation Through Cultural Survival: Indigenous Peoples and Protected Areas*, Island Press, Washington, DC; Nietschmann, B. (1997) 'Protecting indigenous coral reefs and sea territories, Miskito Coast, RAAN, Nicaragua', pp. 193–224, in Stevens, S. (ed) *Conservation Through Cultural Survival: Indigenous Peoples and Protected Areas*, Island Press, Washington, DC; Gray, A., Parellada, A. and Newing, H. (eds) (1998) *From Principles to Practice: Indigenous Peoples and Biodiversity Conservation in Latin America*, Document 87, Forest Peoples Programme, the Interethnic Association for the Development of the Peruvian Amazon, and the International Work Group for Indigenous Affairs, Copenhagen; Schwartzman, S., Moreira, A. and Nepstad, D. (2000) 'Rethinking tropical forest conservation: Perils in parks', *Conservation Biology*, 14(5): 1351–1357; MacKay, F. and Caruso, E. (2004) 'Indigenous lands or national parks?', *Cultural Survival Quarterly*, 28(1): 14–16; Colchester, M. (2000) 'Self-determination or environmental determinism for indigenous peoples in tropical forest conservation', *Conservation Biology*, 14(5): 1365–67; Carino, J. (2004) 'Indigenous voices at the table: Restoring local decision-making on protected areas', *Cultural Survival Quarterly*, 28(1): 23–27; La Rose, J. (2004) 'In Guyana, indigenous peoples fight to join conservation efforts', *Cultural Survival Quarterly*, 28(1) 34–37; Newing, H. and Wahl, L. (2004) 'Benefiting local populations?', *Cultural Survival Quarterly*, 28(1): 38–42.

20   Brandon, K., Redford, K.H. and Sanderson, S.E. (1998) 'Introduction', in pp. 1–23, *Parks in Peril: People, Politics, and Protected Areas*, The Nature Conservancy and Island Press, Washington, DC; Redford, K.H. and Sanderson, S.E. (2000) 'Extracting humans From nature', *Conservation Biology*, 14(5): 1362–1364; Terborgh, J. (2000) 'The fate of tropical forests: A matter of stewardship', *Conservation Biology*, 14(5): 1358–1361.

21   Schwartzman, S., Moreira, A. and Nepstad, D. (2000) 'Rethinking tropical forest conservation: Perils in parks', *Conservation Biology*, 14(5): 1351–1357.

22   World Wildlife Fund (2000) *A Guide to Socioeconomic Assessments for Ecoregion Conservation*, Ecoregional Conservation Strategies Unit, Washington, DC; World Wildlife Fund (2004) *Communities and Large-Scale Conservation – Challenges and Opportunities*, Background Note for Discussion (Draft); Carr, A. (2004) 'Utopian bubbles: What are Central America's parks for?', *Wild Earth*, Spring/Summer, pp. 34–39.

23   Carr, ibid.

24   Several people explained that this was simply meant to be an 'internal' meeting between donors and NGOs, a first cut to chart future directions. Beyond this, several people noted that they had no idea of which 'representative' indigenous people who could.

25   Bray, D.B. (2004) Personal communication.

Chapter 22

Conservation, Development and Poverty Alleviation: Time for a Change in Attitudes

John F. Oates

In a book published in 1999, I presented my views on the root causes of what I considered to be a crisis for wildlife conservation in the forest zone of West Africa, and argued the need for changes in international conservation policy.[1]

In that book, I argued that the challenges faced by conservation in West Africa (which are not unique to that region) were related in part to large human population increases since World War II, along with economic development and associated road-building, increased forest exploitation, farming, mining and the hunting of wildlife. These forces had led to severe reductions in the extent of forest, and in the numbers of forest animals. Some species that are particularly sensitive to hunting and habitat disturbance (such as red colobus monkeys, *Procolobus badius waldroni*) had been driven to the brink of extinction in many areas.[2]

I suggested that international conservation policies had exacerbated the crisis. Despite evidence that traditional protected areas can conserve tropical nature, new international conservation policies formulated in the 1970s and 1980s de-emphasized the importance of protecting wild nature because of its intrinsic value and, instead, stressed the importance of regarding conservation as a component of economic and social development. In my book, I argued that such policies were based on political considerations and financial expediency, and that they were in part a response to large sums of money being made available by development agencies for projects that included a conservation component. The widely accepted policy of encouraging sustainable development emphasized the management of natural resources to promote human material well-being, rather than the protection of nature.

Projects I witnessed in West Africa that attempted to integrate conservation and development had not evidently improved the status of wild animal populations. Wildlife populations had continued to decline as internationally sponsored projects, generally managed by highly-paid foreign consultants, emphasized development efforts around protected areas without significantly increasing law-enforcement efforts against poachers. These projects tended to raise the expectations of local people that 'development' was being brought to them, only to leave them frustrated when short-term foreign aid grants and contracts ran out. I also saw that conservation-and-development projects located in the surroundings of protected areas could slow emigration, while encouraging immigration by people attracted to the possibilities of short-term material gain.

I noted that in the 1990s, further elaboration of human-centred conservation policy began to stress the idea that integrated conservation-and-development projects were most effectively carried out at the level of loosely-defined human 'communities', and community-based natural resource management schemes became popular. Policy-makers argued that local communities of rural people in Africa and elsewhere were inherently 'wise users' of nature (in the proper sense of the term) and that, if more power was devolved to them, they would do a better job of conservation than government agencies.

In fact, rural communities in West Africa are rarely egalitarian or especially cooperative, and their members will exploit wildlife populations without regard to long-term sustainability, just as most human populations have done throughout history. Humans are eclectic foragers, and are prepared to exploit any given resource to a point of exhaustion, and then switch to other sources.[3]

Although it was argued in the 1980s and 1990s that traditional conservation, involving the enforcement of hunting laws and the establishment of strictly protected areas, is incompatible with the realities of life for people in poor rural areas in developing countries, I noted that the example of India shows that this is not so. While having one of the densest human populations in the world, and persistent rural poverty, India managed to create and maintain effective nature reserves and to stave off the extinction of endangered species like the tiger.

Based on my personal experiences in West Africa and India, I called for a greater emphasis in international conservation policy on the strict protection, by governments, of nature. This protection, I argued, is of importance not only because of the aesthetic value of nature to people now and in the future, but also for ethical reasons, because of nature's intrinsic value and because of the 'right' of other species to exist. And I argued that one mechanism to pay for conservation, in cases where it is not generating revenue from some kind of harvesting, is through the establishment of trust funds, established with money from rich countries.

In the same year that my book appeared, John Terborgh of Duke University published *Requiem for Nature*, in which independently he made many of the same points, and stressed his own concerns.[4] Arguing on the basis of many years of experience in tropical forest ecology and conservation, especially in South America, Terborgh also pointed to a large and rapidly growing human population as the underlying cause of the rapid disappearance of tropical forests and their fauna, and for general environmental degradation.

Like me, Terborgh argued that nature and biodiversity must be conserved for their own sake, not because of their utilitarian value. No country, he pointed out, has achieved truly sustainable development, and he suggested that, when conservation organizations advocate sustainable use, conservation principles are being abandoned. The best hope, Terborgh argued, for the perpetuation of tropical nature lies in parks and similar protected areas; these should be located in key areas of high species richness and endemism, and they must be large if they are to retain their biodiversity (in part because of the significant role of top predators in ecosystems).

Terborgh agreed that integrated conservation and development projects are flawed by short funding cycles and tend to attract people to the edges of parks, thus increasing destructive pressures. Conservation projects that focus on local people miss the fact, he said, that such people are generally minor players in a larger theatre in which powerful figures in central government and business have most influence on environmental policy. Terborgh also warned that the policy of supporting the rights of indigenous people to remain inside forest parks and exploit park resources is likely to lead to the gradual destruction of the parks from within.

Although Terborgh argued that nature conservation works best when it is in the hands of national governments, he also noted that many tropical parks exist only on paper, and that others are generally poorly protected. This is because national institutions are often weak in developing countries, corruption and lawlessness are common, ethnic conflict is widespread, and inequities in power and wealth are the norm.

Based on these observations, Terborgh concluded that, for the foreseeable future, people in rich Western countries will probably have to pay for the protection of tropical parks. He suggested that this might best be done through trust fund mechanisms, and perhaps through supporting elite protection forces. He argued that nature protection is of such importance that internationalizing it under the United Nations should be considered, while keeping in mind the key role of national governments.

Trends in International Conservation Since 1999

Do the arguments presented by John Terborgh and myself in 1999 still hold today? Have there been significant changes in international conservation policy? Have there been obvious gains or losses for conservation, especially in the tropical forest systems on which we focused? It is my perception that there has been some progress, but also many setbacks. I will first summarize what I see as positive trends, then consider what I perceive as less positive developments.

Positive Trends

In recent years there has been ever-increasing attention in popular and professional media to 'biodiversity' and conservation. For instance, among new professional journals in the field, *Animal Conservation* began publication in 1998, and *Conservation in Practice* (a journal of applied conservation, sister to the more theoretical *Conservation Biology*) appeared in 2000. *Conservation Biology* itself contained 1540 published pages in 1999, and 1884 in 2003. In 2003 The Association for Tropical Biology was renamed the Association for Tropical Biology and Conservation.

More money than ever has flowed to conservation. For instance, the annual operating budgets of three large international conservation NGOs have increased by more than 50 per cent from 1999 to 2003, from US$332 million to $502 million. Operating expenditures for the World Wide Fund for Nature's (WWF) International Network in its 2003 financial year were CHF 521,631,000 ($386,007,000 at 30 June 2003 exchange rate), compared to CHF 456,010,000 ($291,846,400) in 1999; Conservation International's operating expenditures jumped from $26,576,000 in 1999 to $83,960,000 in 2003; and the international programmes division of the Wildlife Conservation Society increased from $13,327,222 in 1999 to $31,843,000 in 2003.[5]

The World Bank reports that in the 12 years prior to 2003, it provided $450 million in biodiversity conservation funding through the Global Environment Facility (GEF).[6] Part of this is presumably accounted for by GEF and World Bank support to the $150 million Critical Ecosystems Partnership Fund (CEPF), launched jointly with Conservation International (CI), the MacArthur Foundation and the government of Japan in 2001. The CEPF provides funding to 'civil society groups' in biodiversity hotspots. Also launched in 2001, with $100 million from the Gordon and Betty Moore Foundation, is the Global Conservation Fund (GCF) which devotes itself to protected area creation and management in hotspots, wilderness areas and important marine regions. Both the CEPF and the GCF are administered through CI.[7]

More meetings and workshops are being held on conservation themes, and these meetings are tending to become larger and more expensive. The World Parks Congress (WPC), convened in Durban, South Africa over 10 days in September 2003, attracted over 2500 participants, and was so large that it took participants hours just to register.[8]

More attention is being given to the importance of protected areas in conservation. At the WPC, it was announced that 11.5 per cent of the planet's land area is now within protected areas. In 2002, the Wildlife Conservation Society and other organizations helped Gabon to establish a network of 13 national parks, where there had been none before; these parks cover 11 per cent of Gabon's land area. Conservation International has sponsored a study that found that in a sample of 93 parks and other protected areas in 21 countries, the protected areas showed less land clearance, higher wildlife populations, less loss of commercial trees, less burning and less grazing than surrounding areas.[9]

'Conservation concessions' have also been introduced as a new protection tool. Under such schemes, a conservation organization arranges to pay government or other landholders for the right to use an area of land for conservation rather than for exploitative use, such as logging. This approach has been developed by CI and others, and has already been put into effect in a 340,000 acre (137,600ha) area of the Peruvian Amazon.[10]

In 2001 the World Bank introduced a new environment strategy, which includes a revised safeguard policy designed to minimize the adverse environmental impacts of projects supported by the bank.[11] The bank has also conducted a third comprehensive review of its environmental impact policies.[12] This review emphasizes the need to make safeguard policies uniform, transparent and effective, and to incorporate them at an early stage of project planning.

Less Positive Trends

Despite the large number of words and relatively very large sums of money now being devoted to conservation, the status of wild places and of wild plants and animals continues to deteriorate, at least over much of the tropics. Although the world appears to be paying more attention than ever to conservation, and although a good deal of this attention pays at least lip service to the importance of protecting nature, there still exists a large constituency for the ideas that (a) conservation should be seen as intimately linked to development, and (b) that people's perceived needs should be given high priority in the planning of conservation areas and projects. Some examples of these less positive trends follow.

Continuing losses of wildlife and habitat

Examples of continued loss of tropical habitat and wildlife come from the three countries with the largest areas of tropical forest: Brazil, Democratic Republic of Congo and Indonesia.

In April 2004 the government of Brazil announced that the rate of Amazonian deforestation rose 2 per cent in 2003, to produce a loss of 9169 square miles (23,750km²) of forest, the second highest annual loss recorded since 1988.[13]

Conflict and anarchy in the eastern Democratic Republic of Congo (especially pronounced from 1997 to 2003) led to increased bushmeat hunting, and some villages had to abandon agriculture and depend almost solely on bushmeat; in the remote Okapi Faunal Reserve, pygmies are reported to have been forced to hunt at greater and greater distances from the road to assure a catch.[14] Assuming a more stable future, over the next decade the government of DRC plans to increase timber production from 44,000m³/yr to around 10,000,000m³/yr.[15] In the forests of central Africa as a whole, the scale of the bushmeat trade has continued to increase, as forests in previously inaccessible areas are opened up by logging operations.[16]

A study of deforestation across Indonesia has predicted that, if current rates of loss continue, all the lowland forest on Sumatra will be gone by 2005, and on Kalimantan by 2010.[17] A separate analysis of remote sensing data from Kalimantan alone has shown that from 1985 to 2001, forest in West Kalimantan's lowland protected areas was reduced by 63 per cent, while in other parts of Kalimantan 48 per cent of forest cover was lost in protected areas, and much of the remaining forest was reduced to small fragments.[18]

Continuing emphasis on integrating conservation with development

Although more money is being spent by international conservation organizations and donor agencies, this has not necessarily translated to better nature protection on the ground.

Conservation organizations have indeed become richer, but a significant part of the increase in their expenditures is accounted for by larger administrative offices (often in neighbourhoods with high rents) and larger numbers of personnel in their headquarters. Meanwhile, there is a tendency for field programmes to be run with short-term grants from foundations and aid agencies, such as US Agency for International Development (USAID), the European Union Development Fund, the Canadian International Development Agency (CIDA), Germany's Gesellschaft für Technische Zusammenarbeit (GTZ) and the UK Department for International Development (DFID, formerly Organization of Development Assistance, ODA). To receive funds from such donors, projects must often satisfy criteria that can include paying attention to such humanitarian issues as community development, poverty alleviation, gender equity and the curbing of HIV/AIDS.

Aid-agency funded projects, which typically have short-term budgets of one million dollars or more, not only promote the fallacy of development as a means to better conservation, they also directly encourage behaviours that are the antithesis of nature conservation. The potential availability of large sums of money over a short period of time incites a clamour from consultants and NGOs eager not to miss their share. Such funding also tends to encourage corruption. The problem of corruption in externally funded conservation-and-development projects has previously been raised by John MacKinnon, who has suggested that donor agencies have been naive about this problem.[19]

In the area of West Africa where my own research and conservation efforts are concentrated, and where wild nature is under very great threat, much of the money and attention in conservation is still being devoted to projects that stress development, poverty alleviation and community-based management, rather than the basic protection of threatened wildlife.

For example, USAID is currently funding a consultancy group to consider agricultural intensification and community-based natural resources management in a zone around Cross River National Park in Nigeria. Local conservation NGOs are participating in this project, as they are with a programme funded by CIDA.

The CIDA-funded programme has as its stated aim the strengthening of NGO capacity to support communities around the Cross River National Park and the Obudu Plateau, and includes projects looking at issues such as community resource mapping, gender equity, and HIV/AIDS awareness. The Nigerian Conservation Foundation, one of the partner NGOs in this programme, and usually considered to be Nigeria's foremost non-governmental wildlife conservation organization, now states that it 'focuses attention on building a harmonious relationship between the natural resources it seeks to conserve and the people who depend directly on these resources for their food, shelter and clothing. NCF's field projects try to integrate conservation with rural development in order to achieve long-term sustainable development of our natural resources for the benefit of all.'[20]

In Cameroon, GTZ has sponsored studies in the Takamanda Forest Reserve, looking at ways to give villagers living inside the forest greater rights to exploit forest resources. There are recent signs, however, that the government of Cameroon may resist this proposal, and support more stringent protection of the area, one of the last homes of the critically endangered Cross River gorilla (*Gorilla gorilla diehli*).

At Cameroon's Korup National Park, WWF, ODA, GTZ and other agencies have been involved for many years with the Ministry of the Environment and Forestry (MINEF) in a conservation-and-development project. Major funding for this Korup Project has come from the European Union and the German government, but much of this funding has gone not to nature protection but to a socio-economic development programme in a zone around the park.[21] The UK's ODA withdrew from Korup in 1998, and GTZ's component of the project ended in late 2003, to be replaced by an organization called Conservation and Development Service (CODEV), which has a much reduced level of funding and technical assistance compared to the earlier Korup Project. The national park, covering an area of 1259km^2, has only 26 guards, and only 2 of these have long-term employment contracts with MINEF. The remaining guards are employed by WWF with short-term funding, and their motivation is low. Only 2 of 26 park guards have contracts from MINEF. Expectations of development assistance to the villages in and around the park have been only partly met, creating resentment and making the villagers uncooperative with park management. Not surprisingly, hunting is reported still to be rife over most of the park away from park headquarters, from which small-scale ecotourism and research efforts operate.

Increasing emphasis on relationships between poverty alleviation and conservation
The United Nations Millennium Declaration in 2000 stressed poverty eradication as a major concern in development policy (UN General Assembly Resolution 55/2, 2000), and poverty eradication or alleviation is now incorporated into most development-agency policies. These policies have a strong influence on conservation strategies because of the linkages that have arisen between conservation organizations and development agencies.

The United Nations Development Programme (UNDP), in particular, has argued that poverty reduction can play a pivotal role in environmental protection; the UNDP's Human Development Report 2003 states:

> *many environmental problems stem from poverty – often contributing to a downward spiral in which poverty exacerbates environmental degradation and environmental degradation exacerbates poverty. In poor rural areas, for example, there are close links among high infant mortality, high fertility, high population growth and extensive deforestation, as peasants fell tropical forests for firewood and new farmland. ... And when poor people degrade their environment, it is often because they have been denied their rights to natural resources by wealthy elites.*[22]

Meanwhile, on its web page describing its policy on biodiversity, the World Bank states that all the activities it supports (including establishing and strengthening protected areas) have important links to poverty alleviation initiatives.[23]

In the same way that United Nations policy formulations played a major role in driving the 1980s combination of conservation with sustainable development, the new stress on poverty, and the funds made available for its alleviation, have led to the design of increasing numbers of projects claiming that they will solve conservation problems by reducing rural poverty. Indeed, in a recent commentary, Sanderson and Redford suggest that poverty alleviation is supplanting biodiversity conservation on the international aid agenda.[24]

Sanderson and Redford express their disagreement with the argument that poverty alleviation on its own will achieve conservation, even when no specific biodiversity protection measures are attempted. I share their scepticism. Poverty eradication is, of course, an important humanitarian goal; and some of the relationships between poverty and environmental degradation laid out by the UNDP may exist in some form. On the other hand, many years of efforts to promote sustainable development in the tropics, and to link development to conservation, have met with little success, or downright failure. I am not aware of good evidence that the linking of poverty-alleviation with conservation will be more successful, either for reducing poverty or for protecting nature.

In the field of environmental economics, it is still a matter of debate whether alleviating poverty (and therefore increasing material wealth) automatically translates into gains for the environment and nature conservation. For instance, the environmental Kuznets curve suggests that as per-capita income rises, environmental degradation initially increases, only to decrease when people become really wealthy.[25]

Support for the idea that increasing wealth can actually lead to increasing pressure on the environment comes from an article by Naidoo and Adamowicz in *Conservation Biology*.[26] They tested relationships between wealth and wildlife conservation by comparing data from over 100 countries on land use and gross national product, with the numbers of threatened plant, invertebrate, fish, amphibian, reptile, bird and mammal species. With the exception of birds and, in some cases, mammals, all taxonomic groups showed increasing numbers of threatened species as the log of per-capita GNP increased. Only bird data conform to the Kuznets curve, with numbers of threatened species first rising with rising GNP, then declining, perhaps related to a public liking for birds in some rich countries.

Such analyses conform to commonplace observations. In general, as people get wealthier they consume more and more products from their environment and, with the use of more technology, they increase their extractive and destructive powers exponentially. Only at levels of high wealth do societies show increasing concern for environmental quality, at which point they may then act selectively to protect preferred species and sites. To quote from John MacKinnon:

> *Every step of the development ladder is accompanied by an overall increase in resource use levels. People never have 'enough.' When a man graduates from a bicycle to a motor bike he suddenly needs money to pay for the fuel. This need forces him to cut even more forest or sell more wildlife than when he was a subsistence farmer.*[27]

Rural poverty in tropical countries is surely much more susceptible to alleviation by large-scale changes in governance and culture than by small-scale NGO conservation projects run on short-term grants. And as with development projects generally, poverty-alleviation efforts conducted close to conservation target areas are likely, if successful, to increase rather than decrease pressures on nature.

Calls for greater rights for indigenous people

Along with poverty alleviation, another issue that has gained salience in conservation policy formulations in recent years, particularly for tropical regions, is the rights of indigenous people in relation to protected areas. This was one of the core issues addressed at the World Parks Congress in Durban in September 2003, and it is reported that the congress gave increased recognition to indigenous peoples' rights.[28] In a declaration to the congress, a coalition of indigenous peoples noted that they should be regarded as 'rights-holders, not merely stakeholders', and called for restitution of lands expropriated as protected areas, for compensation to be provided, and for indigenous peoples to be able to participate in all aspects of protected area administration and management.[29]

This complex and vexing issue cannot be addressed adequately in a short paper of general scope. A particularly useful discussion on the issue can be found in the pages of the journal *Oryx* in 1998 and 1999. In this exchange, John Burton pointed out the difficulty in defining which people are indigenous in any given area.[30]

In searching for a definition of indigenous people, I found that the United Nations refers to Article 1 of the International Labour Organization's Convention on Indigenous and Tribal Peoples which states that people may be regarded as indigenous:

> *on account of their descent from the populations which inhabited the country, or a geographical region to which the country belongs, at the time of conquest or colonisation or the estab-*

lishment of present state boundaries and who, irrespective of their legal status, retain some or all of their own social, economic, cultural and political institutions.[31]

This is obviously a very broad definition, that can be interpreted to give very many people indigenous status, especially since Article 2 of the convention states that 'Self-identification as indigenous or tribal shall be regarded as a fundamental criterion for determining the groups to which the provisions of this Convention apply.' With regard to the declaration made to the World Parks Congress, this interpretation of 'indigenous' could allow almost any group of people to claim rights to occupy and/or manage a protected area. As John Henshaw pointed out in the discussion published in *Oryx*, this highlights the inadequacy of approaching wildlife and habitat conservation, and its necessary biological underpinnings, from the standpoint of political doctrines.[32]

Social scientists writing about conservation often make the argument that the creation of protected areas involves removing indigenous or local people from their land.[33] This argument ignores the fact that many tropical parks have been established in precisely those areas that have contained few or no resident humans in recent times, and that it is the low densities of people in these areas that has led to the survival of the rich biodiversity which the parks have been created to protect. Almost all regional and national land-use planning that is designed to produce long-term benefits for a majority of people has some adverse consequences for a small number of people. Plans to create new roads, railways, airports and reservoirs will generally displace some local residents, and it is well-established policy that such residents receive appropriate compensation when they relocate. I see no obvious reason why national protected-area planning should proceed according to a different philosophy.

More conservation workshops – but do they help?

Projects that emphasize linkages between conservation and development, and between conservation and poverty alleviation, often have a series of workshops as a major component. In places like West Africa, frequent workshops of this kind over the last decade have been a powerful mechanism for inculcating in local conservationists the notion that wildlife conservation is part and parcel of sustainable development and poverty alleviation. To me, there are parallels with missionary activity. Frequent preaching of the same message often does lead to its widespread adoption, especially when rewards are attached. Workshop attendees expect to be paid relatively handsome per diems to attend workshops and to be put up in good hotels, and these are strong incentives in countries where the average daily income is $1–$2/day. Well-funded, comfortable meetings also reinforce the idea that large funds are potentially available for projects that combine conservation with development. Workshops also seem to be favoured by their sponsors, because they are a discrete activity, easier to administer and report on than are the difficult long-term realities of trying to make a tropical protected area work better. Most of those involved in a workshop probably feel that something worthwhile has occurred, when nothing has changed actually on the ground, and may not change.

The Need to Change Attitudes

Nature conservation continues to face huge challenges, especially in the tropics. Since 1999, tropical conservation has received plenty of attention (at least on paper and in digital form) and there has been increased acknowledgement of the importance of protected areas, but the balance of evidence suggests that actual wildlife and habitat conservation in the tropics continues to lose ground. Not only in general public discourse, but also within conservation circles, the rights and needs of one species, *Homo sapiens*, continue to be stressed relative to those of the millions of other species with which we share the planet. There is widespread acceptance of the propositions that conservation is part of something called sustainable development, that community-based conservation works (despite much evidence to the contrary), and that conservation can be achieved through projects to alleviate poverty. This dogma has been adopted by conservation practitioners in tropical countries, to the general detriment of effective nature conservation.

In my view, wildlife in West Africa and other similar parts of the tropics will continue to lose ground unless we can do a better job of changing attitudes as to what conservation is about. If we continue to regard conservation as just another aspect of efforts to increase the material well-being of humans, we will not retain many other species or the complex ecosystems and processes which sustain them. Rather than continuing to follow this inappropriate course, we need to go back to basics and examine why it is that people interested in wildlife and nature have the concern they do for conservation. Frequently, the root cause of this concern is the aesthetic value of nature; finding animals, plants and wild places beautiful and inspiring. This valuation is often combined with a belief that nature has an intrinsic value, and that other species have some right to exist, to find some corner of the planet where they can live freely.

We know that aesthetic and ethical values towards nature can be nurtured in young people. As I said in my book, such distinguished individuals as Richard Leakey, George Schaller and Edward Wilson, who have all thought deeply about conservation, have independently made the point that one can find an inherent appreciation of nature in people everywhere.[34] This is widely seen in the fascination of young people everywhere with animals.

The need to reduce poverty and to increase human well-being, especially in tropical countries, should not be minimized. But this issue has become too closely entangled with nature conservation. Of course there are some linkages between development and conservation, but conservation has also to be seen as very important in its own right. Many people today value nature for aesthetic and ethical, rather than economic reasons, and this is likely to be the case in the future. Quite apart from the right of other species to exist, preserving nature now can therefore be seen as a benefit for future generations of humans.

For these reasons, I think that conservationists should not be afraid of trying to persuade others of the importance of their core values. Changing the attitudes of those who shape policies will not be an easy task, however, especially because these policy-makers reflect the increasingly materialistic attitudes of the constituents they represent.

It is my perception that in the last 30–40 years, people in many parts of the world seem to have become more rather than less selfish and materialistic, and selfish materialism is not a sturdy foundation on which to build real conservation. The emphasis of a link between conservation and development, and the widespread use of professional consultancy companies to implement conservation-and-development projects, have tended to promote a materialistic approach to conservation at the expense of an aesthetic and ethical one.

These realities, the fact that it can take a long time to change attitudes, and the fact that nature faces a crisis in many parts of the tropics, suggest to me that, in the short term, we are probably going to have to rely on parks as a last refuge for much of tropical nature, and employ a rather hard-nosed monetary approach to park protection. As John Terborgh and others have suggested, those people in rich Western countries who are concerned about tropical nature will probably have to pay for its protection, at least for the time being.[35] Money is needed both to compensate people whose livelihoods may be disrupted by the existence of a park (fair compensation is more compatible with conservation than user rights), and to cover the direct costs of protection (including staff salaries, equipment and infrastructure). Payments by people and organizations in Western countries for the protection of tropical parks is probably best achieved by using long-term trust-fund mechanisms rather than by short-term grants.[36] Such payments, and any necessary outside technical assistance, require the full cooperation of national governments, who can be resentful of too direct a Western role in the management of their natural resources.

This approach is essentially short-term crisis management. In the long run, conservation seems likely to fail unless there is a strong constituency of people urging that nature be protected because of its aesthetic and intrinsic values.

Notes

1   Oates, J.F. (1999) *Myth and Reality in the Rain Forest: How Conservation Strategies are Failing in West Africa*, University of California Press, Berkeley.
2   Oates, J.F., Abedi-Lartey, M., McGraw, W.S., Struhsaker, T.T. and Whitesides, G.H. (2000) 'Extinction of a West African red colobus monkey', *Conservation Biology*, 14: 1526–1532.
3   See Brooks, Chapter 16 of *Gaining Ground: In Pursuit of Ecological Sustainability*, International Fund for Animal Welfare, pp. 243–264, for a Darwinian explanation of such behaviour.
4   Terborgh, J. (1999) *Requiem for Nature*, Island Press, Washington, DC.

5   According to financial statements on the organizations' websites and personal communications from staff of CI, WCS and WWF. The money spent by international conservation organizations is still modest compared with the revenues and expenditures of major international business corporations.

6   Available at http://lnweb18.worldbank.org/ESSD/envext.nsf /48ByDocName/Biodiversity.

7   From the website of Conservation International, www.conservation.org.

8   Salafsky, N. (2003) 'The ghost of SCB future', *Society for Conservation Biology Newsletter,* 10(4): 1–12.

9   Bruner, A.G., Gullison, R.E., Rice, R.E. and da Fonseca, G.A.B. (2001) 'Effectiveness of parks in protecting tropical biodiversity', *Science,* 291: 125–128.

10   Rice, R. (2002) *Conservation Concessions – Concept Description,* Center for Applied Biodiversity Science, Conservation International, Washington, DC.

11   World Bank (2001) *Making Sustainable Commitments: An Environment Strategy for the World Bank,* World Bank, Washington, DC.

12   World Bank (2002) *Third Environmental Assessment Review (FY96–00),* World Bank, Washington, DC.

13   Downie, A. (2004) 'Amazon destruction rising fast', *Christian Science Monitor,* 22 April 2004.

14   Wildlife Conservation Society (2003) *Democratic Republic of Congo Environmental Analysis. Final Report,* Report to USAID, Washington, DC, for more on the bushmeat issue, see Eves, Chapter 9, pp. 141–52, and Milner-Gulland, Chapter 20 of *Gaining Ground: In Pursuit of Ecological Sustainability,* International Fund for Animal Welfare.

15   Wildlife Conservation Society (2003) *Democratic Republic of Congo Environmental Analysis. Final Report,* Report to USAID, Washington, DC.

16   Fa, J.E., Currie, D. and Meeuwig, J. (2003) 'Bushmeat and food security in the Congo Basin: Linkages between wildlife and people's future', *Environmental Conservation,* 30: 71–78.

17   Jepson, P., Jarvie, J.K., MacKinnon, K. and Monk, K.A. (2001) 'The end for Indonesia's lowland forests?', *Science,* 292: 859–861.

18   Curran, L.M., Trigg, S.N., McDonald, A.K., Astiani, D., Hardiono, Y.M., Siregar, P., Caniago, I. and Kasischke, E. (2004) 'Lowland forest loss in protected areas of Indonesian Borneo', *Science,* 303: 1000–1003.

19   MacKinnon, J. (2002) *'Avenues of Futility in Conservation',* unpublished presentation to annual meeting of Society for Conservation Biology, Canterbury, England.

20   From http://www.onesky.ca/Nigeria/partners.html

21   MINEF (2003) *A Management Plan for Korup National Park and its Peripheral Zone,* Ministry of the Environment and Forestry, Yaounde, Cameroon; Oates, J.F. (1999) *Myth and Reality in the Rain Forest: How Conservation Strategies are Failing in West Africa,* University of California Press, Berkeley.

22   UNDP (2003) *Human Development Report 2003,* Oxford University Press, New York.

23   Available at http://lnweb18.worldbank.org/ESSD/envext.nsf/48BYDocName/Biodiversity.

24   Sanderson, S.E. and Redford, K.H. (2003) 'Contested relationships between biodiversity conservation and poverty alleviation', *Oryx,* 37: 389–390.

25   Barbier, E.B. (1997) 'Introduction to Environmental Kuznets Curve special issue', *Environment and Development Economics,* 2: 369–382.

26   Naidoo, R. and Adamowicz, W.L. (2001) 'Effects of economic prosperity on numbers of threatened species', *Conservation Biology,* 15: 1021–1029.

27   MacKinnon, J. (2002) *'Avenues of Futility in Conservation',* unpublished presentation to annual meeting of Society for Conservation Biology, Canterbury, England.

28   DeRose, A.M. (2003) *Fifth IUCN World Parks Congress,* Special Bulletin on Global Process, no. 5, World Resources Institute Washington, DC. Available at: http://governance.wri.org/project_description2.cfm?ProjectID=148

29 'The Indigenous Peoples' Declaration to the World Parks Congress', September 2003. Available at: www.treaty-council.org/section_211812142.htm

30 Burton, J.A. (1999) 'Traditional rights – what do they mean?', *Oryx*, 33: 2–3.

31 International Labour Organization (1989) *C169 Indigenous and Tribal Peoples Convention*, International Labour Organization, Geneva, Switzerland. Available at: http://www.ilo.org/ilolex/english/convdisp1.htm

32 Henshaw, J. (1999) 'Indigenous people and conservation', *Oryx*, 33: 4–5.

33 Brockington, D. and Schmidt-Soltau, K. (2004) 'The social and environmental impacts of wilderness and development', *Oryx*, 38: 140–142.

34 Oates, J.F. (1999) *Myth and Reality in the Rain Forest: How Conservation Strategies are Failing in West Africa*, University of California Press, Berkeley.

35 Terborgh, J. (1999) *Requiem for Nature*, Island Press, Washington, DC.

36 Global Environment Facility (1999) *Experience with Conservation Trust Funds*, GEF Evaluation Report no. 1–99, UNDP, UNEP, World Bank, Washington, DC.

Chapter 23

Conserving What and for Whom? Why Conservation Should Help Meet Basic Needs in the Tropics

David Kaimowitz and Douglas Sheil

Conservation poses tough choices. We cannot prevent every species from going extinct or from losing genetic diversity, so we must prioritize what to save. Those priorities should also take into account human health, well-being and culture. We argue that conservation activities designed to meet people's basic needs deserve more attention. This, to some extent, implies a different *kind* of conservation and conservation science: one that has subsistence needs at its core.

Current Conservation Priorities

Conservation NGOs have played a major role in setting the priorities that drive the global conservation agenda (Redford et al., 2003; Brooks et al., 2006). These priorities emphasize protecting species and ecosystems – not the needs of local people – in part because saving charismatic animals and plants from extinction appeals to those on whom conservation agencies traditionally rely for financial support. It is true that conservation agencies have devoted some attention to generating income for poor people through ecotourism and the sale of natural products. For example, thanks in part to their efforts, the Serengeti tourism industry now employs about 50,000 Tanzanians and benefits at least another 50,000 people in the park buffer zone (Wolanski, 2004); various similar efforts are under way elsewhere. The emphasis and motivation, however, remains the conservation of charismatic species.

In contrast, much less is being done to maintain wild and semi-wild species and habitats specifically to fulfil human needs. Despite persuasive technical arguments, NGOs and governments make relatively little effort to protect the wild relatives of crops, potential sources of new pharmaceuticals, genetic diversity in commercially important plants other than crops, or organisms that recycle nutrients

Reprinted from *Biotropica*, vol 39, no 5, by Kaimowitz, D. and Sheil, D., 'Conserving what and for whom? Why conservation should help meet basic needs in the tropics', pp. 567–574, copyright © (2007) with permission from Blackwell Publishing Ltd, Oxford.

or pollinate crops (International Plant Genetic Resources Institute, 2004; Meilleur and Hodgkin, 2004). Even fewer resources go into ensuring that disadvantaged people retain access to species on which they have traditionally relied for food, livelihoods, shelter, and medicines.

Poor People's Biodiversity

For several billion people, wild plants and animals are not just objects of admiration, but the essential elements of daily life. While most of these people grow crops and raise animals, they still depend to a surprising degree on wild resources obtained through hunting, gathering and fishing.

Ethnographic studies typically find these people use hundreds of species for a wide range of purposes. Wild meat, fish and insects provide much of their protein, while forest fruits and vegetables are a source of vitamins (Scoones et al., 1992). In fact, in 62 developing countries, wild meat and fish provide more than 20 per cent of all protein (Bennett and Robinson, 2000). Studies show it is also common for 'wild' plants and animals to provide 20–30 per cent of rural peoples' income in developing countries (Vedeld et al., 2004).

Many of the estimated two billion people that lack adequate access to Western medicine rely largely on wild and semi-wild plants and animals for much of their treatment (Farnsworth and Soejarto, 1991; WHO, 2003). Moreover, families facing individual or social hardships, such as poverty, sickness, droughts, wars and economic crisis, are most dependent on 'wild resources' (World Resources Institute, 2005). If these species become scarcer or disappear, these people's already difficult lives will be made even harder.

That is precisely what is happening in many places: plants and animals on which poor people depend are disappearing. An estimated 4160 to 10,000 medicinal plants are endangered by habitat loss or overexploitation (Hamilton, 2004), and many more have become hard to find in places where rural families traditionally collected them. In many regions, overexploitation of fish and game along with forest destruction and water pollution have depleted the supply of fish and wild meat, and local people have lost a valuable source of nutrition. In many places, fuel wood has become scarcer (Arnold et al., 2006). Species of cultural and symbolic significance have also been lost.

Sometimes people find substitutes. They may cultivate or purchase alternatives, or come to depend on charitable assistance. But substitutes are not always available and people suffer. It is well established that environmental degradation impacts heavily on the poor causing greater poverty (Millennium Ecosystem Assessment, 2005). This often leads to migration from rural to urban areas, forest frontiers, or marginal lands. Desperation forces people to adopt unsustainable short-term survival tactics – leading to further environmental damage and a cycle of decline (Millennium Ecosystem Assessment, 2005; World Resources Institute, 2005).

A Pro-Poor Approach to Conserving Biodiversity

So, what specifically might pro-poor conservation actually require? In our view, the basic principles are finding, developing, maintaining and safeguarding managed landscapes that include adequate areas to serve as sources of fauna and flora for local people, especially those who are vulnerable and marginalized.

Conservation programmes that address basic human needs will often invest in different places and ways than those focused on saving species from extinction. The emphasis needs to be on places where many people rely on declining wild resources with few substitutes. These areas may often be drier, more heavily disturbed, and more densely populated than the species-centric hotspots identified by the large conservation agencies (Brooks et al., 2006). For instance, they are likely to be in sub-Saharan Africa and the upland areas of Asia and the Pacific.

A pro-poor approach also implies investing resources outside large, strictly protected areas. Biodiversity must be accessible and people must have some rights to use it. For example, instead of buffer zones serving primarily to protect core areas in parks, protected areas can be established and justified by their ability to help sustain tangible local benefits, such as breeding grounds for animals and sources of pollinators, seeds, clean water, or valued products, within a larger land-scape. Smaller strategically located reserves might incur lower opportunity costs for the poor, and might meet their conservation needs better than fewer large areas (Zuidema et al., 1996). Greater emphasis would be placed on conservation in multiple-use 'protected areas' including IUCN categories IV ('Habitat/Species Management Area: Protected Area managed mainly for conservation through management intervention') and VI ('Managed Resource Protected Areas: Protected Area managed mainly for the sustainable use of natural ecosystems'). These now account for nearly half the land in officially designated and categorized protected areas globally (Chape et al., 2003).

Some of the best examples of the effectiveness of such conservation approaches come from the Pacific Islands, where traditional no-fishing zones helped to maintain fish stocks and other marine resources (Johannes, 1978; Cinner et al., 2005). These approaches are increasingly being replicated in marine areas elsewhere (Johannes, 2002; United Nations Food and Agriculture Organization, 2002; Gell and Roberts, 2003). Though initially built on folk ecology, the approaches are becoming more science-led (Lubchenco et al., 2003; Pikitch et al., 2004), with researchers now claiming to satisfy both fishermen and conservationists (Meester et al., 2004).

Changing the practices of both local people and external actors in ways that help maintain the plants and animals that local people use will often be essential.

This implies working with communities to design and enforce rules about hunting, fishing, and gathering plant material, limiting outsiders' access to local resources and giving poor people greater control over them, and protecting the places where animals breed, and obtain food and salt. It means promoting corridors, agroforestry, fire management, and reduced-impact logging (Schroth et al., 2004). It may also require domestication or more intensive management of traditionally wild plants and animals.

Needless to say, a pro-poor approach to conservation inevitably implies working closely with communities rather than fencing them out. It goes beyond most (though by no means all) previous 'community', 'participatory' or 'development' efforts intended primarily to win local acceptance of other people's conservation agendas. It involves focusing on the weak and vulnerable, not only the politically perceptive and influential.

While conservation actions developed wholly without local engagement might occasionally benefit the poor, pro-poor conservation will generally require local engagement to help to determine an agenda that meets their concerns.

Biodiversity assessments that privilege the viewpoints of those directly dependent on wild resources will differ from global perspectives (Table 23.1). Differences reflect distinct perceptions and motivations; they need not imply discordant judgements of desirable versus undesirable conservation outcomes. One fundamental advantage of working with local, in contrast to external, viewpoints, is that local priorities directly engage local understandings and interests. An apparent disadvantage is that these local goals do not attract the same external support as many international perspectives can muster.

A pro-poor approach offers prospects of finding new opportunities for conservation, to attract new supporters and to access new resources. A pro-poor approach alone cannot conserve everything. Some species require large areas of intact habitat and may not survive in fragmented or modified ecosystems, and some do not coexist readily with people (Redford and Richter, 1999). In some cases it may be necessary to compensate poor people for strict protection, so they can meet their needs from other sources. All the same, protected areas will never make up more than a fraction of the planet's surface. The future of many, if not most, species depends on what happens outside strictly protected areas and wilderness areas.

Synergy with Conventional Conservation

Despite common prejudices, human impacts in the tropics are not always wholly detrimental, and many land-use alternatives have biodiversity benefits as well as costs. Conservationists have often viewed modified habitats as a 'glass part empty' rather than a 'glass part full'. This bias reduces the recognition of opportunities. Many species can and do flourish in non-pristine environments (Robbins et al., 2006). Bwindi Forest in Uganda (now a National Park) contains half the world's

Table 23.1 *Contrasting global and local perspectives on biodiversity*

	Dominant global perspectives adopted by most conservation authorities	Dominant perspectives of local communities
Major biodiversity value	Rare and endemic species and species belonging to charismatic taxa	Species used for livelihood and cultural purposes. Some species may be considered undesirable (pests or dangerous species)
Main rationale for conservation	Maintain ecological integrity on basis of scientific criteria	Maintain products and cultural values based on local criteria
Major objective for maintaining biodiversity	Preserving option and bequest values for future generations	Maintaining present use and guaranteeing future supplies
Species considered	All taxonomically reasonably known species	Species locally recognized to provide valuable products and services, including cultural uses, and the species those species depend on.
Main conservation approach	In situ preservation by prohibiting/or limiting	Controlled sustainable use and gradual domestication
Clients/user groups	A continuum from unclear to 'global' or 'future generations'	Clearly defined
Wild and domesticated species	Treated differently	Form a continuum

Source: based on ideas presented in Vermeulen and Koziell (2002) and Wiersum (2003).

mountain gorillas (*Gorilla beringei beringei*) despite once being a productive timber forest (McNeilage et al., 2001). These gorillas like to feed where thick herbaceous growth follows disturbance and so they may have benefited from logging. Logged-over forests in Borneo maintain significant wildlife conservation values that can be further improved by appropriate management (Meijaard and Sheil, 2007). While no one is arguing that oil palm (*Elaeis guineensis*) estates are 'good for conservation', those in Sumatra have some value as habitat for tigers (*Panthera tigris sumatrae*) and other endangered species (Maddox et al., 2005). From the community forests in Mexico (Johnson and Nelson, 2004) to the tree-dominated agroforestry systems in Sumatra (Thiollay, 1995; Garcia-Fernandez et al., 2003; Beukema and van Noordwijk, 2004), studies continue to highlight the diverse biodiversity present in multifunctional landscapes that poor people also depend upon.

Multiple-use landscapes have various conservation values. These values will often be affected by management choices. Trade-offs are inevitable, but land-use mosaics with a mix of different use and conservation intensities could be central to effective conservation strategies, whether to protect globally endangered charismatic species or species relied upon by rural people.

Some opportunities for synergy may not be immediately apparent, but they are important nonetheless. Thus, for example, in East Kalimantan, Indonesia, current regulations require loggers to clear away the undergrowth after timber has been removed. This has a negative impact on both plant species that local people often use, such as medicinals, rattan and wild vegetables, as well as various types of wildlife, and it has little silvicultural value. Moreover, the rules prescribe clearing in a blanket fashion, and it is practised even in areas left unlogged due to rugged terrain. Local people helped researchers understand how this treatment harms both local needs and the forest. Research suggests that any silvicultural benefits are indeed outweighed by the costs; and the practice should be halted (Sheil et al., 2006). Such examples show that incorporating local concerns into management and planning while good for people can also benefit conservation.

In traditional conservation projects, conflicts with local people are often due to the manner in which conservation projects are implemented. Hasty interventions that fail to build local trust are perceived by local people as just one more attempt to gain control over valued land and resources. On the other hand, working with local people to identify local needs can build trust. By building a basis for mutual understanding, oversights and misunderstandings can be avoided. Nearly everyone accepts the need for some form of conservation and most cultures have their own conservation ethic. In many cases, local and external goals have much in common (e.g. Sheil and Boissiere, 2006).

National governments in the tropics may be more willing to support interventions tailored to meet local needs (but see Sekhsaria, 2007). Indeed conservation with democratic support is likely to be more acceptable and thus often more effective than conservation that is imposed (Schwartzman et al., 2000).

Resting our hopes on finding local and national support is not simply wishful thinking. The growth of environmentally concerned movements throughout the developing world is among the most profound political developments of recent decades. Public opinion polls in poor tropical countries consistently show a concern about the environment that is similar to the levels found in wealthier industrialized countries (Steinberg, 2005). Thousands of citizen groups in developing countries are increasingly campaigning in favour of various environmental causes (Steinberg, 2005), while discussions with people living in biodiverse tropical regions reveal a widespread desire for effective, but democratically accountable, conservation (Padmanaba and Sheil, 2007). Such support will benefit conservation more generally, but it is especially likely to favour, and to arise from, activities that bring local benefits.

Learning Lessons

Conservation by using rather than locking up biodiversity has had a bumpy history. This enticing vision gained widespread credibility with the publication of *Caring for the Earth* (IUCN et al., 1991) and the discussions at the 1992 Earth Summit in Rio de Janeiro, and led to the first generation of official integrated conservation and development projects (ICDPs). For a time, almost every new conservation project seemed to support development goals: local people would be allowed to hunt in the Serengeti and the forests of the Amazon basin would become a mosaic of self-supporting extractive reserves. But naive enthusiasm outstripped abilities, and these early ICDPs often failed to provide the anticipated benefits, both in terms of conservation and development. These disappointments generated a backlash, leading various commentators to suggest such efforts are inherently doomed (reviewed in Wilshusen et al., 2002).

ICDPs were not wholly failures (see Schwartzman et al., 2000; Hughes and Flintan, 2001). Those that fell short did so for reasons that are now understood (Hughes and Flintan, 2001; Brown, 2002; Wilshusen et al., 2002; Wells and McShane, 2004; Spiteri and Nepal, 2006; Brooks et al., 2006). One lesson was that these projects remained essentially protectionist, seeking to sever rather than maintain local access to natural resources. The projects were designed and imposed by outsiders to meet predefined goals, with little local control. The development components compensated local peoples' losses to some degree, but the benefits and degrees of engagement were generally insufficient to counter local resentment and opposition, and often accrued inequitably adding to perceived injustice. Besides, the key threats were often external, and the projects had few tools with which to address these. Many of the forces that undermined ICDPs also pose serious challenges to traditional protectionist (guards and fences) conservation approaches (Wilshusen et al., 2002).

So how do we improve projects to benefit the poor? Two requirements that emerge clearly are the need for varied approaches (a 'pro-poor approach' is certainly no panacea to every conservation challenge) (Robinson, 1993; Medellin, 1999) and the need to better engage people (Brown, 2002; Wells and McShane, 2004; Brooks et al., 2006). Even when conservation is the primary goal, greater efforts are needed to ensure compensation and incentives are better targeted, and address those with few livelihood alternatives (Spiteri and Nepal, 2006). Such targeting becomes doubly vital in a pro-poor approach.

Efforts to clarify what works in complex environmental projects repeatedly underline the need to avoid inflexible systems, and instead develop management strategies that learn and respond (Sayer and Campbell, 2003). Though scattered, the sum-total of past experience working on poverty, conservation and environmental management begins to provide a good foundation for what might work (Hughes and Flintan, 2001; Brown, 2002; Fisher et al., 2005).

What Does Pro-Poor Conservation Look Like?

Effective pro-poor conservation projects may not look much like conservation projects at all. Sometimes, the main threats that must be addressed are external. For example, in many tropical countries, governments have claimed natural forests as state land, and have allowed these to be exploited and converted with little reference to their inhabitants (Sekhsaria, 2007). Innovative approaches to recognize and defend such regions and their values against external threats will often be crucial to a pro-poor conservation approach.

When the major threats include local actors, the challenge will be more complex. Excessive exploitation often results from a 'free for all' or a 'tragedy of the commons' situation, in which local people may become their own enemies. Restraint is desirable, and may even be acceptable as long as the rules are fair. Communities have often developed sophisticated traditions and practices to safeguard their access to vulnerable resources, and while these systems may not always be robust to the challenges of the 21st century, they can provide a foundation (Ostrom et al., 1999). Besides the embodied technical understanding, rules based on traditional approaches are often more likely to be understood and respected locally (Johannes, 1978). Acceptance of new rules is not impossible. One example is the crocodile hunters of Mamberamo, Papua (Irian Jaya, Indonesia), who have, despite initial opposition, accepted externally suggested size-based rules on trading in skins, condemn those who breach these rules, and chase away poachers (D. Sheil, pers. obs.). A pro-poor approach will often require the development of such local rules and the means to enforce them.

Elements of pro-poor conservation activities can be drawn from successful community-based resource management projects, where key players agree to develop, implement, and periodically review procedures, assess needs, and gauge effectiveness. Promising examples may be drawn from many regions and biomes from marine fisheries to arid lands (Schwartzman et al., 2000; Campbell and Shackleton, 2001; Johannes, 2002). Community-based forest landscape restoration in Nepal has seen reforested hills boosting wildlife diversity and productivity (Pokharel et al., 2006). Success reflects participation by local actors, the development of suitable local institutions, and the technical and financial support to initiate and nurture the process (Pokharel et al., 2006). Such projects can also focus on wildlife. For example, effective game ranching projects have been developed by and for communities (Le Bel et al., 2004).

In short, for pro-poor conservation, the needs of the poor and the threats to these needs must be better recognized, understood and addressed. Beyond that, a plurality of alternatives and options seems possible. The best options will depend on local needs and circumstances. We still have a lot to learn, but we know enough to make a start.

Support: Partnerships and Research

What role can researchers, conservationists, development professionals, funding agencies, and other external groups play? All the elements of 'pro-poor conservation' mentioned already might benefit from external support. All conservation initiatives can benefit from long-term defenders and champions. Funds, guidance, awareness raising, and capacity building will also be necessary. Two specific aspects, partnerships and research, could greatly facilitate the process and warrant a special consideration.

In an ideal democratic world, conservation might always be conceived as a partnership of conservation organizations with local people. Partnerships require shared decision-making, shared risks, and a balance of rights and responsibilities between external agencies and local groups. In the real world, this can be difficult and time consuming. It is hard to reach the poor and marginalized. Nonetheless, partnerships offer outcomes that are often more ethical and more practicable than most alternatives. Partnering can also help build local institutions and develop people's sense of their own worth and that of their environment (van Rijsoort and Zhang, 2005; Vermeulen and Sheil, 2007).

Pro-poor conservation will benefit from research. Promising initiatives may, as in the case of the traditional Pacific fisheries, be discovered rather than created (Seymour, 1994; Johannes, 2002). The social and political institutions needed to effectively regulate resources must also be characterized and developed to ensure that adequate numbers of affected people find the benefits of involvement outweigh the costs (Dietz et al., 2003). As with any conservation investments experiences should be reviewed, shared and learned from (Kleiman et al., 2000; Ferraro and Pattanayak, 2006).

Working with local people requires effective communication. This is far from trivial (Sheil and Lawrence, 2004). To define the scope and goals of an intervention requires a sound basis of understanding of local needs, preferences and value systems. Assessments to support pro-poor conservation will focus on which species local people use or value, their location, where they can be accessed, their threats, and which management approaches are required to maintain them. It can also seek synergies with more conventional conservation goals. Both communications and assessment can benefit from diagnostic research that sets out to develop the required understanding between locals and outsiders (Sheil et al., 2006).

Research to support pro-poor conservation must draw upon a broad range of disciplines. Biological sciences will remain crucial to guide the conservation and sustainable utilization of wild and managed populations. Whether equally successful approaches to those of marine reserves in maintaining fisheries can be developed for terrestrial systems remains uncertain, and urgently needs attention (e.g. Novaro et al., 2000). Integration across disciplines is also needed. For example valuable work on the sustainability of subsistence hunting (e.g. Robinson and Bennett, 2004; Siren et al., 2004) is especially helpful when biology, incentives and controls are combined to show which species are vulnerable and where, and which cause no concern (e.g. Cowlishaw et al., 2005).

Research can and should allow us to better predict and forestall crises. In a 'pro-poor conservation' guise this implies a stronger recognition of the often vital role of local biodiversity in alleviating human suffering during drought, famine, and other humanitarian crises.

Will Pro-Poor Conservation Work?

What are the chances of success? Since few resources have been devoted to pro-poor conservation, we still know relatively little about the best practices. It also remains to be seen whether investing in pro-poor conservation can lead to better outcomes, for people or conservation, than other programmes.

The task seems easiest when global and local conservation agendas overlap or create synergies (Kremen et al., 2000). Where that happens, supporting local priorities can greatly strengthen these agendas' effectiveness. Such 'win–win' solutions are also possible if local people are compensated for helping to achieve global conservation objectives (Wunder, 2005). However, in other cases divergent objectives may imply incompatible policies and practices. Better recognizing these trade-offs will improve the search for solutions and compromises.

Some conservationists feel that time is too short to negotiate every intervention. While they doubtless regret the hardships local people experience, their main concern is to save species. But even these conservationists may benefit from building closer links with local people. As poor people are frequently identified as part of conservation problems, working with them must often be integral to the solution. Building these links takes time and has no guarantees. There can be various stumbling blocks, both conceptual and practical. Yet building such links is not necessarily as hard as it sounds, though it does require a willingness to try (Sheil and Lawrence, 2004).

Sceptics will probably point out the expense involved in ensuring that rural families retain access to wild and semi-domesticated plants and animals, and harvest these sustainably – much less achieve the institutional presence required on the ground to work with large numbers of geographically dispersed households. Given the relatively low market value of the products and services, the investment might not be worth it, at least in a narrow financial sense.

One important argument in favour of a pro-poor approach, and one that should interest development agencies committed to addressing poverty, is that the poorest families and indigenous peoples are likely to benefit the most, as they depend most heavily on wild resources. One cannot say the same for many other development activities.

Final Words

Conventional conservation choices often emphasize Western preferences including perhaps increasing distaste for harvesting wild species. But the world's poor can seldom afford such misgivings and conservationists need to be pragmatic. Protecting nature where it is being exploited maintains future options.

We have come a long way since the 1992 Earth Summit in Rio de Janeiro offered a vision of sustainable development in which conservation benefited the poor and assisting the poor would benefit the environment. Yet, as the authors of both the recent Millennium Ecosystem Assessment and the Millennium Development Goals underline, a disaggregated approach to conservation and development serves the interests of neither (Sachs and Reid, 2006). If conservation organizations cannot offer real benefits to local people or gain popular approval, retaining public funding or political support from governments in the tropics will prove increasingly difficult. Conservationists will focus on strictly protected areas and abandon biodiversity elsewhere. For their part, development agencies will have a hard time helping poor rural families find substitutes for all the lost natural foods, medicines, fuels, housing materials, soil nutrients, fodder, clean water, and other products and services. Simply letting these natural safety nets disappear could condemn many people to even greater poverty, and undermine many of the development agencies' broader agendas.

We are not suggesting that species that do not benefit poor people should be allowed to disappear forever. But we are suggesting that conservation can and should address broader, more diversified, and more democratically defined goals, and should recognize and address the needs and aspirations of local people: especially the poor and vulnerable. Such efforts might allow people to live happier and more productive lives, and could also strengthen local support for conserving species for their own sake.

Some questions remain controversial whichever approach is adopted. What are acceptable changes in ecosystems? Where do we draw the line between human welfare and conservation? Do we let people cultivate in national parks when they run out of other land? Different people will wish to draw the line in different places, and lines are needed. But there are good ethical and practical reasons why conservationists should not assume poverty is someone else's problem. And as long as people depend heavily on wild and semi-domesticated species, we should try to ensure that those species remain available.

For hundreds of millions of people, biodiversity is about eating, staying healthy, and finding shelter. Such needs, in addition to those of the tiger and other endangered species, must also be considered a conservation priority. Clearly it is not a question of 'either/or', but rather of finding a better balance.

References

Arnold, J.E.M., Kohlin, G. and Persson, R. (2006) 'Woodfuels, livelihoods, and policy interventions: Changing perspectives', *World Development*, 34: 596–611.

Bennett, E.L. and Robinson, J.G. (2000) *Hunting of Wildlife in Tropical Forests, Implications for Biodiversity and Forest Peoples*, Environment Department Papers No. 76, World Bank, Washington DC.

Beukema, H. and Van Noordwijk, M. (2004) 'Terrestrial pteridophytes as indicators of a forest-like environment in rubber production systems in the lowlands of Jambi, Sumatra', *Agriculture, Ecosystems and Environment*, 104: 63–73.

Brooks, J.S., Franzen, A.M. Holmes, C.M. Grote, M.N. and Borgerhoff Mulder, M. (2006) 'Testing hypotheses for the success of different conservation strategies', *Conservation Biology*, 20: 1528–1538.

Brooks, T.M., Mittermeier, R.A., Da Fonseca, G.A.B., Gerlach, J., Hoffmann, M., Lamoreux, J.F., Mittermeier, C.G., Pilgrim, J.D. and Rodrigues, A.S.L. (2006) 'Global biodiversity conservation priorities', *Science*, 313: 58–61.

Brown, K. (2002) 'Innovations for conservation and development', *Geography Journal*, 168: 6–17.

Campbell, B.M. and Shackleton, S. (2001) 'The organizational structures for community-based natural resource management in Southern Africa', *Afr. Stud*, Q. 5: http://web.africa.ufl.edu/asq/v5/v5i3a6.htm.

Chape, S., Blyth, S., Fish, L., Fox, P. and Spalding, M. (compilers) (2003) *United Nations List of Protected Areas*, IUCN, Gland, Switzerland and Cambridge.

Cinner, J.E., Marnane, M.J. and McLanahan, T.R. (2005) 'Conservation and community benefits from traditional coral reef management at Ahus Island, Papua New Guinea', *Conservation Biology*, 19: 1714–1723.

Cowlishaw, G., Mendelson, S. and Rowcliffe, J.M. (2005) 'Evidence for post-depletion sustainability in a mature bushmeat market', *Journal of Applied Ecology*, 42: 460–468.

Dietz,T., Ostrom, E. and Stern, P. (2003) 'The struggle to govern the commons', *Science*, 302: 1907–1912.

Farnsworth, N.R. and Soejarto, D.D. (1991) 'Global importance of medicinal plants', pp. 25–51, in Akerle, O., Heywood, V. and Synge, H. (eds) *The Conservation of Medicinal Plants*, Cambridge University Press, Cambridge.

Ferraro, P.J. and Pattanayak, S.K. (2006) 'Money for nothing? A call for empirical evaluation of biodiversity conservation investments', *PLoS Biol*, 4: 482–488.

Fisher, R.J., Maginnis, S., Jakson, W.J., Barrow, E. and Jeanrenaud, S. (2005) Poverty and Conservation: Landscapes, People and Power, IUCN, Gland, Switzerland

Garcia-Fernandez, C., Casado, M.A. and Ruiz Pérez, M. (2003) 'Benzoin gardens in North Sumatra, Indonesia: Effects of management on tree diversity', *Conservation Biology*, 17: 829–836.

Gell, F.R. and Roberts, C.M. (2003) 'Benefits beyond boundaries: The fishery effects of marine reserves', *Trends in Ecology and Evolution*, 18: 448–455.

Hamilton, A.C. (2004) 'Medicinal plants, conservation, and livelihoods', *Biodiversity Conservation*, 13: 1477–1517.

Hughes, R. and Flintan, F. (2001) *Integrating Conservation and Development Experience: A Review and Bibliography of the ICDP Literature*, International Institute for Environment and Development, London.

International Plant Genetic Resources Institute (IPGRI) (2004) *Diversity for Well-Being: Making the Most of Agricultural Biodiversity*, IPGRI, Rome.

IUCN (World Conservation Union), WWF and UNEP (1991) *Caring for the Earth: A Strategy for Sustainable Living*, IUCN, Gland.

Johannes, R.E. (1978) 'Traditional marine conservation methods in Oceania and their demise', *Annual Review of Ecology and Systematics*, 9: 349–364.

Johannes, R.E. (2002) 'The renaissance of community-based marine resource management in Oceania', *Review of Ecology and Systematics*, 33: 317–340.

Johnson, K.A. and Nelson, K.C. (2004) 'Common property and conservation: The potential for effective communal forest management within a national park in Mexico', *Human Ecology*, 32: 703–733.

Kleiman, D.G., Reading, R.P., Miller, B.J., Clark, T.W., Scott, J.M., Robinson, J., Wallace, R.L., Cabin, R.J. and Felleman, F. (2000) 'Improving the evaluation of conservation programs', *Conservation Biology*, 14: 356-365.

Kremen, C., Niles, J.O., Dalton, M.G., Daily, G.C., Ehrlich, P.R., Fay, J.P., Grewal, D. and Guillery, R.P. (2000) 'Economic incentives for rain forest conservation across scales', *Science*, 288: 1828–1832.

Le Bel, S., Gaidet, N., Mutake, S., Le Doze, S. and Nyamugure, T. (2004) 'Communal game ranching in Zimbabwe: Local empowerment and sustainable game meat production for rural communities', *Game and Wildlife Science*, 21: 275–290.

Lubchenco, J., Palumbi, S.R., Gaines, S.D. and Andelman, S. (2003) 'Plugging a hole in the oceans: The emerging science of marine reserves', *Ecol. Appl.*, 13: S3–S7.

Maddox, T.M., Priatna, Gemita, D., and Selampassy, E. (2005) *Pigs, Palms, People and Tigers: Survival of the Sumatran Tiger in a Commercial Landscape*, Jambi Tiger Project Report 2002–2004, Conservation Programmes, Zoological Society of London, Regents Park, London.

McNeilage, A., Plumptre, A.J., Brock-Doyle, A. and Vedder, A. (2001) 'Bwindi Impenetrable National Park, Uganda: Gorilla census 1997', *Oryx*, 35: 39–47.

Medellin, R.A. (1999) 'Sustainable harvest for conservation', *Conservation Biology*, 13: 225–225.

Meester, G.A., Mehrotra, A., Ault, J.S. and Baker, E.K. (2004) 'Designing marine reserves for fishery management', *Management Science*, 50: 1031–1043.

Meijaard, E. and Sheil, D. (2007) 'The persistence and conservation of Borneo's mammals in lowland rain forests managed for timber: Observations, overviews and opportunities', *Ecology Research*, 23(1): 21–34.

Meilleur, B.A. and Hodgkin, T. (2004) 'In situ conservation of crop wild relatives: Status and trends', *Biodiversity Conservation*, 13: 663–684.

Millennium Ecosystem Assessment, (2005) *Ecosystems and Human Well-being: Biodiversity Synthesis*, World Resources Institute, Washington, DC.

Novaro, A.J., Redford, K.H. and Bodmer, R.E. (2000) 'Effect of hunting in source-sink systems in the Neotropics', *Conservation Biology*, 14: 713–721.

Ostrom, E., Burger, J., Field, C.B., Norgaard, R.B. and Policansky, D. (1999) 'Sustainability – revisiting the commons: Local lessons, global challenges', *Science*, 284: 278–282.

Padmanaba, M. and Sheil, D. (2007) 'Finding and promoting a local conservation consensus in a globally important tropical forest landscape', *Biodiversity Conservation*, 16: 137–151.

Pikitch, E. K., Santora, C., Babcock, E.A., Bakun, A., Bonfil, R., Conover, D.O., Dayton, P., Doukakis, P. Fluharty, D., Heneman, B., Houde, E.D., Link, J., Livingston, P.A., Mangel, M., McAllister, M.K., Pope, J. and Sainsbury, K.J. (2004) 'Ecosystem-based fishery management', *Science*, 305: 346–347.

Pokharel, B.K., Stadtmuller, T. and Pfund, J.-L. (2006) *From Degradation to Restoration: An Assessment of the Enabling Conditions for Community Forestry in Nepal*, Intercooperation, Swiss Foundation for Development and International Cooperation, Kathmandu.

Redford, K.H. and Richter, B.D. (1999) 'Conservation of biodiversity in a world of use', *Conservation Biology*, 13: 1246–1256.

Redford, K., Coppolillo, P., Sanderson, E., da Fonseca, G., Dinerstein, E., Groves, C., Mace, G., Maginnis, S., Mittermeier, R., Noss, R., Olson, D., Robinson, J., Vedder, A. and Wright, M. (2003) 'Mapping the conservation landscape', *Conservation Biology*, 17: 116–131.

Robbins, P., McSweeney, K., Waite, T. and Rice, J. (2006) 'Even conservation rules are made to be broken: Implications for biodiversity', *Environmental Management*, 37: 162–169.

Robinson, J.G. (1993) 'The limits to caring: Sustainable living and the loss of biodiversity', *Conservation Biology*, 7: 20–28.

Robinson, J.G. and Bennett, E.L. (2004) 'Having your wildlife and eating it too: An analysis of hunting sustainability across tropical ecosystems', *An. Conserv.*, 7: 397–408.

Sachs, J.D. and Reid, W.V. (2006) 'Investments toward sustainable development', *Science*, 312: 1002.

Sayer, J. and Campbell, B. (2003) *The Science of Sustainable Development: Local Livelihoods and the Global Environment*, Cambridge University Press, Cambridge.

Schroth, G., Fonseca, G.A.B., Harvey, C.A, Gascon, C., Vasconcelos, H.L. and Izac, A.-M.N. (eds) (2004) *Agroforestry and Biodiversity Conservation in Tropical Landscapes*, Island Press, Washington, DC.

Schwartzman, S., Moreira, A. and Nepstad, D. (2000) 'Rethinking tropical forest conservation: Perils in parks', *Conservation Biology*, 14: 1351–1357.

Scoones, I., Melnyk, M. and Pretty, J. (1992) *The Hidden Harvest: Wild Foods and Agricultural Systems, A Literature Review and Annotated Bibliography*, International Institute for Environment and Development, London.

Sekhsaria, P. (2007) 'Conservation in India and the need to think beyond "tiger vs. tribal"', *Biotropica*, 39(5):575–577.

Seymour, F. (1994) 'Are successful community-based conservation projects designed or discovered?', pp. 472–496, in Western, D. and Wright, R.M. (eds) *Natural Connections: Perspectives in Community-Based Conservation*, Island Press, Washington, DC.

Sheil, D. and Lawrence, A. (2004) 'Tropical biologists, local people and conservation: New opportunities for collaboration', *Trends in Ecology and Evolution*, 19: 634–638.

Sheil, D., Puri, R., Wan, M., Basuki, I., Van Heist, M., Liswanti, N., Rukmiyati, Rachmatika, I. and Samsoedin, I. (2006) 'Local people's priorities for biodiversity: Examples from the forests of Indonesian Borneo', *Ambio*, 35: 17–24.

Sheil, D. and Boissiere, M. (2006) 'Local people may be the best allies in conservation', *Nature*, 440: 868.

Siren, A., Hamback, P. and Machoa, J. (2004) 'Including spatial heterogeneity and animal dispersal when evaluating hunting: A model analysis and an empirical assessment in an Amazonian community, *Conservation Biology*, 18: 1315–1329.

Spiteri, A. and Nepal, S.K. (2006) 'Incentive-based conservation programs in developing countries: A review of some key issues and suggestions for improvement', *Environmental Management*, 37: 1–14.

Steinberg, P.F. (2005) 'From public concern to policy effectiveness: Civic conservation in developing countries', *Journal of International Wildlife Law and Policy*, 8: 341–365.

Thiollay, J.M. (1995) 'The role of traditional agroforests in the conservation of rain-forest bird diversity in Sumatra', *Conservation Biology*, 9: 335–353.

United Nations Food and Agriculture Organization (FAO) (2002*) Pacific Island Fisheries – Regional and Country Information*, Asia-Pacific Fishery Commission, FAO Regional Office, Bangkok, Thailand.

Van Rijsoort, J. and Zhang, J.F. (2005) 'Participatory resource monitoring as a means for promoting social change in Yunnan, China', *Biodiversity Conservation*, 14: 2543–2573.

Vedeld, P., Angelsen, A., Sjaastad, E. and Kobugabe Berg, G. (2004) *Counting on the Environment, Forest Incomes and the Rural Poor*, Environment Economics Series Paper 98, World Bank, Washington, DC.

Vermeulen, S. and Koziell, I. (2002) *Integrating Global and Local Biodiversity Values: A Review of Biodiversity Assessment*, International Institute for Environment and Development, London.

Vermeulen, S. and Sheil, D. (2007) 'Partnerships for tropical conservation', *Oryx*, 41: 434–440.

Wells, M. and McShane, T.O. (2004) 'Integrating protected area management with local needs and aspirations', *Ambio*, 33: 513–519.

WHO (World Health Organization) (2003) *Annual report 2002*, WHO, Geneva, Switzerland. http://whqlibdoc.who.int/hq/2003/test.pdf

Wiersum, K.F. (2003) 'Use and conservation of biodiversity in East African forested landscapes', pp. 33–39, in Zuidema, P.A. (ed) *Tropical Forests in Multi-functional Landscapes*, Prince Bernard Centre for International Nature Conservation, Utrecht University, The Netherlands.

Wilshusen, P.R., Brechin, S.R., Fortwangler, C.F. and West, P.C. (2002) 'Reinventing a square wheel: Critique of a resurgent 'protection paradigm' in international biodiversity conservation', *Society and Natural Resources*, 15: 17–40.

Wolanski, E. (2004) 'The Serengeti: An example of successful development through conservation made possible by north-south partnership', *Bull. Seances Acad. R. Sci. Outre Mer*, 50: 261–269.

World Resources Institute (WRI) (2005) *World Resources 2005: The Wealth of the Poor – Managing Ecosystems to Fight Poverty*, WRI, Washington, DC.

Wunder, S. (2005) *Paying for Environmental Services: Some Nuts and Bolts*, Occasional Paper 42, Center for International Forestry Research, Bogor, Indonesia.

Zuidema, P.A., Sayer, J.A. and Dijkman, W. (1996) 'Forest fragmentation and biodiversity: The case for intermediate-sized conservation areas', *Environmental Conservation*, 23: 290–297.

Chapter 24

Disentangling the Links between Conservation and Poverty Reduction in Practice

Matt Walpole and Lizzie Wilder

Introduction

The extent to which biodiversity conservation can, does, or should be expected to contribute to poverty reduction efforts has been the subject of vigorous debate (Roe, 2008). Some argue that it is inappropriate or ineffective for conservationists to attempt to address poverty issues and diverts attention and resources away from core conservation missions (Sanderson and Redford, 2003; 2004; Kiss, 2004; Terborgh, 2004). Others imply that there is no choice but for conservation organizations to engage, for both ethical and pragmatic reasons (Roe and Elliot, 2004, 2006; Kaimowitz and Sheil, 2007).

Critiques of protected areas as engines of socio-economic marginalization (Brockington and Schmidt-Soltau, 2004; Lockwood et al., 2006) and of conservation NGOs as corporations riding roughshod over human rights (Chapin, 2004), alongside a shift in donor funding away from environmental matters and towards poverty reduction (Roe, 2008), has led to a scramble within parts of the conservation community to demonstrate its pro-poor credentials and its relevance to the international poverty reduction agenda. At both the World Parks Congress (in 2003) and World Conservation Congress (in 2004), resolutions were passed that urged conservationists and protected area managers to ensure conservation is of benefit to the poor, and similar proposals are being developed for the Convention on Biological Diversity (Mapendembe et al., 2008). Conservationists are increasingly promoting the argument that biodiversity underpins poverty reduction because of the importance of natural resources to the livelihoods and well-being of the poor (Ash and Jenkins, 2007), and highlighting cases where conserving threatened biodiversity benefits the poor (WWF, 2006).

Reprinted from *Oryx*, vol 42, no 4, Walpole, M. and Wilder, L., 'Disentangling the links between conservation and poverty reduction in practice', pp. 539–547, copyright © Fauna & Flora International (2008) with permission from Cambridge University Press, Cambridge.

Others are less sure. Case studies illustrating either the positive or negative social impacts of conservation abound, alongside broader-scale analyses of the level of geographical association between poverty and areas of conservation priority (Gorenflo and Brandon, 2006; de Sherbinin, 2008; Upton et al., 2008; Redford et al., 2008). Yet there remains little universal clarity over whether and in what ways conservation in practice could be a mechanism for reducing poverty.

One of the problems is that the academic debate and the analyses surrounding it often oversimplify the complexity inherent in the concepts of conservation and poverty (what conservation does, and what poverty is, are both very broad topics) and variation in the ways that they interact (Agrawal and Redford, 2006). There may be good reasons for simplifying the arguments to create marketable messages for donors, policy-makers and the general public. However, in a world of increasing accountability and public scrutiny such messages must still be based on fact and, in reality, poverty–conservation relationships are more complex. Conservation researchers and practitioners need to grapple with that complexity if the debate, and conservation performance, is to progress.

Numerous theoretical frameworks to categorize poverty–conservation relationships exist (Nadkarni, 2000; Adams et al., 2004; Roe and Elliot, 2005). These outline a range of rationales for conservationists to engage with the poor, which in turn dictate the approaches taken by practitioners and the likely outcomes, not all of which will necessarily reduce poverty (Table 24.1). This is not always understood, particularly amongst conservation biologists. To achieve greater clarity we must disentangle the links by exploring how the rationales in these conceptual frameworks are played out in practice, and which elements of poverty are at the fore (Sunderlin et al., 2005; Robinson, 2006).

Using the portfolio of one international conservation organization, Fauna & Flora International (FFI), as an example, this paper explores how, if at all, conservation activities may contribute to poverty reduction. We ask two principal and related questions. First, what are the rationales being used at field level for engaging, or not engaging, with the poor? This is important because it dictates the extent to which conservation is likely to provide local benefits as opposed to simply offsetting costs. Second, which aspects of poverty are being addressed? Identifying which elements of poverty are most relevant to conservation in practice will help us focus our efforts and ensure we have the right skills to do it, the right research to evaluate impact, and the right arguments to put before critics, thereby improving conservation performance and impact.

Table 24.1 *Framework of rationales for engaging with poverty and their implications for conservation activities*

Rationale[1]	Implications
1. Conservation underpins poverty reduction	Biodiversity provides ecosystem goods and services which, if conserved and used sustainably, will underpin livelihoods and provide long-term security and resilience. This is the argument behind the ecosystem approach to conservation and implies a passive, longer-term contribution to poverty reduction.
2. Poverty reduction leads to conservation	Reducing poverty reduces pressure on biodiversity by reducing the need for unsustainable use, providing opportunities for alternative livelihoods and placing people in a position where they can choose to conserve. This is the argument behind integrated conservation and development projects, and has resulted in conservationists becoming actively involved in more-immediate livelihoods-focused initiatives.
3. Conservation hinders poverty reduction	Conservation inflicts costs on the poor that limits their options and ability to rise out of poverty. This is the argument levelled in particular at protected areas by some social commentators, and can lead to conservationists taking a moral position to 'do no harm' and attempting to offset the costs of conservation, through outreach and benefit-sharing programmes.
4. Poverty reduction hinders conservation	Increased affluence and opportunity, or an overtly economic-oriented development policy, fuels environmental degradation and biodiversity loss. This is the argument that environmentalists and conservationists have levelled at the development lobby for decades, and is the principal fear of those who see environmental concerns marginalized in the race to meet the relatively short-term targets of the MDGs.
5. Poverty reduction generates goodwill and trust	Some projects address local priorities and needs even if they are not directly related to conservation outcomes, in order to generate a local constituency of support for conservation. Livelihoods or poverty reduction interventions act as an entry point and mechanism to engender that support at grass roots levels. This can be extremely important given that the traditional development actors (government, aid agencies and the private sector) are often conspicuously lacking in the poor, rural areas in which conservation NGOs operate. Projects can find themselves either taking the place of such traditional actors, or operating as a facilitator linking communities to development opportunities.

Source: adapted from Nadkarni (2000); Adams et al. (2004); Roe and Elliot (2005)

Number of projects[2]	Example projects
2 (13)	Protecting or restoring forest habitat to improve freshwater provision, the supply of traditionally harvested NTFPs and ecotourism potential in Cambodia, Brazil and Nicaragua
18 (23)	Support to alter and improve agricultural practices where they threaten natural forests and critical wildlife habitats in Belize, Ecuador and Cambodia
8 (13)	Developing people-focused policies, participatory management plans and human–wildlife conflict mitigation strategies for protected areas in Mozambique, DRC and Kenya
5 (10)	Averting the transformation of Fynbos habitat to cultivation by promoting the development of a market for sustainably-harvested wild flowers in South Africa
1 (5)	Supporting social enterprise development to provide a platform for future conservation engagement in Kyrgyzstan

Notes: 1 These various rationales are not necessarily mutually exclusive and may apply simultaneously in a particular place or situation, involving different people or between different elements of poverty and conservation and over different timescales.

2 Frequency of occurrence of different rationales within a sample of 34 FFI livelihoods-focused projects. Number in parentheses refers to total number of projects where rationale is mentioned.

Methods

Founded in 1903, FFI's mission is to 'conserve threatened species and ecosystems worldwide, choosing solutions that are sustainable, based on sound science and take account of human needs' (FFI, 2008a). FFI is active in about 40 countries, developing, implementing and managing biodiversity conservation projects in partnership with host country organizations, to protect and conserve species and ecosystems using a genuinely participatory approach, based upon a strong commitment to building local capacities and to long-term sustainability of conservation achievements.

FFI's mission refers explicitly to human needs, and to address this it established a Biodiversity and Human Needs thematic programme in 2004 'to reflect on how and why we are addressing human needs, to improve our monitoring and analysis of our achievements, and to develop good practice to ensure that we achieve our mission effectively and universally' (FFI, 2006).

Analysis of a livelihoods portfolio

Two main sources of internal FFI documentary information were used to explore livelihood linkages in FFI's work. First, to assess the breadth of engagement with livelihoods and poverty issues, the entire set of annual reports from FFI projects for 2006 were examined (n 588). The annual reporting instrument for 2006 was developed by ourselves and others to focus on outcomes, impacts and lessons learned, broken down into a series of conservation activity areas including livelihoods and human needs. It also asked project managers to record what they felt was the most significant achievement of their project during 2006.

Second, for a detailed understanding of project rationales and approaches, documents from a self-selected sample of 34 projects with a distinct livelihoods component directly supported by FFI's Biodiversity and Human Needs programme during 2004–2007 were examined. Each of these projects was required to submit a detailed plan outlining its rationale for engaging with local livelihoods, its objectives and activities, and its intended outcomes and impacts for livelihoods and for conservation. Using these project plans, associated documentation (project profiles and biannual progress reports), and comprehensive internal evaluation reports submitted in early 2008, the following information was extracted:

(1) conservation focus: species, terrestrial landscape, marine, non-specific/broader scale.
(2) rationale for engaging with livelihoods: using the five categories in Table 24.1.
(3) approach taken: whether direct, field-based livelihoods interventions (either linked to or uncoupled from biodiversity) or indirect institutional-strengthening and policy-related activities at local, national or international scales.
(4) livelihoods outcomes: planned or in some cases actual, using the UK Department for International Development's Sustainable Livelihoods framework (Appendix).
(5) role of livelihoods interventions in the context of the wider conservation strategy.

In addition to this documentary evidence, insights were gathered from site visits, interviews with project managers and a series of regional meetings during 2005–2007 where these projects were presented and discussed with other staff and partners.

It should be noted that this study does not seek to assess the success or failure of different approaches to poverty reduction in conservation projects. Whilst some insights are drawn from projects where outcomes could be demonstrated, in most projects it was too early to do so. The primary aim of this study was to explore the breadth of both the logical and operational links between poverty and conservation within FFI's portfolio, and what they mean, to help conservation researchers and practitioners refine their thinking.

Results

Of the 88 annual reports, 85 per cent recorded some kind of engagement with local communities and poverty issues as part of their conservation activities. The more detailed analysis of 34 projects spanning 22 countries across four continents included some of the poorest places on Earth (Appendix). The majority of projects focused on terrestrial landscape conservation (n 521), with about 25 per cent being species-focused (n 59). A minority of projects (n 53) were unspecific, working indirectly at broader scales. Marine projects were under-represented (n 51). Differences in the rationale and approach of species projects versus landscape projects are identified below.

Rationales underpinning project strategies and interventions

In the majority of cases there was more than one rationale for engaging with liveli-hoods. Many projects were simultaneously attempting to reduce threats to biodiver-sity, offset costs for people locally, and increase support for conservation. However, reducing threats to biodiversity by improving livelihoods/reducing poverty (Rationale 2; Table 24.1) was the most common primary rationale, followed by offsetting the costs of conservation for local people (Rationale 3). A higher proportion of species (33 per cent) than landscape projects (19 per cent) adopted the latter.

The argument that conservation underpins poverty reduction (Rationale 1) was used exclusively in relation to the provision of ecosystem goods, i.e. the sustain-able use of elements of biodiversity by the poor (through tourism or consumptive use), rather than in relation to the provision of supporting/regulating ecosystem services and ecological resilience.

The argument that poverty reduction threatens conservation efforts (Rationale 4) was used primarily in response to the planned activities of governments and develop-ment agencies that risked overlooking environmental concerns in the face of economic or humanitarian expediency. It was less related to fears of over-consumption with increased affluence as a result of poverty reduction, although this could become an issue in some cases in the future. Some projects recognized that external (rather than local) consumer demand was a driver of biodiversity decline but had no direct means to address it.

Few projects appeared to be using an indirect rationale for livelihoods interventions as a means of entry and engagement with poor rural communities to generate a constituency of support (Rationale 5). However, when rationales were discussed at a workshop session with one of FFI's regional teams, this was considered to be a much more common reason for engaging with livelihoods than is often recognized or written in funding proposals.

Approaches used in engaging with local livelihoods and poverty

The full spectrum of approaches was illustrated across the portfolio, and several (n 58) involved multiple strategies, combining direct (field-based) and indirect (institutional and policy-related) approaches. However, most projects appeared to focus on direct interventions (n 518), with about 25 per cent (n 58) taking only indirect approaches. Of the latter, local institutional strengthening was more common than policy interventions.

Amongst direct interventions there was an even balance of projects aiming to strengthen existing livelihoods (mainly agriculture and pastoralism), provide alternative livelihoods not linked to the landscape or species of conservation concern (mainly agriculture/agroforestry), and provide alternative livelihoods based on sustainable extractive use of the biodiversity in question (mainly plants or plant parts). Nature-based tourism as a non-consumptive linked livelihood only featured in a minority of projects, most of which were species-focused (Table 24.2).

Table 24.2 *Frequency of occurrence of different approaches to engaging directly with livelihoods and poverty reduction within a sample of 34 FFI livelihoods-focused projects.*

Type of direct livelihoods approach	Frequency (number of projects)	Project examples
Strengthen existing livelihoods	11	Improving rice farming techniques to reduce food insecurity in Cambodia
Alternative linked livelihood (tourism)	5	Developing community involvement in Pemba flying fox tourism in Zanzibar
Alternative linked livelihood (sustainable use)	12	Implementing sustainable management of native fruit and nut forests in Kyrgyzstan
Alternative non-linked livelihoods	12	Supporting small, service-based enterprises as alternatives to Saiga poaching in Kazakhstan
Multiple livelihoods strategies	8	Influencing national government forest policy, diversifying local farming and building capacity for community-forest management in Liberia
No direct livelihoods strategies	3	Raising awareness of conservation–poverty linkages amongst NGOs in the Philippines

Poverty reduction and livelihoods outcomes

A wide range of livelihoods effects were anticipated across the portfolio (Table 24.3). The most common impacts were on human skills and social networks as a result of the training, capacity building, network development and facilitation that projects undertake. It was less common for projects to invest directly in the more tangible natural, physical or financial assets, although a minority did provide infrastructure, access to loans or micro-finance, or greater access to natural resources. About 30 per cent of projects focused on influencing structures and processes (building organizational capacity and developing appropriate policies), and a similar proportion aimed to increase local empowerment, mainly through participatory approaches to increase local engagement in conservation decision-making. In terms of livelihoods outcomes, there was an even spread of attention to income, food security, sustainable resource management and reduced vulnerability.

Table 24.3 *Frequency of occurrence of different livelihoods effects (number of projects) within a sample of 34 FFI livelihoods-focused projects.*

Livelihoods effect		No. of projects
Assets:	Human	20
	Financial	7
	Natural	7
	Physical	8
	Social	14
Structures/processes:		10
Empowerment:		9
Outcomes:	Increased income	15
	Food security	10
	Sustainable NRM	14
	Reduced vulnerability	15

More detailed evaluation of actual outcomes from a number of these projects revealed evidence that responding to local needs (such as food, water and land tenure), improving institutional and policy environments and enhancing local capacity and empowerment served to reduce local vulnerability in a variety of ways (Table 24.4). Furthermore these had tangible conservation benefits by stimulating local action to reduce threats to biodiversity. Although just under 50 per cent of all projects included increased income as a likely outcome, only 10 per cent were able to demonstrate this within the timeframe of the study.

Across FFI's wider project portfolio more than 33 per cent of project managers reported that their most significant project achievements in 2006 related to work supporting local communities. These fell into three broad categories: (1) changing government perceptions to accept the legitimacy of bottom-up approaches and to embrace community participation in biodiversity management, (2) seeing local organizations empowered to take action and influence others, and (3) generating local trust, support and behaviour change through local benefits.

Livelihoods interventions in context

Although many projects considered livelihoods interventions as a strategic approach to reduce threats (Table 24.1), in very few cases (n 55) were livelihoods interventions the only activity being undertaken within conservation projects. A range of other conservation activities were being implemented concurrently, the most common being awareness raising (n 518), conservation capacity building (n 518), and management planning (n 515). Less common activities included formulating conservation policy (n 55), directly undertaking or supporting security patrols in protected areas (n 58), or direct species management (n 52).

Discussion

This study has unravelled the complexity in the conservation–poverty nexus across a broad geographic and thematic range of conservation projects within a single organization. Although based on reported plans and perspectives more than on actual measures of impact, and therefore influenced to some extent by respondents' understanding and interpretation, the results still reveal much about how conservation and poverty are linked in real-world project situations. Moreover, although based on the experiences of a single international conservation organization, it does represent a wide cross-section of such projects and is thus likely to reflect the spectrum of scenarios that other international conservation organizations will experience. In that sense the findings should have some resonance for the wider conservation community.

This study reveals that, even within a single project, the relationship is rarely simple, and disentangling the links to determine appropriate actions is not straightforward. The real-world situations described here suggest that taking account of human needs in conservation is not unreasonable and often strategically paramount. Yet this is not the same as reducing poverty. The principal questions that arise are whether and how conservation strategies really do have the potential to reduce poverty and, depending on the answer, what conservation organizations should do about it.

Are global conservation efforts reducing poverty?

It is clear that the activities of international conservation organizations are unlikely to make a significant impact on global poverty. Although the chronically poor are largely found in rural, forested and arid lands (Hulme and Shepherd, 2003), the majority of the world's poor live in peri-urban areas. The threatened biodiversity and protected areas of interest to international conservation organizations in the developing world tend to be in areas of low rural population density (Redford et al., 2008) and low agricultural potential (Gorenflo and Brandon, 2006) and where poverty may be no more acute than elsewhere in these countries (de Sherbinin, 2008).

Moreover many livelihoods-focused projects may not be about reducing poverty at all (Table 24.1). This is certainly true where projects are working primarily to offset the costs of conservation, where the logical conclusion is that people will be no worse off, but also by implication no better off, than if biodiversity was not being conserved. In practice the balance of trade-offs between accepting the limits on livelihoods imposed by living with wildlife, protected areas and resource restrictions, and the alternative benefits that conservation projects bring to offset those costs, is unlikely to be exact. Whether it yields a net benefit could be extremely hard to determine.

Yet this does not mean that conservation activities are irrelevant to the poor. The results of this study suggest that, at a local scale, conservation activities have the potential to make a difference where local poverty (i.e. a lack of choice) threatens biodiversity (Table 24.3). Giving people livelihoods choices and the potential to improve their well-being in ecologically sustainable ways is clearly beneficial but this is rarely just about alternative livelihoods providing income and jobs (Tables 24.2 and 24.3). Ecotourism, for example, despite being amongst the highest-profile alternative livelihood approaches in conservation (Agrawal and Redford, 2006), was being promoted in less than 20 per cent of projects examined.

The majority of projects involved training and capacity building to improve food security and sustainable resource management outcomes and to strengthen and diversify livelihoods strategies. However in about 40 per cent of projects the focus was on improving social networks and strengthening policies and institutions to build connectedness, empowerment and voice, and thereby reduce vulnerability (Tables 24.3 and 24.4). These are harder to conceptualize and less easily measurable, in terms of their impact on poverty, than material measures such as income and jobs.

There are many ways in which conservation activities can subtly influence the poor. Pride, happiness, feelings of responsibility, empowerment and security can all enrich well-being in ways not well captured in standard indicator frameworks like the Human Development Index (World Bank, 2008) or the Millennium Development Goals (Millennium Ecosystem Assessment, 2005). Just because they are not easy to measure does not mean that they should be ignored (Dasgupta, 2004).

Conservation can also benefit people in less obvious ways. The argument that conservation reduces poverty because biodiversity underpins human well-being through its contribution to ecosystem services such as pollination, clean air and flood control (Ash and Jenkins, 2007) was rarely cited in the projects examined here (Table 24.1; see Swiderska et al., 2003, for similar findings). Yet as such services decline the poor suffer more than the rich because of their greater direct dependence on locally sourced ecosystem goods and services such as food, fibre, medicines and watershed protection (Shackleton et al., 2007). In many cases natural resources act as a safety net for the poor rather than a route out of poverty (Wunder, 2001) but, either way, conserving functioning natural ecosystems will benefit the poor. In contrast, conservation that focuses on particular elements of biodiversity will only benefit the poor where those elements of biodiversity are of significance in the livelihoods of the poor. As much conservation activity focuses on globally threatened species rather than locally utilized biodiversity, this is not always the case (Roe and Walpole, in press).

Table 24.4 *Examples of demonstrated livelihoods impacts and associated conservation outcomes in selected FFI livelihoods-focused projects*

Project	Livelihoods impacts	Conservation outcomes
Developing participatory forest management in southern Tanzania	Improved knowledge, awareness and local institutions enabling communities to assert their tenurial rights and increase the price paid for sustainably harvested logs by 200 per cent	Community members are patrolling the forest and, for the first time, are turning away illegal loggers and imposing fines on their own members for misdemeanours
Enhancing livelihoods and engaging communities in species and habitat conservation in the Cardamom mountains, Cambodia	Better farming techniques have more than doubled rice yields, reducing vulnerability to food shortages from seven months to three months per annum. Local land rights are being respected, social cohesion has improved, and support for traditional NTFP harvesting as increased prices paid at market	Communities are acting to deter poaching, logging and habitat clearance. The critically endangered Siamese crocodile population is recovering
Engaging buffer zone communities to support protected area conservation in the southern Amazon, Brazil	Improving pasture management has improved milk productivity whilst developing local agricultural networks has improved access to markets. Forest restoration around natural springs has secured the flow of fresh water	Increased awareness of the value of forests has increased local commitment to conservation. Active forest restoration and protection in buffer zones now taking place

Note: Reducing vulnerability and increasing empowerment are common features of successful projects. In that regard, addressing immediate local needs and building on existing livelihoods and traditional practices yields results more quickly than attempting to develop unfamiliar and unproven alternative livelihoods. Ensuring a tangible link between livelihoods benefits and conservation is important.

How should conservation organizations respond?

The diversity of rationales, approaches and outcomes is a consequence of the varied contexts in which biodiversity exists and conservation operates. Understanding why to engage with local communities will help practitioners to identify how to do so, and what the goals should be. In that sense it is important for the poverty–conservation linkages and rationales to be made explicit. This will help in communicating honestly with partners, donors and critics about project goals, and ultimately will ensure greater clarity that will improve conservation actions.

In terms of actions, some key themes emerge. Often, addressing immediate needs such as food security rather than income, and strengthening or building on existing, familiar livelihood options before introducing alternatives, is a good place to start. These are the areas where FFI's projects have generally had most demonstrable impact (Table 24.4). It is also clear from project evaluation reports that training, social network development (including local institutions and access to markets), partnership development, and mediation are very important elements of livelihoods-focused projects. The skills and experience to deliver these will not all be available within conservation organizations but we must know where to look to find them.

Where commercial livelihoods are being developed an understanding of markets and enterprise development is critical but often lacking. Although, 50 per cent of projects included market-based income generation, the better performing ones were those with commercial expertise built in (Walpole and Thouless, 2005; for a more detailed discussion of experiences with enterprise development see FFI, 2008b).

In our experience, however, and as revealed in the project reports examined here, most demonstrable outcomes were achieved not through enterprise development but through other forms of empowerment. In that sense supporting people-centred policy development and building staff and partner capacity in social impact assessment and other tools is relevant. However, four important caveats, arising either from the results of the study or from workshops and discussions during the course of the study, should frame the way that the relationship between conservation and poverty reduction is viewed.

First, the immediacy of the human issues and the difficulty of identifying conservation impacts in the short-term can lead to mission creep, whereby addressing human needs becomes a de facto project goal, but it is important not to lose sight of conservation goals when focusing on what projects are achieving in livelihoods terms. Although community-based livelihoods and local empowerment approaches generally take longer to mature and to yield tangible results, it should still be possible to measure some form of biodiversity threat reduction in the short-to medium-term (Table 24.4; Salafsky and Margoluis, 1999). Regularly reviewing the rationale and impacts of the approach and adapting actions accordingly will help to keep it on track.

Second, conservation organizations are not the only bodies working in this area, and we need to be working much harder to convince the humanitarian and development sectors to take notice of environment and biodiversity more clearly than they currently do. This means working more closely in partnership with these sectors (Walpole, 2006; Adams, 2007) but also requires stronger rationales for why biodiversity loss is an important issue for them to tackle.

Third, livelihoods-focused interventions are only part of the conservation toolkit alongside direct site and species management, education, capacity building, policy and legislative initiatives and research. In all the projects examined here, on average one or two of these other activities were being employed besides livelihoods-focused activities. In these projects the achievement of conservation goals does not rely solely on livelihoods interventions and poverty reduction but on multiple approaches. Success, for conservation or poverty reduction, is not well captured by focusing on simple cause and effect models.

Fourth, whilst it is clear from this study that community engagement is widespread, this does not mean that focusing on poverty or poverty reduction is applicable in all conservation situations. In some, site and species management and protection may be more appropriate approaches than livelihoods, education and empowerment. The answer will be context specific and conservation should not be viewed, enacted or judged solely through the lens of poverty reduction.

Conclusions and Recommendations

Conservation and poverty reduction are different societal goals that in particular contexts may come together in mutually supportive or conflicting ways. Relationships between poverty and conservation are complex but this is not always manifest in the wider debate.

Conservation organizations need to distance themselves from the generic debate about whether conservation actions are beneficial or detrimental to poor people, and likewise from oversimplified attempts to prove or disprove assumptions of causality between poverty reduction and conservation.

Conservation organizations have been criticized for their social record, and at the same time are expected to contribute positively to poverty reduction efforts. This study of a sample of conservation projects has shown that there is widespread social responsibility and a wide range of potential and actual benefits for the poor. On the one hand conservation organizations could do more to promote the wider societal benefits of their activities, whether direct or indirect, tangible or intangible, passive or active, short-term or long-term. On the other hand, if they are claiming to be generating benefits then they need to be sure that they can demonstrate them. To negotiate the minefield, address the critics, and do justice to their achievements without resorting to unsubstantiated rhetoric, conservation organizations could adopt the following recommendations:

- Be clear in each specific context about why they are engaging with livelihoods or poverty reduction, and how poverty and conservation interact, both positively and negatively.
- Be clear about which elements of biodiversity and which elements of poverty they are dealing with in each case.

- Be clear about who they are dealing with and why, and who will benefit or not, considering potential trade-offs. If acting to offset costs, it is important to know who the poor are and how they are affected by conservation activities.
- Be clear about underlying assumptions, and test them wherever necessary.
- Be clear about the timescale over which benefits and costs may ensue. There are not always short-term increases in income. When dealing with issues such as sustainable use, reduced vulnerability, and increased resilience there may be short-term tangible costs to achieve longer-term but less tangible security.
- Be clear about where livelihoods interventions fit within broader conservation strategies in each particular case. Reductionist causal-chain arguments focused on single types of conservation activity mask the complexity of conservation and the effects and importance of other areas of a strategy in achieving goals.
- Attempt to measure and demonstrate the broader range of possible impacts for people, rather than just focusing on one or two simple, tangible, material examples.

There is a range of assessment, research, monitoring and evaluation tools available to assist these tasks, including stakeholder analyses, social risk assessments, poverty mapping, and both indicator-based and non-indicator-based approaches to monitoring and evaluation (Wilder and Walpole, 2008). A lot can be learned from the development sector in this regard (Walpole et al., 2007), and conservation scientists of every discipline and persuasion should be devoting their efforts to further our understanding and improve our impact in situations where poverty and conservation coincide.

References

Adams, W.M. (2007) 'Thinking like a human: Social science and the two cultures problem', *Oryx*, 41: 275–276.

Adams, W.M., Aveling, R., Brockington, D., Dickson, B., Elliott, J., Hutton, J., Roe, D., Vira, B. and Wolmer, W. (2004) 'Biodiversity conservation and the eradication of poverty', *Science*, 306: 1146–1149.

Agrawal, A. and Redford, K. (2006) *Poverty, Development and Biodiversity Conservation: Shooting in the Dark?*, WCS Working Paper No. 26, Wildlife Conservation Society, New York.

Ash, N. and Jenkins, M. (2007) *Biodiversity and Poverty Reduction: The Importance of Ecosystem Services*, UNEP-World Conservation Monitoring Centre, Cambridge.

Brockington, D. and Schmidt-Soltau, K. (2004) 'The social and environmental impacts of wilderness and development', *Oryx*, 38, 140–142.

Chapin, M. (2004) 'A challenge to conservationists', *World Watch*, 71(6): 17–31.

Dasgupta, P. (2004) *Human Wellbeing and the Natural Environment*, Oxford University Press, Oxford.

de Sherbinin, A. (2008) 'Is poverty more acute near parks? An assessment of infant mortality rates around protected areas in developing countries', *Oryx*, 42: 26–35.

DFID (2000) *Sustainable Livelihoods Guidance Sheets*, Department for International Development, London.

FFI (2006) *The Case for Integrating Conservation and Human Needs*, Livelihoods and Conservation in Partnership Series No. 1, Fauna & Flora International, Cambridge.

FFI (2008a) *Fauna & Flora International*, www.fauna-flora.org (accessed 2 July 2008).

FFI (2008b) *The Role of Enterprise Development in Conservation*, Livelihoods and Conservation in Partnership Series No. 5. Fauna & Flora International, Cambridge.

Gorenflo, L.J. and Brandon, K. (2006) 'Key human dimensions of gaps in global biodiversity conservation', *Bioscience*, 56: 723–731.

Hulme, D. and Shepherd, A. (2003) 'Conceptualising chronic poverty', *World Development*, 31: 399–402.

Kaimowitz, D. and Sheil, D. (2007) 'Conserving what and for whom? Why conservation should help meet basic needs in the tropics', *Biotropica*, 39: 567–574.

Kiss, A. (2004) 'Is community-based ecotourism a good use of biodiversity conservation funds?', *Trends in Ecology and Evolution*, 19: 232–237.

Lockwood, M., Worboys, G. and Kothari, A. (2006) *Managing Protected Areas: A Global Guide*, Earthscan, London.

Mapendembe, A., Thomas, D. and Dickson, B. (2008) *Conservation and Poverty: A Review of Existing Commitments*, FFI and BirdLife International, Cambridge.

Millennium Ecosystem Assessment (2005) *Ecosystems and Human Well-Being: Biodiversity Synthesis*, Island Press, Washington, DC.

Nadkarni, M.V. (2000) 'Poverty, environment, development – a many-patterned nexus', *Economic and Political Weekly*, 35: 1184–1190.

OECD (2001) *The DAC Guidelines: Poverty Reduction*, Organisation for Economic Co-operation and Development, Paris.

Redford, K.H., Levy, M.A., Sanderson, E.W. and de Sherbinin, A. (2008) 'What is the role for conservation organizations in poverty alleviation in the world's wild places?', *Oryx*, 42: 516–528.

Robinson, J.G. (2006) 'Conservation biology and real world conservation', *Conservation Biology*, 20: 658–669.

Roe, D. (2008) 'The origins and evolution of the conservation-poverty debate: A review of key literature, events and policy processes', *Oryx*, 42: 491–503.

Roe, D. and Elliott, J. (2004) 'Poverty reduction and biodiversity conservation: Rebuilding the bridges', *Oryx*, 38: 137–139.

Roe, D. and Elliott, J. (2005) *Poverty-Conservation Linkages: A Conceptual Framework:* Poverty and Conservation Learning Group, International Institute for Environment and Development, London.

Roe, D. and Elliott, J. (2006) 'Pro-poor conservation: The elusive win-win for conservation and poverty reduction?', *Policy Matters*, 14: 53–63.

Roe, D. and Walpole, M.J. (in press) 'Whose value counts? Trade-offs between biodiversity conservation and poverty reduction', in Leader-Williams, N., Adams, W.M. and Smith, R. (eds) *Trade-offs in Conservation: Deciding What to Save*, Blackwells, Oxford.

Salafsky, N. and Margoulis, R. (1999) 'Threat reduction assessment: A practical and cost-effective approach to evaluating conservation and development projects', *Conservation Biology*, 13: 830–841.

Sanderson, S. and Redford, K. (2003) 'Contested relationships between biodiversity conservation and poverty alleviation', *Oryx*, 37: 1–2.

Sanderson, S. and Redford, K. (2004) 'The defence of conservation is not an attack on the poor', *Oryx*, 38: 146–147.

Shackleton, C.M., Hackleton, S.E., Buiten, E. and Bird, N. (2007) 'The importance of dry woodlands and forests in rural livelihoods and poverty alleviation in South Africa', *Forest Policy and Economics*, 9: 558–577.

Sunderlin, W.D., Angelsen, A., Belcher, B., Burgers, P., Nasi, R., Santoso, L. and Wunder, S. (2005) 'Livelihoods, forests, and conservation in developing countries: An overview', *World Development*, 33: 1383–1402.

Swiderska, K., Roe, D., Maganga, F. and Wilder, L. (2003) *Voices from the South: The Role of Civil Society in Linking Biodiversity Conservation and Poverty Reduction*, International Institute for Environment and Development, London.

Terborgh, J. (2004) 'Reflections of a scientist on the World Parks Congress', *Conservation Biology*, 18: 619–620.

Upton, C., Ladle, R., Hulme, D., Jiang, T., Brockington, D. and Adams, W.M. (2008) 'Are poverty and protected area establishment linked at a national scale?', *Oryx*, 42: 19–25.

Walpole, M.J. (2006) 'Partnerships for conservation and poverty reduction', *Oryx*, 40: 245–246.

Walpole, M.J. and Thouless, C.R. (2005) 'Increasing the value of wildlife through non-consumptive use', pp. 122–139, in Woodroffe, R., Thirgood, S. and Rabinowitz, A. (eds.) *People and Wildlife: Conflict or Coexistence?*, Cambridge University Press, Cambridge.

Walpole, M.J., Wilder, L., Granziera, A., Thomas, D. and Elliott, J. (2007) *Measuring the Impact of Livelihoods Initiatives in the Conservation Context*, Fauna & Flora International/BirdLife International/African Wildlife Foundation, Cambridge.

Wilder, L. and Walpole, M.J. (2008) 'Measuring social impacts in conservation: Experience of using the Most Significant Change method', *Oryx*, 42: 529–538.

World Bank (2008) *World Development Indicators*, The World Bank, Washington, DC.

Wunder, S. (2001) 'Poverty alleviation and tropical forests – what scope for synergies?', *World Development*, 29: 1817–1833.

WWF (2006) *Species and People: Linked Futures*, WWF International, Gland, Switzerland.

Appendix

The appendix for this article is available online at http://journals.cambridge.org

Part 5

New Developments:
Ecosystem Services, Carbon
and Climate Change

Editors' Introduction

In **Part 5** we seek to explore the concept of ecosystem services and their links to both biodiversity conservation and poverty reduction. We look at the approach of payments for ecosystem services (PES) and the extent to which this strategy for conservation incentives is also providing benefits for poor people. The Millennium Ecosystem Assessment (MA) brought to global attention the concept of 'ecosystem services' and the contribution these make to human well-being. According to the MA, biodiversity underpins the supply of ecosystem services and its conservation is thus critical to their delivery over the long term (Chapter 25).

There is some confusion around the use of the terms 'ecosystem services' and 'PES' in the literature. The MA for example describes ecosystem services as the benefits that people obtain from ecosystems and classify these into four types: (i) provisioning services (e.g. food, fuel, fibre); (ii) regulating services (e.g. climate stabilisation, water quality); (iii) cultural services (e.g. aesthetics, spirituality); and (iv) supporting services (e.g. soil formation, nutrient cycling). The concept of PES – which emerged before the MA – was originally used to mean payments for *environmental services*. These were categorized differently from the MA typology. A global review of markets for forest-based environmental services, for example, identified four key categories: carbon sequestration, biodiversity protection, landscape beauty and watershed protection (Landell-Mills and Porras, 2002). Clearly these are not the same as the benefits described by the MA. However, the term PES is now used interchangeably to cover both definitions (e.g. Ravnborg et al., 2007).

The Intergovernmental Panel on Climate Change (IPCC) recently concluded that the resilience of many ecosystems is likely to be exceeded this century as a result of global warming and related climate impacts such as wildfires and floods (IPCC, 2007). This detrimental impact is likely to affect the ability of biodiverse ecosystems to help poor people adapt to climate change: for example, through maintenance of natural protection against floods and increased resilience provided by diverse traditional crops (Reid and Swiderska, 2008) – thus exacerbating the direct impact of climate change on the poor. At the same time, because of the potential threats to biodiversity posed by climate change, there are calls for renewed support for, and expansion of, protected areas (Hansen et al., 2003) – which would also have potentially negative implications for poor people, as we have discussed in **Part 3**. Add to this the fact that the carbon markets have to date largely ignored social issues, and it is clear that climate change is a highly relevant issue for the conservation–poverty debate.

The maintenance of one particular ecosystem service, carbon sequestration, has significant implications both for the climate change agenda and the conservation–poverty agenda. The Stern Review (Stern, 2007) estimated that land use change is responsible for 18 per cent of greenhouse gas emissions, and that this land use change arises almost entirely from deforestation. Rapidly increasing attention has thus been paid to including mechanisms for reduced emissions from deforestation and degradation (REDD) under the UN Framework Convention on Climate Change (UNFCCC). Yet REDD schemes have potentially huge implications for both biodiversity conservation and local people's livelihoods. Proposed REDD schemes, for example, may prioritize carbon sequestration irrespective of biodiversity considerations and risk exacerbating tensions over land and resource rights, and yet if well designed, could in theory enhance all three areas (see the work of the Climate, Community and Biodiversity Alliance, for example).

More generally, the concept of PES, of which REDD is one example, is increasingly gaining credibility as a market mechanism for resource conservation which seeks to reward resource providers and managers for conservation services. One of the largest and best-known PES programmes was introduced in Costa Rica in 1996, where the national government compensates landowners for keeping forests intact and reforesting degraded areas (WRI, 2008). Wunder (2005) notes that there is a lack of agreement as to the likely beneficiaries of such schemes in terms of both conservation and poverty impacts:

> PES advocates stress that innovation is urgently needed because current approaches provide too little value for declining funding; that PES can provide new (especially private-sector) funding; and that poor communities selling these services can improve their livelihoods. Sceptics, however, fear that PES will 'bring back the fences' by decoupling conservation from development; that asymmetric power distribution means powerful conservation consortia may deprive communities of their legitimate land-development aspirations; and that commercial conservation may erode culturally rooted, not-for-profit conservation values.

Chapter 25 is an extract from the MA and provides an overview of ecosystem services and their links with biodiversity and with human well-being. Published in 2005, the MA is widely acknowledged for its scientific authority, and has brought considerable policy attention to the value and vulnerability of ecosystem services, underpinning arguments for including biodiversity conservation as key to both mitigation of and adaptation to climate change. The concept of ecosystem services provides a mechanism for linking biodiversity conservation with climate change, land degradation and other environmental concerns, strengthening the case that individual environmental problems cannot be treated in isolation.

However, not all are happy with the growing focus on ecosystem services, in particular with the perceived emphasis on the utilitarian values of 'wild nature'. In Chapter 26, McCauley (2006) regards the focus on ecosystem services as 'selling out on nature'. This prompts a response from Marvier et al. (2006) who point out that it is the poorest who suffer most from degraded ecosystems, yet it is also the poorest who are most affected by efforts to protect nature. Attention to ecosystem services can thus ensure that consideration for poor people is built into the design of conservation projects thus building 'a broader constituency for conservation that reaches beyond the affluent Western world'.

Attention to ecosystem services and their economic values does not necessarily mean a win–win for conservation and poverty reduction. In Chapter 27, Wunder (2008) reviews the extent to which the poor can really benefit from PES schemes. He points out that the poor can be both service providers (and hence benefit from payments) and service users (and hence be expected to pay for previously free services which they can ill-afford). Overall, the welfare effects of PES are small compared to national poverty-alleviation goals and Wunder concludes that the prime focus of PES should thus remain on the environment, not on poverty.

In Chapter 28, Roe et al. (2007) set PES in the context of climate change and its links to international conservation and local communities. They explore the potentially negative implications of carbon offset markets and REDD schemes for poor people, in terms of their ability to be 'hijacked' by a protectionist conservation agenda, and emphasize the importance of integrating biodiversity conservation and poverty reduction into efforts to tackle climate change. Campbell et al. (2008) take this further in Chapter 29, focusing on the experience of protected areas as an example of the impacts that can be expected from REDD. Forest carbon schemes face similar problems to those of protected areas, namely lack of established tenure and inequitable resource distribution, and the authors call for careful treatment of livelihoods issues, sound assessment of past experience, community involvement in planning and ensuring sharing of financial benefits if REDD is to become a sustainable solution to deforestation.

Griffiths (2008) expresses further concerns about REDD in Chapter 30 in terms of its likely impacts on forest-dependent communities. These include: renewed or increased top-down approaches to forest conservation, notably through exclusionary models such as strictly protected areas with no human habitation; unjust targeting of local communities as drivers of deforestation; land speculation, land grabbing and land conflicts; violations of customary land and territorial rights; corruption and embezzlement of international funds by national elites; and inequitable and abusive community contracts. Each of these concerns has previously featured in different elements of the conservation–poverty debate.

References

Campbell, A., Clark, S., Coad, L., Miles, L., Bolt, K. and Roe, D. (2008) 'Protecting the future: Carbon, forests, protected areas and local livelihoods', *Biodiversity*, 9 (3&4): 117–121.

Griffiths, T. (2008) *Seeing RED? Avoided Deforestation and the Rights of Indigenous Peoples and Local Communities*, Update for Poznan, Forest Peoples Programme, Moreton-in-Marsh.

Hansen, L.J., Biringer, J.L. and Hoffmann, J.R. (2003) *Buying Time: A User's Manual for Building Resistance and Resilience to Climate Change in Natural Systems*, WWF Climate Change Programme, Berlin.

IPCC (2007) *Climate Change 2007: Climate Change Impacts, Adaptation and Vulnerability. Summary for Policymakers*, Working Group II Contribution to the Intergovernmental Panel on Climate Change Fourth Assessment Report, Intergovernmental Panel on Climate Change, Geneva, Switzerland.

Landell-Mills, N. and Porras, I. (2002) *Silver Bullet or Fools' Gold? A Global Review of Markets for Forest Environmental Services and their Impact on the Poor*, IIED, London.

McCauley, D. (2006) 'Selling out on nature', *Nature*, 443: 27–28.

Marvier, M., Grant, J., and Karieva, P. (2006) 'Nature: poorest may see it as their economic rival', *Nature*, 443: 749–750.

Ravnborg, H.M., Damsgaard, M.G. and Raben, K. (2007) *Payments for Ecosystem Services Issues and Pro-Poor Opportunities for Development Assistance*, DIIS Report 2007(6), Danish Institute for International Studies, Copenhagen.

Reid, H. and Swiderska, K. (2008) *Biodiversity, Climate Change and Poverty: Exploring the Links*, IIED Briefing, International Institute for Environment and Development, London.

Roe, D., Reid, H., Vaughan, K., Brickell, E. and Elliott, J. (2007) *Climate, Carbon, Conservation and Communities*, An IIED/WWF Briefing, International Institute for Environment and Development, London, UK.

Stern, N. (2007) *The Economics of Climate Change: The Stern Review*, Cambridge University Press, Cambridge.

WRI (2008) *Protecting Forests to Save the Climate: REDD Challenges and Opportunities*, WRI Earth-Trends, April 2008 Monthly Update.

Wunder, S. (2005) *Payments for Environmental Services: Some Nuts and Bolts*, CIFOR Occasional Paper No. 42, Center for International Forestry Research, Bogor, Indonesia.

Wunder, S. (2008) 'Payments for environmental services and the poor: Concepts and preliminary evidence', *Environment and Development Economics*, 2008, 13(3): 279–297.

Chapter 25

Ecosystems and Human Well-Being: Current State and Trends

Millennium Ecosystem Assessment

Introduction

Humanity has always depended on the services provided by the biosphere and its ecosystems. Further, the biosphere is itself the product of life on Earth. The composition of the atmosphere and soil, the cycling of elements through air and waterways, and many other ecological assets are all the result of living processes – and all are maintained and replenished by living ecosystems. The human species, while buffered against environmental immediacies by culture and technology, is ultimately fully dependent on the flow of ecosystem services.

In his April 2000 Millennium Report to the United Nations General Assembly, in recognition of the growing burden that degraded ecosystems are placing on human well-being and economic development and the opportunity that better managed ecosystems provide for meeting the goals of poverty eradication and sustainable development, United Nations Secretary-General Kofi Annan stated that:

> *It is impossible to devise effective environmental policy unless it is based on sound scientific information. While major advances in data collection have been made in many areas, large gaps in our knowledge remain. In particular, there has never been a comprehensive global assessment of the world's major ecosystems. The planned Millennium Ecosystem Assessment, a major international collaborative effort to map the health of our planet, is a response to this need.*

The Millennium Ecosystem Assessment was established with the involvement of governments, the private sector, non-governmental organizations, and scientists to provide an integrated assessment of the consequences of ecosystem change for

,human well-being and to analyse options available to enhance the conservation of ecosystems and their contributions to meeting human needs. The Convention on Biological Diversity, the Convention to Combat Desertification, the Convention on Migratory Species, and the Ramsar Convention on Wetlands plan to use the findings of the MA, which will also help meet the needs of others in government, the private sector, and civil society. The MA should help to achieve the United Nations Millennium Development Goals and to carry out the Plan of Implementation of the 2002 World Summit on Sustainable Development. It has mobilized hundreds of scientists from countries around the world to provide information and clarify science concerning issues of greatest relevance to decision-makers. The MA has identified areas of broad scientific agreement and also pointed to areas of continuing scientific debate. The assessment framework developed for the MA offers decision-makers a mechanism to:

- *Identify options that can better achieve core human development and sustainability goals. All countries and communities are grappling with the challenge of meeting growing demands for food, clean water, health and employment.* And decision-makers in the private and public sectors must also balance economic growth and social development with the need for environmental conservation. All of these concerns are linked directly or indirectly to the world's ecosystems. The MA process, at all scales, was designed to bring the best science to bear on the needs of decision-makers concerning these links between ecosystems, human development, and sustainability.
- *Better understand the trade-offs involved – across sectors and stakeholders – in decisions concerning the environment.* Ecosystem-related problems have historically been approached issue by issue, but rarely by pursuing multi-sectoral objectives. This approach has not withstood the test of time. Progress toward one objective such as increasing food production has often been at the cost of progress toward other objectives such as conserving biological diversity or improving water quality. The MA framework complements sectoral assessments with information on the full impact of potential policy choices across sectors and stakeholders.
- *Align response options with the level of governance where they can be most effective.* Effective management of ecosystems will require actions at all scales, from the local to the global. Human actions now directly or inadvertently affect virtually all of the world's ecosystems; actions required for the management of ecosystems refer to the steps that humans can take to modify their direct or indirect influences on ecosystems. The management and policy options available and the concerns of stakeholders differ greatly across these scales. The priority areas for biodiversity conservation in a country as defined based on 'global' value, for example, would be very different from those as defined based on the value to local communities. The multi-scale assessment framework developed for the MA provides a new approach for analysing policy options at all scales – from local communities to international conventions.

What is the Problem?

Ecosystem services are the benefits people obtain from ecosystems, which the MA describes as provisioning, regulating, supporting and cultural services (see Box 25.1). Ecosystem services include products such as food, fuel and fibre; regulating services such as climate regulation and disease control; and nonmaterial benefits such as spiritual or aesthetic benefits. Changes in these services affect human well-being in many ways (See Figure 25.1).

The demand for ecosystem services is now so great that trade-offs among services have become the rule. A country can increase food supply by converting a forest to agriculture, for example, but in so doing it decreases the supply of services that may be of equal or greater importance, such as clean water, timber, ecotourism destinations, or flood regulation and drought control. There are many indications that human demands on ecosystems will grow still greater in the coming decades. Current estimates of 3 billion more people and a quadrupling of the world economy by 2050 imply a formidable increase in demand for and consumption of biological and physical resources, as well as escalating impacts on ecosystems and the services they provide.

Box 25.1 *Key definitions*

Ecosystem. An ecosystem is a dynamic complex of plant, animal and micro-organism communities and the non-living environment interacting as a functional unit. Humans are an integral part of ecosystems. Ecosystems vary enormously in size; a temporary pond in a tree hollow and an ocean basin can both be ecosystems.

Ecosystem services. Ecosystem services are the benefits people obtain from ecosystems. These include provisioning services such as food and water; regulating services such as regulation of floods, drought, land degradation, and disease; supporting services such as soil formation and nutrient cycling; and cultural services such as recreational, spiritual, religious and other non-material benefits.

Well-being. Human well-being has multiple constituents, including basic material for a good life, freedom of choice and action, health, good social relations, and security. Well-being is at the opposite end of a continuum from poverty, which has been defined as a 'pronounced deprivation in well-being.' The constituents of well-being, as experienced and perceived by people, are situation-dependent, reflecting local geography, culture, and ecological circumstances.

The problem posed by the growing demand for ecosystem services is compounded by increasingly serious degradation in the capability of ecosystems to provide these services. World fisheries are now declining due to over-fishing, for instance, and a significant amount of agricultural land has been degraded in the past half-century by erosion, salinization, compaction, nutrient depletion, pollution and urbanization. Other human-induced impacts on ecosystems include alteration of the nitrogen, phosphorus, sulphur and carbon cycles, causing acid rain, algal blooms, and fish kills in rivers and coastal waters, along with contributions to climate change. In many parts of the world, this degradation of ecosystem services is exacerbated by the associated loss of the knowledge and understanding held by local communities – knowledge that sometimes could help to ensure the sustainable use of the ecosystem.

This combination of ever-growing demands being placed on increasingly degraded ecosystems seriously diminishes the prospects for sustainable development. Human well-being is affected not just by gaps between ecosystem service supply and demand but also by the increased vulnerability of individuals, communities and nations. Productive ecosystems, with their array of services, provide people and communities with resources and options they can use as insurance in the face of natural catastrophes or social upheaval. While well-managed ecosystems reduce risks and vulnerability, poorly managed systems can exacerbate them by increasing risks of flood, drought, crop failure, or disease.

Ecosystem degradation tends to harm rural populations more directly than urban populations and has its most direct and severe impact on poor people. The wealthy control access to a greater share of ecosystem services, consume those services at a higher per-capita rate, and are buffered from changes in their availability (often at a substantial cost) through their ability to purchase scarce ecosystem services or substitutes. For example, even though a number of marine fisheries have been depleted in the past century, the supply of fish to wealthy consumers has not been disrupted since fishing fleets have been able to shift to previously underexploited stocks. In contrast, poor people often lack access to alternative services and are highly vulnerable to ecosystem changes that result in famine, drought or floods. They frequently live in locations particularly sensitive to environmental threats, and they lack financial and institutional buffers against these dangers. Degradation of coastal fishery resources, for instance, results in a decline in protein consumed by the local community since fishers may not have access to alternative sources of fish and community members may not have enough income to purchase fish. Degradation affects their very survival.

Changes in ecosystems affect not just humans but countless other species as well. The management objectives that people set for ecosystems and the actions that they take are influenced not just by the consequences of ecosystem changes for humans but also by the importance people place on considerations of the intrinsic value of species and ecosystems. Intrinsic value is the value of something in and for itself, irrespective of its utility for someone else. For example, villages in India protect 'spirit sanctuaries' in relatively natural states, even though a strict cost-benefit calculation might favour their conversion to agriculture. Similarly, many countries have passed laws protecting endangered species based on the view that these species have a right to exist, even if their protection results in net economic costs. Sound ecosystem management thus involves steps to address the utilitarian links of people to ecosystems as well as processes that allow considerations of the intrinsic value of ecosystems to be factored into decision-making.

The degradation of ecosystem services has many causes, including excessive demand for ecosystem services stemming from economic growth, demographic changes, and individual choices. Market mechanisms do not always ensure the conservation of ecosystem services either because markets do not exist for services such as cultural or regulatory services or, where they do exist, because policies and institutions do not enable people living within the ecosystem to benefit from services it may provide to others who are far away. For example, institutions are now only beginning to be developed to enable those benefiting from carbon sequestration to provide local managers with an economic incentive to leave a forest uncut, while strong economic incentives often exist for managers to harvest the forest. Also, even if a market exists for an ecosystem service, the results obtained through the market may be socially or ecologically undesirable. Properly managed, the creation of ecotourism opportunities in a country can create strong economic incentives for the maintenance of the cultural services provided by ecosystems, but poorly managed ecotourism activities can degrade the very resource on which they depend. Finally, markets are often unable to address important intra- and intergenerational equity issues associated with managing ecosystems for this and future generations, given that some changes in ecosystem services are irreversible.

The world has witnessed in recent decades not just dramatic changes to ecosystems but equally profound changes to social systems that shape both the pressures on ecosystems and the opportunities to respond. The relative influence of individual nation-states has diminished with the growth of power and influence of a far more complex array of institutions, including regional governments, multinational companies, the United Nations, and civil society organizations. Stakeholders have become more involved in decision-making. Given the multiple actors whose decisions now strongly influence ecosystems, the challenge of providing information to decision-makers has grown. At the same time, the new institutional landscape may provide an unprecedented opportunity for information concerning ecosystems to make a major difference. Improvements in ecosystem management to enhance human well-being will require new institutional and policy arrangements and changes in rights and access to resources that may be more possible today under these conditions of rapid social change than they have ever been before.

Like the benefits of increased education or improved governance, the protection, restoration and enhancement of ecosystem services tends to have multiple and synergistic benefits. Already, many governments are beginning to recognize the need for more effective management of these basic life-support systems. Examples of significant progress toward sustainable management of biological resources can also be found in civil society, in indigenous and local communities, and in the private sector.

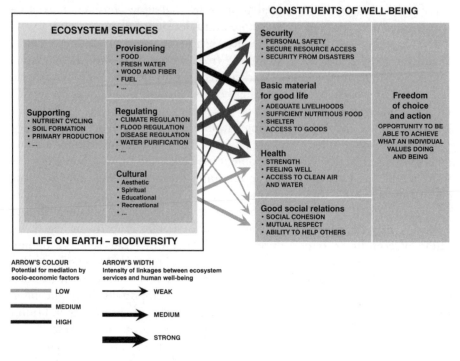

Source: Millennium Ecosystem Assessment

Figure 25.1 *Linkages between ecosystem services and human well-being*

Figure 25.1 depicts the strength of linkages between categories of ecosystem services and components of human well-being that are commonly encountered and includes indications of the extent to which it is possible for socio-economic factors to mediate the linkage (for example, if it is possible to purchase a substitute for a degraded ecosystem service, then there is a high potential for mediation). The strength of the linkages and the potential for mediation differ in different ecosystems and regions. In addition to the influence of ecosystem services on human well-being depicted here, other factors – including other environmental factors as well as economic, social, technological, and cultural factors – influence human well-being, and ecosystems are in turn affected by changes in human well-being (Millennium Ecosystem Assessment).

Conceptual Framework

The conceptual framework for the MA places human well-being as the central focus for assessment, while recognizing that biodiversity and ecosystems also have intrinsic value and that people take decisions concerning ecosystems based on considerations of well-being as well as intrinsic value (see Box 25.2). The MA conceptual framework assumes that a dynamic interaction exists between people and other parts of ecosystems, with the changing human condition serving to both directly and indirectly drive change in ecosystems and with changes in ecosystems causing changes in human well-being. At the same time, many other factors independent of the environment change the human condition, and many natural forces are influencing ecosystems.

The MA focuses particular attention on the linkages between ecosystem services and human well-being. The assessment deals with the full range of ecosystems – from those relatively undisturbed, such as natural forests, to landscapes with mixed patterns of human use and ecosystems intensively managed and modified by humans, such as agricultural land and urban areas.

A full assessment of the interactions between people and ecosystems requires a multi-scale approach because it better reflects the multi-scale nature of decision-making, allows the examination of driving forces that may be exogenous to particular regions, and provides a means of examining the differential impact of ecosystem changes and policy responses on different regions and groups within regions.

This section explains in greater detail the characteristics of each of the components of the MA conceptual framework, moving clockwise from the lower left corner of the Figure in Box 25.2.

Ecosystems and their services

An ecosystem is a dynamic complex of plant, animal and micro-organism communities and the non-living environment interacting as a functional unit. Humans are an integral part of ecosystems. Ecosystems provide a variety of benefits to people, including provisioning, regulating, cultural and supporting services. Provisioning services are the products people obtain from ecosystems, such as food, fuel, fibre, fresh water, and genetic resources. Regulating services are the benefits people obtain from the regulation of ecosystem processes, including air quality maintenance, climate regulation, erosion control, regulation of human diseases, and water purification. Cultural services are the non-material benefits people obtain from ecosystems through spiritual enrichment, cognitive development, reflection, recreation, and aesthetic experiences. Supporting services are those that are necessary for the production of all other ecosystem services, such as primary production, production of oxygen, and soil formation.

Biodiversity and ecosystems are closely related concepts. Biodiversity is the variability among living organisms from all sources, including terrestrial, marine and other aquatic ecosystems, and the ecological complexes of which they are part. It includes diversity within and between species and diversity of ecosystems. Diversity is a structural feature of ecosystems, and the variability among ecosystems is an element of biodiversity. Products of biodiversity include many of the services produced by ecosystems (such as food and genetic resources), and changes in biodiversity can influence all the other services they provide. In addition to the

Box 25.2 Millennium Ecosystem Assessment conceptual framework

Changes in factors that indirectly affect ecosystems, such as population, technology and lifestyle (upper right corner of figure), can lead to changes in factors directly affecting ecosystems, such as the catch of fisheries or the application of fertilizers to increase food production (lower right corner). The resulting changes in the ecosystem (lower left corner) cause the ecosystem services to change and thereby affect human well-being. These interactions can take place at more than one scale and can cross scales. For example, a global market may lead to regional loss of forest cover, which increases flood magnitude along a local stretch of a river. Similarly, the interactions can take place across different time scales. Actions can be taken either to respond to negative changes or to enhance positive changes at almost all points in this framework (black cross-bars).

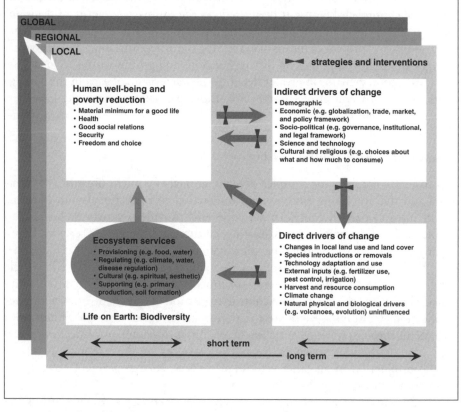

important role of biodiversity in providing ecosystem services, the diversity of living species has intrinsic value independent of any human concern.

The concept of an ecosystem provides a valuable framework for analysing and acting on the linkages between people and the environment. For that reason, the 'ecosystem approach' has been endorsed by the Convention on Biological Diversity, and the MA conceptual framework is entirely consistent with this approach. The CBD states that the ecosystem approach is a strategy for the integrated management of land, water and living resources that promotes conservation and sustainable use in an equitable way. This approach recognizes that humans, with their cultural diversity, are an integral component of many ecosystems.

In order to implement the ecosystem approach, decision-makers need to understand the multiple effects on an ecosystem of any management or policy change. By way of analogy, decision-makers would not make a decision about financial policy in a country without examining the condition of the economic system, since information on the economy of a single sector such as manufacturing would be insufficient. The same need to examine the consequences of changes for multiple sectors applies to ecosystems. For instance, subsidies for fertilizer use may increase food production, but sound decisions also require information on whether the potential reduction in the harvests of downstream fisheries as a result of water quality degradation from the fertilizer runoff might outweigh those benefits.

For the purpose of analysis and assessment, a pragmatic view of ecosystem boundaries must be adopted, depending on the questions being asked. A well-defined ecosystem has strong interactions among its components and weak inter-actions across its boundaries. A useful choice of ecosystem boundary is one where a number of discontinuities coincide, such as in the distribution of organisms, soil types, drainage basins, and depth in a water body. At a larger scale, regional and even globally distributed ecosystems can be evaluated based on a commonality of basic structural units. The global assessment being undertaken by the MA reports on marine, coastal, inland water, forest, dryland, island, mountain, polar, culti-vated and urban regions. These regions are not ecosystems themselves, but each contains a number of ecosystems.

People seek multiple services from ecosystems and thus perceive the condition of given ecosystems in relation to their ability to provide the services desired. Various methods can be used to assess the ability of ecosystems to deliver particular services. With those answers in hand, stakeholders have the information they need to decide on a mix of services best meeting their needs. The MA considers criteria and methods to provide an integrated view of the condition of ecosystems. The condition of each category of ecosystem services is evaluated in somewhat different ways, although in general a full assessment of any service requires considerations of stocks, flows and resilience of the service.

Human well-being and poverty reduction

Human well-being has multiple constituents, including the basic material for a good life, freedom of choice and action, health, good social relations, and security. Poverty is also multidimensional and has been defined as the pronounced depriva-tion of well-being. How well-being, ill-being, or poverty are experienced and expressed depends on context and situation, reflecting local physical, social, and personal factors such as geography, environment, age, gender, and culture. In all contexts, however, ecosystems are essential for human well-being through their provisioning, regulating, cultural, and supporting services.

Human intervention in ecosystems can amplify the benefits to human society. However, evidence in recent decades of escalating human impacts on ecological systems worldwide raises concerns about the spatial and temporal consequences of ecosystem changes detrimental to human well-being. Ecosystem changes affect human well-being in the following ways:

- *Security* is affected both by changes in provisioning services, which affect supplies of food and other goods and the likelihood of conflict over declining resources, and by changes in regulating services, which could influence the frequency and magnitude of floods, droughts, landslides or other catastrophes. It can also be affected by changes in cultural services as, for example, when the loss of important ceremonial or spiritual attributes of ecosystems contributes to the weakening of social relations in a community. These changes in turn affect material well-being, health, freedom and choice, security, and good social relations.
- *Access to basic material for a good life* is strongly linked to both provisioning services such as food and fibre production and regulating services, including water purification.
- *Health* is strongly linked to both provisioning services such as food production and regulating services, including those that influence the distribution of disease-transmitting insects and of irritants and pathogens in water and air. Health can also be linked to cultural services through recreational and spiritual benefits.
- *Social relations* are affected by changes to cultural services, which affect the quality of human experience.
- *Freedom of choice and action* is largely predicated on the existence of the other components of well-being and are thus influenced by changes in provisioning, regulating or cultural services from ecosystems.

Human well-being can be enhanced through sustainable human interactions with ecosystems supported by necessary instruments, institutions, organizations, and technology. Creation of these through participation and transparency may contribute to freedoms and choice as well as to increased economic, social, and ecological security. By ecological security, we mean the minimum level of ecological stock needed to ensure a sustainable flow of ecosystem services.

Yet the benefits conferred by institutions and technology are neither automatic nor equally shared. In particular, such opportunities are more readily grasped by richer than poorer countries and people; some institutions and technologies mask or exacerbate environmental problems; responsible governance, while essential, is not easily achieved; participation in decision-making, an essential element of responsible governance, is expensive in time and resources to maintain. Unequal access to ecosystem services has often elevated the well-being of small segments of the population at the expense of others.

Sometimes the consequences of the depletion and degradation of ecosystem services can be mitigated by the substitution of knowledge and of manufactured or human capital. For example, the addition of fertilizer in agricultural systems has been able to offset declining soil fertility in many regions of the world where people have sufficient economic resources to purchase these inputs, and water treatment facilities can sometimes substitute for the role of watersheds and wetlands in water purification. But ecosystems are complex and dynamic systems and there are limits to substitution possibilities, especially with regulating, cultural and supporting services. No substitution is possible for the extinction of culturally important species such as tigers or whales, for instance, and substitutions may be economically impractical for the loss of services such as erosion control or climate regulation.

Moreover, the scope for substitutions varies by social, economic and cultural conditions. For some people, especially the poorest, substitutes and choices are very limited. For those who are better off, substitution may be possible through trade, investment, and technology.

Because of the inertia in both ecological and human systems, the consequences of ecosystem changes made today may not be felt for decades. Thus, sustaining ecosystem services, and thereby human well-being, requires a full understanding and wise management of the relationships between human activities, ecosystem change, and well-being over the short, medium and long term. Excessive current use of ecosystem services compromises their future availability. This can be prevented by ensuring that the use is sustainable.

Achieving sustainable use requires effective and efficient institutions that can provide the mechanisms through which concepts of freedom, justice, fairness, basic capabilities, and equity govern the access to and use of ecosystem services. Such institutions may also need to mediate conflicts between individual and social interests that arise.

The best way to manage ecosystems to enhance human well-being will differ if the focus is on meeting needs of the poor and weak or the rich and powerful. For both groups, ensuring the long-term supply of ecosystem services is essential. But for the poor, an equally critical need is to provide more equitable and secure access to ecosystem services.

Chapter 26

Selling Out on Nature

Douglas J. McCauley

Probably the most important trend in conservation science at the moment is 'ecosystem services', typically seen as economic benefits provided by natural ecosystems.[1] They form the basis of most market-oriented mechanisms for conservation. The underlying assumption is that if scientists can identify ecosystem services, quantify their economic value, and ultimately bring conservation more in synchrony with market ideologies,[2] then the decision-makers will recognize the folly of environmental destruction and work to safeguard nature.

But market-based mechanisms for conservation are not a panacea for our current conservation ills. If we mean to make significant and long-lasting gains in conservation, we must strongly assert the primacy of ethics and aesthetics in conservation. We must act quickly to redirect much of the effort now being devoted to the commodification of nature back towards instilling a love for nature in more people.

Gold Rush

The proponents of market-based mechanisms for conservation bolster their argument by repeatedly citing one example: the Catskill/ Delaware watershed. Through this project, New York City invested in conserving a watershed that filters its water as effectively as a filtration plant, and more cheaply.

A growing number of ecologists, economists and environmental scientists hold this shining example aloft and proclaim that where there is one golden nugget, there must be others. They describe, mostly in hypothetical terms, a world of win–win scenarios. It is a message with broad appeal: for the public, which is notoriously averse to bad news; for business-oriented politicians, who see an opportunity to further liberalize markets while appeasing the environmentally anxious; for philanthropists who wish to do good without straying too far from their economic comfort zones; and for foundations that want to use the familiar capitalist rhetoric of ecosystem services to draw out new or wary donors.

It is both true and obvious that 'ecosystems', in some sense of the word, are necessary for human survival. It is also true that there will be cases in which it will be lucrative to protect nature, and that people will derive benefits from this conservation effort. However, ecosystem services are rapidly assuming an importance in discussions on conservation that is far out of proportion to their actual utility.

As conservation tools, ecosystem services are limited in four fundamental ways. First, the logic of ecosystem-service-based conservation rests on the implicit assumption that the biosphere is benevolent – that it provides us with useful services and protects us from malevolent abiotic forces such as hurricanes, floods and rising temperatures. This reasoning ignores basic ecology: environments don't act for the benefit of any single species. There are myriad examples of what might be labelled 'ecosystem disservices'. Trees take water out of watersheds;[3] forests may be contributing to global temperature increases;[4] wild animals kill people and destroy property;[5] and wetlands can increase the risk of disease.[6] Market-based conservation strategies, as currently articulated, offer little guidance on how we are to protect the chunks of nature that conflict with our interests or preserve the perhaps far more numerous pieces of nature that neither help nor harm us.

Markets in Flux

Second, although most conservationists would argue that nature should be conserved in perpetuity, the strength and direction of market forces that are now being called upon to motivate nature conservation are anything but perpetual. The often illusory and ephemeral relationship of the market to conservation is well illustrated by the case of a former coffee plantation, Finca Santa Fe, in the Valle del General of Costa Rica.[7] A recent study found that native bees from two forest fragments adjacent to Finca Santa Fe yielded approximately US$60,000 a year in pollination services to the coffee plants. This was hailed as an example of how conservation can yield 'double benefits' for biodiversity and agriculture.

Shortly after the conclusion of the study, however, Finca Santa Fe, probably affected by one of the worst dips in coffee prices this century, cleared its coffee and planted pineapple instead. Pollinators are irrelevant to pineapple production. So simple logic suggests that over a period of several years, the monetary value of the pollinators in forest fragments around Finca Santa Fe dropped from $60,000 per year to zero.

To make ecosystem services the foundation of our conservation strategies is to imply – intentionally or otherwise – that nature is only worth conserving when it is, or can be made, profitable. The risk in advocating this position is that we might be taken at our word. Then, if there is a 'devaluation' of nature, as in the case of Finca Santa Fe, what are we to tell local stewards who have invested in our ideology, and how can we protect nature from liquidation?

Watershed Down

Third, conservation based on ecosystem services commits the folly of betting against human ingenuity. The entire history of technology and human 'progress' is one of producing artificial substitutes for what we once obtained from nature, or domesticating once-natural services. One of the primary selling points for protecting the Catskill/Delaware Watershed was that the costs associated with constructing and operating a filtration plant would have driven up water prices in New York City. However, recent reports[8] indicate that increased turbidity might ultimately force New York to turn to technology to filter its water, in essence negating this much-ballyhooed economic incentive for conservation.

Several other major US cities still rely on natural filtration, and in some of these cases it is difficult to imagine that technology will soon produce a cheaper artificial alternative to these natural watersheds. Yet it would also once have been difficult to imagine cost-effective manufactured alternatives to rubber and timber. Although we will never replicate all of the 'services' offered by nature, I would argue that conservation plans that underestimate the technological prowess of humans are bound to have short lifespans.

Lastly, although it has been suggested that in most cases the services that come from nature are valuable enough to make conservation profitable, making money and protecting nature are all too often mutually exclusive goals. Take the case of Africa's Lake Victoria, where the introduction of the invasive Nile perch (*Lates niloticus*) contributed significantly to the decimation of local biodiversity while dramatically boosting the economic value of the lake. Local people profiting from trade in the fish hail its introduction as a success, whereas biologists have condemned the event as 'the most catastrophic extinction episode of recent history'.[9] John Terborgh,[10] discussing similar issues in tropical-forest conservation, remarked that these forests are 'worth more dead than alive'. If Terborgh's assessment is not always true, it is true all too often. So we must directly confront the reality that conservation may be expensive and stop deceiving ourselves and partners in conservation with hopes that win–win solutions can always be found.

Infinite Value

Are there other socially viable paths for conservationists besides the commodification of nature? Yes. Nature has an intrinsic value that makes it priceless, and this is reason enough to protect it. The idea is not new. We view certain historical artefacts and pieces of art as priceless. Nature embodies the same kind of values we cherish in these man-made media. Some ecologists claim that these intrinsic values, often referred to as cultural services, figure prominently enough in their valuation programmes. However, this co-option seems in many cases incongruous. I suggest that the aggregate value of a chunk of nature – its aesthetic beauty, cultural importance and evolutionary significance – is infinite, and thus defies incorporation into any ecosystem service programme that aims to save nature by approximating its monetary value.

All of this is not to deny a role for ecosystem services in our general efforts to protect nature. Individual ecosystem services will occasionally prove to be useful bargaining chips in specific conservation plans and, as such, can meaningfully support programmes aimed at protecting nature for nature's sake. However, to avoid trading in significant long-term conservation successes for marginal short-term gains, philosophical clarity is essential and caution is needed. When we employ the aid of ecosystem services to help pay the bills of conservation, we must make it abundantly clear that our overall mission is to protect nature, not to make it turn a profit.

Some will argue that this view is simply too optimistic. They may believe that the best way to meaningfully engage policy-makers driven by the financial bottom line is to translate the intrinsic worth of nature into the language of economics. But this is patently untrue – akin to saying that civil-rights advocates would have been more effective if they provided economic justifications for racial integration. Nature conservation must be framed as a moral issue and argued as such to policy-makers, who are just as accustomed to making decisions based on morality as on finances.

The track record of achievements by conservationists motivated by a moral imperative to protect nature for nature's sake is impressive: consider the international ban on commercial whaling, the national parks of the United States, and the CITES ivory-trade ban. Meanwhile, the only 'successful' large-scale ecosystem-service-based conservation project yet achieved is the imperilled Catskill watershed. But this 'nugget' may turn out to be fool's gold.

We will make more progress in the long run by appealing to people's hearts rather than to their wallets. If we oversell the message that ecosystems are important because they provide services, we will have effectively sold out on nature.

Notes

1   Daily, G.C. (1997) *Nature's Services*, Island Press, Washington, DC.

2   Millennium Ecosystem Assessment (2003) *Ecosystems and Human Well-Being: A Framework for the Assessment*, Island Press, Washington, DC.

3   Hayward, B. (2005) *From the Mountain to the Tap: How Land Use and Water Management Can Work for the Rural Poor*, NR International.

4   Gibbard, S., Caldeira, K., Bala, G., Phillips, T.J. and Wickett, M. (2005) 'Climate effects of global land cover change', *Geophys. Res. Lett*, 32, L23705.

5   Woodroffe, R., Thirgood, S. and Rabinowitz, A. (eds) (2005) *People and Wildlife: Conflict or Co-existence?*, Cambridge University Press, New York.

6   Willott, E. (2004) 'Restoring nature, without mosquitoes?', *Restor. Ecol.* 12, 147–153.

7   Ricketts, T.H., Daily, G.C., Ehrlich, P.R. and Michener, C.D. (2004) 'Economic value of tropical forest to coffee production', *Proc. Natl. Acad. Sci. USA* 101: 12579–12582.
8   DePalma, A. (2006) 'New York's water supply may need filtering', *New York Times.*
9   Wilson, E.O. (1992) *The Diversity of Life*, Belknap Press of Harvard University Press, Cambridge, Massachusetts.
10   Terborgh, J. (1999) *Requiem for Nature*, Island Press, Washington, DC.

Response
Nature: Poorest May See It as their Economic Rival

Sir – The moral imperative of saving species and protecting nature as put forward by Douglas J. McCauley ('Selling out on nature', *Nature*, 443: 27–28; 2006) must be weighed against the moral imperative of saving people. Typically it is the poorest members of our world community who are most affected by efforts to protect nature, and who suffer the most when ecosystems are degraded.

The conservation debate cannot be reduced to a choice between protecting nature or making an extra million for a yacht or villa. If it were, then perhaps moral arguments alone would be enough to protect the environment. The reality is that poor people are deforesting vast areas of tropical forest for subsistence agriculture, members of indigenous tribes are killing endangered wildlife and out-of-work fishermen are converting mangrove forests to shrimp farms. Moreover, biodiversity is greatest in the very areas where human populations are most dense, most rapidly growing and most impoverished (Cincotta, R.P, Wisnewski, J. and Engelman, R., *Nature* 404: 990–992; 2000).

McCauley does not acknowledge that economic valuation of ecosystem services can provide the data and tools needed to make human well-being part of the design of conservation projects. Although win–win scenarios are hard to find, it is important that we take care to quantify ecosystem services so that those situations in which both humans and biodiversity benefit can be identified and promoted. Moreover if fundamental economic concepts such as GNP could be reformulated to reflect ecosystem services, then nations might embark on policies that better protect their natural capital assets. The economic valuation of ecosystem services is simply a way of getting everyone's moral imperatives on the same page. It is a way of recognizing that conservation must be accomplished in a just and fair manner, in a way that does not pit the basic needs of humans against nature.

Attention to ecosystem services is not equivalent to venal worship of the dollar. Instead it provides an entry into market incentives, government policies, better-designed conservation projects and a broader constituency for conservation that reaches beyond the affluent Western world.

Conservationists who promote valuation of ecosystem services have no intention of selling out on nature – we just want to make sure it is correctly valued.

Michelle Marvier, Joy Grant and Peter Karieva

Chapter 27

Payments for Environmental Services and the Poor: Concepts and Preliminary Evidence

Sven Wunder

Introduction

At a time when overseas development assistance has become increasingly focused on poverty reduction, it is no surprise that innovative management tools like payments for environmental services (PES) are also scrutinized for their potential to contribute to this goal. Much hope exists that poor providers of environmental services (ES), such as remote upland farmers, can raise their incomes by receiving PES from the allegedly richer ES buyers, such as urban water users or global carbon-sequestration buyers. Indeed, some donors are only interested in PES for their hoped-for pro-poor effects, rather than their environmental impacts.

The purpose of this article is to provide a conceptual framework for analysing to what extent the poor participate in and benefit from PES – questions that under closer scrutiny are more comprehensive than is often assumed. This will be spiced with preliminary empirical evidence from developing-country case studies portrayed in the PES literature, and from fieldwork done by the Center for International Forestry Research (CIFOR) in Bolivia, Colombia, Ecuador, Venezuela and Vietnam. An overall conclusion is that poor people can widely participate in PES schemes, that this participation usually makes them better off (though seldom yielding huge gains), and that poverty concerns in selected cases should rather be with poor non-participants, especially landless people. There is no reason to believe that PES could, at the one extreme, risk becoming a poverty trap nor, at the other, a massive contribution to the poverty-alleviation Millennium Development Goals. It is recommended that less emphasis be given to direct PES poverty targeting, and more to increasing the scale of well-functioning PES schemes, which probably has more important welfare implications.

The article is organized as follows. The next section will frame the concepts of PES and poverty, and hypothesize on how they are interlinked. Following sections look at the ability of the poor to participate in PES schemes as sellers; describe how they are likely to fare if they pass the participation filters; explain the welfare effects on poor ES buyers; and that of PES-derived effects on poor non-participants. The final section summarizes the main arguments and discusses policy implications.

Definitions and Concepts

In CIFOR's applied work, PES has been defined as (1) voluntary transaction where (2) a well-defined ES (or corresponding land use) is (3) being 'bought' by a (minimum one) ES buyer (4) from a (minimum one) ES provider (5) if and only if ES provision is secured (conditionality). This narrow yet simple definition draws on the theoretical PES literature (Simpson and Sedjo, 1996; Ferraro and Kiss, 2002; Ferraro and Simpson, 2002). In practice, there are many 'PES-like' compensation schemes in the tropics that satisfy several but not all five criteria. One global review identified a gross list of 287 such cases, some of them in planning stages (Landell-Mills and Porras, 2002). However, there are probably not more than a couple of dozens of experiences globally that fit all five criteria above.[1]

This PES definition includes several sub-dimensions and categories (Wunder, 2005), of which two particularly should be distinguished for poverty-assessment purposes. First, public-sector schemes (central State or municipalities) tend to have different access filters and less payment-differentiation mechanisms than ones with private sector buyers (see 'To what extent do poor people sell environmental services?'). Second, people can be paid either for conservation of pre-existing environmental services (use-restricting schemes) or for their restoration (asset-building schemes). Whether PES is for doing something or for not doing something has likely implications for local economic activity, employment, and thus also for poverty (see 'How do poor non-participants fare?').

In the same vein, conceptual clarity about 'poverty' and 'the poor' is needed. In the following, we will be mainly concerned with absolute poverty, defined as a shortfall in welfare below a commonly defined standard, for instance a national poverty line. However, in some rural environments all households live below the national poverty line, but are still heterogeneous in terms of their assets, income and entitlements. This makes it necessary to look also at distribution and poverty depth; in particular, PES effects on 'the poorest of the poor' differ from those on smallholders (see 'How do poor non-participants fare?'). There is now a widespread consensus that poverty has multiple dimensions, thus integrating also broader entitlements (World Bank, 2000). In fact, PES also has non-income effects on participants, which tend to be positive (see 'Non-income gains'). Finally, one can split up the concept of poverty alleviation into poverty reduction, i.e. lifting people above the poverty line, and poverty prevention, i.e. impeding people from falling into (deeper) poverty through safety nets, seasonal gap fillers, etc. (Angelsen and Wunder, 2003). Since PES will typically accrue as a regular, fixed income flow, its potential will mostly be in poverty reduction, rather than its prevention.

The links between PES and poverty can be summarized in four sequential questions:

1. Participation filters: To what extent do poor people participate in PES schemes as buyers and sellers of environmental services?
2. Effects on sellers: If the poor become service sellers, does this make them better off?
3. Effects on users: Do poor service buyers (and non-paying poor service users) become better off from PES?
4. Derived effects: How are other, non-participant poor affected by PES outcomes?

The answers to these questions provide us with three categories of poor to scrutinize:

(a) poor environmental service sellers (supply side);
(b) poor environmental service users (demand side); and
(c) other poor people potentially being impacted by PES implementation (derived effects)

In the existing literature on PES and poverty, most discussion has been limited to questions 1 and 2, both of which are exclusively concerned with the fate of group (a). As will be shown below, it is important to broaden the view to the other two questions and groups for a more complete view of PES effects on poverty. Let us start by looking at question 1, i.e. the requirements for participation of the poor in PES schemes.

To What Extent do Poor People Sell Environmental Services?

This section will look at access to and 'market share' in PES schemes by poor potential ES providers. Poor people face explicit PES access rules and underlying structural constraints, but will also consider whether they desire to participate or not. Figure 27.1 gives a graphical illustration of the selection process leading to participation of the poor in PES schemes, or not.[2]

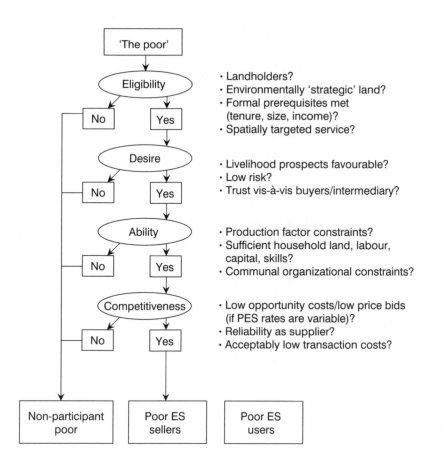

Figure 27.1 *Participation of the poor in PES schemes*

Eligibility

A first hurdle concerns the eligibility of the poor. Normally only landholders can participate in a PES programme, leaving out the landless that tend to be among 'the poorest of the poor': without control over land, it is impossible to guarantee the continuous delivery of an ES.[3] Among those owning land, only lands with a 'strategic environmental value' will find buyers' interest. In other words, the land has to be located vitally for service delivery (e.g. on a steep slope bordering a stream with important downstream water users) and the ES has to be either threatened (e.g. deforestation pressures that would accelerate the slope's soil erosion) or there has to be an opportunity to recuperate ES (e.g. planting trees to reduce ongoing soil erosion).

Note that the land-based eligibility criterion already excludes billions of poor people and directs them to the group of 'non-participant poor': the urban poor, the rural landless, those with land without environmental value, or land without 'strategic ES value' – i.e. where non-action does not make much difference for service provision. The degree of strategic spatial targeting will be larger for biodiversity protection, landscape beauty, and watershed protection – all of which are very space-specific. This contrasts with forest carbon sequestration, which can be done anywhere on the globe where trees can grow – a much less restrictive enrolment filter. Spatial targeting is also more common in private than in public PES schemes; the state is usually reluctant to strongly discriminate participant access throughout space.

Whereas spatial targeting thus filters out a large absolute number of poor, it will normally increase the poor's relative participation, because environmentally sensitive lands often spatially coincide with remote, sparsely populated, poverty-struck areas. Recent comparative poverty mapping in seven tropical developing countries showed a marked spatial correlation between closed forests and high poverty rates – although seldom high population numbers, and thus not high poverty densities (Sunderlin et al., 2007). In absolute numbers, provision of most ES is thus strongly targeted and exclusionary, but among the few eligible, the share of poor people is likely to be high, as exemplified by the Mexican national watershed PES.[4]

Public sector PES schemes are normally less spatially targeted, but tend to have more formal requirements for enrolment – some of which are pro-poor, others anti-poor. In a study examining six carbon and two watershed projects in Latin America, we reconfirmed this mixed picture (Grieg-Gran et al., 2005). Some rules discriminated against smallholders, such as formal land-tenure requirements and the exclusion of agroforestry and silvopasture (both being land uses favoured by the poor); others such as maximum farm-size enrolled and targeting of under-developed regions were pro-poor. Probably the requirement of formal land titles is the most common anti-poor enrolment criterion. Costa Rica abandoned a previous formal land-title requirement for PES to eliminate this bias (Pagiola, 2007). This shows that enrolment without formal title is possible, as long as landholders have locally recognized tenure and a proven ability to exclude potential intruders. On the other hand, all national-level public PES-like programmes in developing countries (Costa Rica, China, Mexico, South Africa, Vietnam) employ pro-poor targeting measures; in the South African Work for Water programme, radical pro-poor screening only makes the poor and unemployed eligible (Turpie et al., 2007).

Desire
Not only do the poor need to be eligible, they also need to have their own motivation and desire to participate in PES: is there an expected gain from participation, i.e. will PES payments more than cover the opportunity costs of buyer-requested land-use adjustments? But beyond income, a broader livelihood assessment of

benefits, costs and risks is pertinent. For instance, a piece of forest land threatened by invasions unless the landholder keeps 'working' it (i.e. gradually deforesting) might not be desirable to enrol in a PES set-aside scheme: rewards may be attractive, but the risks of losing the land might be too high unless land-tenure security is simultaneously strengthened (see 'Do poor environmental service users benefit from PES?'). Similarly, landholders are often suspicious of outsiders offering contracts that involve land-use caps, mistaking these for the first step towards land expropriation – in particular, in settings where land tenure remains insecure and PES contracts are a completely untested initiative. Initial trust-building through PES intermediaries or ES buyers may be necessary to convince landowners to participate. Finally, ES providers' transaction costs of participating are also relevant: does enrolment require so much paperwork and permits from the authorities that the effort is not worthwhile?

Ability

Poor people may be both eligible and willing to join a PES scheme, but still lack the ability to enrol. This applies in particular to what above was called 'asset-building PES', i.e. schemes where active investments are required to establish, for instance, biodiversity-friendly silvopastoral systems (Pagiola et al., 2008). Poor households may lack the necessary capital, skills or labour, as well as access to credit or technical assistance, to implement the changes required by the PES scheme. In Ecuador and Guatemela, Southgate et al. (2007) found that the smallest farmers were less willing to enrol land into conservation set-aside PES, since they perceived their food security to be compromised.

Other ability constraints may be at the village level, external to household decision-making. For instance, under loosely defined land tenure and access regimes, neighbours may exert strong pressures on the landowner not to fence off access to a land area proposed for set-aside conservation. In Bolivia, in one small-scale biodiversity-conservation PES the landowner had already agreed to the proposal, but backed off when his off-farm-living sons opposed it due to fears of losing future land access (Robertson and Wunder, 2005, pp. 115–116).

Competitiveness

A final question determining the poor's PES participation is whether the willing, able and eligible poor constitute competitive ES providers, or whether ES buyers are actually better off looking for non-poor providers. A first sub-question here is whether the farm-specific opportunity costs of the poor are sufficiently low to enable them to make a net profit from PES. If the PES scheme offers a single fixed rate per land area enrolled or per ES output unit, the farmer will have a 'take it or leave it' offer, and this competitiveness factor will already be captured under the 'desire' heading above. However, with variable rates in a bidding/auctioning system, a lower ES supply bid from the landowner will also increase enrolment chances.

What does this mean in practice? If poor landholders possess marginal lands, are strongly capital- and technology-constrained, and labour remuneration is low, their opportunity costs for changing land use are probably also low. Yet, if they work their smaller plots more intensively (e.g. labour-intensive crops) while large landholders prefer land-extensive, low-input activities with low per-hectare returns (e.g. extensive cattle ranching), this situation may be reversed. One watershed study in Guatemala found large differences between farmers' PES-relevant conservation opportunity costs, with poor farmers exhibiting lower costs and higher competitiveness (Costa and Zeller, 2003). Results are bound to be site-specific, but in general the poor are more likely to have lower opportunity costs.

A second competitiveness factor is the reliability of poor farmers as service suppliers. If they have de facto insecure land tenure and low control – a feature not uncommon for poor people – they may not be able to exclude outside intruders extracting resources or even taking over the land entirely. This risk would decisively jeopardize competitiveness vis-à-vis alternative ES suppliers who effectively control third-party access to their land.

The third, and often most important competitive factor, is the high PES transaction costs ES buyers face in working with smallholders. Imagine a water plant looking to secure the supply of clean urban drinking water, with options for investing in the conservation of two sub-watersheds. Both comprise an area of 3000ha, face the same degree of threat from erosion, and potential participants are equally eligible, willing and able. But the first watershed has three large landholders with 1000ha each, while the second holds 1000 poor landholders with 3ha each. The transaction costs of working in the second, poverty-struck watershed, in terms of PES negotiation, contracts, monitoring, enforcement and sanctions are bound to be much higher than those in the first.

The transaction-cost factor can be a 'killer assumption' for an intended pro-poor PES scheme, as experienced in the field of carbon services (Smith and Scherr, 2002). This effect will be stronger the higher are the economies of scale in service provision. For instance, some carbon-sequestration buyers requiring certification under the Kyoto Protocol have so elevated fixed costs that they operate with a minimum project size of around US$50,000, which may effectively exclude smallholders. The Ecuadorian PROFAFOR carbon sequestration programme decided after some years of operation to introduce a minimum plot size of 50ha to reduce excessive transaction costs. This has excluded some poor smallholders as potential participants, although the scheme still includes many collective contracts with marginalized highland communities (Wunder and Albán, 2007).[5]

Do competitiveness constraints affect all ES equally? Making smallholders sufficiently competitive to participate in PES is often simpler for highly spatially targeted services (watershed and biodiversity protection, landscape beauty) where buyers have to work with whoever happens to occupy the targeted space – e.g. if in the above example it is only feasible to work in one single watershed, not two.[6] However, the dilemma of transaction costs becomes prime for homogeneous services with a high degree of spatial mobility and competition (carbon sequestration, in particular).

What can be done to address competitiveness problems of poor ES suppliers in general, and their transaction-cost problem in particular? Creative schemes design to 'bundle' smallholder contracts, as currently experimented with in Costa Rica, might alleviate that constraint. 'Bubble projects' for carbon sequestration are similar cost-saving attempts to make ES commitments for an entire region, rather than individual landholders (Smith and Scherr, 2002). Obviously, this will move at least part of the transaction costs from the buyer to those seller institutions that have to make sure collective commitment is converted into individual compliance. These measures may thus reduce transaction costs and increase competitiveness, but can hardly eliminate the structural constraint proper.

Do Poor People Gain from Selling Environmental Services?

Voluntary participants – rational sellers?

Once poor people have made it through the narrow eye of the PES enrolment selection needle, the next question is: does participation make them better off? In a recent study, we scrutinized the full spectrum of potential welfare effects using the Sustainable Livelihood Approach as a general framework (Grieg-Gran et al., 2005). The following will instead distinguish only between income and non-income effects, and concentrate on the empirically most important impacts, illustrated by site-specific examples.

The welfare effects on ES sellers will generally be determined by 'the rules of the PES game' (payment rates and modes, conditionality, monitoring), which can either be preset by the buyers (as in most public, nationwide schemes) or be negotiated up front among buyers and sellers (see Figure 27.2), but will either way normally be well-known prior to ES providers' participation decision. As explained in the section on 'Definitions and concepts', PES contracts are voluntary agreements, so individual service providers can only be made outright worse off if they were de facto forced into participation (thus violating PES criterion (1)), being cheated, or just surprised by the ex-post livelihood impacts (e.g. due to underestimated opportunity costs) and local-economy derived effects (e.g. changing land or labour markets) – or simply make irrational decisions.

In the Chinese Sloping Land Conversion Program, some farmers have experienced net welfare losses, i.e. the tree planting on their land produced on aggregate fewer benefits than the previous land use; public payments were not enough to tip the balance. In general, this happened not because farmers wrongly predicted returns, but because many 'received a payment offer they could not refuse', i.e. they were forced to participate in the tree-planting scheme (Bennett, 2007). In similar public forest-protection contracts in Vietnam,[7] we found that payments of around US$3/ha/yr typically made up only 1–2 per cent of total household income (with a few high-end exceptions), which was typically not enough to significantly improve rural livelihoods. However, most payment-receiving farmers were not full-fledged landowners but received long-term allocations of public land that had already been declared 'protection forest'. The Vietnamese case was thus not a voluntary scheme, and not a PES programme in the strict sense, but rather an economic side-incentive functioning as 'the oil that greases the wheel' of the pre-existing command-and-control machinery (Wunder et al., 2005).

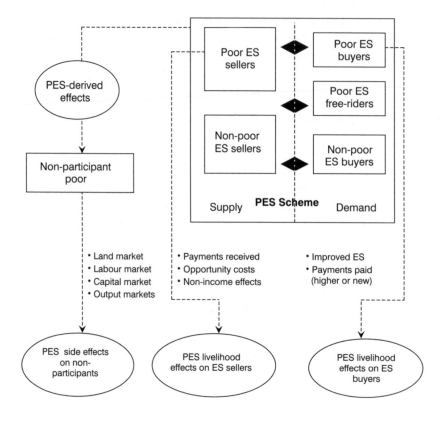

Figure 27.2 *The impacts of PES schemes on the poor*

It has been conjectured that poor service sellers could become 'PES trapped' into lasting negative livelihood outcomes, e.g. when long-term land-use deals were signed under asymmetric access to information (Landell-Mills and Porras, 2002). Long PES contract horizons do occur; e.g. in the Ecuadorian PROFAFOR case carbon buyers increased contract length from 25 to 99 years to raise permanence (Wunder and Albán, 2007). But so far, convincing real-world examples of 'PES trap' cases with systematic welfare losses on behalf of poor ES sellers notably seem to be missing. Not only does PES offer a new income source in often cash-poor areas with low diversification, the cash flow is potentially also more stable than common alternative sources, such as cash crops with heavily fluctuating output prices (Wunder, 2006). At least, this is the case if the PES programme is well administered and continuously funded, allowing ES buyers to fully meet their obligations (Pagiola et al., 2005).

Income gains

Even if poor PES providers are likely to become better off, questions remain as to 'how much' and 'in what way' they will gain from participation. As in any commercial transaction, there is an inherent conflict over price between ES buyers maximizing consumer surplus ('biggest conservation bang for the buck') and ES providers boosting their provider surplus (PES minus opportunity costs). In other words, a PES contract produces an economic rent, the distribution of which to buyers and sellers will depend on their respective negotiation power.

ES buyers will often, though not always, be in a better negotiating position – on account of being fewer in number, better informed and more initiative-seeking than ES providers. The use of provider price differentiation, inverse auctions and other bidding tools is designed by the buyers to squeeze the provider share of the rents, thus also reducing their welfare gains. Increasing organization and information levels among ES providers may sometimes improve their negotiating position. However, exceptionally there are also reverse cases where relatively few sellers hold unique assets that many buyers are willing to compete for. For instance, in the Zimbabwean CAMPFIRE programme, which can be scrutinized as a PES-like programme, communities controlling land areas with attractive wildlife and landscape-beauty values have been able to auction off land-access rights for safaris and trophy hunting to the highest-bidding tour operators (Frost and Bond, 2007).

Notwithstanding possible power asymmetries, in many cases PES comes to constitute a noteworthy share of participants' household income – as far as we can tell from preliminary evidence. In Costa Rica, PES payments accounted for more than 10 per cent of household income in more than one quarter of participants (E. Ortiz, cited in Pagiola et al., 2005); in the Virilla watershed PES payments averaged 16 per cent of cash household incomes, but three-quarters of households there earned more than US$820 monthly and were thus far from poor in the first place (Miranda et al., 2003). However, in poverty-struck zones the situation can be quite different. In Costa Rica's Osa Peninsula, a small survey found that of those PES recipients that were under the poverty line, the scheme lifted half of them above it and became the primary household cash income source in 44 per cent of cases (Muñoz, 2004). In Pimampiro, watershed-protection payments to poor upland settlers made up 30 per cent of recipient households' spending on food, medicine and schooling (Echavarria et al., 2004). PROFAFOR carbon projects in low-income, high-altitude areas of Ecuador, and the Huetar Norte project in a disadvantaged region of Costa Rica, both created some employment in the short run and a valuable plantation asset for future incomes (Albán and Argüello, 2004; Milne, 2000; Miranda et al., 2003), with expected internal rates of return of 12–27 per cent over a 30-year horizon (Grieg-Gran et al., 2005). In Bolivia, we found that four of five PES-like schemes jointly targeting biodiversity conservation and landscape beauty through communal ecotourism produced local annual income gains of between US$77 and US$640 per household.[8] At least for poor people living in remote, disadvantaged regions, the relative size of income contributions from PES or PES-like schemes seems thus likely to have been quite significant.

Obviously, all gains reported in the above studies are gross PES-income figures; we do not know the size of landowners' opportunity costs (income forgone due to PES-induced land-use restrictions). Relatively few PES studies have explicitly calculated opportunity costs, but the few that do confirm that voluntary PES schemes produce benefits in excess of opportunity costs. For instance, the PES scheme in the Bolivian Los Negros watershed produced in-kind benefits from beehive transfers (the locally preferred PES payment modality) with the low monetary equivalent of US$3.5–7/ha/yr. But so far the opportunity costs were likely to be negligible, so the voluntary participants of the scheme are thus likely to receive small but positive net gains (Robertson and Wunder, 2005).

A larger-scale PES-like example is the Noel Kempff Mercado Climate Action Project (NKMCAP), also in Bolivia. A national park was extended by 634,000ha into a logging-concession area. The credits from the avoided-logging carbon loss were bought by North American companies investing in carbon-emission offsets. Three local communities lost their jobs in the bought-out timber companies, and received in compensation economic benefits from park-ranger employment, investments in improved agriculture and ecotourism. Gross benefits over three years were estimated at US$96,782–260,695 (Milne et al., 2001) and US$128,580 (Asquith et al., 2002), respectively.[9] Deducting opportunity costs, the 1050 community members received a modest but positive net per-capita gain of US$100–250.

Non-income gains

Frequently PES recipients gain more than just income from participation; non-monetary side benefits can be equally important (Rosa et al., 2003). Three factors stand out: land-tenure consolidation, increases in human and social capital, and higher visibility vis-à-vis external investors.

Regarding tenure, one global review had feared that PES could induce more powerful groups to crowd out smallholders from their land whenever insecure property rights existed (Landell-Mills and Porras, 2002). While in theory this could have happened – and certainly land-appropriation fears exist among peasants (see 'To what extent do poor people sell environmental services?') – in various Latin American cases, PES participation actually increased smallholder land-tenure security vis-à-vis neighbours or squatters. Conversely, most PES gains are not large enough to really attract the interest of the powerful (Rosa et al., 2003; Robertson and Wunder, 2005).

There are two avenues for a PES scheme to increase land-tenure security, which may work jointly or separately. First, tenure-consolidation efforts can explicitly be enabled by the PES scheme – as an up-front requirement or as an accompanying result. For instance, in CIFOR's efforts to promote a community conservation concession in East Kalimantan (Indonesia), a process towards land-tenure clarification among different villages' overlapping land claims was started up front, acknowledged as a necessary PES precondition (Wunder et al., 2007). Mapping, demarcating and legalizing land claims is also often done as PES implementation progresses, either because PES receipts help finance the required legalization process (as for the Bolivian Chalalan Ecolodge) or because ES buyers use land-tenure formalization as a reward for ES sellers' compliance, as in the NKMCAP (Robertson and Wunder, 2005).

A second PES-induced pathway toward more secure land tenure is a perceptional one. Local acceptance of land tenure often depends on proof of 'economic use' of that piece of land. A major tenure-securing effect of a PES scheme can be to create local recognition that land set aside for conservation has tangible economic value and is not just idle 'reserve land' up for grabs by immigrants or neighbours. This was confirmed in our Bolivian case of Los Negros where forested land is threatened by an influx of landless migrants from the highlands. Landowners confirmed that the fact they received maps with demarcated boundaries and could demonstrate income-generating activity from the conserved land, gave it a de facto higher protection from invasions (Robertson and Wunder, 2005).

Beyond land-tenure effects, experiences show that PES participants tend to increase their human and social capital by improving internal organization, e.g. through collective bargaining and action vis-à-vis the service buyers (Rosa et al., 2003; Grieg-Gran et al., 2005). Again, some benefits are provided in advance (training courses, help in starting an association, etc.); others accrue through PES 'learning-by-doing' (e.g. through negotiating with ES buyers or intermediaries). The Chalalan Ecolodge showed both effects: substantial up-front training was provided by Conservation International to the community that now fully controls the operation, and significant internal coherence and entrepreneurial spirit has been added (Robertson and Wunder, 2005). This empowerment is to the advantage of local people in any other business dealings with the outside world.

Finally, the PES programme can also work as a strategic 'site propaganda', increasing the visibility of the village or community vis-à-vis both donors and public entities. For instance, in Bolivia we found that several villages involved in PES-like initiatives suddenly found it easier to attract a donor for a health clinic, road improvement, or land-tenure recognition by the municipality, because the PES scheme had put the community 'on the map' of these external agents. In the Los Negros case, the PES scheme has served as an effective negotiation platform to mediate long-standing conflicts between upstream land-colonizing farmers and downstream irrigation users (Robertson and Wunder, 2005).

Inequality and social costs
Despite the predominance of positive socio-economic PES outcomes, some negative social side-effects can also occur. Paying some and not others (e.g. enrolling only 'strategically located' landowners) can create jealousies and raise inequality.

This is probably a feature shared with most development initiatives: not every individual is equally equipped and motivated to take advantage of new income-generation options. In addition, in some hybrid cases between PES and traditional projects, focusing on communal development rather than conditional payments (e.g. NKMCAP and tourism payments in the Eduardo Avaroa Reserve), flows of non-conditional benefits can create paternalistic expectations of even greater flows, and tensions when these hyper-expectations are not met (Robertson and Wunder, 2005).

Nevertheless, some collective PES payments benefiting all households may create equality but not equity: households that bear disproportionate opportunity costs are under-compensated and are made worse off, but cannot individually reject the PES deal. This can create social tensions, as in the case of the Zimbabwean CAMPFIRE programme where landowners and users directly adjacent to wildlife-priority areas often lost out (Frost and Bond, 2007), and in the NKMCAP where one community particularly dependent on logging (Florida) was disproportionably hit (Asquith et al., 2002). Fine-tuning compensation payments in collective deals to individual opportunity costs may thus be an important step to prevent social tensions.

Do Poor Environmental Service Users Benefit from PES?

It is frequently assumed that ES providers/sellers are much poorer than ES users/ buyers, so that PES-related poverty-alleviation efforts should focus on the former. Empirically this key assumption seems to hold quite well, for three reasons. First, as mentioned, the poor often occupy fragile lands that are economically less developed but strategic for ES provision. Second, various environmental services are in a way luxury goods that only the rich northern-hemisphere countries (carbon, biodiversity services) and the more well-off strata of people in southern-hemisphere countries (landscape beauty) can afford to pay for. Third, groups of poor potential buyers often lack the internal coordination to act as ES buyers, even if it would be rational for them to compensate ES providers. For instance, a recent PES feasibility analysis in the Philippines found that payments in one watershed dominated by many poor lowland rice farmers were unlikely to materialize, whereas chances were much better in a similar watershed were the users included municipal water plants and the ecotourism industry (PREM, 2005). In practice, most existing PES schemes are therefore monopsonies or oligopsonies, without direct poverty-alleviation scope on the buyer side.

If downstream areas are populous, the number of poor ES buyers represented by one municipal water plant may often exceed that of upstream poor ES sellers by orders of magnitude, which also has poverty implications. In a recently started PES scheme in Chaina (Colombia), about 5600 water users, many of them poor farmers, depend for their water quality on the action of 15 potential 'ES providers'

– upstream settler households currently increasing sedimentation through defor-estation of a 440ha sub-watershed (Blanco et al., 2005). At a larger scale, the aqueduct of Tachira (Western Venezuela) serves about 90,000 people, but is simi-larly being threatened by sedimentation from about 90 upstream households' farming, and a small-scale PES scheme has recently been piloted to reverse the trend (Blanco et al., 2006). Hence, maximizing sellers' PES rates alone would here have little poverty-alleviation effect: the major welfare benefits from PES accrue through reducing drinking-water fluctuations and pollution, thus improving the numerous poor water users' health. Helping the poor is thus here best achieved by making sure the PES scheme is efficient in delivering the service it promises.

Far from all ES users are also ES buyers, especially so if they are poor: many disadvantaged ES users free-ride on others' payments to receive improved services. Poor tropical farmers are likely to suffer most from global warming (water short-ages, declining crop yields, disease-proneness) since they lack the means to adapt their farming systems, and are thus particularly helped by current mitigation efforts – which they are not paying for (IPCC, 2001). Poor urban water users often receive their drinking water for free since their taps are not metered; in poor countries, non-payment shares easily reach 50–90 per cent. Hence, free-riders benefit from any PES-led improvement in water quality or availability.[10]

How Do Poor Non-participants Fare?

What happens to those impoverished people who are not participating in PES? For most, PES effects will be neutral, but some may be significantly affected by the scheme through its effect on land, labour, capital and output markets. Let us look at each of these separately.

PES schemes will usually directly affect the market for or the availability of land. To the extent that PES schemes are achieving effective conservation – e.g. reducing open-access lands and stabilizing agricultural frontiers – they could particularly hurt the landless who are looking for opportunities to invade land for homesteading – the scenario prevalent, for instance, in the aforementioned Los Negros watershed. While most landowners there were disadvantaged, the landless people were among 'the poorest of the poor', thus pointing to important conflicts of interest between different strata of poor (Robertson and Wunder, 2005).

Regarding labour-market effects, other subgroups of poor usually self-engage (or are being employed) in some of the environmentally most threatening activi-ties, such as logging-company workers, firewood cutters and charcoal makers, extractors overharvesting non-timber forest products (NTFPs), or farm hands hired for clearing land and for cultivating converted soils. These poor people often depend on environmental degradation for their livelihoods. To the extent that the PES scheme is 'use-restricting' (see 'Definitions and concepts'), i.e. it caps total economic activity levels (as in the Los Negros conservation set-aside PES), the poor are likely to lose out in terms of employment or informal sector income. For instance, PES restrictions were found to probably hurt traditional herder and NTFP harvester groups in India (Kerr, 2002). Conversely, if ES provision is 'asset-building', such as establishing silvopastural systems in treeless pastures (Pagiola et al., 2008) or planting trees in degraded landscapes with few productive alternatives (Albán and Argüello, 2004), one can expect a net expansion in rural jobs that benefits unskilled rural labour, thus alleviating poverty.

Prospective employment-contraction effects in use-restricting schemes have to be weighed against the local multiplier effects from their inflows of cash – the main limiting production factor in many remote rural areas. This concerns the financial inflows from recurrent PES payments, but also accompanying up-front invest-ments. In five of the nine PES or PES-like schemes we reviewed in Bolivia, significant up-front investments in infrastructure, training, negotiation, etc. were made, which partially also reflected the 'project-PES hybrid' character of these schemes. In various cases, direct causal links could be made from cash inflows to local livelihood gains (Robertson and Wunder, 2005, pp. 121–127). On the down-side, if logging produces valuable timber rents that, say, end up in the country's capital, then restricting timber harvests through PES could indirectly harm poor people working in, say, the urban service sector previously stimulated by the recy-cling of these rents.

Finally, PES can also change output markets. For instance, a successful ecotourism scheme could raise local demand and prices of certain protein-rich foodstuffs (fish, meat, etc.), making them unavailable for especially those on-site poor that do not receive higher incomes. Some output-market effects can be off site; cutting off raw-material supply may have notable downstream development impacts. For instance, the urban poor buying charcoal could face higher prices if an important peri-urban charcoal-production area was set aside in a conservation PES scheme. Yet, conversely, these higher prices would benefit poor charcoal producers at other sites, showing the complexity of these PES-derived welfare effects.

How important are these PES-derived effects from production-factor and output markets for the poor? Few empirical studies on these linkages exist; in most cases one would expect effects to be small, especially the off-site effects, although timber rents could be a prominent exception. Local effects can sometimes be size-able. For instance, laid-off logging and sawmill workers constituted the most weighty local welfare loss, and the main reason for community compensations being implemented in NKMCAP (Asquith et al., 2002). In other words, the non-participating poor, especially the landless and the unemployed, should not be forgotten in livelihoods-impact assessments of PES schemes, since in some cases effects can be substantial.

Conclusions and Perspectives

The empirical evidence on welfare impacts of PES in developing countries remains sketchy, both because many schemes are still young and because little systematic 'with and without PES' welfare data have been gathered. Yet, as suggested in this article, some patterns are emerging. Let us return to our four initial questions from the section on 'Definitions and concepts', provide some tentative answers, and discuss policy implications.

First, to what extent can poor people participate as sellers in PES schemes? We know that their access depends upon eligibility, desire, ability and competitiveness. Among these filters, two conditions tend to be anti-poor: informal and/or insecure land tenure (affecting all four filters) and high buyer-transaction costs of working with numerous smallholders (reducing competitiveness). Options to address these conditions may be to skip or modify inappropriate access restrictions (such as formal land-title requirements), or to develop collective smallholder-bundling schemes that reduce transaction costs. If ample participation of poor providers is a prime concern, explicit poverty targeting (e.g. maximum-income thresholds) and subsidies (e.g. pro-poor carbon premiums) may be considered, though targeting tends to come at the cost of environmental efficiency losses.[11] Nevertheless, other pre-existing filtering conditions are clearly pro-poor, such as formal caps on land size enrolled in most public PES schemes, and in particular the spatial overlap between marginal production areas and environmentally sensitive lands. To the extent that these pro-poor filters dominate in the first place, we may not need to worry much about the poor's seller access to PES schemes.

Second, do ES sellers become better off? Whenever poor people are selected as sellers, they are also very likely to benefit from getting paid – unless they were forced to participate in the first place. As for the payment mode, large singular cash transfers often can have detrimental local development impacts, but there is growing evidence from other fields (e.g. education, emergency aid, demobilization) that well-designed conditional cash transfers can be an efficient way to simultaneously achieve targeted sectoral goals and stimulate general recipient welfare gains.[12] In terms of outcomes, typically PES income gains beyond the (rarely quantified) opportunity costs do materialize, but asset transfers (e.g. tree plantations) or non-income gains (training, improved organization, land-tenure recognition, etc.) can also be important. Yet, it seems that per-capita provider income gains are seldom impressively large: typically ES buyers are in a better negotiating position to appropriate the 'gains from trade'. What could be done to increase poor providers' share of the environmental rent from PES deals? Again, pro-poor premiums can be one pathway to increase provider incomes. One can also provide communities and smallholders with more information about the value of the service at stake, and realistic compensation levels for land-use changes. Sometimes poor communities actually overestimate buyers' willingness to pay, thus endangering the deal per se.

Third, what about the demand side? Poor ES users – in some cases ES buyers, in most cases free-riders – can benefit significantly, so PES poverty assessments should not focus exclusively on ES sellers. Sometimes these poor ES users outnumber poor sellers by orders of magnitude, especially for watershed protection. If so, making sure that the promised service is delivered is certainly the best way to help the poor. In particular cases, donors and NGOs could help organize multiple poor service users so they can become ES buyers – say, poor fishermen paying for mangrove conservation. Although 'the poor paying the non-poor' could be a highly remunerative strategy for the former, it is usually very challenging to implement.

Fourth, how are non-participants affected? In most cases, these effects are mixed, and minor in size. However, sometimes the impacts of use-restricting PES on the non-participating poor are noteworthy. Especially landless colonists can suffer if open access to land is closed, and people working in environmentally degrading activities can lose their job. This feature is not exclusive to PES; it is shared with any efficient conservation initiative. If implementers on fairness or political feasibility accounts are highly concerned with these derived effects, it may be advisable to undertake compensatory measures that minimize third-party losses.

How important is PES thus on aggregate for poverty alleviation? In most cases, PES has positive but point-wise, quantitatively small poverty-reduction effects. Those claiming that PES will become a poverty trap are clearly barking up the wrong tree. Those believing in its major poverty-alleviation potential underesti-mate the limitations posed by narrow spatial targeting and by the 'naturally' supe-rior negotiation position of ES buyers. Arguably, the main bottleneck impeding PES from reducing poverty more is their hitherto reduced implementation scale. Analogous to the growth vs. distribution development debate, the key trick is probably not how to redistribute the PES cake towards a greater share for the poor, but how to increase the size of the entire cake. External donors can ease the scale bottleneck by helping to finance PES start-up costs (trust-building, negotiation, baseline studies, monitoring systems, etc.), if PES operational costs are likely to remain sustainably low.

Yet, to the extent that multiple side objectives (e.g. concerns for poverty, human rights, gender, indigenous people) are increasingly squeezed into the PES equation, the schemes will lose efficiency in achieving their main target: to deliver an improved environmental service. If schemes become over-regulated and efficiency is lost, the outreach to the private sector – globally a prime target for PES schemes so far (Landell-Mills and Porras, 2002) – would be reduced. PES would increasingly become 'old wine in new bottles', subsumed into the generic family of altruistic development projects to which they were actually meant to be an alterna-tive. Reduced PES scale would not only limit environmental impacts, but eventu-ally also pro-poor effects. Policy- and decision-makers should thus not 'put the (poverty) carriage before the (PES) horse'. Poverty reduction is an important PES side objective, and safeguards can be taken to address it properly – but it should never become the primary goal of PES.

Notes

1   This was concluded from the international workshop 'Design of Payments for Environmental Services in Developed and Developing Countries' (University of Bonn and CIFOR, 14–16 June 2005, Titisee, Germany), and is confirmed by CIFOR's various national PES assessments.

2   The first three levels (eligibility, desire and ability) draw partially on Pagiola et al. (2005).

3   An exception is PES-like schemes such as the South African Work for Water programme, where unemployed labour is paid to undertake lasting environmental improvements, mostly elimination of exotic vegetation that harms water and biodiversity services (Turpie et al., 2007).

4   The PSAH scheme is explicitly targeted to areas with significant natural forest areas. This criterion alone means that the target population of landholders is to more than two-thirds represented by the lowest income quintile, i.e. the poorest of the poor in Mexican national income distribution (Muñoz-Piña et al., 2007).

5   In terms of our conceptual framework, strictly speaking PROFAFOR introduced an 'eligibility' filter, but the factor underlying that decision was smallholder-inflated transaction costs.

6   Even if there is only one watershed management option, there may still be alternatives to PES (water treatment, new infrastructure, etc.) that force smallholders to be concerned with competitiveness.

7   The following refers to the Vietnamese Government Program 327, and its successor Program 661.

8   Based on 2003 tourism income figures (net cash profits and intra-community wages) for La Chonta, Mapajo, Chalalan and Reserva Eduardo Avaroa operations (Robertson and Wunder, 2005).

9   Asquith et al. used a narrower benefit definition than Milne et al., thus lowering the estimate.

10 Obviously, extensive free-riding reduces the chances of creating a PES scheme in the first place, since the payment base is reduced. However, if PES introduction increases pressure to start paying (e.g. by introducing more water meters), the previous free-riders could also be turned into net losers.

One example is the Mexican PSAH programme, which since 2004 has progressively achieved higher poverty-targeting levels, but correspondingly has become less focused on zones truly threatened by deforestation, which ceteris paribus lowers the programme's additionality (Muñoz-Piña et al., 2007).

11 These cash-transfer programmes include conditional payments for school enrolment in Mexico, Brazil and Argentina (e.g. Heinrich, 2007). In two Mozambican programmes, flood victims and demobilized soldiers receiving cash have generally used their money wisely, administrative costs were low at 5–10 per cent, and the overall poverty-alleviation impact was impressive (Hanlon, 2004). A recent cash-transfer programme in Malawi has had similar positive experiences (Ellis, pers. comm., 2007).

References

Albán, M. and Argüello, M. (2004) 'Un analisis de los impactos sociales y economicos de los proyectos de fijacion de carbono en el Ecuador, El caso de PROFAFOR – FACE', IIED, London.

Angelsen, A. and Wunder, S. (2003) 'Exploring the poverty–forestry link: Key concepts, issues and research implications', *CIFOR Occasional Papers*, no.42,58

Asquith, N., Vargas-Rios, M. and Smith, J. (2002) 'Can forest-protection carbon projects improve rural livelihoods? Analysis of the Noel Kempff Mercado Climate Action Project, Bolivia', *Mitigation and Adaptation Strategies for Global Change*, 7: 323–337.

Bennett, M.T. (2007) 'China's Sloping Land Conversion Program: Institutional innovation or business as usual?', *Ecological Economics*, 65(4): 699–711.

Blanco, J., Wunder, S. and Navarrete, F. (2005) *La experiencia colombiana en esquemas de pagos por servicios ambientales*, Ecoversa and CIFOR, Bogotá (unpublished).

Blanco, J., Wunder, S. and Sabogal, S. (2006) *Potencialidades de implementacion de esquemas de pagos por servicios ambientales en Venezuela*, Ecoversa & CIFOR, Bogota (unpublished).

Costa, M.M. and Zeller, M. (2003) 'Peasants' production systems and the integration of incentives for watershed protection: a case study of Guatemala', Paper presented at the International Conference on Forests, Livelihoods and Biodiversity, CIFOR, Bonn, pp. 23.

Echavarria, M., Vogel, J., Albán, M. and Meneses, F. (2004) *The Impacts of Payments for Watershed Services in Ecuador*, Rep. No. 1 84369 484 0, IIED, London.

Ferraro, P. and Kiss, A. (2002) 'Direct payments to conserve biodiversity', *Science*, 298: 1718–1719.

Ferraro, P. and Simpson, R. (2002) 'The cost-effectiveness of conservation payments', *Land Economics*, 78: 339–353.

Frost, P.G.H. and Bond, I. (2007) 'The CAMPFIRE programme in Zimbabwe: Payments for wildlife services', *Ecological Economics*, 65(4): 776–787.

Grieg-Gran, M., Porras, I.T. and Wunder, S. (2005) 'How can market mechanisms for forest environmental services help the poor? Preliminary lessons from Latin America', *World Development*, 33: 1511–1527.

Hanlon, J. (2004) 'It is possible to just give money to the poor?', *Development and Change*, 35: 375–383.

Heinrich, C.J. (2007) 'Demand and supply-side determinants of conditional cash transfer program effectiveness', *World Development*, 35: 121–143.

IPCC (2001) *Summary for Policy Makers. Climate change 2001: Impacts, Adaptation, and Vulnerability*, Intergovernmental Panel on Climate Change.

Kerr, J. (2002) 'Watershed development, environmental services, and poverty alleviation in India', *World Development*, 30: 1387–1400.

Landell-Mills, N. and Porras, I.T. (2002) *Silver Bullet or Fool's Gold? A Global Review of Markets for Forest Environmental Services and their Impact on the Poor*, IIED, London.

Milne, M. (2000) *Forest Carbon, Livelihoods and Biodiversity: A Report to the European Commission*, CIFOR, Bogor.

Milne, M., Arroyo, P. and Peacock, H. (2001) *Assessing the Livelihood Benefits to Local Communities from Forest Carbon Projects: Case Study Analysis Noel Kempff Mercado Climate Action Project*, (unpublished) CIFOR, Bogor.

Miranda, M., Porras, I. and Moreno, M. (2003) *The Social Impacts of Payments for Environmental Services in Costa Rica*, IIED, London.

Muñoz, R. (2004) *Efectos del Programa de Servicios Ambientales en las Condiciones de Vida de los Campesinos de la Peninsula de Osa*, Masters Thesis, Universidad de Costa Rica, San Jose.

Muñoz-Piña, C., Guevara, A., Torres, J.M. and Braña, J. (2007) 'Paying for the hydrological services of Mexico's forests: Analysis, negotiation and results', *Ecological Economics*, 65(4): 725–736.

Pagiola, S. (2007) 'Payments for environmental services in Costa Rica', *Ecological Economics*, 65(4): 712–724.

Pagiola, S., Arcenas, A. and Platais, G. (2005) 'Can payments for environmental services help reduce poverty? An exploration of the issues and the evidence to date', *World Development*, 33: 237–253.

Pagiola, S., Rios, A.R. and Arcenas, A. (2008) 'Can the poor participate in payments for environmental services? Lessons from the Silvopastoral Project in Nicaragua', *Environment and Development Economics*, 13: 99–325.

PREM (2005) *Compensating Upland Forest Communities for the Provision of Watershed Protection Services: Using 'Payments for Environmental Services' Instruments in the Philippines*, PREM Policy Brief No. 8.

Robertson, N. and Wunder, S. (2005) *Fresh Tracks in the Forest: Assessing Incipient Payments for Environmental Services Initiatives in Bolivia*, CIFOR, Bogor.

Rosa, H., Kandel, S. and Dimas, L. (2003) *Compensation for Environmental Services and Rural Communities*, PRISMA, San Salvador.

Simpson, R. and Sedjo, R.A. (1996) 'Paying for the conservation of endangered ecosystems: A comparison of direct and indirect approaches', *Environment and Development Economics*, 1: 241–257.

Smith, J. and Scherr, S. (2002) *Forest Carbon and Local Livelihoods: Assessment of Opportunities and Policy Recommendations*, CIFOR, Bogor, Indonesia.

Southgate, D., Haab, T., Lundine, J. and Rodriguez, F. (2007) *Responses of Poor, Rural Households in Ecuador and Guatemala to Payments for Environmental Services*, Ohio State University (unpublished).

Sunderlin, W.D., Dewi, S.D. and Puntodewo, A. (2007) *Poverty and Forests: Multi-Country Analysis of Spatial Association and Proposed Policy Solutions*, CIFOR Occasional Paper No. 47, 43.

Turpie, J.K., Marais, C. and Blignaut, J.N. (2007) 'The Working for Water Programme: Evolution of a payments for environmental services mechanism that addresses both poverty and ecosystem service delivery in South Africa', *Ecological Economics*, 65(4): 788–798.

World Bank (2000) *World Development Report 2000–2001: Attacking Poverty*, Oxford University Press, Oxford and New York.

Wunder, S. (2005) *Payments for Environmental Services: Some Nuts and Bolts*, CIFOR Occasional Paper No. 42, 24.

Wunder, S. (2006) 'Are direct payments for environmental services spelling doom for sustainable forest management in the tropics?', *Ecology and Society*, 11: 23.

Wunder, S. and Albán, M. (2007) 'Decentralized payments for environmental services: Comparing the cases of Pimampiro and PROFAFOR in Ecuador', *Ecological Economics*, 65(4): 685–698.

Wunder, S., The, B.D. and Ibarra, E. (2005) *Payment is Good, Control is Better: Why Payments for Environmental Services so Far Have Remained Incipient in Vietnam*, CIFOR, Bogor, pp. 86.

Wunder, S., Campbell, B., Frost, P.H.G., Iwan, R., Sayer, J.A. and Wollenberg, L. (2007) 'When donors get cold feet: The community conservation concession in Setulang (Kalimantan, Indonesia) that never happened', *Ecology and Society*, 13(1): 12.

Chapter 28

Climate, Carbon, Conservation and Communities

Dilys Roe, Hannah Reid, Kit Vaughan, Emily Brickell and
Joanna Elliott

Key Messages

- The new generation of carbon funds must address the need for a sustained reduction in carbon emissions, while also building good governance and strengthening the resilience and adaptive capacity of ecosystems and local communities in the face of increased vulnerability to climate change.
- To tackle climate change effectively, we need to 'join the dots' between biodiversity loss, local livelihoods and land use changes such as deforestation.
- There is a strong need for credible standards that link curbing emissions with forest conservation to ensure they provide robust carbon benefits while incorporating biodiversity conservation and benefits to local communities.
- Conservation-based strategies that address carbon emissions, which include afforestation, reforestation and curbing deforestation, must be made robust.
- Forest carbon stores are vulnerable to disease or fire, and carbon-emitting activities can be displaced elsewhere.

Carbon: Linking Climate and Conservation

With climate change riding high on the political and economic agenda, more and more attention is being paid to different mechanisms for offsetting, reducing and preventing carbon releases into the atmosphere. The UK's 2006 Stern Review on the Economics of Climate Change[1] estimated that land use change – and deforestation in particular – is responsible for 18 per cent of global emissions.

Yet so-called 'avoided deforestation' or 'reduced emissions from deforestation and degradation' (REDD) projects are not yet recognized under the Clean Development Mechanism (CDM) of the United Nations Framework Convention on Climate Change (UNFCCC) during the first commitment period (2008–2012) of its Kyoto Protocol.

The exclusion of standing forests from the CDM stemmed from a number of concerns, including:

- the risk of deflecting attention from the need to curb industrial emissions; and
- technical issues relating to whether forests can deliver robust carbon benefits. For example, forest carbon stores can succumb to disease, fire or logging, making them less than permanent, with a risk that emissions from forest conversion are often displaced to other locations.

Discussions on the development of a new post-2012 Kyoto framework have reignited debate on whether to include REDD projects. This is in large part due to the increasing recognition of the significance of emissions from deforestation and also to the technical improvements in monitoring carbon stocks – for example through better satellite imagery. There is growing international consensus that any future agreement under the UNFCCC to combat climate change must include measures seeking to reduce deforestation in tropical countries. Limiting global warming to 2°C above pre-industrial levels will mean that all major sources of potential reductions in emissions, including those from deforestation and land degradation, will need to be considered.

The WWF Energy Task Force concluded that curbing emissions from land use change is a key part of tackling climate change while the Stern Review stated that 'curbing deforestation is a highly cost-effective way of reducing greenhouse gas (GHG) emissions and has the potential to offer significant reductions fairly quickly'. In addition to deforestation, the UNFCCC Subsidiary Body for Scientific and Technological Advice acknowledged that forest degradation needs to be addressed when developing mechanisms to reduce emissions from land use.

Along with climate change, biodiversity loss is another environmental issue of international concern. The Millennium Ecosystem Assessment (MA) highlights how biodiversity underpins the delivery of a range of 'ecosystem services' on which human well-being depends but is being degraded at an unprecedented rate. Although the complex links between biodiversity loss and climate change are not yet well understood, there are some clear overlaps:

- Land conversion contributes to GHG emissions and has been identified by the MA as a major driver of biodiversity loss.
- The MA estimates that by the end of the century, climate change will be the main driver of biodiversity loss.

Efforts to tackle climate change are thus becoming increasingly entwined with efforts to address biodiversity loss. A common solution appears to lie in efforts to curb carbon emissions through forest conservation. This should be good news for biodiversity conservation. For a number of years, conservation organisations have been lamenting the decline in available funding. Carbon funds, however, are growing at a phenomenal rate, and offer the potential to make up some of the shortfall. Forest carbon thus provides a tool for mitigating climate change and financing forest conservation.

It is vital, however, not to overlook local development issues. An effective, sustainable approach demands an examination of the overlap between the *three* areas. For instance, can forests provide robust carbon benefits? Will the growing volume of carbon funds invested in land use improvements for climate purposes take biodiversity conservation into account? And what are the implications for local communities living in and around areas earmarked for carbon sequestration?

Different Mechanisms for Linking Carbon Emissions and Biodiversity Conservation

Carbon trading

Under the Kyoto Protocol, industrialized countries in Annex B to the Protocol are able to address emission reduction obligations through three mechanisms:

1. trading carbon credits with other Annex B countries (emissions trading);
2. offsetting emissions through investment in emission-reduction projects in other Annex B countries (Joint Implementation); and
3. offsetting emissions through investment in emission-reduction projects in developing countries (CDM).

In addition to these so-called 'compliance' mechanisms, a 'voluntary' carbon market has emerged through which individuals and organizations can choose to offset their carbon emissions for various purposes, often linked to individual or corporate responsibility. These include:

- Government-led mechanisms such as the New South Wales GHG Abatement Scheme.
- Schemes run by specialist carbon brokers and/or retailers. Carbon funds operate like any project-based investment fund: a set of partners invests in the fund, the fund invests in a portfolio of emissions-reducing projects (for

example, renewable energy and energy efficiency projects) and the fund manager or broker sells the carbon credits generated, with profits going to investors.
- Individual carbon-offset projects run by NGOs.

This voluntary market is growing rapidly, is largely unregulated and is often confused with official 'compliance' mechanisms by consumers. Although many schemes purport to offer sustainable development benefits in addition to carbon offsetting, some have been criticized for lack of transparency, accountability and rigorous carbon measurement systems. There is a strong need for voluntary emission reductions to be verified against clear standards to ensure that they provide a robust carbon benefit, alongside any additional co-benefits they promote.

A number of means exist through which investments in these compliance or voluntary mechanisms can link payments for carbon emissions with biodiversity conservation:

- Individual projects can be designed to meet CDM criteria, registered with the CDM and sold on the international market. Sellers include government agencies, conservation organizations and community groups. CDM projects are intended to secure firm carbon reductions and also contribute to sustainable development, and have to meet certain standards to be eligible.
- Outside the CDM, retailers may invest in a portfolio of projects for sale to individuals or organizations on a 'pay as you go' basis – for example, planting trees to offset emissions from air travel.
- The Climate, Community and Biodiversity Alliance – a partnership convened under the Center for Environmental Leadership in Business – has developed a set of standards for land-based carbon projects that simultaneously address climate change, support local communities and conserve biodiversity. WWF helped develop the Gold Standard to measure sustainable development benefits (including biodiversity) of offset projects, but this does not currently include forestry projects. Both are applicable to the compliance and the voluntary markets.
- The World Bank BioCarbon Fund is an example of a carbon fund specifically aimed at projects in forests and agro-ecosystems, with a view to securing climate and biodiversity co-benefits.

Conservation funds

Because of concerns over biodiversity loss, conservation organizations have long invested in projects that tackle tropical deforestation through the various sources of funding available to them. These include official development assistance, corporate donations, contributions from philanthropic foundations and member donations. Funding for conservation is likely to increase significantly if projects that reduce emissions from deforestation and degradation are accepted under the second commitment period of the Kyoto Protocol, which is expected to start by 2012.

Estimates of likely revenue streams vary widely, depending on which costs and benefits are included and which carbon pools and mitigation options are assessed. One review noted that as much as US$43 billion could flow into developing countries for conservation if REDD projects are approved.[2] A recent World Bank report[3] estimated that forested land could be worth between US$1500 and US$10,000 per hectare if returns to forest land were funded through the carbon market. The top-end value is based on a price of US$20 per tonne of carbon, which was the price within the Emissions Trading Scheme at the time the report was written.

Meanwhile, substantial conservation funds are already beginning to emerge alongside the carbon market. For example:

- As part of its £800 million Environmental Transformation Fund, the UK Department for International Development recently announced a £50 million UK contribution to a new fund to help conserve the Congo Basin rainforest.
- The World Bank is developing a Global Forest Alliance to address key international forestry challenges, including climate change mitigation. Linked to this, a new funding mechanism – the Forest Carbon Partnership Facility – is proposed to generate payments for efforts to reduce emissions from deforestation and to build national capacity to establish baselines, analyse drivers and monitor impacts of measures to reduce emissions from deforestation and degradation.

Other proposals also exist for various forms of conservation trust funds. The Brazilian government, for example, has called for the establishment of an international trust fund to which industrialized countries make voluntary contributions and which can be used to provide compensation for slowing or preventing deforestation.[4]

Conservation-based strategies to address carbon emissions

A wide range of forest-based projects can help reduce, prevent or offset carbon emissions. These include:
- Afforestation:
  - large-scale commercial plantations;
  - smaller-scale tree planting schemes;
  - agroforestry; and
  - community woodlots.
- Reforestation:
  - large-scale plantations on deforested land;
  - tree planting on degraded land; and
  - forest restoration.
- Slowing or preventing deforestation:

– establishment, expansion or enforcement of protected areas; and
– sustainable forest management.

To date, afforestation and reforestation projects have attracted relatively little investment, with the bulk of carbon funding going towards industrial and energy projects. Under the CDM, for example, only one such project has been registered. This is largely to do with problems of guaranteeing the 'permanence' of forest stock and of 'leakage' or 'displacement' – that is, displacing the carbon-emitting activity elsewhere.

Dialogue within the UNFCCC is beginning to move away from the term 'permanence' towards 'time bound sequestration agreements', whereby a resource owner commits to maintaining carbon stocks for an agreed period. Issues around displacement can be reduced through setting national and, where appropriate, regional targets (rather than a project-based approach) and gaining broad participation of countries with significant forest areas to avoid the potential risk of displacement between neighbouring countries. 'Additionality' refers to the requirement that activities under the CDM project should be additional to those which would have happened without the carbon finance. This is a problematic concept with all CDM projects and is not specific to forests.

One criticism of many forestry projects is that the biodiversity value is the primary reason for the project and that, therefore, the activity would have taken place even without carbon finance. Projects can demonstrate 'additionality' if they face barriers that cannot be overcome without carbon finance or when the activity without carbon finance is not financially the most attractive and, therefore, will not happen on its own.

Under the current CDM, assessment of 'additionality' generally focuses on establishing whether a reforestation activity is economically viable without the CDM. The issue of economic viability is relevant to REDD projects, as the economic incentives to convert forests are often greater than the incentives to conserve or manage them responsibly. However, this is a complicated area. Overcoming concerns relating to 'additionality' requires careful control to ensure that only projects proven to meet these requirements receive finance.

Who benefits from conservation-carbon projects?

Conservation-carbon projects have different implications for different stakeholders – national governments, conservation NGOs, private companies and local communities. Overall, the carbon-trading market is dominated by large-scale projects with little community ownership and benefit. Large-scale monoculture plantations are an efficient way of sequestering carbon, due to their rapid growth rates and minimal management regimes, but they have negative impacts on biodiversity and ecosystem functioning. They present high barriers to entry for poor producers because they are capital intensive and scale dependent. These producers may also lose access to land that is designated for a plantation or other carbon-related activity. As noted by the Center for International Forestry Research (CIFOR), 'A number of countries have targeted "degraded areas" for CDM plantations. In many cases, however, these may be lands held under traditional common property systems that are used by local people for a variety of purposes.'[5]

With potentially high rates of return from carbon offset projects, opportunities are being seized by powerful elites, while local communities often lack the secure tenure and resource rights to stake their claim. In Uganda, for example, a project entailing the planting of trees for carbon offsets in Mount Elgon National Park has been criticized for ignoring local people's land rights and exacerbating the conflict between the park authorities 'guarding' the trees and adjacent communities claiming rights over the land.[6]

Projects aimed at reducing deforestation appear to have greater long-term potential for attracting investment, but again the likely distribution of costs and benefits raises concerns. It is estimated the largest income flows would accrue to only a few countries. The *Stern Review* reports that eight countries are responsible for 70 per cent of emissions from land use change (Bolivia, Brazil, Cameroon, Democratic Republic of Congo, Ghana, Indonesia, Malaysia and Papua New Guinea), with Brazil and Indonesia accounting for 20 and 30 per cent respectively.[7] A framework which also includes incentives for maintaining low levels of deforestation would expand the number of countries that could benefit from a forest carbon market, such as India, and also reduce the risk of transnational displacement.

Concerns have also been raised that benefits are likely to be captured by government ministries, private companies and conservation NGOs. Local communities will probably bear a disproportionate share of the cost in terms of restrictions on resource use while reaping little of the benefit. Simply increasing investment in forestry through funding for carbon storage and sequestration is unlikely to generate more sustainable forest management or greater benefits to biodiversity and poverty elimination, without first addressing critical governance issues.[8] A few of the common pitfalls are outlined below.

Reducing emissions from deforestation, by reinforcing protected areas without the full participation of local communities, could be a form of 'protectionism by the back door' and reopen decades of discussion on the livelihood and poverty impacts of protected areas. For these schemes, the Overseas Development Institute highlights two key concerns for local, forest-dependent people:[9]

1. How will incentive or payment schemes be targeted to ensure that the benefits reach those whose livelihoods are affected by changes in land use practice?
2. How will displacement be addressed and what are the implications for local resource rights and livelihood needs?

These concerns are echoed by the Forest Peoples Programme (FPP), which fears states may use REDD funds to reinforce state and private sector control over forests and revert to a 'guns and guards' approach to forest protection. FPP also highlights the risk of REDD funds fuelling land speculation and the appropriation of community land – either by external actors or by more powerful individuals within a community.[10]

Connecting carbon, conservation and community benefits

While there are certainly risks to local communities from the rapidly growing interest in carbon conservation, there are an increasing number of fledgling schemes that could benefit local communities and generate income streams in areas with very little alternative economic potential, particularly where explicitly designed to do this.

Little attention has been paid to such 'bottom-up' approaches to date, but some good examples exist of projects which provide both carbon and biodiversity benefits.[11] The BioCarbon Fund portfolio includes a number of community-based projects. In Niger, for example, local communities enter into a partnership agreement with a private company to grow *Acacia senegalensis* for the production of gum arabic.

Plan Vivo is a good example of a scheme specifically designed with community benefits in mind, and supports small-scale initiatives with local communities that can be used to generate tradable carbon credits. One is a Community Carbon Project in the N'hambita community in the buffer zone of the Gorongosa National Park, Mozambique. The project improves the livelihoods of this very poor community by introducing agroforestry systems that provide income from carbon finance and a range of other benefits such as fruit, timber, fodder, fuelwood and improved soil structure. The community also benefits from improved organisational capacity, education and awareness about forest stewardship and conservation, and the introduction of novel income through beekeeping, cane rat production and craft making.

The Forest Stewardship Council (FSC) provides accreditation for sustainably managed forest products, which takes into account the rights of indigenous people, local communities and workers. FSC requires that:

- The legal and customary rights of indigenous peoples to own, use and manage their lands, territories and resources are recognized.
- Forest management operations enhance the long-term social and economic well-being of forest workers and local communities. FSC's principles and criteria provide an example of how local community benefits can be linked to forest conservation.

Next steps: Beyond carbon conservation?

The urgent need to reduce carbon emissions is generating exciting new initiatives. While these offer a big increase in investment flows for conservation, there are a number of critical concerns. Our preliminary review suggests the need to understand the role of biodiversity and impacts on local communities of carbon management within these initiatives: in their prioritization of projects, and in the process of agreeing to include 'avoided deforestation' as a legitimate carbon reduction approach. These new mechanisms have yet to include the lessons from the past few decades of biodiversity conservation and sustainable forest management. As yet, they pay scant attention to governance issues and the rights of poor local people, particularly those with limited livelihood diversification options and those critically dependent on forest resources.

It is vital that biodiversity, social and cultural values are taken into account in the design and implementation of afforestation/reforestation (A/R) and REDD projects. The concept of high conservation value forests (HCVFs) aims to ensure that forests of outstanding and critical importance are maintained, given their high environmental, socio-economic, biodiversity or landscape values. The aim is to identify HCVFs and ensure that management decisions are consistent with maintaining those attributes of high conservation value. The concept was originally developed within the Forest Stewardship Council certification process, but is increasingly being used by timber purchasers, land use planners, conservation advocates and within policy debates. It would provide useful elements to incorporate in standards for A/R and REDD projects to ensure that these values were respected and maintained.

Encouraging innovation through a 'seed-bed' approach by supporting small-scale projects is part of the answer, as is greater attention to rights, equity and livelihoods within all initiatives. Equally important is to recognize that sustainable resource management mitigates climate change through reducing carbon emissions, and also helps local communities adapt to the effects of climate change.

In Vietnam, for example, tropical cyclones have damaged the livelihoods of those living near the coast, and climate change is likely to increase the frequency and severity of such tropical storms. Since 1994, the Vietnam National Chapter of the Red Cross has worked with local communities to plant and protect mangrove forests in northern Vietnam. Nearly 12,000 hectares of mangroves have been planted, and the benefits have been remarkable.

Although planting and protecting the mangroves cost US$1.1 million, it has saved US$7.3 million per year in dyke maintenance. During the devastating Typhoon Wukong in 2000, project areas remained unharmed while neighbouring provinces suffered huge loss of life, property and livelihoods. The Vietnam Red Cross estimates that 7750 families have benefited from mangrove rehabilitation. The mangroves are also a reservoir for carbon sequestration and family members can now earn additional income from selling crabs, shrimp and molluscs while increasing the protein in their diets.[12]

In Sudan, local farmers harvest gum from gum arabic trees. The trees seed themselves naturally on farmland, and the farmers leave the seedlings to grow for five years until they can be tapped for gum. Local people are also selecting varieties with greater resistance to drought and hotter temperatures, both associated with climate change. These activities enhance livelihoods, help local people adapt to a changing climate, sequester carbon in tree growth and support good land management and biodiversity conservation.[13] The UNFCCC Adaptation Fund will expand the number of such projects.

The wise development of carbon funds offers a major opportunity to respond to climate change in ways that blend mitigation and adaptation. However, for these new carbon funds to succeed, they must bridge local and international interests, and engage with local people to ensure these partnerships for sustainable forest management are transparent and accountable. They need to deliver tangible livelihood benefits, maintain biodiversity and ensure long-term gains from forests, rather than rapid disbursement of funds.

Notes

1   HM Treasury (2006) *Stern Review on the Economics of Climate Change*. See: www.hm-treasury.gov. uk/independent_reviews/stern_review_economics_climate_change/stern_review_report.cfm.

2   'Avoided deforestation could help fight third world poverty under global warming'. See: http:// news.mongabay.com/2006/1031-deforestation.html.

3   Chomitz, K.M. (2007) *At Loggerheads? Agricultural Expansion, Poverty Reduction, and Environment in the Tropical Forests*, World Bank, Washington, DC.

4   Griffiths, T. (2007) *Seeing RED? Avoided Deforestation and the Rights of Indigenous Peoples and Local Communities*, Forest Peoples Programme, Moreton-in-Marsh.

5   Smith, J. and Scherr, S. (2002) *Forest Carbon and Local Livelihoods: Assessment of Opportunities and Policy Recommendations*, CIFOR, Bogor, Indonesia.

6   'Human rights abuses, land conflicts, broken promises – the reality of carbon "offset" projects in Uganda', FERN press release, 12 January 2007.

7   This list varies slightly from the FAO's list of 10 countries with the largest annual net loss of forest. The differences between the two are potentially due to the Stern Review looking beyond net forest loss. Both lists indicate that deforestation and associated emissions are largely accounted for by a small number of countries.

8   Griffiths, T. (2007) *Seeing RED?* Forest Peoples Programme.

9   Peskett, L., Brown, D. and Luttrell, C. (2006) *Can Payments for Avoided Deforestation to Tackle Climate Change Also Benefit the Poor?* Forestry Briefing 12, ODI, London.

10 Griffiths, T. (2007) *Seeing RED?* Forest Peoples Programme.

11 Reid, H. (2004) 'Climate change – biodiversity and livelihood impacts', pp. 37–54, in Roe, D. (ed) *The Millennium Development Goals and Conservation*, IIED, London.

12 International Federation of Red Cross and Red Crescent Societies (2001) *Coastal Environmental Protection: A Case Study of the Vietnam Red Cross*, IFRC, Geneva.

13 Personal communication, Dr Sumaya Ahmed Zaki-Eldeen, Sudanese Environment Conservation Society, June 2007.

Chapter 29

Protecting the Future: Carbon, Forests, Protected Areas and Local Livelihoods

Alison Campbell, Sarah Clark, Lauren Coad, Lera Miles,
Katharine Bolt and Dilys Roe

Background

Reducing emissions from deforestation and forest degradation (REDD) in developing countries was first raised at a UN Framework Convention on Climate Change (UNFCCC) meeting in 2005. The UNFCCC aims to *stabilize greenhouse gas concentrations* in the atmosphere at a level that prevents dangerous interference with the climate system. Decisions made under UNFCCC can therefore be expected to focus on stabilizing emissions of carbon dioxide and other greenhouse gases, and not to make explicit provision for maximizing any other benefits of reduced deforestation and forest degradation. The prospect that forest issues could be tackled through the Convention has been welcomed by many conservationists, but also sparked an increasing amount of controversy, especially amongst forest user groups. Whilst there are some risks both for conservation, and for the livelihoods of people dependent on forests or forest conversion, participatory planning and monitoring of the effects of REDD activities on these co-benefits could help to minimize the risks.

A UNFCCC decision on compensation to developing countries for REDD is only likely to arise as part of an overall post-2012 agreement on greenhouse gas emissions. Major issues yet to be decided include whether the international agreement involves a forest carbon market or fund, and to what extent broader forest conservation efforts and carbon stocks in non-forest ecosystems would be accounted for. At the December 2007 Conference of Parties in Bali, Parties to the Convention agreed a 'demonstration' phase to test REDD methodologies and share experiences. Various donors, tropical forest countries, non-governmental organizations and private sector players are now investing in this pilot phase.

Reprinted from *Biodiversity*, vol 9, no 3&4, Campbell, A., Clark, S., Coad, L., Miles, L., Bolt, K. and Roe, D., 'Protecting the future: Carbon, forests, protected areas and local livelihoods', copyright © (2008) with permission from TC-Biodiversity, Kullu, India.

Whilst REDD is likely to involve national-scale policy changes and planning, forest management changes will have to be implemented at a site scale. Although protected areas are by definition (IUCN, 1994) established for biodiversity conservation rather than climate mitigation purposes, they can offer existing experience in the effectiveness of different approaches to reducing deforestation and supporting co-benefits. Protected area experience could thus help to inform REDD decision-making at local to national scales.

How Successful are Protected Areas at Reducing Deforestation?

Successful implementation of REDD is likely to require the reduction of deforestation rates on a national scale. It is therefore useful to know the effects of forest designation and management on deforestation rates, and to consider the design and management-related factors that influence protected area effectiveness in reducing deforestation and forest degradation. Here, we focus on deforestation, as there is little research on the impacts of protected areas on the degradation of forest carbon stocks.

The evidence suggests that protected areas are an effective tool for reducing deforestation within their boundaries. That is, there is usually less deforestation within formally protected areas than in their immediate surroundings (Sánchez-Azofeifa et al., 1999, 2003; Pelkey et al., 2000; Bruner et al., 2001; Deininger and Minten, 2002; Helmer, 2004; Curran et al., 2004; DeFries et al., 2005; Mas, 2005; Naughton-Treves et al., 2005, 2006; Sommerville, 2005; Bleher et al., 2006; Nepstad et al., 2006; Chowdhury, 2006; Gaveau et al., 2007; Oliveira et al., 2007; Phua et al., 2008). A minority of studies have reported that protection status had no significant impact on deforestation, indicating that legal designation alone is insufficient when land-use change pressures are high and governance limited (Marizán, 1994; Cropper et al., 2001; Rautner et al., 2005; Roman-Cuesta and Martinez-Vilalta, 2006). In addition, the extent to which deforestation is merely displaced to surrounding areas is unclear. This issue is particularly relevant in the context of REDD, where the aim is to reduce total greenhouse gas emissions.

Whilst protected areas tend to reduce the rate of deforestation *relative to their surroundings*, forest may still be cleared at high rates. In an extreme example, Gunung Raya Wildlife Sanctuary in Sumatra lost nearly 81 per cent of its forest cover between 1972 and 2002, with a deforestation rate only 0.1 per cent less than that of the surrounding area (Gaveau et al., 2007). Annual deforestation rates in excess of 3–6 per cent have been reported within protected area borders (Achard et al., 2002; Linkie et al., 2004). Such vulnerable protected areas could offer useful test sites for reducing deforestation within the REDD demonstration phase, as the necessary land designations and legislative frameworks are already in place, and the biodiversity co-benefits are already identified.

This raises the question of what factors influence protected area effectiveness in reducing deforestation, assuming an equal degree of pressure. Effectiveness in reducing deforestation is commonly linked to the level of funding (Wilkie et al., 2001; Jepson et al., 2002; Aung, 2007). Without adequate funding, protected areas lack the necessary infrastructure and management resulting in 'paper parks'. Dudley et al. (2004) suggest that legal gazettement does immediately confer some protective effect, but that active management (including planning, monitoring and evaluation) improves this. Strong involvement of NGOs can be a significant factor in protected area success, probably as a result of their contribution to management practices and employee accountability (Sommerville, 2005). Staff education, training and salaries are all often listed as weaknesses in protected area management that limit effectiveness (Aung, 2007).

The World Conservation Union (IUCN) describes six management categories for protected areas, based on the reasons for establishment. In general, protected areas with a higher IUCN category (I–II) are more (and sometimes completely) restrictive of resource exploitation and land use change than the lower categories (V–VI). Protected areas designated under categories (I–II) seem to be more effective at reducing deforestation than those which include a focus on sustainable use (V–VI) (Jones, 1990; Sánchez-Azofeifa, 1999; Pelkey et al., 2000; Dudley et al., 2004; Naughton-Treves et al., 2005; Bleher et al., 2006; Nepstad et al., 2006). However, there are comparatively few studies on deforestation rates within category V–VI protected areas, so further investigation would be useful.

These comparative studies typically make use of remote sensing to assess deforestation levels, and rarely consider the forms of governance within the protected areas, or the level of community involvement. Protected area management and governance regimes can differ both within and between IUCN categories (Naughton-Treves et al., 2006). The land and resources in any of the six management categories can be owned and/or directly managed, alone or in combination, by government agencies, NGOs, communities and private parties (Borrini-Feyerabend, 2007). At one end of the governance spectrum, the state has ownership of the area and may involve the surrounding communities in some decision-making through representation in stakeholder groups; at the other end, protected areas are owned and run by the communities themselves. Some insight can be gained through studies of indigenous lands and community forestry areas, which indicate success in reducing deforestation (Bray et al., 2003, 2004; Ruiz Perez et al., 2005; Hayes, 2006; Murdiyarso and Skutsch, 2006; Nepstad et al., 2006; Stocks et al., 2007). These factors need further investigation if the potential for REDD to provide carbon, biodiversity and livelihood benefits is to be assessed.

Land tenure and land use rights differ across protected areas, as do the number of people living in and around the area. Thousands of people, indigenous or otherwise, may live within individual protected areas. These protected areas vary in their governance and in the level of community involvement. From a conservation perspective, the rationale for community involvement is that denying locals access to protected area resources or decision-making leads to tension between protected area officials (where present) and residents (Hayes, 2006). When government agencies allocate land for certain purposes without consulting local residents, they may simply ignore the restrictions (Werner, 2001), or violent conflict may erupt (Naughton-Treves et al., 2006). There are various effective approaches to involving local people, ranging from compensation for costs incurred (Bruner et al., 2001) to full co-management (Brown, 1999). Environmental education can help communities to understand the benefits of protected areas and increase local support for their protection. This type of outreach has been found to correlate strongly with management effectiveness (Dudley et al., 2004), though not in all cases (Struhsaker et al., 2005). The strength of public support has also been correlated with overall conservation success (Mugisha and Jacobson, 2004; Struhsaker et al., 2005), although again, not in all cases (Bruner et al., 2001).

A protected area network that incorporates all levels of protection, as appropriate for the situation at site level, could be a valuable component of a national REDD strategy. Unless a country's protected area network includes a high proportion of remaining forest, it can form only part of a successful REDD strategy, as the local reduction in carbon emissions resulting from the success of a protected area may be offset by an increase in deforestation outside of the area (Ewers and Rodrigues, 2008).

What are the Livelihood Impacts of Forest Protected Areas?

The majority of the rural poor make use of forest resources: in Africa alone, 600 million people have been estimated to rely on forests and woodlands for their livelihoods (Anderson et al., 2006). The benefits of protected areas for local communities can include direct revenue from environmental protection, livelihood diversification, security of access to given resources, and the maintenance of ecosystem services such as watershed protection. Costs can range from significant crop damage by wildlife (e.g. Bajracharya et al., 2006) to displacement of local communities from their customary lands (West et al., 2006), and may include restricted access to resources and disadvantageous changes in land tenure. The nature of these costs and benefits depends largely upon the protected area's status and governance, as well as its history of use. Some protected areas restrict access to resources, whereas others allow sustainable use; and land tenure arrangements and benefit sharing vary across the six IUCN management categories.

The *net* livelihood impacts of protected areas are not easy to summarize, as standardized assessment methodologies are lacking, and because it is difficult to place a monetary value on some aspects. However, general patterns can be identified from the literature. Livelihood impacts vary with protected area status, management strategies and community involvement in governance. Management structures can provide direct benefits, for example through employment, but can restrict access to resources, alter local power structures, and change social/traditional values and behaviours. Strictly protected areas with top-down management structures (often associated with IUCN management categories I–II) can result in major livelihood costs, generating conflict with local communities. Community management schemes, and protected area management allowing sustainable use of forest resources (often associated with IUCN management categories V–VI), have been shown to provide tangible livelihoods benefits. However, significant costs can still be incurred by communities if management and institutional capacity is lacking or if issues of governance, particularly benefit sharing and tenure, are not resolved.

Attitudinal surveys are sometimes used to measure local perception of protected areas. Even with high costs, communities can support protected areas, citing the forest use benefits that they receive (Sekhar, 1998). Positive or negative attitudes are sometimes correlated with measurable costs and benefits (Allendorf et al., 2006), but communities may undervalue protected areas, as many of the benefits of protected areas (such as forest products and ecosystem services) are future use values, and may not be perceived to be under threat by the community. Wealth, ethnicity, age, gender and occupation have all been shown to be important in predicting attitudes, often as a result of differential impacts on livelihoods (Infield, 1988; Infield and Namara, 2001; McClanahan et al., 2005; Allendorf et al., 2006; Kideghesho et al., 2007). The impact of protected area designation on an individual is likely to depend on his or her use of the forest, tenure rights and political power within the community. Those with high dependency on the forest, few land-tenure rights and little political influence will be most at risk from protected area designation, which in turn is likely to influence their attitude towards conservation.

The inequitable distribution of livelihood costs and benefits between and within communities and households is thus an obvious barrier to sustainable reduction of deforestation as well as a direct issue for human development. Although richer members of forest communities are often the biggest harvesters of forest products, the poor can be more dependent on these resources, relying on the collection of forest products as a safety net during times of low employment and food production (Ferraro, 2002). Forest restrictions can therefore have large impacts on the poorest sections of forest communities. Resource restrictions may also differentially affect the livelihoods of men and women: such as allowing collection of non-timber forest products and firewood, but banning hunting (e.g. Sekhar, 1998; Allendorf et al., 2006). Overall, however, the more prominent members of society tend to capture most of the benefits from protected areas whilst suffering less of the costs. This is often true regardless of the protected area status or the level of community involvement in governance.

In contrast with the norm of government planning, some protected areas are designated in response to the desire of local communities to safeguard local resources (De Lacy, 1994; Catton, 1997; Naughton-Treves, 1998; Chapin, 2000;

Colchester, 2000; Lawrence, 2000; Schwartzmann and Zimmerman, 2005; Sohn, 2007). Whilst the direct benefits depend upon protected area management strategy, designation is likely to be more favourable to local livelihoods than the transfer of land ownership to external companies. For example, when the Peruvian government declared that the Madre de Dios region of the Amazon was to be opened up to oil and gas exploration, locals and conservation groups objected to the plans (Chicchón, 2000). The outcome included the designation of the Bahuaja Sonene National Park in 1996, and an agreement that the exploration activities in adjacent regions would return any land not desired for extraction programmes for inclusion in the protected area.

Increased efforts are required into the standardization of methodologies for social impact assessment, to facilitate further assessment of the costs and benefits of protected areas to local livelihoods. Further study into the combined effects of protection status and governance on the costs and benefits of forest protection would also be a valuable input into the development of REDD strategies.

Lessons for REDD

There is still much uncertainty regarding the factors influencing effectiveness of protected areas in reducing deforestation and impacts on local livelihoods, and a clear need for a detailed assessment of these factors in order to inform climate change policy. Although strictly protected areas are often effective in reducing deforestation, it is clear that protected areas allowing some resource extraction can still reduce deforestation whilst imposing fewer livelihood costs. The type and quantity of resources extracted will determine the effect on forest carbon stocks. Further research is required into the impact of the relationship between protected area status, community involvement and governance within protected areas on forest carbon stores and livelihoods.

An agreement on REDD could create an international market or fund for avoided emissions of greenhouse gases from forest loss or damage. The impact on protected areas and livelihoods will depend upon the national as well as global approaches selected. The potential exists for REDD to remove the large-scale drivers of deforestation, secure land tenure rights in forest areas, and increase the potential benefits to local people from conservation through community management regimes. The carbon market offers increasing opportunities for payments for restoration and retention of forest carbon. However, existing forest carbon schemes share many of the issues seen in protected area management, including lack of established tenure and the inequitable distribution of resources (Nelson and de Jong, 2003; May et al., 2004; Griffiths, 2007). The transaction costs of projects tend to favour large operators at the expense of small landholders (Pfaff et al., 2007). Clear governance, including well-defined property rights, is critical for emerging international markets (Landell-Mills and Porris, 2002), and these issues need careful consideration as REDD policy develops. Currently, carbon forestry projects are particularly weighted against those whose livelihoods are dependent upon less formal rights to forest resources, such as poor or landless households and women (Brown et al., 2004; Grieg-Gran et al., 2005); leading to the capture of most of the benefits by elite groups (Brown and Corbera, 2003; Brown et al., 2004). Increased finance could exacerbate these issues, and protection of carbon areas could intensify livelihood impacts if a strict 'fences and fines' approach was employed. Where strict protection is implemented, local people need to be involved in management and compensated for losses if they are expected to cooperate with the goal of reducing emissions.

If livelihoods issues are treated with care, avoided deforestation and other carbon storage schemes could provide much needed funds for conservation and development. Addressing the root causes of deforestation is likely to require improved governance of forest areas rather than heavy restrictions on the activities of local communities (Chomitz, 2006). Consideration of the potential impacts of REDD approaches based on past experience is therefore required, including an assessment of the management and governance strategies that facilitate provision of livelihood benefits. REDD implementation could provide the incentive for governments to strengthen policies for forest protection and settle tenure issues. An increase in the economic value of standing forests could also have positive impacts on the livelihood benefits of protected areas. Involvement of local communities in planning and implementation of REDD, and ensuring sharing of the benefits from REDD finance is likely to result in a more sustainable solution to deforestation and forest degradation.

References

Achard, F., Eva, H.D., Stibig, H-J, Mayaux, P., Gallego, J., Richards, T. and Malingreau, J-P. (2002) 'Determination of deforestation rates of the world's humid tropical forests', *Science*, 299(5583): 999–1002.

Allendorf, T., Swe, K.K., Oo, T., Htut, Y., Aung, M., Aung, M., Allendorf, K., Hayek, L., Leimgruber, P. and Wemmer, C. (2006) 'Community attitudes toward three protected areas in Upper Myanmar (Burma)', *Environmental Conservation*, 33(4): 344–352.

Anderson, J., Benjamin, C., Campell, B. and Tiveau, D. (2006) 'Forests, poverty and equity in Africa: New perspectives on policy and practice', *International Forestry Review*, 8(1): 44–53.

Aung, U.M. (2007) 'Policy and practice in Myanmar's protected area system', *Journal of Environmental Management*, 84(2): 188–203.

Bajracharya, S.B., Furley, P.A. and Newton, A.C. (2006) 'Impacts of community-based conservation on local communities in the Annapurna Conservation Area, Nepal', *Biodiversity and Conservation*, 15(8): 2765–2786.

Bleher, B., Uster, D. and Bergsdorf, T. (2006) 'Assessment of threat status and management effectiveness in Kakamega Forest, Kenya', *Biodiversity and Conservation*, 15(4): 1159–1177.

Borrini-Feyerabend, G. (2007) *The 'IUCN Protected Area Matrix'- A Tool Towards Effective Protected Area Systems*, Summit on the IUCN categories, Andalusia, Spain 7–11 May 2007.

Bray, D.B., Merino-Perez, L., Negreros-Castillo, P., Segura-Warnholtz, G., Torres-Rojo, J.M. and Vester, H.F.M. (2003) 'Mexico's community-managed forests as a global model for sustainable landscapes', *Conservation Biology*, 17(3): 672–677.

Bray, D.B., Ellis, E.A., Armijo-Canto, N. and Beck, C.T. (2004) 'The institutional drivers of sustainable landscapes: A case study of the "Mayan Zone" in Quintana Roo, Mexico', *Land Use Policy*, 21: 333–346.

Brown, D. (1999) *Principles and Practice of Forest Co-management: Evidence from West-Central Africa*, European Union Tropical Forestry Paper 2, Overseas Development Institute, London.

Brown, K. and Corbera, E. (2003) 'Exploring equity and sustainable development in the new carbon economy', *Climate Policy* 3(S1): 41–56.

Brown, K., Adger, N., Boyd, E., Corbera-Elizalde, E. and Shackley, S. (2004) *How do CDM Projects Contribute to Sustainable Development?*, Tyndall Centre for Climate Change Research Technical Report 16.

Bruner, A.G., Gullison, R.E., Rice, R.E. and da Fonseca, G.A.B. (2001) 'Effectiveness of parks in protecting biodiversity', *Science*, 291(5501): 125–128.

Catton, T. (1997) *Inhabited Wilderness: Indians, Eskimos, and National Parks in Alaska*, University of New Mexico Press, Albuquerque.

Chapin, M. (2000) *Defending Kuna Yala*, USAID Biodiversity Support Program, Washington, DC.

Chicchón, A. (2000) 'Conservation theory meets practice', *Conservation Biology*, 14(5): 1368–1369.

Chomitz, K.M. (2006) *Policies for National-Level Avoided Deforestation Programs: A Proposal for Discussion*, Background paper for policy research report on tropical deforestation, Revised Draft, www.rainforestcoalition.org/documents/ChomitzAvoidedDeforestationrev1.3.pdf.

Chowdhury, R.R. (2006) 'Landscape change in the Calakmul Biosphere Reserve, Mexico: Modeling the driving forces of smallholder deforestation in land parcels', *Applied Geography*, 26: 129–152.

Colchester, M. (2000) 'Self-determination or environmental determinism for indigenous peoples in tropical forest conservation', *Conservation Biology*, 14(5): 1365–1367.

Cropper, M., Puri, J. and Griffiths, C. (2001) 'Predicting the location of deforestation: The role of roads and protected areas in North Thailand', *Land Economics*, 77(2): 172–186.

Curran, L.M., Trigg, S.N, McDonald, A.K., Astiani, D., Hardiono, Y.M., Siregar, P., Caniago, I. and Kasischke, E. (2004) 'Lowland forest loss in protected areas of Indonesian Borneo', *Science*, 303(5660): 1000–1003.

DeFries, R., Hansen, A., Newton, A.C. and Hansen, M.C. (2005) 'Increasing isolation of protected areas in tropical forests over the past twenty years', *Ecological Applications*, 15(1): 19–26.

Deininger, K. and Minten, B. (2002) 'Determinants of deforestation and the economics of protection: An application to Mexico', *American Journal of Agricultural Economics*, 84(4): 943–960

De Lacy, T. (1994) 'The Uluru/Kakadu Model – Anangu Tjukurrpa, 50,000 years of Aboriginal law and land management changing the concept of national parks in Australia', *Society and Natural Resources*, 7: 479–498.

Dudley, N., Belokurov, A., Borodin, O., Higgins-Zogib, L., Hockings, M., Lacerda, L. and Stolton, S. (2004) *Are Protected Areas Working? An Analysis of Protected Areas*, WWF International, Gland.

Ewers, R.M. and Rodrigues, A.S.L. (2008) 'Estimates of reserve effectiveness are confounded by leakage', *Trends in Ecology and Evolution*, 23(3): 113–116.

Ferraro, P.J. (2002) 'The local costs of establishing protected areas in low incomenations: Ranomafana National Park, Madagascar', *Ecological Economics*, 43(2): 261–275.

Gaveau, D.L.A., Wandono, H. and Setiabudi, F. (2007) 'Three decades of deforestation in South-west Sumatra: Have protected areas halted forest loss and logging, and promoted re-growth?', *Biological Conservation*, 134(4): 495–504.

Grieg-Gran, M., Porras, I. and Wunder, S. (2005) 'How can market mechanisms for forest environmental services help the poor? Preliminary lessons from Latin America', *World Development*, 33(9): 1511–1527.

Griffiths, T. (2007) *Seeing 'RED'? 'Avoided Deforestation' and the Rights of Indigenous Peoples and Local Communities*, Forest Peoples Programme.

Hayes, T.M. (2006) 'Parks, people, and forest protection: An institutional assessment of the effectiveness of protected areas', *World Development*, 34(12): 2064–2065.

Helmer, E.H. (2004) 'Forest conservation and land development in Puerto Rico', *Landscape Ecology*, 19(1): 29–40.

Infield, M. (1988) 'Attitudes of a rural community towards conservation and a local conservation area in Natal, South Africa', *Biological Conservation*, 45(1): 21–46.

Infield, M. and Namara, A. (2001) 'Community attitudes and behaviour towards conservation: An assessment of a community conservation programme around Lake Mburo National Park, Uganda', *Oryx*, 35(1): 48–60.

IUCN (1994) *Guidelines for Protected Areas Management Categories*, IUCN, Cambridge, and Gland.

Jepson, P., Mornberg, F. and van Noord, H. (2002) 'A review of the efficacy of the protected area system of East Kalimantan Province, Indonesia', *Natural Areas Journal*, 22(1): 28–42.

Jones, J.R. (1990) *Current Management of Tropical Forest Areas in Costa Rica from Colonization and Environment: Land Settlement Projects in Central America*, United Nations University Press.

Kideghesho, J.R., Roskat, E. and Kaltenborn, B.P. (2007) 'Factors influencing conservation attitudes of local people in Western Serengeti, Tanzania', *Biodiversity and Conservation*, 16(7): 2213–2230.

Landell-Mills, N. and Porras, I.T. (2002) *Silver Bullet or Fool's Gold? A Global Review of Markets for Forest Environmental Services and their Impact on the Poor*, International Institute for Environment and Development, London.

Lawrence, D. (2000) *Kakadu: The Making of a National Park*, Melbourne University Press, Melbourne.

Linkie, M., Smith, R.J. and Leader-Williams, N. (2004) 'Mapping and predicting deforestation patterns in the lowlands of Sumatra', *Biodiversity and Conservation*, 13(10): 1809–1818.

Mas, J.F. (2005) 'Assessing protected area effectiveness using surrounding (buffer) areas environmentally similar to the target area', *Environmental Monitoring and Assessment*, 105: 69–80.

Marizàn, G.R. (1994) *Deforestation in Protected Areas: Case Study of Los Haitises National Park*, Third International Conference on Environmental Enforcement, 1: 253–260. Available at: www.inece.org/3rdvol1/pro1toc.htm (accessed 9 May 2008).

May, P.H., Boyd, E., Veiga, F. and Chang, M. (2004) *Local Sustainable Development Effects of Forest Carbon Projects in Brazil and Bolivia: A View from the Field*, International Institute for Environment and Development, London.

McClanahan, T., Davies, J. and Maina, J. (2005) 'Factors influencing resource users and managers' perceptions towards marine protected area management in Kenya', *Environmental Conservation*, 32: 42–49.

Mugisha, A.R. and Jacobson, S.K. (2004) 'Threat reduction assessment of conventional and community-based conservation approaches to managing protected areas in Uganda', *Environmental Conservation*, 31(3): 233–241.

Murdiyarso, D. and Skutsch, M. (eds) (2006) *Community Forest Management as a Carbon Mitigation Option: Case Studies*, CIFOR, Indonesia.

Naughton-Treves, L. (1998) 'Predicting patterns of crop damage by wildlife around Kibale National Park, Uganda', *Conservation Biology*, 12(1): 156–168.

Naughton-Treves, L.M., Holland, B. and Brandon, K. (2005) 'The role of protected areas in conserving biodiversity and sustaining local livelihoods', *Annual Review Environmental Resources*, 30: 219–252.

Naughton-Treves, L.M., Alvarez-Berríos, N., Brandon, K., Bruner, A., Holland, M.B., Ponce, C., Saenz, M., Suarez, L. and Treves, A. (2006) 'Expanding protected areas and incorporating human resource use: A study of 15 forest parks in Ecuador and Peru', *Sustainability: Science, Practice, and Policy*, 2(2): 32–44.

Nelson, K. and de Jong, B. (2003) 'Making global initiatives local realities: Carbon mitigation projects in Chiapas, Mexico', *Global Climate Change: Human Dimensions*, 13: 19–30.

Nepstad, D., Schwartzman, S., Bamberger, B., Santilli, M. and Ray, D. (2006) 'Inhibition of Amazon deforestation and fire by parks and indigenous lands', *Conservation Biology*, 20(1): 65–73.

Oliveira, P.J.C., Asner, G.P., Knapp, D.E., Almeyda, A., Galván-Gildemeister, R., Keene, S., Raybin, R.F. and Smith, R.C. (2007) 'Land-use allocation protects the Peruvian Amazon', *Science*, 31: 1233–1236.

Pelkey, N.W., Stoner, C.J. and Caro, T.M. (2000) 'Vegetation in Tanzania: Assessing long term trends and effects of protection using satellite imagery', *Biological Conservation*, 94: 297–309.

Pfaff, A., Kerr, S., Lipper, L., Cavatassi, R., Davis, B., Hendy, J. and Sanchez-Azofeifa, G.A. (2007) 'Will buying tropical forest carbon benefit the poor? Evidence from Costa Rica', *Land Use Policy*, 28(3): 600–610.

Phua, M.-H., Tsuyuki, S., Furuya, N. and Lee, J.S. (2008) 'Detecting deforestation with a spectral change detection approach using multitemporal landsat data: A case study of Kinabalu Park, Sabah, Malaysia', *Journal of Environmental Management*, 88(4): 784–795.

Rautner, M., Hardiono, M. and Alfred, R.J. (2005) *Borneo: Treasure Island at Risk*, Report for WWF Germany.

Roman-Cuesta, R.M. and Martinez-Vilalta, J. (2006) 'Effectiveness of protected areas in mitigating fire within their boundaries: Case study of Chiapas, Mexico', *Conservation Biology*, 20(4): 1074–1086.

Ruiz-Pérez, M., Almeida, M., Dewi, S., Costa, E.M.L., Pantoja, M.C., Puntodewo, A., de Arruda Postigo, A. and de Andrade, A.G. (2005) 'Conservation and development in Amazonian extractive reserves: The case of Alto Juruá', *Ambio*, 34(3): 218–223.

Sánchez-Azofeifa, G.A., Quesada-Mateo, C., Gonzalez-Quesada, P., Dayanandan, S. and Bawa, K.S., (1999) 'Protected areas and conservation of biodiversity in the tropics', *Conservation Biology*, 13(2): 407–411.

Sánchez-Azofeifa, G.A., Daily, G.C., Pfaff, A.S.P. and Busch, C. (2003) 'Integrity and isolation of Costa Rica's national parks and biological reserves: Examining the dynamics of land-cover change', *Biological Conservation*, 109(1): 123–135.

Schwartzmann, S. and Zimmerman, B. (2005) 'Conservation alliances with indigenous peoples of the Amazon', *Conservation Biology*, 19: 721–727.

Sekhar, N.U. (1998) 'Crop and livestock depredation caused by wild animals in protected areas: the case of Sariska Tiger Reserve, Rajasthan, India', *Environmental Conservation*, 25(2): 160–171.

Sohn, J. (2007) *Protecting the Peruvian Amazon and its People from the Risks of Oil and Gas Development*, World Resources Institute. Available at: www.wri.org/stories/2007/10/protectingperuvian-amazon-and-its-people-risks-oil-and-gas-development

Sommerville, M. (2005) *An Analysis of Deforestation Trends across Madagascar's Protected Area System (1980–2000) and Implications for Future Management*, MSc thesis, Oxford University.

Stocks, A., McMahan, B. and Taber, P. (2007) 'Indigenous, colonist, and government impacts on Nicaragua's Bosawas Reserve', *Conservation Biology*, 21(6): 1495–1505.

Struhsaker, T.T., Struhsaker, P.J. and Siex, K.S. (2005) 'Conserving Africa's rainforests: Problems in protected areas and possible solutions', *Biological Conservation*, 123(1): 45–54.

Werner, S. (2001) *Environmental Knowledge and Resource Management: Sumatra's Kerinci-Seblat National Park*, PhD Dissertation, Technischen Universität Berlin. Available at: http://edocs.tuberlin.de/diss/2001/werner_silvia.pdf (accessed 11 February 2008).

West, P., Igoe, J. and Brockington, D. (2006) 'Parks and peoples: The social impact of protected areas', *Annual Review of Anthropology*, 35: 251–277.

Wilkie, D.S., Carpenter, J.F. and Zhang, Q. (2001) 'The under-financing of protected areas in the Congo Basin: So many parks and so little willingness to pay', *Biodiversity and Conservation*, 10: 691–709.

Chapter 30

Seeing 'REDD'? Forest, Climate Change Mitigation and the Rights of Indigenous Peoples and Local Communities

Tom Griffiths

Introduction and Background

After repeated warnings from scientists, civil society and indigenous peoples that climate change is already under way and set to accelerate, there are signs that most governments today accept that more effective measures must be taken to tackle global warming. It is increasingly recognized that deforestation, particularly in the tropics, contributes between 18 and 20 per cent of all annual global emissions of CO_2, and that in some countries like Brazil it accounts for up to 75 per cent of the country's annual release of CO_2 from human activity each year. Consequently, there is international consensus that future policies to combat climate change must include measures that seek to reduce deforestation in tropical countries.

In late 2007, governments in the UN Climate Convention decided to try to adopt a new forest and climate regime that could include policies for reducing emissions from deforestation and forest degradation (REDD) by the end of 2009. As these complex negotiations gather pace in 2008, indigenous peoples and civil society organizations continue to emphasize that recognizing the rights of indigenous peoples and forest dependent communities must be an essential precondition in the design and implementation of national and international efforts to protect forests and curb emissions.[1] They stress that without proper involvement of forest communities and respect for peoples' rights, REDD policies and global carbon and other commodity markets threaten to generate land grabs, displacement, conflict, corruption, impoverishment and cultural degradation.[2]

At the same time, there is a growing realization that REDD policies as currently proposed contain serious moral hazards because they plan to reward polluters with a history of forest destruction, but would fail to recognize and reward the role of indigenous and local forest custodians who protect and sustainably use standing forests.

There is broad agreement among forest policy specialists that sustainable and just REDD policies and incentives must fulfil criteria for *effectiveness, efficiency and fairness*.[3] To be effective and fair, REDD policies at all levels must respect human rights, including the rights of indigenous peoples, and respect the principle of free, prior and informed consent. Effective policies must also deliver local benefits and require governance reforms and measures to secure land and resource tenure. Policies must be based on transparency, equitable benefit sharing, biodiversity protection, maintenance of ecosystem integrity and must be accountable to the public and affected forest peoples and forest dependent communities.[4] They must also tackle the underlying causes of deforestation, require independent monitoring of social and governance performance, and promote legal and policy reforms in the forest sector and in other sectors affecting forests. With these preconditions and with a genuine commitment to forest policy reforms, there is a possibility that international forest and climate agreements could deliver local and global benefits and empower forest peoples.

Ongoing Rights, Equity and Accountability Concerns

Civil society and indigenous peoples' organizations point out that there are still risks that ill-conceived REDD interventions could harm communities and generate perverse outcomes, not least because the evolving global legal framework has so far failed to establish intergovernmental commitments on rights and equity issues as an essential part of a new forest and climate regime.[5] At the same time, *if* forests become part of an international regime that respects peoples' rights and promotes genuine progressive people-centred tenure and governance reforms in the forest sector, and if moral hazards and other problems can be addressed (see below), then many agree that there could be potential benefits to be gained by indigenous peoples and forest-dependent communities.[6]

The social risks associated with top-down REDD policies are increasingly acknowledged by international agencies like the UN and by government advisers and bilateral initiatives on REDD.[7] It is significant that several recent governmental and NGO reviews of international forests and climate finance have recognized that REDD will not work without recognising the rights of forest-dependent peoples.[8] For example, while the 2008 Eliasch Review has been criticized for its problematic analysis in favour of carbon markets,[9] the study does note that alongside REDD incentives:

> There will be a danger of customary rights being violated in the interests of inward investment, and abusive contracts and land speculation acting to the detriment of community

interests. Thus without clear tenure and use rights, sustainable forest management will be impossible and carbon finance may increase social conflict.[10]

Nevertheless, such reviews advocating REDD, or agencies that plan to fund REDD, only propose voluntary standards. They do not seem willing to require recipient countries to meet human rights standards. Although countries like Papua New Guinea have publicly talked about the need to respect community rights in the UNFCCC and other forums, they have pressed donors hard not to attach strings to international REDD funds.

Top-down REDD policies

Most REDD proposals in 2008 continued to flow from governments, international agencies, carbon finance companies and large conservation NGOs. Communities are not well informed about REDD at the local level. In some cases, like Panama, governments are claiming that they have *already* consulted the public and forest communities on measures to tackle deforestation in related previous consultations on national environmental plans. Government officials suggest that the fundamentals of REDD strategy are more or less already formulated through existing national forest or environmental plans.[11] Some governments therefore seem to see REDD primarily as a new source of funding for their *existing* forest policies as well as an opportunity to add carbon stocks to their protected area and concession portfolio (see 'The local benefits of existing and proposed REDD initiatives').

A 2008 FPP-FERN review of nine readiness plan idea notes (R-PINs) submitted to the World Bank's Forest Carbon Partnership Facility (FCPF) found that most had been developed with only minimal or no consultation with forest peoples. In the case of Paraguay, indigenous organizations have protested strongly that the government has so far developed REDD policies internally without consultation with indigenous peoples.[12] In another case, the governments in Vietnam and the Lao People's Democratic Republic (Lao PDR) openly admit that they developed their REDD concepts in 2008 without public consultation.[13]

History shows that any global plans to save the world's forests devised without the full knowledge and agreement of forest peoples and local communities are doomed to failure and such top-down policy-making often serves to reinforce the unequal status quo in forest politics at the international, national and local levels. A prime example of a previous failed global solution designed by the World Bank and FAO, which at one point involved no less than 73 developing country governments, was the Tropical Forestry Action Plan (TFAP) which was planned and implemented in the 1980s and early 1990s.

Though the TFAP talked a lot about participation and local livelihoods it ended up serving the interests of government agencies and the logging industry, despite its claims of support for 'social forestry'. The TFAP experience showed clearly that it is a mistake to develop forest policy from the top down and that sustainable solutions can only come from the bottom up, from forest owners and forest peoples who actually live in and depend on the forest.[14]

While some indigenous organizations and UN bodies have started to prepare community training materials on REDD,[15] few governments have yet consulted properly with forest peoples and community organizations on their plans for new forest and climate policies. Most consultations have so far been based in towns and involved conservation NGOs and government officials.

Rushed or minimal consultations in voluntary initiatives

At the same time, there are indications that voluntary REDD and avoided defor-estation initiatives are failing to properly consult and obtain consent from affected forest communities. In Guyana, Canopy Capital signed an agreement with the Iwokrama International Centre to pilot payments for environmental services in an effort to protect the rainforest and fund the protected area.

The first that most Makushi communities knew about the deal that covers their ancestral forests, came from announcements in the national and interna-tional press issued after the agreement had already been made. The failure of Canopy Capital and the Iwokrama Centre to consult local people beforehand is arguably in violation of the collaborative co-agreement between the park and local Amerindian communities. Canopy Capital explains that the limited transparency and rushed process stemmed from commercial confidentiality requirements and the need to maintain a competitive advantage – a commercial concept and fast-practice that is at odds with due process and prior consent requirements for deci-sions affecting indigenous forest communities.

Unless indigenous peoples, communities and civil society in tropical forest countries are able to secure full and effective participation in the development of public policies on forests and climate change mitigation, there is a real risk that REDD policies and interventions will end up reinforcing the status quo and serving the interest of forest departments, conservation organizations and local elites.

Lack of essential governance and tenure reforms

Indeed, self-serving central government-oriented REDD plans are already emerging. There is a mounting body of new evidence to show that many of the initial plans for REDD drawn up by governments have disregarded concerns raised by indigenous peoples, NGOs and social development specialists relating to human rights, land tenure, customary rights, free, prior and informed consent (FPIC), good governance and equity.

The problems with weak governance and corruption in the forest sector in developing countries and widespread unjust treatment and exploitation of forest communities by government forest departments are well documented.[16] Dealing with these deep-rooted problems requires far-reaching reforms to respect commu-nity rights and enable changes to forest, land and forest product laws and regulations. Yet in many cases it seems such reforms are not planned under current national REDD proposals.

The same FPP–FERN review of REDD concept notes referred to above shows a disturbing tendency towards 'business as usual' in government environmental ministries and forest departments elaborating REDD policies.[17]

While countries like Liberia and Ghana have rightly acknowledged the need to address tenure reform in their REDD concept notes, other countries like Guyana and Democratic Republic of Congo portray State ownership of forests as unproblematic. In these latter countries, outline REDD plans do not acknowledge that extensive areas are under customary possession and claimed by indigenous peoples and forest-dependent communities.[18] In the case of Guyana, the official REDD concept note paints an overly positive and arguably 'misleading' picture of the state of forest governance and progress towards sustainable forest management.[19]

Some government REDD plans propose to provide support for 'community-based forest management', but what would that really mean in practice? Who would really benefit from these REDD funds? Experience in India has shown that such schemes have in certain ways *increased* state control over forests, and increased unwanted government interventions in local customary systems of forest governance, land tenure and natural resource management.[20]

Narrow focus on carbon accounting, monitoring, measurement and verification

Rather than tenure and legal reforms to empower communities for forest protection many REDD plans focus on requirements for complex carbon accounting and monitoring systems, new forest inventories and actions to verify emissions reductions. Very few suggest monitoring of social impacts or governance performance as has been recommended by civil society.

For their part, international agencies seem to be focused on actions in developing countries, but are not addressing underlying causes related to international trade and global consumption of agricultural commodities, timber and pulp products. As one indigenous leader from Indonesia cautions, a business as usual approach will not solve deforestation problems:

> Setting up carbon forests, national parks and protected areas, or developing legality standards for timber and timber trading, will be just dealing with the symptoms of deforestation. In contrast, addressing inequalities in land tenure, discrimination against Indigenous Peoples, corruption, over-consumption and uncontrolled industrialization will tackle the underlying causes of deforestation. We do have examples from all over the world, showing that customary forest management is a long term solution in safeguarding and ensuring sustainability.[21]

Risk of moral hazards and perverse outcomes

Indigenous peoples, forestry experts, economists and social scientists increasingly point to the 'moral hazard' in REDD financial incentives as currently proposed, which would target payments (compensation) and rewards toward *polluters* (forest destroyers), while effective custodians, like indigenous peoples, who are already protecting forests, would go unrewarded or receive only token benefits.[22]

REDD-based inequities may also emerge between different regions within a country – where some districts or provinces have high deforestation, while others retain intact forests (e.g. the States of Mato Grosso *versus* Amazonas in Brazil).[23]

In Central America, as in many other regions, most intact forests with low or zero deforestation rates, like those in Nicaragua and Panama – for example, are located on the traditional lands and territories of indigenous peoples or in well-managed protected areas. A recent study of the potential for REDD policies to deliver emissions reductions and local benefits in Central America has found that REDD policies as currently proposed would deliver few benefits to indigenous peoples and local communities. Instead, REDD incentives would likely focus on areas with deforestation threats and therefore mainly benefit large-scale deforesters like cattle ranchers.[24]

Indigenous peoples' organizations and forest and development experts caution that REDD policy proposals that only target incentives and actions in deforestation areas, will inevitably set up an unfair environmental incentive system that will increase rural inequality and almost certainly attract widespread public condemnation and even generate local conflicts.[25]

REDD plans that risk disregarding historical and existing community efforts to protect forests can be seen in the case of Panama. Initial government plans for REDD, for example, appear to concentrate incentives on cattle ranchers in areas at risk from deforestation in the province of Darién, the eastern province of Panama and Ngöbe Buglé territory (suffering deforestation by outsiders).[26] REDD incentives apparently will not extend to those areas with intact forests where Kuna and other indigenous peoples have historically organized to defend their territory and halt unauthorized deforestation.[27] There is little doubt that unless the government of Panama addresses these equity issues regarding the use of REDD incentives, their scheme will come in for heavy public criticism.

At the end of 2008, while the moral hazards associated with planned REDD incentives have been publicly acknowledged by some of its major proponents and architects,[28] so far few solutions have been put forward by REDD advocates to address fairness issues. One recent proposal suggests fairness might be achieved through a three-fund approach. This would consist of a government fund (for capacity building and readiness activities), a forest stewardship fund (for indigenous peoples and communities) and a private stewardship fund to compensate private forest owners with options to deforest for economic gains.[29]

Even this tripartite approach, however, may feature moral hazards and cause perverse outcomes. Without safeguards, payments to some private landowners (e.g. in Brazil and Paraguay where 'property owners' have often obtained their land illegally) might end up rewarding law breakers and illegitimate landholders.[30]

It is thus essential that rules for distribution of REDD incentives are based on just and credible principles and criteria, including legality criteria – otherwise the payments will end up going to the wrong people, including people who might occupy and grab forest lands in anticipation of receiving REDD benefits.

Unjust and unlawful targeting of shifting cultivators

Weak and unscientific analysis of the drivers of deforestation and degradation in government REDD concepts also reveals a worrying tendency for governments to blame shifting cultivators for deforestation and forest degradation. Of the nine REDD concepts studied by FPP and FERN, no less than eight (Panama, Guyana, Paraguay, Democratic Republic of Congo, Liberia, Ghana, Lao PDR and Vietnam) identify 'traditional agriculture' or 'shifting agriculture' as a major cause of forest loss.[31]

None of the REDD concepts distinguish between permanent and temporary forest loss and none acknowledge that these practices are often carbon neutral or even carbon positive – and also sustain important biodiversity and cultural values. They also fail to recognize that sustainable rotational agriculture and agroforestry systems are protected under international environmental and human rights laws. In the same way, flawed proposals by governments and NGOs for monitoring deforestation, like that developed by the Woods Hole Research Center for Democratic Republic of Congo,[32] ignore the long-term dynamics of swidden farming systems that maintain a mosaic of fields, regrowth and secondary forest in which much deforestation may be *local* and *temporary*.[33]

Application of these defective analyses of forest loss and degradation risks depriving people of their legitimate means of livelihood security and way of life. Forest activists and local leaders will have to be alert to detect and reject false and dangerous 'trade-off' REDD policies promoted by forest departments and NGOs (i.e. stop swidden farming in the forest and you will gain benefits and cash). REDD policies that seek to convert shifting cultivators to off-farm workers or settled farmers or to provide 'alternative' cash-based livelihoods risk exposing people to the vagaries of local food markets. In the case of traditional forest-based hunting and farming groups, narrow monetary compensation for forgoing use of forest land and resources is never likely to fully compensate for loss of food security and cultural integrity.

In short, governments, international agencies and NGOs must avoid falling into the trap of promoting simplistic and scientifically and legally questionable policies seeking to provide alternatives to slash and burn (ASB) and crude 'no-smoke' REDD policies. Unfortunately, there are disturbing signs that some agencies and NGOs are already heading down this ill-thought-out route.[34]

Land grabs, land conflicts and violation of customary rights

The availability of REDD financial incentives for 'owners' of standing forests creates a risk that governments, companies and conservation NGOs will 'zone' (carve up) forests by demarcating protected areas, biological corridors, forest reserves and sustainable forest management zones (certified logging) to receive REDD payments to the exclusion or disadvantage of indigenous peoples and traditional communities and local people. Thus, the same potential problems of top-down land-use planning and forest zonification exist with REDD schemes as they do with other approaches that depend on land-use zoning and land classification – like the application of the high conservation value or 'critical forests' concepts.[35]

In many tropical forest countries, states fail to recognize the collective customary rights of indigenous peoples over their ancestral forests, or only recognize a small portion of their traditional lands – legally defining the remaining forests as so-called 'State land'.[36] Given the potential earning capacity of standing forests, REDD compensation payments to governments may create a *dis*incentive for forest and conservation and other government authorities to resolve long-standing land disputes in forest areas.

At the same time forests are under pressure worldwide from the growing international demand for food, fibre and agrofuels which is driving up crop prices and increasing the value of rural land.[37] Add to this incentives for REDD and there is a danger that relatively lucrative compensation rates per hectare of forest might drive land speculation on forest frontiers and even in more remote forest areas. Unless REDD schemes take measures to secure and recognize customary collective lands for communities, forests risk being taken over by outsiders and commercial interests.

Increased inequality and social conflict

Forests under top-down demarcation REDD schemes might generate conflict over boundaries and benefits both within and between rural landholders and forest owners. There is also the risk that without careful measures to ensure equitable benefits in rural areas, REDD payments could create rifts between those communities or households receiving payments and those that are excluded, which may include those without formal legal title to their lands and 'landless' people. In other words, REDD compensation might increase inequality in rural forest areas and risk creating intra- and inter-community conflicts.

Support for outdated and unjust exclusionary conservation practices

Despite important advances in international (CBD) and best practice (IUCN) standards for participatory and inclusive conservation models, application of these principles in the practice of park authorities in some tropical countries remains patchy or limited. For example, a United Organisation for Batwwa Development in Uganda (UOBDU)–FPP study found in 2008 that:

> *The Batwa continue to suffer multiple forms of marginalisation in protected area management. Not only were they arbitrarily evicted from their homeland, thereby suffering the greatest injustices, they also now get the least amount of attention from government in the ongoing efforts to make protected area management more socially responsible ... protected area managers in SW Uganda still perceive indigenous peoples as external to conservation and, as a result, the translation of the Durban Action Plan and CBD's Programme of Work on Protected Areas on the ground is far from satisfactory.*[38]

In Cameroon, a 2008 FPP-Okani study documented that:

> *little progress has been made ... to secure forest communities' rights. Conservation organisations and donors, and the government, have done little in Cameroon to implement their international commitments to protect community rights in their conservation projects. Most of the new standards to which they have agreed remain unknown at the local level. Yet it is government people at the local level who most need to be informed about these new standards, and be given support to implement them. However, in addition to being impeded by a persistent lack of information and support, they are also constrained by outdated laws which contradict the government's international commitments.*[39]

The slow pace of change on the ground in many countries means that, without requirements for reform, REDD funds risk reinforcing unjust conventional forest protection models and policies. There are real risks that where REDD funds are used to promote and *ensure* forest conservation, a significant proportion could be used by the state to equip forest protection agencies with jeeps, walkie talkies, arms, helicopters and GPS in an outdated and anti-people 'guns and guards' approach to forest protection.

Significant financial REDD rewards may induce state forest agencies and protected area authorities to start overzealous enforcement of existing unjust forest protection laws using measures that will unequally target marginal and vulnerable groups, including indigenous peoples and traditional forest-dependent communities.[40] This is a significant risk, particularly in Africa and Asia, as numerous studies have shown that forest law enforcement initiatives have a tendency to target communities and poor people, while disregarding larger commercial interests involved in harmful or illegal extraction.[41]

The Local Benefits Potential of Existing and Proposed REDD Initiatives

Could local people receive worthwhile benefits?

Existing REDD proposals are often vague about *which* bodies, entities or persons would receive compensation payments under a national REDD scheme.[42] Though most governments mention the need for communities to receive benefits they do not contain proposals on how and according to what principles local benefits would be distributed.[43]

Many national REDD plans propose that REDD payments would be made to *government* ministries or treasuries, and these central government bodies plan to control the use and distribution of REDD funds or REDD concessions for the private sector based on outdated large-scale logging concession models.

There are disturbing signs that REDD policies will reinforce the status quo in the forest sector in many countries and largely benefit forest departments and powerful commercial or conservation interests with the resources to cover the transaction costs of purchasing concession rights.

REDD proposals made by the government of Indonesia, for example, plan to allocate carbon rights under the existing concession model. Indigenous peoples fear that REDD will entrench the power and hegemony of the forest authorities and block their claims to secure their customary rights over community forests:

> There is a fear also REDD could become a business like any other, and that developers can pay a fee/rent to the government for the use of a carbon as a commodity, including on Indigenous territories. REDD is e.g. drawing high interests of various players such as the sectoral Ministries, and they tend to monopolize information and decision making.[44]

Similar concerns are expressed about the government's REDD plans in Papua New Guinea:

> Lack of proper governance, corruption, illegal logging and lack of implementation of existing laws are the main problems which would also affect the implementation of REDD. A lack of transparency and lack of benefit sharing mechanism could impede the roll-out of REDD. It is unclear how benefits would reach the local level. Any REDD income should go towards infrastructure development for indigenous peoples and local communities.[45]

Lessons from PES schemes

Studies by economists and advocates of avoided deforestation and payments for environmental services (PES) show that livelihood impacts on communities vary according to different schemes, but in general benefits for communities and small-holders have tended to be low.[46] A study of the Climate Action Project in Noel Kempff Mercado National Park in Bolivia and its Rio Bravo Conservation and Management Area in Belize carried out by IIED found that benefits were initially captured by state agencies, local governments and conservation NGOs rather than indigenous peoples and local communities.[47]

A study of PES in Central Amercia has found that under publicly funded PES programmes in Mexico local communities have received benefits.[48] In Costa Rica, on the other hand, PES schemes have mainly benefited large wealthy landholders and absentee landlords, while indigenous peoples, smallholders and the rural poor have been largely excluded.[49] Larger and commercial landholders have had privi-leged access to these schemes in Costa Rica because they have the resources to cover the costs and legal fees for accessing such schemes. Small landholders and rural communities consider that PES schemes lack incentives for engagement, deliver only minimal benefits and are unprofitable. They also perceive the PES administrative process as long and complicated.[50]

Studies of other PES schemes in Brazil and Bolivia have found these programmes have tended to be top down and have suffered 'inadequate stakeholder participa-tion' and thus have been plagued by 'barriers to sustainability'.[51] In Ecuador, the 'socio-bosque' programme has come under criticism for applying differential compensation rates for avoided deforestation depending on the type of land-holders. Under the existing scheme indigenous peoples with extensive forests receive a much lower rate per hectare than other small property owners in the same region.[52]

In Asia, the World Agroforestry Centre points to its Rewarding Upland Poor for Environmental Services (RUPES) programme that operates in Indonesia, Nepal and the Philippines as a positive example.[53] In the case of indigenous communities with subsistence and barter economies it is suggested that non-monetary benefits in-kind might be more culturally appropriate, while those indigenous communities with some degree of monetisation might be compensated or 'rewarded' with small and regular payments into community funds or to community projects.[54]

While positive PES experiences do exist, economists warn that future public PES and REDD schemes are likely to target financial incentives on areas suffering deforestation and severe degradation to meet *efficiency* criteria (reducing GHG emissions), while private investors will seek maximum returns and efficiency and so are unlikely to take equity concerns into consideration. As noted in the section on 'Ongoing rights, equity and accountability concerns' above, effective forest stewards who have historically maintained forests may not see many benefits from REDD-PES schemes unless they contain stringent components to ensure fair-ness.[55]

Critics of market-based PES also argue that the commodification of life forms and 'biodiversity' (biodiversity credits, etc.) undermines local (non-monetary) cultural, conservation and sustainable use values.[56]

Preconditions for securing local benefits

Economists suggest that, based on emerging experience with PES schemes in some parts of Latin America, at least some local livelihood gains can be expected if the right terms and conditions are in place.[57] In one recent detailed study, based on 233 field sites in forest areas, scientists have confirmed that positive local livelihood and biodiversity outcomes and local benefits increase with community forest size, community ownership, and community control and autonomy in forest management.[58]

Under PES initiatives, land regularization and secure property rights are an essential precondition for generation of local benefits for indigenous peoples and local communities.[59] To meet fairness criteria, regional or national PES schemes must include rewards and incentives for indigenous peoples, traditional forest dwellers and small forest owners.[60]

Key preconditions for improving the likelihood of communities securing worthwhile benefits include:

- secure tenure and community rights to lands and forest resources;
- control over substantial and extensive areas of standing forest for each community;[61]
- strong community organization;
- effective negotiating capacity of community representatives;
- transparent and mutually agreed procedures for FPIC and good-faith negotiation;
- early and balanced information provision to communities explaining pros and cons, livelihood, economic and cultural risks, and potential costs and benefits;
- full information on the external parties (including private sector) seeking an agreement;
- access to and funding for legal and technical assistance to communities;
- flexible and adjustable contracts that may be periodically reviewed and amended;
- prior agreement and clarity on land and resource rights, including carbon rights;
- mutual agreements on definitions of 'forests' and 'degradation' so that customary resource use is protected and sustainable traditional practices are not unjustly targeted (e.g. agreements on permissible emissions, etc.);
- application of minimum social standards, including standards for cultural and social impact assessment, poverty-risk analysis and vulnerability analysis;
- effective, transparent and accountable benefit distribution and grievance mechanisms;
- compliance with relevant international social, human rights and sustainable development standards; and
- strong mechanisms for community monitoring and verification of delivery of local benefits.

To meet these preconditions, avoid potential adverse impacts and help maximize the possibility of positive outcomes for local people, it will be essential that REDD policies and actions, among other measures:

- establish new mechanisms to ensure indigenous peoples and local communities are involved in the design and implementation of REDD schemes;
- implement measures to remove legal obstacles so that customary tenure and local governance structures are recognized;
- make long-term and focused investments for land tenure reforms;
- integrate natural resource management with tenure security;
- include mechanisms to address the elite capture (outside and inside communities);
- train communities and their leaders in FPIC, consultation and negotiation techniques; and
- provide legal assistance to communities.[62]

Notes

1   See, for example, Seymour, F. (2008) *Forests, Climate Change, and Human Rights: managing risks and Trade Offs*, CIFOR, Bogor.

2   See White, A. (2008) *Seeing People Through the Trees: Scaling Up Efforts to Advance Rights and Address Poverty, Conflict and Climate Change*, Rights and Resources Initiative, Washington, DC.

3   Humphreys, D. (2008) 'The politics of "avoided deforestation": Historical context and contemporary issues', *International Forestry Review*, 10(3).

4   See, RRI (2008) *Foundations for Effectiveness: A Framework for Ensuring Effective Climate Change Mitigation and Adaptation in Forest Areas Without Undermining Human Rights and Development*, http://rightsandclimatechange.files.wordpress.com/2008/10/foundations-for-effectiveness-14-oct-final-4-pages.pdf; See also Fry, I. (2008) 'Reducing emissions from deforestation and forest degradation: opportunities and pitfalls in developing a new legal regime', *Reciel*, 17(2): 166–166.

5   Friends of the Earth International (2008) *REDD Myths: A Critical Review of Proposed Mechanisms to Reduce Emissions from Deforestation and Forest Degradation in Developing Countries*, Issue 114.

6   RRI (2008) *Foundations for Effectivenes: A Framework for Ensuring Effective Climate Change Mitigation and Adaptation in Forest Areas Without Undermining Human Rights and Development*, http://rightsandclimatechange.files.wordpress.com/2008/10/foundations-for-effectiveness-14-oct-final-4-pages.pdf

7   See, for example, 'Message 4' on forest and climate issues made by a consortium of international forest-related agencies that recognizes that REDD and climate mitigation policies could harm forest peoples and 'swamp' recent progress towards more people-centred forest policies – Collaborative Partnership on Forests (2008) *Strategic Framework for Forests and Climate Change: A Proposal of the CPF for a Coordinated Forest-Sector Response to Climate Change* FAO, UNDP, UNEP, UNFCCC, UNCCD, CBD, GEF, World Agroforestry Centre, IUFRO, IUCN, ITTO, CIFOR www.fao.org/forestry/cpf-climatechange. On the other hand, these agencies do not acknowledge the social and other risks associated with their calls for support for 'alternative livelihoods' in forest and climate initiatives in 'Message 3', or their calls for 'tree planting' on smallholder farms and continuation and simplification of CDM tree planting projects (Message 2). See also, UN REDD Programme (2008) *UN Collaborative Programme on Reducing Emissions from Deforestation and*

Forest Degradation in Developing Countries (UN REDD) Framework Document, 20 June 2008, FAO, UNDP, UNEP at page 5.

8   See, for example, Campbell, A., Clark, S., Coad, L., Miles, L., Bolt, K. and Roe, D. (2008) 'Protecting the future: Carbon, forests, protected areas and local livelihoods', *Biodiversity*, 9(3–4): 117–121.

9   REDD Monitor (2008) *The Eliasch Review: Decent Analysis, Shame About the Conclusions*, www.redd-monitor.org/2008/10/14/eliasch-review-decent-analysis-shame-about-the-conclusions/

10 Eliasch, J. (2008) *Climate Change: Financing Global Forests. The Eliasch Review*, Office of Climate Change, London.

11 ANAM (2008) *FCPF R-PIN: Panama*, 7 April 2008

12 www.forestpeoples.org/documents/s_c_america/paraguay_capi_wb_redd_oct08_sp.pdf

13 Dooley, K. et al. (2008) op. cit.

14 Colchester, M. and Lohmann, L. (1990) *The Tropical Forestry Action Plan: What Progress?*, WRM and *The Ecologist*, Penang and Sturminster Newton; see also Hildyard, N., Hegde, P., Wolverkamp, P. and Reddy, S. (1998) *Same Platform, Different Train: The Politics of Participation*, www.thecornerhouse.org.uk/item.shtml?x=51958

15 See, for example, Tebtebba (2008) *Guide on Climate Change and Indigenous Peoples*, Tebtebba Foundation, Baguio; see also Barnesly, I. (2008) *Pocket Guide to Reducing Emissions from Deforestation and Forest Fegradation in Developing Countries: A Guide for Indigenous Peoples*, United Nations University Institute of Advanced Studies (UNU-IAS), Yokohama.

16 Larson, A.M. and Ribot, J.C. (2007) 'The poverty of forestry policy: Double standards on an uneven playing field', *Sustainability Science*, 2(2): 189–204.

17 Dooley, K. et al. (2008) op. cit.

18 Dooley, K. et al. (2008) op. cit.

19 Bulkan, J. (2008) 'Not all the information reported from Minister Robert Persaud's address to the joint meeting of the IDB, GFC, CI is found on the GFC website' *Stabroek News, Sunday 23 November 2008*, www.stabroeknews.com/letters/not-all-the-information-reported-from-minister-robert-persaud%E2%80%99s-address-to-the-joint-meeting-of-the-idb-gfc-ci-is-found-on-the-gfc-website/

20 See, for example, Griffiths, T., Rebbapragada, R. and Kalluri, B. (2005) 'The great "community forest management" swindle si India – critical evaluation of an ongoing World Bank-financed project in Andhra Pradesh' in *Broken Promises: How World Bank Policies Fail to Protect Forests and Forest People' Rights*, World Rainforest Movement, FPP, RF-UK, EDF, Global Witness, www.forestpeoples.org/documents/ifi_igo/wb_forests_joint_pub_apr05_eng.pdf

21 Nababan, A. (2008) *Keynote Speech: Inclusive Climate Change Solutions*, Presentation made by the Secretary General of Aliansi Masyarakat Adat Nusantara (Indigenous Peoples' Alliance of the Archipelago), Indonesia to the Global Forest Leaders Forum, Preston Auditorium, World Bank, Washington, DC, 17 September 2008.

22 Sunderlin, W., Angelsen, A. and Roberts, T. (2008) *Rights: An Essential Precondition for Effectiveness, Efficiency and Equity in REDD*, Presentation to 'Rights, Forests and Climate Change' joint conference convened by Rights and Resources Initiative and Rainforest Foundation Norway, Oslo, 15–17 October 2008; see also Humphreys, D. (2008) 'The politics of 'avoided deforestation': historical context and contemporary issues', *International Forestry Review*, 10(3): 433–442.

23 Persson, U.M. and Azar, C. (2007) 'Tropical deforestation in a future international climate policy regime – lessons from the Brazilian Amazon', *Mitigation, Adaptation Strategies Global Change*, 12: 1277–1304.

24 Kaimowitz, D. (2008) 'The prospects for REDD in Mesoamerica', *International Forestry Review*, 10(3): 485–495.

25 Seymour, F. (2008) *Forests, Climate Change and Human Rights: Managing Risk and Trade Offs*, CIFOR, Bogor.

26 Government of Panama (2008) *FCPF R-PIN: Panama*, 7 April 2008.

27 While the Panama REDD concept does plan to support measures to 'strengthen indigenous peoples and other forest dwellers who reside or work in critical areas of deforestation, through community investment projects', it seems this applies primarily to areas in the Ngöbe-Buglé region, cf. Richa, G. (2008) *REDD: Complement to the Future Climate*, ANAM Environmental Economics Unit, Panama – Presentation to joint conference convened by Rights and Resources Initiative and Rainforest Foundation Norway, Oslo, 15–17 October 2008.

28 www.newscientist.com/article/mg19726481.400-save-the-climate-by-saving-the-forests.html

29 Johns, T., Merry, F., Stickler, C., Nepstad, D., Laporte, N. and Goetz, S. (2008) 'A three-fund approach to incorporating government, public and private forest stewards into a REDD funding mechanism', *International Forestry Review*, 10(3): 458–464.

30 Karsenty, A. (2008) The architecture of proposed REDD schemes after Bali: Facing critical choices, *International Forestry Review*, 10(3): 443–457.

31 Dooley, K. et al. (2008) op. cit.

32 Laporte, N., Merry, F., Baccini, Goetz, S., Stabach, J. and Bowman, M. (2007) *REDD: Reducing CO₂ Emissions from Deforestation and Degradation in the Democratic Republic of Congo – a First Look*, (report for UNFCCC COP 13, Bali) Woods Hole Research Center, Falmouth, MA

33 For a critique of the flawed Woods Hole REDD analysis, see REDD Monitor (2008) *Woods Hole Research Centre: A Reliable Advisor on REDD?*, www.redd-monitor.org/2008/10/19/woods-hole-research-centre-a-reliable-advisor-on-redd/

34 See, for example, ASB (2007) *Opportunities for Avoided Deforestation with Sustainable Benefits: An Interim Report of the ASB Partnership for the Tropical Forest Margins*, ASB (Alternatives to Slash and Burn) Partnership for the Tropical Forest Margins, Nairobi

35 'Focus on high conservation value forests', *WRM Bulletin No. 114*, January 2007, www.wrm.org.uy/bulletin/114/viewpoint.html#Policy

36 See especially, International Alliance of Indigenous and Tribal Peoples of the Tropical Forests (2005) *Our Knowledge Our Survival: Traditional Forest Related Knowledge and the Implementation of Related International Commitments*, IAITPTF and CIFOR, Chiang Mai and Bogor; see also: Colchester, M. (ed) (2001) *A Survey of Indigenous Land Tenure*, FPP, Moreton-in-Marsh

37 White, A. (2008) op. cit. note 2.

38 Colchester, M., Farhan Ferrari, M., Nelson, J., Kidd, C., Zaninka, P., Venant, M., Regpala, L., Balawag, G.T., Motin, B. and Lasimbang, B. (2008) *Conservation and Indigenous Peoples: Assessing the Progress since Durban*, FPP, Moreton-in-Marsh (Draft report), www.forestpeoples.org/documents/conservation/wcc_conservation_and_ips_interim_rep_sept08_eng.pdf

39 Venant, M. with Nelson, J. (2008) *Securing Indigenous Peoples' Rights in Conservation: Reviewing and Promoting Progress in Cameroon*, FPP and Okani, Moreton-in-Marsh.

40 Colchester, M., Boscolo, M., Contreras-Hermosilla, A., Del Gatto, F., Dempsey, J., Lesccuyer G., Obidzinski, K., Pommier, D., Richards, M., Sembiring, S.N., Tacconi, L., Vargas Rios, M.T. and Wells, A. (2006) *Justice in the Forest: Rural Livelihoods and Forest Law Enforcement*, CIFOR, Bogor.

41 See Colchester, M. (2007) *Beyond Tenure, Rights-Based Approaches to Peoples and Forests: Some Lessons from the Forest Peoples Programme*, Paper presented to the conference 'Towards a New Global Forest Agenda' organized by the Rights and Resources Initiative, Swedish International Development Cooperation Agency, and the Stockholm School of Economics, 29 October 2007.

42 Blomley, T. (2008) *Avoided Deforestation, Community Forestry and Options for Channeling Payments to the Community Level: Lessons from Tanzania*, Presentation to 'Rights, Forests and Climate Change' A joint conference convened by Rights and Resources Initiative and Rainforest Foundation Norway, Oslo.

43 Dooley, K., et al. (2008) op. cit.

44 Statement by Mina Setra to the UN REDD Programme – see UN REDD Programme (2008) *Global Indigenous Peoples' Consultation on Reducing Emissions from Deforestation and Forest Degradation (REDD)* Baguio City, Philippines, 12–14 November 2008 at page 9.

45 Kajir, A. (2008) Statement to UN REDD Programme – see UN REDD Programme (2008) *Global Indigenous Peoples' Consultation on Reducing Emissions from Deforestation and Forest Degradation (REDD)*, Baguio City, Philippines, 12–14 November 2008 at page 10.

46 Bond, I. (2008) *Compensation and incentives for the Maintenance of Ecosystem Services: A Review of Current Knowledge*, Presentation to 'Rights, Forests and Climate Change' A joint conference convened by Rights and Resources Initiative and Rainforest Foundation Norway, Oslo, 15–17 October 2008

47 May, P.H., Boyd, E., Veiga, F. and Chang, M. (2004) *Local Sustainable Development Effects of Forest Carbon Projects in Brazil and Bolivia*, Environmental Economics Programme, IIED, London; Robertson, N. and Wunder, S. (2005) op. cit. note 57.

48 Kaimowitz, D. (2008) 'The prospects for REDD in Mesoamerica', *International Forestry Review*, 10(3): 485–495.

49 Ibid.

50 Camacho, S.M.A., Reyes, G.V., Miranda, Q.M. and Segura, B.O. (2003) *Gestión local y participación en torno al Pago por Servicios Ambientales: Estudios de caso en Costa Rica*, Fundación Prisma.

51 May, P., Boyd, E., Chang, M. and Veiga Neto, F.C. (2005) Incorporating sustainable development in carbon forest projects in Brazil and Bolivia, *Estudios Sociedade e Agricultura 1 (2005)*

52 Cerda, J. (2008) Statement to UN REDD global consultation meeting, November 2008 – see UN REDD Programme (2008) *Global Indigenous Peoples' Consultation on Reducing Emissions from Deforestation and Forest Degradation (REDD)*, op. cit. note 44.

53 ICRAF (2006) 'Clean rivers, lighted lights: Monetary rewards for reducing sediment', *RUPES Sumberjaya Brief No. 2*, World Agroforestry Centre, Bogor; ICRAF (2007) 'In Bakun, indigenous peoples use modern mechanisms for selling environmental services to preserve a traditional way of life without its poverty traps', *Site Profile: RUPES Bakun* ICRAF, Baguio City.

54 Wunder, S. (2006) 'Are direct payments for environmental services spelling doom for sustainable forest management in the tropics?', *Ecology and Society*, 11 (2): 23.

55 Wunder, S. (2008) 'The efficiency of payments for eenvironmental services in tropical conservation', *Conservation Biology*, 21(1): 48–58.

56 Karsenty, A. (2004) 'Des rentes contre le développment? Les nouveaux instruments d'acquisition mondiale de la biodiversité et l'utilisation des terres dans les pays tropicaux', *Mondes en development*, 127(3): 1–9. See also, Friends of the Earth International (2005) *Nature for Sale: Privatization – the Impacts of Privatizing Water and Biodiversity*, FOEI, Amsterdam, www.foei.org/en/publications/pdfs/privatization.pdf. See also, Global Forest Coalition (2007) *Potential Policy Approaches and Positive Incentives to Reduce Emissions from Deforestation in Developing Countries*, A submission to the Secretariat of the Framework Convention on Climate Change, www.wrm.org.uy/GFC/material/Incentives_Reduce_Emissions.html.

57 See, for example, Robertson, N. and Wunder, S. (2005) *Fresh Tracks in the Forest: Assessing Incipient Payments for Environmental Services Initiatives in Bolivia*, CIFOR, Bogor.

58 Agrawal, A. (2008) Livelihoods, Carbon and Diversity of Community Forests: Trade Offs and Win Wins? Presentation to 'Rights, Forests and Climate Change' A joint conference convened by Rights and Resources Initiative & Rainforest Foundation Norway Oslo, Norway, 15–17 October 2008

59 Rubens, H.B., Talocchi, S. et al. (2002) *Payment for Environmental Services: Brazil*, Fundación Prisma.

60 E.g. Hall, A. (2008) 'Better RED than dead: Paying the people for environmental services in Amazonia', *Philosophical Transactions of the Royal Society*, 363: 1925–1932.

61 Agrawal, A. (2008) 'Livelihoods, carbon and diversity of community forests: trade offs and win wins? Presentation to 'Rights, Forests and Climate Change' A joint conference convened by Rights and Resources Initiative & Rainforest Foundation Norway Oslo, Norway, 15–17 October 2008.

62 Norfolk, S. (2008) *Securing Rights to Territories Through Participatory Land Delimitation: Lessons for Scaling p*, Presentation to 'Rights, Forests and Climate Change' A joint conference convened by Rights and Resources Initiative and Rainforest Foundation Norway, Oslo, 15–17 October 2008.

Part 6

Moving Beyond the Debate:
The Need for Conservation–Poverty
Partnerships

Editors' Introduction

Parts 1 to **5** of this Reader have illustrated how the conservation and development communities have both been urged to recognize and address the links between biodiversity conservation and poverty reduction. We note in the editors' introduction to **Part 1** that one source of disagreement in the conservation and poverty debate arises from the tendency to generalize and to disregard complexities or different contexts when passing judgement on the links between conservation and poverty. Other sources of divergence arise from failures to understand the different agendas and ways of working of different organizations; the lack of knowledge of different academic disciplines and so on.

In order to address these limitations, partnerships have been urged between the conservation and development communities; between natural and social scientists; and between those who make or implement policy and those who are affected by it. Vermeulen and Sheil (2007) note 'Partnerships are no panacea, but a real commitment to partnership offers conservation outcomes that are more ethical and often more practicable than current models.'

Many of our earlier readings make reference to partnerships and in **Part 6** we present a final set of readings that focus specifically on this issue.

In Chapter 31, Walpole (2006) highlights the practical reality that, ethical concerns aside, there is a missed opportunity for biodiversity conservation if conservation organizations don't engage with development and humanitarian agencies where there is geographical overlap between areas of high biodiversity and high poverty. Developing meaningful partnerships with development agencies doesn't mean that conservation organizations should try to fulfil the role of governments, donor agencies or development organizations but rather that they could seize an opportunity to 'harness' development processes for symbiotic benefits with conservation and ensure that, just as development agencies ask conservationists to contribute to their poverty reduction agenda, so conservationists can ask development agencies to ensure biodiversity is not marginalized. Achieving this requires much better levels of understanding on both sides and deeper local-level collaboration than has been the case to date.

Similarly in Chapter 32, Brosius (2006) calls for constructive engagement – this time challenging anthropologists to move on from critique (e.g. Chapters 17 and 21) to providing practical evidence and examples of how their analyses can inform and improve conservation practice: 'Rather than standing on the outside, we need to work with conservation practitioners and offer our analyses in ways that subject our own critiques to examination.' At the same time Brosius recognizes this has to be two-way process and that conservation organizations need to recognize the value and validity of the social scientists and their potential contribution to more effective conservation. The overall challenge is to search for areas of consensus – however modest – rather than positions at opposing ends of contentious debates.

Finally in Chapter 33, Adams (2007) concludes that the 'real challenge for today's conservationist is to learn to think like a human'. The issue is not so much about interdisciplinary teams or partnerships, but about 'interdisciplinary people', a form of inner partnership.

At the heart of the debates highlighted and explored in this book lies a challenge to conservation organizations to articulate and integrate the 'human' element back into conservation decision-making. But there is also a challenge to development agencies and social scientists to recognize the intrinsic value of biodiversity and the fundamental necessity for conservation in an uncertain and unstable world. Linking conservation and poverty reduction will continue to be difficult and complex and will require clear and fair decision-making where there are trade-offs. But the need for practical progress is paramount – it is not enough to sit and comment from the sidelines.

References

Adams, W.M. (2007) 'Thinking like a human: Social science and the two cultures problem', *Oryx*, 41(2): 275–276.

Brosius (2006) 'Common ground between anthropology and conservation biology', *Conservation Biology*, 20(3): 683–685.

Vermeulen, S. and Sheil. D. (2007) 'Partnerships for tropical conservation', *Oryx*, 41(4): 434–440.

Walpole, M. (2006) 'Partnerships for conservation and poverty reduction', *Oryx*, 40(3): 245–246.

Chapter 31

Partnerships for Conservation and Poverty Reduction

Matt Walpole

Most of us probably think of Chad as somewhere dry and dusty in the heart of the Sahara, and it may be a surprise to discover that it has just designated the world's third largest RAMSAR wetland site. The floodplains of the Aouk and Salamat rivers, covering 50,000km in southern Chad, are the breeding grounds for several migratory water birds and numerous large mammals, including the largest remaining elephant population in the Sahel.

This area is not far from the conflict-ridden Darfur region of Sudan, and violence and refugees frequently spill over the border. As Chad also tops Transparency International's list of the world's most corrupt governments, and is fourth from bottom of the UN's Human Poverty Index, the prospects for conservation, and for people, may seem bleak. But Chad has discovered oil, and World Bank funding has been tied to government commitments to spend oil revenues on health, education and rural development (but not the environment). Inevitably the government is backtracking, and the World Bank suspended funding in January. Nevertheless, in the UN Year of Deserts and Desertification (Fisher, 2006) it is a development worth watching.

It also prompts a question. Whilst most responsible governments are expected to invest their resources in raising people out of poverty, to what extent does this responsibility extend to big business or, for that matter, to conservationists? Although this was debated extensively in *Oryx* in 2004 (38: 119–120, 137–147), the answer remains elusive.

As with oil companies, international conservation organizations have been criticized over their record on poverty and human rights. Protectionist conservation strategies can impose disproportionate costs on people. Where conservation conflicts with local interests, so the argument goes, local interests lose out, and with them goes any local support for conservation. This is bad for everyone, and there are both ethical and strategic reasons for ensuring that the costs of conservation, whatever they may be, do not fall disproportionately on the poor.

Reprinted from *Oryx*, vol 40, no 3, Walpole, M., 'Partnerships for conservation and poverty reduction', pp. 245–246, copyright © Fauna & Flora International (2008) with permission from Cambridge University Press, Cambridge.

Of particular relevance, and highlighted in this issue, is human–wildlife conflict mitigation. Threatened large mammals are rarely loved by the people living with them. Global conservation flagships can be local pests, and if livestock predation and crop raiding are not addressed, such species are persecuted (Altrichter et al., 2006). Fortunately a great deal of conservation science and practice is being brought to bear to find solutions to offset the costs borne by poor rural communities. Two papers in this issue of *Oryx* focus on crop-raiding African elephants, one testing the effects of farm-based crop protection methods (Sitati and Walpole, 2006) and the other exploring the viability of alternative cash crops that are less palatable to wildlife (Parker and Osborn, 2006). Both suggest that local solutions can be found.

Tackling the costs of conservation for the poor is one thing, but whether conservation organizations should be involved in poverty reduction remains hotly contested. Every conservation organization is keen to demonstrate how biodiversity conquers poverty, to keep the door to development funding unlocked and ensure that the environment is not the forgotten Millennium Development Goal. Yet for some, pledging to improve lives and livelihoods is straying beyond the conservation mandate into areas where we are ill-equipped to deliver. How far should we go, and under what circumstances is it legitimate to do so?

It is clear that poverty and conservation are often interlinked. Two papers in the previous issue of *Oryx* revealed the importance to poorer rural households in Madagascar of harvesting bats (Goodman, 2006) and crayfish (Jones et al., 2006). A study of turtle harvesting in China in this issue points to the financial benefits of illegal trade in otherwise low-income villages as a powerful incentive to continue the practice (Shiping et al., 2006).

It is less clear whether conservation can offer people a genuine route out of poverty, or whether poverty reduction efforts will bring conservation gains. We know that simplistic models that predict benefits for both conservation and poverty reduction are generally unrealistic and unattainable. In some cases conservation efforts can bring benefits to the poor but there are inevitably trade-offs that can shift the balance considerably in the wrong direction. At the same time a dogged adherence to livelihoods-focused initiatives may reduce poverty and increase well-being in ways that are counterproductive to conservation if increased affluence and opportunity simply fuel increased resource degradation. Poverty is rarely the only, or even the most urgent, threat to biodiversity.

Does this mean that we shouldn't bother, that attempts by conservationists to address poverty are misguided? There is no doubt that if we are blinkered to the practical challenges and the naivety of some of the assumptions then we risk undermining the ultimate goals of conservation and sustainable use of biodiversity. But there are good reasons why we should bother, and why in some cases we have little alternative.

In the poverty-stricken places where we work there is often no one else: no development agency, no government support programme, no opportunity. Can we justify ignoring the issue? Conservation needs a local constituency of support, and poverty reduction acts as an entry point and mechanism to engender that support at grassroots levels.

Where there are full-scale poverty reduction and development programmes being implemented by the 'experts', are we prepared to let them take the usual, short-cut route to development that sidelines environmental concerns in the face of humanitarian expediency? Many high-biodiversity areas are also sites of human-itarian emergency, such as Cambodia, Liberia, Congo and Indonesia. If it is not the aftermath of civil conflict then it is a natural disaster, with the unluckiest, like Aceh, suffering both. These areas witness a flood of development assistance from an army of humanitarian organizations, but how often is any consideration given to longer-term concerns for biodiversity and environmental sustainability when short-term needs for food and shelter and means to make a living appear so much more pressing? Conservation organizations will have a much louder voice if they engage with recovery and reconstruction efforts, if they take human needs seri-ously and act to address them in a way that demonstrates to humanitarian agencies that it can be done with due consideration for biodiversity, the environment and the longer term, than if they sit on the sidelines lamenting the destruction of the forests for the rebuilding of houses.

Ultimately, of course, we cannot and should not try to fulfil the role of govern-ments, development agencies or even the private sector when it comes to disaster relief, poverty reduction and the provision of livelihood opportunities for the poor. But if we want to put the environment and biodiversity back at the heart of sustain-able development we are going to have to do two things. First, we must become much more sophisticated in how we assess our impacts on people, and a lot clearer about which aspects of biodiversity really contribute to the well-being of the poor and which aspects require alternative rationales for their conservation. Second, and here I echo Sanderson and Redford's Editorial (2003), we must work harder to develop meaningful cross-sectoral partnerships with those who do development. Harnessing development in the name of conservation, and ensuring conservation is not marginalized by development, requires both sides to work together and understand each other more emphatically than has been the case to date.

To help achieve these two things, Fauna & Flora International has established a Livelihoods Programme that is enabling us to reflect on how and why we are addressing human needs, improving our monitoring and impact analysis across a range of projects worldwide, and providing tools and guidelines to ensure that we achieve our mission effectively. A major component of the programme is evalu-ating and enhancing cross-sectoral partnerships for conservation and human well-being in the wake of natural disasters and civil conflict. The challenge is finding the right partners and making the partnerships work. Learning from our experi-ences to date will be the first step in meeting that challenge.

References

Altrichter, M., Boaglio, G. and Perovic, P. (2006) 'The decline of jaguars *Panthera onca* in the Argentine Chaco', *Oryx*, 40: 302–309.

Fisher, M. (2006) 'Don't desert drylands', *Oryx*, 40: 1–2.

Goodman, S.M. (2006) 'Hunting of *Microchiroptera* in southwestern Madagascar', *Oryx*, 40: 225–228.

Jones, J.P.G., Andriahajaina, F.B., Ranambinintsoa, E.H., Hockley, N.J. and Ravoahangimalala, O. (2006) 'The economic importance of freshwater crayfish harvesting in Madagascar and the potential of community-based conservation to improve management', *Oryx*, 40: 168–175.

Parker, G.E. and Osborn, F.V. (2006) 'Investigating the potential for chilli to reduce human-wildlife conflict in Zimbabwe', *Oryx*, 40: 343–346.

Sanderson, S.E. and Redford, K.H. (2003) 'Contested relationships between biodiversity conservation and poverty reduction', *Oryx*, 37: 389–390.

Shiping, G., Jichao, W., Haitao, S., Riheng, S. and Rumei, X. (2006) 'Illegal trade and conservation needs of freshwater turtles in Nanmao, Hainan Province, China', *Oryx*, 40: 331–336.

Sitati, N.W. and Walpole, M.J. (2006) 'Assessing farm-based measures for mitigating human-elephant conflict in Transmara District, Kenya', *Oryx*, 40: 279–286.

Chapter 32

Common Ground between Anthropology and Conservation Biology

J. Peter Brosius

In recent years, a remarkable florescence of environmental scholarship across a range of disciplines has occurred. One manifestation of this trend is a proliferation of studies by anthropologists focused on conservation at various sites around the globe. A starting premise for many anthropologists is that many of the practices that define conservation – establishing and enforcing boundaries, curtailing subsistence activities, negotiating benefits – are inherently political.

Our interest in the political dimensions of conservation derives in part from recent theoretical trends. Anthropologists have lately recognized that the contours of power are more convoluted and more implicit than was once thought. Across a range of disciplines the theoretical landscape is defined by a concern with questions of the links between the production of knowledge and the exercise of power. Anthropologists want to know how knowledge is produced and who is empowered to produce it, how it circulates, and how some forms of expertise are considered authoritative whereas others are marginalized. In the view of many anthropologists, a critical perspective alert to matters of culture, power and history can lead to conservation practices that are both more effective and more just (Brosius et al., 2005). In planning for conservation, these anthropologists believe it is vital that conservation practitioners understand not only the human impact on the environment but also how that environment is constructed, represented, claimed and contested.

Conservation scientists also recognize that conservation is inherently political, but this means different things to anthropologists and conservation practitioners. Whereas conservation biologists recognize political processes at particular sites, anthropologists see politics in other places as well. Conservation is a nexus of relationships – between large organizations and donors, between organizations and governments, between scientists and local people, and so forth. In the very act of biological knowledge making about the world and in techniques for visualizing and managing ecosystems, anthropologists see a cultural politics of nature they regard as too obvious to ignore. When we hear conservation scientists ask, 'At what scale should we assess the state of biodiversity and work to protect it? How much is enough?' or 'What are the best available techniques for achieving conservation goals at particular sites?' anthropologists ask, 'Who speaks for nature?'

Anthropologists' critical commentaries sometimes frame conservation issues in ways that challenge fundamental assumptions held by the conservation community, and they are usually not well received. I write this as one who has produced just these kinds of critiques (Brosius and Russell, 2003; Brosius, 2006) in ongoing research focused on what might be termed the *strategic turn* in conservation, evident most notably in the linked enterprises of ecoregional conservation planning and conservation finance, and supported by new mechanisms to measure success and ensure accountability. The comprehensive visions being produced in the emerging complementarities of spatial planning, investment and social-ecological metrics are reshaping the strategic visions of major conservation organizations and have transformed the practice of conservation. It is worth asking what is at stake, and for whom, in this proliferation of blueprints for the future of the planet. As major conservation organizations working at these larger scales are compelled to provide ever more rigorous metrics of accountability to donors, do they not become less accountable to local actors? Are these organizations consolidating their authority over global conservation practices and monopolizing conservation funding through the very complexity of the methods, metrics and administrative techniques they employ?

Questions such as these present certain difficulties for the relationship between anthropologists and conservation practitioners. Whatever value anthropologists see in such studies, conservation practitioners have rarely found them useful. Conservation practitioners are compelled by a well-founded sense of urgency. Anthropological critiques are therefore perceived as a luxury that conservationists cannot afford. Anthropologists are seen to be fiddling while Rome burns. Furthermore, what anthropologists view as critiques derived from a particular set of theoretical premises, those in the conservation community view as criticisms, and this creates resentment. The fact that anthropologists, although prepared to critique, often fail to provide alternatives, only reinforces the perception that their criticisms are corrosive, irresponsible and without validity.

Another source of difficulty in the relationship between anthropologists and the conservation community emerges when anthropologists position themselves as spokespersons for local communities. This leads many conservation practitioners to regard anthropologists as persistent obstructionists. What to anthropologists seems self-evident – that ethnographic research can provide rich, textured accounts of local lives – appears to many in the conservation community as noise, eruptions of particularity against the smooth sine wave of conservation policy. Anthropologists are forever sounding the discordant note, and for conservationists this gets old.

Additionally, there is an inherent set of assumptions about the value and role of the social sciences that results in certain incommensurability of research agendas. Because the first priority of conservation biologists is to preserve biodiversity, they see that the value of the social sciences lies in their ability to help them achieve this goal more effectively. When anthropologists provide data conservation biologists find useful (i.e. deliverables) their participation is welcomed. However, differences often emerge between anthropologists and conservation scientists over the question of what constitutes useful data. Because anthropologists stress the importance of understanding the complexities that appear when conservation initiatives encounter local communities and national political cultures, they believe they should have a role beyond that of data providers. For many anthropologists, developing an understanding of those engaged in saving biodiversity is as critical a task as trying to understand the local communities that are the focus of most conservation efforts. When anthropologists examine the practices of conservation practitioners, their contributions are rarely welcomed.

Finally, anthropologists and conservation practitioners have very different perceptions of who is privileged and who is marginalized in the conservation domain. Anthropologists who study conservation often see conservation scientists as embodying power both through their knowledge-making activities and in the assumption that they speak authoritatively for nature and how it should be managed. Likewise anthropologists who have worked at conservation sites see the social sciences – especially anthropology – treated as an afterthought, and they feel thoroughly marginalized. Conservation biologists, on the other hand, see themselves as the ones who are marginalized. They are engaged in a struggle against extractive industries, developers, well-armed bushmeat cartels, corrupt governments, and others. Furthermore, they feel compelled to respond to agendas set by social scientists situated in donor agencies that mandate addressing concerns such as livelihood issues, gender equity, and community participation. They find the suggestion that they exercise inordinate power ridiculous.

As an anthropologist who views the world through a critical lens, I am drawn to questions of the sort I have described. Anthropologists cannot simply will these kinds of critical questions away, nor should we. We have good reason to operate in a critical mode and to be hesitant about merely providing deliverables. Ours is a discipline that has devoted a good deal of effort coming to terms with our involvement in colonial projects, the Cold War, Vietnam and the Green Revolution, and we are wary of participating in projects that might position us to once again be co-opted. This hesitation was given theoretical shape when, a couple of decades ago, anthropology went through a crisis of representation that compelled us to interrogate our knowledge-making practices and our presumption of representing or speaking for others. Whatever else anthropology is today, it is not about figuring out how to manage people better. However, as one of my students pointed out, conservation biology has not had and cannot afford to have a crisis of representation. Conservation organizations fighting the sixth great extinction have a clear mandate to do something about the erosion of biodiversity, and research by social scientists must therefore be judged on its utility. Little wonder then that, compared with other environmental social sciences that have produced powerful analytical tools that conservation organizations and government agencies can use to shape or judge the success of conservation initiatives, anthropology comes up short. Anthropological critiques of conservation typically offer little to those engaged in the work of preserving biodiversity.

Given such a great epistemological gulf, is there any hope for fruitful engagement? I believe there is. But it requires that anthropologists rethink the convergence zone between their critiques and the forms of practice promoted by conservation scientists. We must premise this effort to bridge critique and engagement on recognition of the value of anthropological assessments of conservation and on recognition that critique alone is not enough. Anthropologists must challenge themselves to take their analyses to the next step: linking critique with engagement by showing in concrete form how their analyses can inform the practices of conservation practitioners and by providing alternatives. A key entailment of this proposition is that anthropologists must identify policies and projects that appear to be working according to criteria they think are important, and they must provide clear and detailed assessments of why those are successful. Furthermore, anthropologists can do a better job in the way they offer their critiques: they must provide them in and through a process of meaningful engagement with those whose practices they are examining. Rather than standing on the outside, we need to work with conservation practitioners and offer our analyses in ways that subject our own critiques to examination.

Productive engagement also places a demand on the conservation community to recognize that, although conservation biology is an important tool, alone it cannot provide answers to the challenges facing contemporary conservation because the questions it asks are too limited. I believe conservation biologists have something to learn from the kinds of questions anthropologists ask.

Anthropologists and conservation biologists alike would also do well to remember that, whatever issues divide them, both have one important thing in common: as Kent Redford reminds us, we are both committed to standing against the forces that are producing a more homogeneous world. Compared with the global forces that are driving this process, neither group is particularly privileged (King and Biggs, 2005). Although the focus and tools may differ, there are many more points of commonality than have been discovered.

Perhaps part of the problem has been that anthropologists have devoted too much attention to positioning themselves in debates about the 'big' issues (e.g. Should conservation aspire to satisfy development goals? Is there ever any justification for strict protection?) that only ever seem to lead to sterile polemics. If the search for new languages of collaboration between conservation biologists and anthropologists is of value, modest points of consensus should be sought – in small ways, in particular places, in 'situated collaborations' (to paraphrase Haraway, 1988). It still will not be easy, but discovering modest agreements in unexpected places is our best hope for creating a foundation of emergent understandings in our efforts to preserve a diverse world.

References

Brosius, J.P. (2006) 'Seeing communities: Technologies of visualization in conservation', in Creed, G. (ed) *Reconsidering Community: The Unintended Consequences of an Intellectual Romance*, School of American Research Press, Santa Fe, New Mexico.

Brosius, J.P. and Russell, D. (2003) 'Conservation from above: An anthropological perspective on transboundary protected areas and ecoregional planning', *Journal of Sustainable Forestry,* 17: 39–65.

Brosius, J.P., Tsing, A. and Zerner, C. (2005) *Communities and Conservation: Histories and Politics of Community-Based Natural Resource Management*, Altamira Press, Lanham.

Haraway, D. (1988) 'Situated knowledges: The science question in feminism and the privilege of partial perspective', *Feminist Studies,* 14: 575–599.

King, N. and Biggs, H. (2005) *Seeking Common Ground: How Natural and Social Scientists Might Jointly Create a Unified Worldview for Sustainable Livelihoods*, Teleseminar, Transboundary Protected Areas Research Initiative, Wits, South Africa.

Chapter 33

Thinking Like a Human: Social Science and the Two Cultures Problem

Wiliam M. Adams

This much we know: most people active in conservation are trained as biologists, yet most of the problems of conservation are to do with people. Ask a room full of conservationists, young and excited or old and world-weary, where the biggest threats to biodiversity and the success of conservation lie, and they will point to the workings of society, economy and politics. People, they always say, are the problem.

And yet we mostly recruit biologists into conservation, not social scientists. There is a Society for Conservation Biology (SCB), but no society for conservation sociology, or conservation anthropology or conservation political science. These disciplines do not exist as such in universities. They have no journals. They train no graduates. Of course, social scientists have made major contributions to conservation (Brosius, 2006) and the SCB has a very active Social Science Working Group. However, it remains a fact that the core expertise needed to solve the problems of global conservation has to be painstakingly learned by people trained in quite different ways of thinking.

Conservation biologists know they need to reach out beyond their base in the core science disciplines. Thus Michael Mascia and his colleagues argue that 'to preserve the earth's natural heritage, the social sciences must become central to conservation science and practice' (Mascia et al., 2003). Amen to that. The question is, how do we do it?

There are numerous barriers to integrating social science and conservation, both in the real world and the minds of conservationists (Fox et al., 2006). What we do reflects what we think, and if we are not trained to understand how society works it is quite likely that what we do about society's demands on nature will be crude, unpopular and ineffective. This is pretty much how conservation's critics describe them (Chapin, 2004).

I believe that conservation suffers from a version of the 'two cultures' problem outlined by the British scientist, novelist and civil servant C.P. Snow in his Rede Lecture in 1959 on *The Two Cultures and the Scientific Revolution*. Snow's purpose was to draw attention to the importance of science and technology in the improvement of the human condition. Scientists, he thought 'had the future in their bones' (Snow, 1998, p. 10). He argued that two distinct cultures were emerging, 'scientists' and 'literary intellectuals'. The latter he described as 'natural luddites' (p. 22), and he mocked their ignorance of the Second Law of Thermodynamics: 'the great edifice of modern physics goes up, and the majority of the cleverest people in the western world have about as much insight into it as their neolithic ancestors would have had' (p. 15).

Snow's lecture stimulated an extensive debate across the world (Collini, 1998). It is clear in retrospect that his concepts of 'literary intellectual', and indeed 'scientist', were straw people, and his rhetorical structure was too slight for the weight of argument subsequently hung upon it. But he captured something important about the power of science in the aftermath of the Second World War, the ignorance of science on the part of the British elite (and the education system that nurtured it), and the lack of mutual comprehension across disciplines.

These factors remain relevant, not least to conservation. Its leaders are mostly highly educated in the biology of organisms and ecosystems. But what do they know of social theory, political economy, and the economics of institutions? As conservationists we mostly lack the knowledge and language to be able properly to understand and talk about the most significant problems we face, and we lack the language to have an effective conversation with those who claim (on the basis of their social science training) they have the understanding we need.

Arun Agrawal and Elinor Ostrom (2006) describe the 'dialogue of the deaf' between political science and conservation biology. This problem stretches right across the social sciences, and has at least three dimensions. First, issues of language and terminology prevent effective communication: much social science is unintelligible to natural scientists because of the complexity of language and concepts; many terms used by conservationists (e.g. 'community', 'tradition', 'household') and many assumptions (e.g. that people will always do what makes material economic sense) are profoundly simplistic and often misleading and misunderstood. Second, there are distinct communities of knowledge between the natural and social sciences, and different traditions of theoretical and historical understanding: without taxonomy, Tardigrades are just 'bugs'; without anthropology, ethnicity is just 'tribe', and any intelligent detailed discussion of biodiversity and society is still-born. Third, there are issues of epistemology, differences in how we know what we think we know, between the safe reductionist conventions of statistical methods and modelling (shared by social science disciplines such as macroeconomics and spatial human geography) and the complexities of qualitative analysis.

Conservation biologists often express bewilderment at the way social scientists revel in theory as something diverse to argue about, and see such argument as a way to enrich understanding of complex questions rather than to reduce them to their essential constituents; many social scientists seem confused over the role of statistical analysis and quantitative techniques, and have an inexplicable reluctance to speak in terms of evidence, facts and proof. On the other hand, social scientists often wince at the clunking number-crunching, the dependence on quantitative questionnaires and the arbitrary definitions involved in conservation scientists' attempts to understand people, and they express amazement at natural scientists' willingness to analyse society without reading relevant literature outside their discipline.

These differences can be expressed in academic terms, but they are also intensely practical. Lisa Campbell (2005) describes the plight of the social scientist on interdisciplinary teams in conservation: typically brought in late, working alone, and assigned a lowly position and confined to tackling tasks pre-specified by natural science colleagues. Social scientists are often asked 'what's the answer to this question?', when they want themselves to ask 'why is that the question you are asking?'

If we are to make real progress in conservation we have to take the challenges of the communication between different academic ways of understanding the world seriously. Deep interdisciplinary chasms are maintained by the apartheid of many university education curricula, and entrenched by the different disciplinary publication requirements and academic reward systems (Fox et al., 2006). There is a prejudice within many academic institutions in favour of issues at the core of disciplines against those at the margins, and in favour of pure and against applied work. Conservation biology, as a 'mission-driven discipline' (Meine et al., 2005), already suffers from this, in a world where science funding and career advancement reward highly specialized work. Yet to meet the needs of conservation we need thinking and education that reaches further, outside the natural and applied sciences altogether.

We have to recognize that what we need in conservation are not interdisciplinary teams, but inter-disciplinary people. Certainly, we must learn about one another's methods, and be prepared to understand and use effectively one another's tools, as the SCB's Catalog of Conservation Social Science Tools encourages (www.conbio.org/workinggroups/sswg/catalog/, or see White et al., 2005). However, our challenge is not to take biologists and equip them with the skills to get by in social surveys. Our real task is to create conservationists for whom these skills are innate, for whom the disciplinary boundaries so beloved of academic researchers are no constraint.

Aldo Leopold starts his essay *Thinking Like a Mountain*, by describing the death of a wolf that he has shot, and through it builds to his famous appeal for wildness as an antidote to 'safety, prosperity, comfort, long life, and dullness'. In the course of it he dismisses the rancher who exterminates wolves without realizing he must take on their job of controlling grazing herd numbers. That cowman has not, he says, learned to 'think like a mountain'. Leopold's point is that unless we think differently, we will not understand our task. Unlike the rancher, the conservationist must learn to think like a mountain if they are to achieve anything worthwhile.

We all know this story, and for my money Leopold is right about wildness. But I would argue that the essay is as important for what it says about the rancher as about the wolf. To me the real challenge for today's conservationist is to learn to think like a human.

References

Agrawal, A. and Ostrom, E. (2006) 'Political science and conservation biology: A dialogue of the deaf?', *Conservation Biology*, 20: 681–682.

Brosius, P. (2006) 'Common ground between anthropology and conservation biology', *Conservation Biology*, 20: 683–685.

Campbell, L.M. (2005) 'Overcoming obstacles to interdisciplinary research', *Conservation Biology*, 19: 574–577.

Chapin, M. (2004) 'A challenge to conservationists', *World Watch*, 17: 17–31.

Collini, S. (1998) 'Introduction', pp. vii–lxxi, in Snow, C.P., *The Two Cultures*, Cambridge University Press, Cambridge.

Fox, H., Christian, C., Nordby, J.C., Pregams, O.R.W., Petersen, G.D. and Pyke, C.R. (2006) 'Perceived barriers to integrating social science and conservation', *Conservation Biology*, 26: 1817–1820.

Mascia, M., Brosius, J.P., Dobson, T.A., Forbes, B.C., Horowitz, L., McKean, M.A. and Turner, N.J. (2003) 'Conservation and the social sciences', *Conservation Biology*, 17: 649–650.

Meine, C., Soule, M. and Noss, R.F. (2005) '"A mission-driven discipline": The growth of conservation biology', *Conservation Biology*, 20: 631–651.

Snow, C.P. (1998) *The Two Cultures*, Cambridge University Press, Cambridge.

White, P.C.L., Vaughan Jennings, N., Renwick, A.R. and Barker, N.H.L. (2005) 'Questionnaires in ecology: A review of past use and recommendations for best practice', *Journal of Applied Ecology*, 42: 421–430.

Additional Resources

There is a large and continually growing body of literature on poverty and conservation linkages. It is impossible to list here all the books, journals and grey literature that might be of interest to the reader. However, the majority of this literature has been captured by the Poverty and Conservation Learning Group (PCLG) and can be easily browsed on the PCLG website (http://povertyandconservation.info/en/bsearch.php).

PCLG is an initiative coordinated by the International Institute for Environment and Development (IIED). The Mission of the PCLG is to promote better understanding on the links between conservation and poverty in order to improve conservation and poverty policy and practice. One of the key strategies for accomplishing this is to collect, synthesize and disseminate relevant information, and this is done primarily through the PCLG website, where you can find:

- a bibliographic database that, with more than 1300 entries, provides details of the literature on conservation–poverty linkages;
- an 'organisations database' that identifies the range of organizations working on conservation–poverty linkages – including donor agencies, conservation organizations, NGOs, indigenous people's organizations and grassroots groups;
- an 'initiatives database' that describes significant international initiatives designed to explore the links between conservation and poverty reduction – from broad poverty–environment programmes to focused single-issue agendas.

The PCLG website also hosts a number of hyperlinks to external databases, websites and information services that might be of interest to the poverty and conservation practitioner. Some of these are included in the additional resource areas for the Reader identified below, organized as lists of newsletters, information services, databases, projects/programmes, professional associations and international initiatives.

If you would like to hear more about the PCLG, become a member, send us additional references, or sponsor the PCLG, please email pclg@iied.org.

Newsletters

Arborvitae is the IUCN/WWF Forest Conservation Newsletter that is published jointly by WWF and IUCN three times a year to disseminate general current information and share knowledge on key issues and events that impact the forestry sector and the conservation and sustainable use of forest resources.
www.iucn.org/about/work/programmes/forest/fp_news_events/fp_news_arborvitae/

BioSoc is an output of the Poverty and Conservation Learning Group (PCLG) – a multi-stakeholder forum facilitated by IIED that is intended to promote mutual learning between key stakeholders on poverty–conservation linkages. BioSoc highlights recently published articles on poverty and conservation linkages.
http://povertyandconservation.info/en/biosoc.php

Biodiversity for Development Newsletter is the newsletter of the CBD Secretariat's initiative on the linkages between biodiversity and development.
www.cbd.int/development

The **Environment & Poverty Times** aims to explain the complex links between poverty and the environment. It shows, through short texts, maps and other illustrations, some of the manifestations of poverty and environmental conditions.
www.grida.no/publications/et

id21 insights is an output of ID21 the research reporting service managed by the Institute of Development Studies in the UK. There are three editions, with the one focusing on natural resources published in paper and online format seven times a year.
www.id21.org/insights

Natural Resource Perspectives are produced by the Overseas Development Institute in the UK and present accessible information on current development issues.
www.odi.org.uk/nrp

Natureandpoverty.net is the IUCN Netherlands platform for practitioners working on ecosystem management and poverty alleviation. Natureandpoverty.net has recently launched its newsletter 'News from Nature and Poverty Knowledge and Learning Network'. This newsletter features updates on the work of Natureandpoverty.net and its network members.
www.natureandpoverty.net

PCLG News is the newsletter of the Poverty and Conservation Learning Group. It provides monthly news on the work of the PCLG and its members.
http://povertyandconservation.info/en/newslist.php

Information Services

Biodiversity Economics is a site managed by IUCN and WWF, which is intended to encourage and assist the use of economics in support of biodiversity conservation and sustainable development. The site provides a library, a search engine which explores authoritative sites, and a 'Basics' section is intended for visitors new to the economics of biodiversity.
www.biodiversityeconomics.org

CBNRM Net is a web portal for information and resources on community-based natural resource management.
www.cbnrm.net

The **Conservation Commons** is a collaborative effort to improve open access to data, information and knowledge related to the conservation and sustainable use of biodiversity.
http://conservationcommons.com

The main objective of **ConservationEvidence.com** is to improve practical conservation by increasing access to the experience of others. It disseminates information on the effectiveness of conservation practice though its collection of case studies and its online peer-reviewed journal.
www.conservationevidence.com

Development Gateway is a web portal on economic development, offering project information, articles, community features and many other resources.
www.developmentgateway.org

Eldis is an information service provided by the Institute of Development Studies. Its aim is to 'Support the documentation, exchange and use of evidence-based development knowledge'. It hosts resources on a wide range of development issues including biodiversity and poverty.
www.eldis.org

FRAMEweb is a USAID-funded programme to build knowledge-sharing networks of natural resource management professionals.
www.frameweb.org

ID21 is a research reporting service aiming to make policy-makers aware of the latest British development research findings. It includes a section dedicated to conservation and biodiversity.
www.id21.org/zinter/id21zinter.exe?a=l&w=e2

Livelihoods Connect is a learning platform for creating sustainable livelihoods to eliminate poverty. It provides a suite of information sharing, learning and management tools for researchers, policy-makers, consultants and practitioners working in a broad range of institutions around the world.
www.livelihoods.org

peopleandplanet.net provides a global review and internet gateway into the issues of population, poverty, health, consumption and the environment. It is published by Planet 21, an independent non-profit company and a registered British charity.
www.peopleandplanet.net

The **People and Wildlife Initiative** is an information and communications forum for matters related to human–wildlife conflict.
www.peopleandwildlife.org.uk

Poverty Environment Net is a dedicated website to promote improved efforts to address poverty–environment relationships globally. The purpose of the website is to collect and share knowledge and experiences on poverty–environment linkages, lessons learned and good practices in responding to poverty–environment challenges.
www.povertyenvironment.net

PovertyNet is a World Bank web portal that provides an introduction to key issues as well as in-depth information on poverty measurement, monitoring, analysis, and on poverty reduction strategies for researchers and practitioners.
www.worldbank.org/poverty

Poverty-wellbeing.net is the internet platform of the Social Development Division (SoDev) of the Swiss Agency for Development and Cooperation (SDC). The platform provides resources on the following themes: sustainable livelihoods approaches, pro-poor policy, empowerment, poverty impact and effectiveness, and focus on poverty.
www.poverty-wellbeing.net

The **Protected Areas Learning Network (PALNet)** is intended to compile and disseminate information relating to protected area management. The site includes databases of protected area experts, projects and documents.
www.parksnet.org

Databases

Case Study Database is an online tool hosted by the Centre for Community-Based Resource Management at the University of Manitoba, providing searchable access to hundreds of case studies of community-based management including papers in scientific journals, book chapters, case studies, and Masters and PhD dissertations.
www.umanitoba.ca/institutes/natural_resources

Produced by the Society for Conservation Biology's Social Science Working Group (SSWG) the '**Catalog of Conservation Social Science Tools**' is a searchable database containing practical tools and other useful resources to help researchers and practitioners to better understand and address the social challenges of biodiversity conservation. The Catalog includes an overview of the main social science disciplines, challenges and methodological approaches related to conservation practice written by expert members of the SSWG.
www.conbio.org/workinggroups/sswg/catalog

The **CBO** database hosted by the African Conservation Centre provides details of over 100 community-based organizations involved in managing natural resources with details of their activities and how to contact them.
www.conservationafrica.org/cbo-database/cbo-database.php

The **Digital Library of the Commons (DLC)** is a gateway to the international literature on the commons. It includes a Comprehensive Bibliography of the Commons; a Keyword Thesaurus, and links to relevant reference sources on the study of the commons.
http://dlc.dlib.indiana.edu

EarthTrends is a database hosted by the World Resources Institute (WRI). It includes data on key environmental and social issues gathered from the world's leading statistical agencies, along with WRI-generated maps and analyses. To facilitate the comparison of data from different sources, EarthTrends supplements its content with detailed metadata that reports on research methodologies and evaluates the information's reliability.
http://earthtrends.wri.org

The **Equator Knowledge Zone** is the Equator Initiative's interactive, map-based best practice database. This online tool provides users with information and resources on innovative community projects working at the interface of biodiversity and poverty reduction around the world.
www.equatorinitiative.net

The **PCLG organizations database** highlights the range of organizations working on conservation–poverty linkages – including donor agencies, conservation organizations, NGOs, indigenous people's organizations and grassroots groups.
http://povertyandconservation.info/en/osearch.php

The **PCLG initiatives database** describes significant international initiatives designed to explore the links between conservation and poverty reduction – from broad poverty–environment programmes to focused single-issue agendas.
http://povertyandconservation.info/en/isearch.php

The **World Database on Protected Areas (WDPA)**, managed by UNEP-World Conservation Monitoring Centre in partnership with the IUCN World Commission on Protected Areas provides the most comprehensive data set on protected areas worldwide. The WDPA allows you to search protected areas data by site name, country, and international programme or convention.
www.wdpa.org

TILCEPA (Theme/Strategic Direction on Governance, Communities, Equity, and Livelihood Rights in Relation to Protected Areas) has initiated a **Worldwide database of Indigenous and Community Conserved Areas (ICCA)**, through voluntary inputs from members who are familiar with policy/legal developments.
www.iucn.org/about/union/commissions/ceesp/topics/governance/icca/ceesp_icca_database

Project/Programme Websites

CIFOR (Center for International Forestry Research)'s Forests and Livelihoods Programme aims to enhance livelihoods by contributing to improved policies and practices related to the management and use of forests and forested landscapes.
www.cifor.cgiar.org/AboutCIFOR/How-we-work/Livelihoods

CIFOR (Center for International Forestry Research)'s Criteria and Indicators Toolbox's initiative aims at empowering local users to develop and apply sets of indicators relevant to their interpretation of sustainable forest management in their specific context.
www.cifor.cgiar.org/acm/pub/toolbox.html

COMACO is an initiative of the Zambia field programme of the Wildlife Conservation Society (WCS), working in close consultation with Community Resources Boards of Luangwa Valley, District Council authorities, and key government institutions. Its objectives are to provide marketing services, trade benefits, and

extension support for farm-based and natural resource-based commodities as a basis for adopting improved land-use practices that promote natural resource conservation.
www.itswild.org

The **Forest Governance Learning Group**, coordinated by IIED, works in Africa and Asia to exchange learning and develop ideas on forest governance – and helps to make them work for practical, just and sustainable forest use.
www.iied.org/natural-resources/key-issues/forestry/forest-governance-learning-group

The **IUCN Livelihoods and Landscapes Strategy (LLS)** is a global initiative that examines the rights and access of the rural poor to forest products in the context of the entire landscape in which people and forests interact.
www.iucn.org/about/union/secretariat/offices/asia/asia_where_work/china/iucnch_work/iucnch_forests/iucnch_lls/index.cfm

ODI Bushmeat is the project website for the Overseas's Development Institute's project on wild meat, livelihoods security and conservation in the tropics.
www.odi-bushmeat.org

WRI's **People & Ecosystems Program** creates innovative, practical and decision-relevant solutions that aim to halt and reverse ecosystem degradation while sustaining their capacity to provide humans with the goods and services we need.
www.wri.org/ecosystems

Policy Powertools is a website hosted by IIED that introduces a range of Power Tools – 'how-to' ideas that marginalized people and their allies can use to have a greater positive influence on natural resources policy.
www.policy-powertools.org

Poverty Mapping is a site hosted by UNEP/GRID-Arendal that includes case studies, graphics and publications relating to poverty mapping. This includes work on poverty–conservation mapping.
www.povertymap.net

Information on **The Economics of Ecosystems and Biodiversity (TEEB)** can be found on the website of the European Commission. This study aims to evaluate the costs of the loss of biodiversity and the associated decline in ecosystem services worldwide, and compare them with the costs of effective conservation and sustainable use.
http://ec.europa.eu/environment/nature/biodiversity/economics

Professional Associations

The **International Association for the Study of Common Property (IASCP)**, founded in 1989, is a non-profit association devoted to understanding and improving institutions for the management of environmental resources that are (or could be) held or used collectively by communities in developing or developed countries.
www.iascp.org

The **International Association for Society and Natural Resources (IASNR)** is an interdisciplinary professional association open to individuals who bring a variety of social science and natural science backgrounds to bear on research pertaining to the environment and natural resource issues. IASNR publishes the journal *Society and Natural Resources*, which includes research articles and policy analyses pertaining to a broad range of topics addressing the relationships between social and biophysical systems. International Symposia on Society and Resource Management are held annually.
www.iasnr.org

The **Society for Conservation Biology (SCB)** is an international professional organization dedicated to promoting the scientific study of the phenomena that affect the maintenance, loss and restoration of biological diversity. The society's membership comprises a wide range of people interested in the conservation and study of biological diversity: resource managers, educators, government and private conservation workers, and students.
www.conbio.org

The **SCB Social Science Working Group (SSWG)** is a global community of conservation scientists and practitioners. Established in 2003, the SSWG is dedicated to strengthening conservation social science and its application to conservation practice.
www.conbio.org/workinggroups/SSWG

International Initiatives

Advancing Conservation in a Social Context (ACSC) is an interdisciplinary research initiative designed to investigate the complex trade-offs that exist between human well-being and biodiversity conservation goals at a variety of spatial and temporal scales, and between conservation and other political, economic and social agendas nationally and internationally through a programme of formative research to generate knowledge about how trade-offs occur and can be resolved. www.tradeoffs.org

Coordinated by UNDP, the **Equator Initiative** is a partnership that brings together the United Nations, civil society, business, governments and communities to help build the capacity and raise the profile of grassroots efforts to reduce poverty through the conservation and sustainable use of biodiversity. www.equatorinitiative.org

The **Poverty Environment Network (PEN)** is an international research network and coordinated research effort on poverty, environment and forest resources. PEN is coordinated by the Centre for International Forestry Research (CIFOR). www.cifor.cgiar.org/pen

The **Poverty Environment Partnership** is an informal network of development agencies which seeks to improve the coordination of work on poverty reduction and the environment within the framework of internationally agreed principles and processes for sustainable development. www.povertyenvironment.net/pep/

The **Poverty and Environment Program (PEP)** is a regional technical assistance programme aimed at accelerating learning about poverty–environment linkages and effective approaches for poverty reduction. www.adb.org/Projects/PEP

UNDP/UNEP Poverty Environment Initiative aims to support country-led efforts to integrate the environmental concerns of poor and vulnerable groups into policy and planning processes for poverty reduction and pro-poor growth. www.unpei.org

Index